15 t ed.

25⁰⁰

Early SPANISH Exploration

QUIVIRA

ARKANSAS R.

ARKANSAS R.

ARKANSAS R.

CANADIAN R.

RED R.

SABINE R.

BRAZOS R.

TRINITY R.

COLORADO R.

SAN ANTONIO R.

RIO GRANDE

NUECES R.

GULF OF MEXICO

palacios

Mainstream of America Series ★

EDITED BY LEWIS GANNETT

GLORY, GOD
and GOLD

By PAUL I. WELLMAN

History

THE INDIAN WARS OF THE WEST
  Death on the Prairie
  Death in the Desert

THE TRAMPLING HERD

GLORY, GOD AND GOLD

Novels

BRONCHO APACHE

JUBAL TROOP

ANGEL WITH SPURS

THE BOWL OF BRASS

THE WALLS OF JERICHO

THE CHAIN

THE IRON MISTRESS

THE COMANCHEROS

THE FEMALE

By PAUL I. WELLMAN

GLORY, GOD
and GOLD

a Narrative History

DOUBLEDAY & COMPANY, INC., *Garden City, N.Y., 1954*

Library of Congress Catalog Card Number 54–10773

PRINTED IN THE UNITED STATES
AT THE COUNTRY LIFE PRESS, GARDEN CITY, N.Y.

FIRST EDITION

To my father

DR. FREDERICK CREIGHTON WELLMAN

Contents

List of Maps

A *Word to the Reader*

"HISTORY," said Sir Walter Scott, "is the essence of innumerable biographies."

Amen to that, say I; and particularly when one seeks to weave into a single skein the countless threads of the story of four hundred years of strife in a sprawling wild land toward the slow goal of civilization.

In this book I have sought to tell, insofar as it can be done, the history of the American Southwest in terms of the lives and deeds of the men and women who played the chiefest roles in it. An army is impersonal; still more so is an economic or a social trend. But when these are reflected in the acts, ambitions and achievements, as well as the disappointments and despairs, of the principal actors, they become personal; and the history therefore more vivid and perhaps comprehensible.

Of necessity I have been debarred from the exhaustive and definitive. This is the story of five different peoples: Indians, Spaniards, French, Mexicans and Americans. It deals with their complicated and some-times confusing collisions and blendings—impelled, in one direction or another, almost always, by one and in some instances all three of the motives suggested in the title of this book—covering four cen-turies of time. When this is considered it will be understood that some details must be barely touched upon, or omitted altogether, in the interests of the main stream of a narrative which must be kept within the bounds of a single volume.

I have, for example, dealt most briefly with California, sketching in barely enough to keep the story in perspective. Fortunately other histories are coming in this series, and one of them will tell the Cali-fornia story in a fuller manner.

The Southwest is old in relation to our national history yet still refreshingly new. It has been the theater for high adventure, for greed and cruelty, for consecration and patient labor, and those who played the leading parts in its drama, as if by the very nature of

their surroundings, were sometimes romantic and passionate, sometimes hard-bitten and wrathful, and always colorful and original, to
a degree seldom encountered in softer lands. So individualistic is
the Southwest as a somewhat homogeneous realm, including the states
of Texas, New Mexico, Arizona, and parts of Oklahoma, Colorado,
Nevada and even Mexico, that it seems surprising that a chronological
history of it as a region has not been attempted before; and in this
may lie some value in this book.

In the matter of proper names I have taken refuge from the inevitable controversies by electing to use in each case the spelling
most popularly remembered, rather than clutter up the text with all
the variations of each.

Formal bibliographies are tedious. The busy man or woman, interested in the subject, wishes to know the *best* places to go for added
knowledge, not *all* the places. I have therefore appended to this volume a reading list of comparatively few books, which for interest and
factual content cover the entire period fairly well and are available
to most. The innumerable primary sources which went into the
preparation of this history will be known already to the serious re-
searcher and historical scholar.

If in these matters I am arbitrary, it is in the interest of the general
reader, for whom, I hope, my story will not be lacking entirely in
moments of interest and perhaps even in added insight into this
America.

                                        PAUL I. WELLMAN

BOOK 1

Liars Sometimes Make History

The Captain in Golden Armor

JUST over the hill—the very next hill—might lie Cathay. Or, if not that fabulous empire of the Grand Khan, some other land of equal opulence, such as India.

There was, in fact, no telling what one might see if he just kept going onward. Perhaps the Strait of Anian, that passage from Europe to Asia through the New World which everyone knew existed simply because it had been so much talked about, and which would assuredly be worth more to its finder than all the gold of the Americas. Or the mysterious domain of the Amazons, warlike women who were said to defend their treasures—of gems and of virtue—from any man, and who (if pretty) thus offered a double challenge to gentlemen of fortune, and also of gallantry. Or even the country of El Dorado, "the Gilded Man," where gold was reputedly so plentiful that the ruler was painted with flakes of the pure metal as an adornment on state occasions.

At the very least one might expect to find, perhaps just beyond the next ridge, another Tenochtitlán, such as had amazed Cortés only twenty years before, or a Cuzco, where Pizarro's mighty lootings were of still more recent vintage—offering an honest Spanish *conquistador* the opportunity, perhaps, of getting for himself whole roomfuls of gold by using the right methods of "persuasion" on a captive Indian monarch.

Not a man in the army which set forth bravely that twenty-third of February, in the year 1540, from the colonial city of Compostela in New Spain (later to be called Mexico) had the slightest doubt that one or many of such wonders would be his reward before he finished his march to the north.

It was a time of credulity almost unbelievable, when a man was willing to swallow anything he heard. And with apparent good reason, for had not the incredible facts already established in the past fifty years—the very existence of this New World, and all the realms explored and "pacified" in less than half a century—made pallid some of the rosiest imaginings of this roseate year of 1540?

The very best map makers of the period helped at once to accentuate the mystery and sharpen the anticipation of the explorers. Two of the most widely circulated current maps of the world differed in almost everything—except inaccuracy.

There was a contemporary Ptolemaic map of the world which showed the *Novus Orbis* as a large island rather than a continent, shaped somewhat like a human stomach and alimentary canal, with its northern shore no farther from the City of Mexico than, say, Yucatán; and separated from "India Superior" by a narrow sea, hardly more than a strait, perhaps a hundred leagues wide.

On the other hand, Orontius Fine's map, published a few years before, disregarded the strait entirely. It showed that America was no more than a landward extension of Asia, the Gulf of Mexico an indentation opposite the Bay of Bengal, and Cuba as much an island of the Orient as Java, and of about equal size and importance. According to this map, if one just marched northward from New Spain, he could hardly miss Cathay (Catay)—it was, apparently, much nearer than Florida.

What if the maps did disagree? A shrug of the shoulders at this. No matter *which* was correct, the results could hardly fail to be much the same—new lands, new adventures, new riches, new glory for deserving Spaniards! Small wonder the army that day set out eagerly northward with blare of trump and tuck of drum, and pennons snapping in the Mexican breeze.

It was a veritable army, rather than a mere expedition, and had been reviewed only the day before by Don Antonio de Mendoza, the all-powerful viceroy, personification of the king's own majesty in Mexico. Mendoza had a large personal financial investment in it, and had gone back to the capital to await with confidence news of its conquests and achievements. In size, organization, provisioning and large ideas it was probably the most elaborate and expensive exploration ever embarked upon in the world's history.

Its muster roll contained the names of 336 Europeans, all Spaniards except for five Portuguese, two Italians, one Frenchman, one German and one Scot. With these went several hundred Indians, some of them warriors in the quilted cotton armor and carrying the primitive weapons —bow and *maquahuitl*—of the Aztecs, but mostly herdsmen or body servants to the Spanish gentlemen.

There were a number of women and even children with the expedition. Most of these were wives and offspring of Indian auxiliaries, but three were spouses of Spanish soldiers. They were Francisca de Hozes,

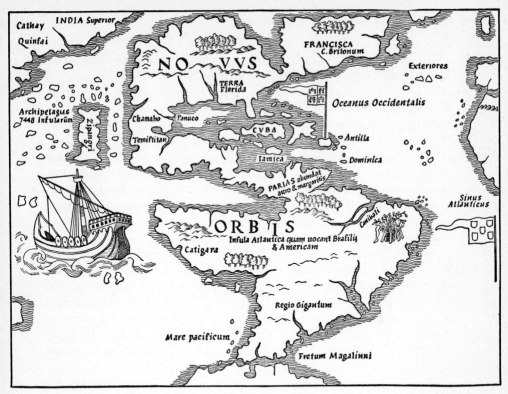

Ptolemaic map

Orontius Fine's Globe of 1531

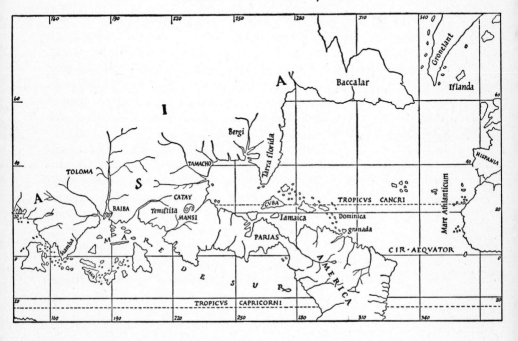

wife of one Alonso Sánchez, who was accompanied by her young son; María Maldonado, wife of Juan de Paradinas; and an Indian woman, wife of Lope de Caballero. Of these, the first two made themselves more or less conspicuous, though for widely different reasons. Señora María Maldonado was a kindly, industrious woman who won the affection of all by becoming a sort of nurse to the expedition, caring for sick or wounded soldiers, mending their ragged garments, and perhaps preparing special broths and foods for them. Señora Francisca de Hozes, on the other hand, was a determined shrew. From the beginning she hectored not only poor Sánchez, her husband, but others about her, even the captain general. Her spouse hardly dared speak, except to echo her assertions, and he may be said to be the first henpecked man who ever entered the borders of the United States: an honor which, though dubious, can hardly be challenged, since the Indians allowed no such latitude to their women. Eventually Señora Francisca and her clacking tongue would mean big trouble for the leader of the expedition.

A great herd of animals accompanied the army. There were more than fifteen hundred horses and mules, including the mounts of the *caballeros* and the pack animals. Also driven behind the marching column went its commissary on the hoof, cattle bawling, sheep bleating, even hogs squealing and grunting; all raising a prodigious dust and clamor as they were herded along by their Indian wardens.

The backbone of the army was its Spaniards. These were mostly young men, many of noble blood—younger sons, chiefly, who, being barred from the family patrimony in Spain by the laws of primogeniture, had come to the New World to seek their fortunes.

In the capital these youthful *hidalgos* had been something of a problem. Being accustomed to obsequious treatment at home, they expected it in New Spain. And being unaccustomed to anything resembling labor at home, they had no intention of soiling their hands with it in New Spain. They were a burden to the substantial Spanish households, for they expected with bland innocence to be entertained lavishly; and with less innocence, though perhaps with equal blandness, they devoted themselves to seducing the daughters and wives of their hosts.

To a young Spanish nobleman only two occupations were honorable: love and warlike adventure. Since there seemed to be no war, feminine virtue was besieged in the City of Mexico as it never before had been besieged; and there must have been a heartfelt sigh of relief from harried fathers of susceptible daughters and husbands with young, pretty and perhaps giddy wives, when what appeared to be prospect of war, or at least glorious adventure, siphoned off more than three hundred gay, handsome and conscienceless young libertines and wastrels into the army of exploration.

Gonzalo de Salazar, royal factor, wrote: "It seemed . . . that it was a very fortunate thing for Mexico that the people who were leaving were about to do so, because they had been injuring the citizens there. For the most part they were young gentlemen who had nothing to do either in the city or in the country."

Not all, of course, were young and lightheaded. There was a fair sprinkling of veterans with scarred visages and graying beards. One, Juan Gallego, a great hand-to-hand fighter, was more than fifty years old. Yet by and large it was a handsomer and more youthful aggregation than the usual collection of battle-worn *conquistadores*, of whom a young lady, newly arrived from Spain, is said to have exclaimed: "One would think by the way they are cut up that they had just escaped from the infernal regions; for some are lame, some with but one hand, others without ears, others with only one eye, others with half their faces gone, and the best of them have one or two cuts across the forehead."

There was one other element: a group of Franciscan friars, setting forth with an eye on the souls of the heathen they might expect to encounter, and ready to use any method—and the latitude allowed them by the Spanish Catholic Church was very wide indeed—to rescue the benighted from hell in the hereafter, even if to do so it required a taste of hell in the present.

Three hundred-odd Spaniards, with three hundred-odd different personalities, thoughts, tastes and characteristics. Yet they were as one in some traits that seemed common to all Spaniards in that day: incredible courage and audacity; religious bigotry and intolerance which made Spain the executioner of the Counter Reformation and nurtured the horror of the Spanish Inquisition from 1478 to 1834; a racial cruelty the more terrifying in its unthinking callousness; and rapacity which was yet hardly avarice, for the Spaniard who seized wealth spent it lavishly, and frequently almost as quickly as he obtained it.

Most of the Spaniards were *caballeros*, although there marched with them a body of footmen—arquebusiers and pikemen—the grim Spanish infantry, at that time the most invincible soldiers of Europe. In the Italian wars they had demonstrated to the world the value of drill and mass tactics in the victory of Garigliano in 1503; and later, in another great triumph at Pavia, in 1525, showed the decisive effect of what is now known as "fire power," in their use of the arquebus, a primitive firearm of the matchlock variety. These infantrymen would do good service in the expedition just starting.

In some regards quite typical of his men was the leader of the army.

Don Francisco Vásquez de Coronado was only thirty years old, quite handsome, a younger son who, like many of his followers, had left Spain to seek his fortune. He was born in Salamanca, a city of Estramadura, that province of Spain which produced also Cortés, Pizarro, Alvarado, De Soto—in fact most of the greatest *conquistadores* of the period of mighty Spanish expansion. His father was a nobleman with a high post in Spain. Francisco, in 1535, when he was twenty-five years old, went to America in the train of Mendoza, the first viceroy of New Spain.

We may assume that he had more than ordinary address and charm, because not only did he make a firm friend and patron of Mendoza, but shortly after arriving in the colony he won the hand of one of the most eligible heiresses in the New World, Doña Beatriz de Estrada. Marrying her, he came into possession of "half of Tlalpa," an estate so immense that the jealous Cortés lodged a protest that it had been "unduly and inconsiderately alienated from the Crown." To this Coronado shortly added another large estate, belonging to Juan de Burgas, who lost it because he was unmarried and hence, under royal decree, could not hold such property.

Doña Beatriz was something more than a lady with a rich dowry. Her father, now dead, was Alonso de Estrada, who had been royal treasurer of New Spain. And Don Alonso, it was freely stated, was a natural son of King Ferdinand of Spain, who had smiled benignly, though left-handedly, upon one of the ladies of his court—perhaps before he was wedded to the strong-willed Isabella of Columbus fame. Throughout his life Estrada held high offices, and his widow felt close enough to the throne to complain in writing to Charles V, Ferdinand's successor, that she could not find suitable husbands for her two daughters. This complaint soon ceased. Coronado married Beatriz and her sister was wedded to Jorge de Alvarado, who succeeded his bride's deceased father as royal treasurer of New Spain. Not for long did the blood royal have to go begging in those days; even when it descended from a dalliance unblessed by the Church, though understood by everyone, since kings were human and frequently more than susceptible to a pretty face.

Coronado proved not only agreeable but efficient. In 1537 he put down an Indian revolt energetically, and the following year, when he was only twenty-eight, was appointed governor of Nueva Galicia. He was brave, though not a particularly good combat fighter, credulous and at times indecisive, and somehow born to bad luck. But he had a grand manner, thought well of himself, and was the only man in his army who wore golden armor. If he *did* meet El Dorado, he could at least offer a suitable auriferous comparison to that gilded prince of fable.

CHAPTER TWO

Fray Marcos, the Mendacious

WHEN the main body of the army set forth from Compostela that February morning, its advance guard had preceded it northward. With it, marching on foot, "in the apostolic manner," and armed only with crucifix and missal, went several friars. Two of them deserve especial attention. One was Fray Marcos de Niza, the newly appointed provincial of the Franciscans of New Spain. The second was Fray Juan de Padilla.

In an age when militant religion was very close to the profession of arms, Padilla was a symbol of his time—a soldier turned priest. He had learned the use of temporal weapons in his youth, and perhaps never quite got over the joy of combat, for we see him leading at least one charge in the campaign to come. Since 1529 he had been in the New World, pioneering on the roughest frontiers, seeing life very much in the raw as a chaplain in the train of the terrible Nuño de Guzmán, who hunted men as other men hunted wild beasts, and also on the Panama peninsula—a thorough adventurer in the best sense, a Spaniard with the stout Spanish lack of fear for his body and a sincere belief in his mission and his faith.

Fray Marcos de Niza was even more important to this expedition, for he was the true genesis of it. A strange mixture of qualities, he was an Italian who had lived at Nice—whence his surname—whose convictions seemed always at war with his timidity. A vaulting imagination led him into gross exaggerations—to use the most charitable word for it—and a nice sense of plausibility enabled him to make his stories most convincing to his listeners. He was ambitious for the conversion of the heathen, and perhaps this laudable ambition is an extenuation for his somewhat loose handling of the facts, for he believed that if he could get the government to send armed authority into the regions north the Church would be better able to bring the message of salvation to the unbelievers there.

Fray Marcos' part in launching the expedition went back to the adventure of Cabeza de Vaca and his three companions, who had suddenly appeared in New Spain four years previously, after a perilous six-year journey among the wild tribes. In the course of his journey, living sometimes as slaves and sometimes as honored guests, they crossed the continent, after having been cast ashore near the present-day Galveston Island on the coast of Texas. They were survivors of the ill-starred, ill-managed expedition of Pánfilo de Narváez, who set out to conquer Florida and wound up by being shipwrecked and lost in the Gulf of Mexico.

Cabeza de Vaca and his companions, Castillo, Dorantes and Estevan —a Negro slave belonging to Dorantes—managed to convince the natives that they were medicine men of magical powers, and so were escorted on their journey into the unknown, until at last they heard that to the south were bearded men who had "horses, lances, and swords, and who had lanced two of the natives." Rejoicing at this indubitable evidence of the presence of Spaniards, the wanderers hastened thither and were received by Diego de Guzmán and his party on the Yaqui River.

Diego was a nephew of Nuño de Guzmán, and he and his men were at the moment engaged in slave driving—rounding up Indians to be sold later on the auction block. The two they had "lanced" no doubt offered some objection to the process—even though Diego, like all his colleagues in the business, offered them the priceless privilege of being baptized into Holy Church, as compensation for their lost liberty and enforced hard labor for the rest of their days.

When Cabeza de Vaca reached the City of Mexico he told his story to Viceroy Mendoza, and it was widely repeated, firing the imagination of Spaniards throughout the province. He reported that to the north were people who lived in large houses (pueblos); cultivated in fertile valleys such crops as maize, squash and beans; made cotton clothing; had plentiful emeralds, turquoises and pearls; and worked in leather from "hump backed cows" living in the region. Cabeza de Vaca, it appears, was the first European to see the American bison.

Further, he said, he had observed signs of gold, antimony, iron, copper and other valuable metals, and there were evidences of still greater riches "farther north" where he had not been.

He was sent to Spain with a letter of commendation from Mendoza, who made up his mind to look further into the northward mystery. The viceroy seems to have proposed that these whilom explorers head a new expedition, but they were weary of exploration. Castillo married, settled down in the capital, and refused to budge. Dorantes, like Cabeza de Vaca, returned to the home land. But Mendoza took the precaution of purchasing from him the Negro, Estevan. Being a slave, Estevan had no volition in the matter and could be sent exploring whether he liked it or not.

At this propitious time Fray Marcos de Niza appeared in the City of Mexico. The good friar had, in the past few years, witnessed the virtual extermination of the Indians in Santo Domingo, and accompanied Alvarado to Guatemala, going thence to South America, where it is said he was present at the treachery of Pizarro, when that odious *conquistador,* after extorting from the Inca Atahualpa a room filled with gold from floor to ceiling as a ransom for which his life and liberty were promised, cruelly murdered the Indian ruler on a pretext. Returning to Guatemala, Fray Marcos wrote to the lord bishop of New Spain, Juan de Zumárraga, and was invited to the City of Mexico. He arrived in 1537 and regaled the good bishop with such tales of barbarities and cruelties practiced by Spaniards that the shocked prelate had him put his statement in writing and took both friar and manuscript to the viceroy.

Mendoza was quite taken by Fray Marcos. He had received authority from Charles V to explore northward, and with the co-operation of the bishop he arranged to send Fray Marcos to look over the lands reported by Cabeza de Vaca, entrusting the supervision of the expedition to Coronado, the new governor of Nueva Galicia.

Friar and governor conferred, but the start north was delayed until 1538, because of an uprising at Culiacán, in the northern part of the province, where a chief named Ayapin entertained some doubts as to the value of the particular kind of heaven promised by the Spaniards in the future, as a substitute for the particular kind of hell proposed by them for the present, and took up arms.

The Spaniards made a nice distinction in words. Culiacán was, to use their phrase, *tierra paz* (pacified land). Ayapin, therefore, was a rebel, and not a defender of his country, since he did not have a country to defend, it having been taken over by His Most Catholic Majesty. Coronado defeated the ungrateful natives, pursued and captured Ayapin, and, according to his report to Mendoza, "After capturing him, I brought him to trial, where he was found guilty and sentenced to death, and I ordered him quartered. This execution completed the task of stabilizing and pacifying the land."

And well it should. Seeing their chief chopped into four pieces while still living was enough to convince the natives of the unprofitableness of resisting the Spaniards, at least for the present.

Two episodes illustrate the fact that Coronado possessed a conscience quite tender on some points. During the pursuit of Ayapin, Melchior Diaz, Coronado's military commander, captured two native women and presented them to the governor to be sent as servants to his beautiful wife, Doña Beatriz. The Indian women were of free status, so Coronado consulted his confessor, Padre Antonio de Castilblanco, disclosing his doubts as to the rectitude of making slaves of them. Holy Church promptly relieved him of his scruples. Padre Antonio charged him "as a matter of conscience" to send the captive women to his wife, pointing out that with Doña Beatriz they would be taught womanly arts and crafts and would become Christians, whereas if Coronado freed them to return to their homes they would remain heathen and fry in the everlasting fires of hell. The women were duly sent to enter a career of bondage, and the incident demonstrates the quite simple manner whereby conscience could be reconciled with practical considerations by the most devout of Spanish Catholics.

The second episode occurred just before Fray Marcos started north from Culiacán after the uprising was put down. The daughters of the natives had always been pleasing to the white invaders, and long before the romantic affair of John Rolfe and Pocahontas there were unions, usually informal, between Spaniards and Indian women. Finding thirty cases of such unwed bliss in Culiacán, Coronado ordered Fray Marcos to marry them all in a wholesale wedding at the church.

Having taken care of both revolt and scandal, Coronado dispatched the friar-led scouting expedition north. With Fray Marcos went another religious, Fray Oronato. The slave, Estevan, was sent by the viceroy as guide, and there was a goodly escort of Indians as servants and perhaps as guards.

Estevan entered thoroughly into the spirit of the occasion. Of all Cabeza de Vaca's party, he alone seems to have enjoyed the long journey across America, perhaps because of the lofty position he occupied —as a magician in the eyes of the Indians. He had a taste for glitter and show, and now he got himself up as impressively as possible, walking with bells jingling at ankles and elbows, and carrying a rattle made of a gourd adorned with bells and red and white feathers—the same he had carried as a "medicine man" with Cabeza de Vaca, and which always had gained him respect on his previous adventures.

Thus they set forth on foot, with Mendoza's instructions still ringing in Fray Marcos' ears: discover the truth of Cabeza de Vaca's report; note the peoples and lands; seek news of both the South and North seas—the Pacific and Atlantic oceans, which some maps of the time indicated as being hardly more than a few miles apart—and particularly the Strait of Anian; take possession in the name of the king of Spain of all lands and rivers, while informing the natives of the new suzerainty over them and theirs; and, finally, send back messengers from time to time to report on progress and discoveries.

Fray Marcos was not the martyr type. By the time he reached what is now Sinaloa, where Fray Oronato fell ill and was sent back, he decided that it would be wise to send Estevan on ahead with an escort, to see if it was safe and to prepare the way for himself and the main expedition.

Nothing loath, Estevan, who, whatever his failings, lacked timidity, departed with instructions: if he heard of a country of importance, he should send back a courier with a white cross "a palm in length"; if it were of great importance, "two palms in length"; and "if it were something greater and better than New Spain, he should send a large cross."

Four days later, to Fray Marcos' surprise and delight, a runner came speeding back on the trail, bearing a cross *as high as a man!*

The messenger was questioned and told the good friar such marvels that he refused to believe them until he saw them himself—so he said in his report. To the north was a new country called Cíbola, in which were seven great cities, and it was thirty days' travel to the first of these cities, which was the smallest of them.

From the record, this is the first appearance of the word "Cíbola." There has been considerable conjecture as to its meaning. The Spaniards later called the buffalo of the Texas and New Mexico plains *cíbolos,* as well as *vacas* (cows), and it has been supposed by some that the name of the towns was from these beasts. But it appears that the reverse was the case. The best theory is that Cíbola was a Spanish corruption of *Shíwona,* in the Zuñi tongue, "Land of the Zuñis," the name of the tribe for themselves being *Ashíwi* (singular *Shíwi*), meaning "the flesh." After the exploration the great plains to the east were called *Llanos de Cíbola,* the animals *vacas de Cíbola,* and finally the name for buffalo was shortened to *cíbolo.*

Untroubled by such etymological questions, but anxious to catch up with Estevan and reach the reported great kingdom with him, Fray Marcos now put on speed where before he had lagged. But the Negro was eager, too, and the excellent padre never overtook him.

Concerning this little impromptu race, Pedro de Castañeda, one of the chroniclers of the Coronado expedition, wrote: "It seems that, after the friars and the Negro had started, the Negro did not get along very well with the friars, because he took the women that were given to him, collected turquoises, and accumulated a stock of everything." Also: "He [Estevan] thought he could get all the reputation and honor himself, and that if he alone should discover those settlements with such famous high houses, he would be considered bold and courageous."

For fifteen days Fray Marcos toiled across the *despoblado* of what is now Arizona. When he emerged at the northern edge of the desert, late in May, he received stunning news. Fleeing for his life came a member of Estevan's party, saying that the Negro had been killed by the Cíbolans. Two others of the party, both wounded, arrived a little later, with word that not only the Negro but all with him save themselves had been massacred—the number, according to different accounts, ranging from sixty to three hundred.

His ambition, his greed and his lust for native women were Estevan's undoing, but even more so was the "medicine rattle" with bells and feathers, in which he put such boundless faith. When his messengers presented it to the chief of the town—Hawikuh, one of the Zuñi pueblos —the chief furiously dashed it to the ground and ordered them away with threats, because the rattle was of a type used by enemies of Cíbola.

Estevan refused to take the warning seriously. Perhaps he had begun to share the belief of the Indians in his own supernatural powers. Arriving at the pueblo before sunset with his main party, he was denied admission and lodged in a house outside the walls where the old men in authority questioned him. They were suspicious because he, being *black,* said he was an emissary of *white* men. Estevan did nothing to gain their friendship. Instead, with a great show of peremptory authority, he added to their resentment by demanding from them turquoises, and that women be sent to him. The last was an insult: the Zuñi women were chaste.

Too late Estevan saw the deadly hostility he had aroused. He tried to flee but was killed, with others of his party—although according to Castañeda the report of the first refugees was exaggerated, most of the Negro's followers escaping back to New Spain unharmed. Thereafter, for a long time, Estevan's bones were kept by the Cíbolans and exhibited to prove that the strangers from the south were not immortal.

Fray Marcos, a timid man at best, was terrified by this news, especially since some of the Indians accompanying him became ugly and threatened his life because of the friends and relatives they had lost.

There has been a dispute for centuries as to what happened next. Castañeda said that Fray Marcos distributed among the Indians everything he had, except his vestments for saying mass, to placate them, and returned "by forced marches" to New Spain, without going any nearer to Cíbola, which was still sixty leagues away.

Fray Marcos said that he went on until he came within sight of the city, which he viewed from "a distant eminence." And because of this assertion his right to the claim of being the discoverer of Cíbola has been accepted by many throughout all these years.

But a brief examination of the good friar's statements throws somewhat more than a shadow of doubt on his story. He described the city as being on a plain at the foot of a round hill. When later Coronado actually reached the pueblo, identified now by every authority as Hawikuh, he found it on top of a low flat mesa—not a "round hill" and not on any plain at its foot.

Fray Marcos also said that "the settlement is larger than the City of Mexico." Inasmuch as Tenochtitlán—the City of Mexico—at the time of Cortés' conquest had, with its suburbs, a population of around 300,000 persons, with 60,000 houses, while Hawikuh had at this date perhaps 1000 inhabitants and 200 houses, it is difficult to understand how, supposing Fray Marcos actually saw the town, even an imagination that multiplied everything by exaggeration would have compared the Zuñi with the Aztec city.

Cortés used a stronger word than "exaggeration" later. He—and others also—called the friar an outright liar.

In one respect Fray Marcos was truthful enough—his reasons for not approaching closer to this Cíbola which he said he saw.

"At times I was tempted to go to it, because I knew that I risked only my life, and this I had offered to God the day I began the expedition. But the fact is that I was afraid, realizing my peril, and that if I should die it would not be possible to have an account of this land, which in my opinion is the largest and best of all those discovered. . . . And so I returned, with much more fear than food, and traveled with all the speed I could make until I came upon the people I had left."

But, he added, before he departed thus hastily he made a pile of stones on the hill from which he viewed distant Cíbola, erected on it a cross, "slender and small, because I lacked equipment for making a larger one," and thus—by remote control, so to speak—he "took possession" of Cíbola, its seven cities, and the "kingdoms" that lay beyond, in the name of God, Charles V of Spain and Viceroy Mendoza.

The Cíbolans remained innocently unaware that they had thus, without even knowing it, become subjects of His Most Catholic Majesty.

The excellent padre made haste now to leave the company of the Indians who had lost relatives and might exact retribution from him, traveling ten leagues the first day—say thirty miles, and that on foot, which shows his eagerness to get out of that unhealthy vicinity. As he caught his breath, however, and continued his southward journey perhaps less precipitately, he began to regain composure. And with that his imagination went to work, and improved on the facts of the case, and by the time he reached Compostela and made his report to Coronado he had a story that made the young governor's head dizzy. And when Coronado took him to the capital to tell his tale to the viceroy, he dazzled even that august dignitary.

The voluble friar, his tongue loosed now that he was out of danger, said that Cíbola was "a land rich in gold, silver, and other wealth, and has great cities; the houses are of stone, terraced like those of Mexico; the people are civilized . . . marry only once, wear woolen clothes,

and ride about on some animals whose name he does not know." Also
—Fray Marcos warmed to his work—"the cities were guarded with
gates, and the people were very rich, the women even wearing belts of
gold. In the country were silversmiths, blacksmiths, slaughterhouses,
baths, sheep, and partridges."

Mendoza was convinced. For some time he had been wishing to
extend his authority northward, and now the opportunity seemed
golden materially as well as figuratively. Unhappily he had competi-
tors. As soon as Fray Marcos' story became known—and it was impossible to muzzle the loquacious friar—gold fever ran through New Spain,
so that the viceroy had to proclaim that nobody might leave the
province without a special license.

A few, however, could hardly be controlled by licenses. One was the
famous Hernando Cortés, the original conqueror of Mexico. Though
now a *marqués,* with a huge estate, he nursed a sense of injury because
he had not been made viceroy. Cortés already had financed some independent exploring expeditions—one of which discovered Lower California—and now he dispatched a small fleet of ships under Francisco
de Ulloa, who sailed up the Gulf of California (then called the Sea of
Cortés), discovered the mouth of the Colorado River, and proved that
Lower California was a peninsula and not an island (a fact which had
to be proved over again later) but found no gold and no cities.

At the same time, in the royal court of Spain, others were seeking
the right to explore, "pacify" and Christianize the new country—and
to direct the robbery which would follow the discovery of gold and
other treasure, as anticipated. One of these was Cabeza de Vaca, who
pleaded his original explorations as justification. Unfortunately for his
ambitions, others were closer to the royal and greedy ear of Charles V.

Nuño de Guzmán, former governor of Nueva Galicia, back in Spain
after nearly two years in jail in the City of Mexico, was a petitioner.
No more horrifying human ogre ever lived than Guzmán. A man of
bottomless cruelty and bottomless greed, he conducted such terrible
slave hunts to enrich himself that Bishop Zumárraga stated that he sold
at least ten thousand inoffensive Indians into slavery, most of whom
soon died because slavery was incompatible with Indian nature. He
crucified and hanged men who opposed his will, and once when a
Spaniard used "insolent language" to him he had him nailed to a post
by the tongue. Mendoza was sent to New Spain as viceroy partly because of Guzmán's atrocities, and he arrested the governor and imprisoned him under grave charges. Regrettably, however, Guzmán's
wealth and connections were so great that by a royal order he was
released and returned to Spain. There he was pleading that he should
be given the right to explore the new Cíbola since he had acted in all

cases "with propriety and for the interests of the Crown"—because his slave hunts had opened northern Mexico!

Yet another petitioner was the famous Pedro de Alvarado, whose flaming red hair and beard caused the superstitious natives to call him Tonatiuh (Child of the Sun). One of Cortés' lieutenants in the conquest, he had later "pacified" Guatemala, which he felt entitled him to explore the north.

None of these rivals gave Mendoza serious trouble. But there was another who did—Hernando de Soto. That *hidalgo* had come to the New World as a youth, and displayed genius in assisting the murderous activities of Pedrarias, the infamous governor of Darien, of whom the chroniclers say, "he joyed in the hunting of savages." With this apprenticeship behind him, in 1532 De Soto reinforced the detestable Pizarro with a troop of horses in Peru and participated in the treacherous capture and later murder of the Inca Atahualpa. De Soto's share of the famous roomful of gold the Spaniards extorted enriched him so that, returning to Spain, he made a great impression by the magnificence of his entourage, and endeared himself to Charles V by lending him a sum which by modern values would be perhaps equivalent to $1,000,000. The loan gained for him the coveted commission—governorship of Cuba and Florida, and the right to explore and "pacify" the lands further (including Cíbola).

In granting this commission—whereby De Soto was to conduct the expedition at his own expense—the king was unusually magnanimous. He reserved to himself *only half* of all the gold to be discovered, together with silver, jewels, pearls and any other objects of value which might be seized in Indian palaces, temples and places of burial. And he regally granted to De Soto one sixth of all "ransoms of chiefs and caciques captured," the rest to be distributed among the soldiers of the expedition—after, of course, reserving the royal fifth for his money-grabbing majesty. De Soto's experience in the ransom business had been delightful. Out of Atahualpa's roomful of gold, De Soto received ingots worth, at present money values, between $5,000,000 and $6,000,000.

The vast grant, covering more than twelve degrees of latitude, made De Soto a rival in power to Mendoza himself. Both were after the same loot—the imagined wealth of Cíbola, which did not grow less as the Spaniards discussed it among themselves. De Soto organized his expedition quickly, and by the middle of May 1539 had landed in Florida, thus gaining a head start on Mendoza; for according to the current maps there was no great distance separating him from Cíbola—no more, indeed, than separated Mendoza from it.

Knowing he must act quickly, Mendoza sent a scouting party under

Melchior Díaz to check Fray Marcos' story; but without waiting for its return, he and Coronado organized the army that was to begin the march as described earlier. He and Coronado shared the chief costs. It is almost impossible to translate the monetary units of that time into modern financial terms. But the viceroy put in 60,000 ducats; the governor 50,000, for which he mortgaged the lands of Doña Beatriz, his wife; and Herbert E. Bolton, whose *Coronado* is the most exhaustive study of the adventure, thinks that, considering the purchasing power of the ducat then and the dollar now, between them Mendoza and Coronado sank in the expedition what would be equivalent to something like $2,000,000 today.

But, after all, how could they lose? The prospects were infinite. That their investment would be returned many times over, nobody doubted. Cíbola, El Dorado, the Strait of Anian, Cathay, India—other lands and peoples of which nobody had even heard—seemed certain. Every Spaniard in the expedition would plunge his arms elbow-deep in gold ingots before he returned—and plunging the arms into gold was an occupation most dear to every Spaniard.

Yet Mendoza differed from some other Spaniards in one marked respect. He was a good man, according to his lights, a just man and a kind man. He had stopped Guzmán's atrocities, and now he set a startlingly new policy for Coronado's expedition. Bishop Zumárraga expressed it in a letter to his nephew: "The viceroy . . . wishes to send friars ahead without arms, and that the conquest may be Christian and apostolic, and not a butchery."

Natives encountered should be required to render obedience to the Spanish Crown, but not be enslaved. No food was to be taken without compensation, and the natives were not to be forced to labor.

Very laudable, all this. But very difficult for the Spanish temperament to carry out, as will be seen.

CHAPTER THREE

The Moment of Great Disappointment

F RAY MARCOS and his fellow friars, all on foot and sandal-shod "in true apostolic fashion," and accompanied by their escort of Spanish horsemen, were overtaken before many days by Coronado and the main army. The details of the northward march to the present borders of Arizona are not important for this history.

Streams were forded, mountains climbed, and the slow progress continued by the mounted cavaliers, the marching Spanish footmen, the
hordes of Indians, the women and children, and the multitude of livestock.

On the way they met Melchior Díaz and his travel-weary scouts,
who had spent the cold months at Chichilticalli, on the Gila River,
which was considered the edge of the *despoblado*. Because of the cold
and snow they could not cross the desert, but Díaz, a good recon-
noiterer, questioned closely and shrewdly the natives he encountered.
Meeting Coronado on his way south, he sent his lieutenant Zaldívar,
with three men, to carry the formal written report to Mendoza, and
with the rest of his men joined the army.

To Coronado he privately imparted information far from rosy. Realistic as he was intelligent, he said bluntly that though there were turquoises in the country ahead he had learned of no gold or other metal.
The people spun cotton cloth, and wore also leather garments, but
there was no evidence, from what he had learned, of any great wealth.

In his written report to Mendoza he characteristically added that
"there are many people . . . but they are not good for anything except
to make them Christians." A soldier's gibe, perhaps, at Fray Marcos—
already some did not fully trust the friar, and his purposes, however
laudable, seemed hardly to justify the glittering yarns he had told.

The general tenor of the scouting party's conclusions could not help
leaking out in the army, through members of Melchior Díaz' command,
and the effect was depressing. Another mishap added to the gloom.
Lope de Samaniego, the army master, took out a foraging party. This
was "pacified" country, and since the natives were technically subjects
of Spain, their rights, as enjoined by Mendoza in his instructions, could
be happily disregarded by the soldiers, who took food or anything else
they saw or wanted. Unfortunately the natives were not as pacified as
had been thought. Several of Samaniego's foragers were wounded in
an ambush, and he himself was killed by an arrow which penetrated
through his eye into the brain. It was the expedition's first fatality, and
removed a popular soldier and important officer.

To cheer up the army, Coronado caused Samaniego to be buried
with full honors, and hanged all the Indians who could be found in the
vicinity from nearby trees, as limp testimonials to their surviving
friends that *they*, at least, were pacified.

The march continued. Culiacán greeted it with a gala celebration,
including a sham battle and a fiesta. It was here that the army fully
realized the task ahead, and many of the young grandees discarded
surplus silks, doublets and other finery, even non-essential extra armor,
some of which, for lack of a better destination, was presented to their

hosts, who thus were in a measure repaid for their trouble and expense in providing the hospitality the visitors had enjoyed. Much baggage of the army was likewise left behind, because the loads of the pack mules were too heavy and the beasts were breaking down. This was placed in warehouses, awaiting the ships of Hernando de Alarcón, Mendoza's chamberlain, who had been ordered to sail with three vessels up the Gulf of California as a naval auxiliary to Coronado. Unhappily the ships failed to make contact, and though Alarcón entered the Colorado River and worked his way up to a point well above the present city of Yuma, he did not further in any manner the expedition's efforts.

At Culiacán a young gentleman named Trujillo reported that while bathing in a nearby stream he had had a vision. In that day a vision was no small matter, and it was brought to the attention of Coronado, to whom the young man related it. Its context was a little startling.

Trujillo said that he saw himself kill Coronado, whereupon everything belonging to the captain general—including his charming young wife, Doña Beatriz—became Trujillo's.

A ridiculous fantasy, one might think today.

But Fray Marcos did not treat it so. He preached some eloquent sermons on it, to the effect that the Devil was dignifying this expedition with his personal attention, being jealous of the good that was to be accomplished, and wishing to prevent it in any way. The other friars with the army all wrote their respective superiors, and so it went all over New Spain by way of pulpit oratory that the expedition was grappling with the Foul Fiend himself, which gave it a new importance, of a Dantesque variety, in the minds of many of the faithful.

Nor did Coronado dismiss it lightly. Some might smile at Trujillo's dream, but it evidently made the general feel a bit self-conscious every time he encountered Trujillo's eye. Was that gleam purposeful or merely jocular? Fanaticism took strange turns, and men had been known to do outlandish things to make visions come true. And *this* vision was so unpleasantly personal . . .

When the army marched on from Culiacán, Trujillo was no longer with it. By official request he remained behind. One is plagued with wonder as to whether Trujillo, having sensed the unprofitable nature of the expedition, did not resort to a stratagem whereby he was enabled to avoid further involvement with it, while at the same time bowing out with his Spanish sense of honor unsmirched.

Meantime Coronado had decided to lead an advance party and depart from Culiacán immediately, leaving Tristan de Arellano to bring along the main army. Arellano was one of the more glittering grandees, listing in his personal baggage and possessions on the march eight horses, a leather jacket, sleeves and neckpieces of mail, arms of the country, chin piece, an arquebus, two crossbows, a two-handed sword, three ordinary swords, and other arms and garments for himself and his servants. In spite of this he proved to be an able army master.

There is no indication that Coronado's decision for a hurried departure had anything to do with a desire to leave Dreamer Trujillo's uncomfortable vicinity, but it just could have been a factor—unadmitted, of course. With about eighty horsemen, perhaps thirty foot soldiers, and all the friars, "since none of them wanted to remain behind with the army," he marched from Culiacán. Naturally the friars wanted to be in on the fun, and besides, the pacifying of the natives must always be accomplished with the proper religious rituals. So unanimously did the friars vote to accompany Coronado that the main army was left to its sins without even a single chaplain.

As it turned out, Coronado's early departure had important effects. Zaldívar had reached Mendoza with Díaz' disquieting report to the effect that Fray Marcos had been somewhat overimaginative in describing the lands to the north. Much worried, the viceroy sent Zaldívar flying back with orders to Coronado to remain at Culiacán until further scouting expeditions were made. But the messenger arrived after the general was gone. For good or ill, the expedition was launched and could not be called back.

It should be remarked here that Coronado was seeing to it that his men obeyed the newfangled order of Mendoza that natives of the country—except those in "pacified" areas—be well treated. He pitched his camps at some distance from Indian villages, to keep his rakish young gallants away from the Indian damsels. In exchange for food, he carefully saw to it that something was given—glass beads and cheap knives, usually. If any of his soldiers proved irresponsible and violated his orders, they were punished. One, who helped himself without permission to some roasting ears, traveled in disgrace for three days, with gyves upon his wrists.

Such unnatural behavior on the part of Spaniards toward Indians excited understandable comment. Amazement turned to grumbling. It was a strain—a heavy strain—and one which could not be borne forever, because it was contrary to all nature, as the Spaniards understood nature. It was like inviting a pack of hungry lobo wolves to walk through a sheepfold and enjoining them not to touch any of the tempting, woolly prizes therein.

As the expedition grew footsore and weary, and the miles dragged behind with little to vary the monotony, grumbling grew louder in another direction—against Fray Marcos. If this was a sample of what he had promised, the army did not think much of it. Yet even the grumblers admitted they had not yet reached the goal he described. For the present, though they grumbled, they would wait and see. Perhaps Cíbola's seven cities would be worth all this marching after all. . . .

Coronado's advance party—followed by the main army—crossed the present international boundary where the San Pedro River crosses it, south of Bisbee, for he followed that stream north for a time. Eventually the general swung off northeast and reached Chichilticalli, where Melchior Díaz had spent the previous winter. The words *Chichilte* and *Calli* mean Red House. Near Eagle Pass, opening between the Pinaleño and Santa Teresa mountains of Arizona, may still be seen ruins of pueblos, one of which may have been the Red House. Castañeda wrote that it was made of red earth and already in ruins when the Spaniards visited it.

This was the edge of the *despoblado,* an area of mountain and desert east of the Mogollon Plateau. At that point Coronado rested a few days, while he sent García Lopez de Cárdenas, one of his best captains, with a small detachment to reconnoiter ahead and locate camping sites. Shortly after, he followed Cárdenas across the *despoblado*—and found that this part of Fray Marcos' narrative was not exaggerated. There was little grass until the White Mountains were reached, and after that much rough country. In later generations this would be Apache country, but those dread warriors had not yet penetrated this far west, and the Spaniards encountered at first no inhabitants. Death came, however, when a Spaniard named Espinosa, two Negro slaves and perhaps some Indian servants died from eating poisonous herbs while they were descending the northern slope of the White Mountains. They were buried beside the road, and the troop marched on. Though the men were pretty hungry, there was no more experimenting with unknown plants for food after this Camp of Death, as it was named.

By July Coronado had been on the march five months. His men were weary and his horses worn and thin. But with Cárdenas still scouting ahead, he pressed on, for now they must be near the longed-for Cíbola. Fray Marcos at this time became conspicuous by his silence. There is no mention of him in the chronicles, although he was with the advance party. Perhaps he was beginning to feel a belated twinge of conscience, coupled with some apprehension concerning his overstatements, for the showdown was coming.

Two days after leaving the White Mountains, Cárdenas and his scouts met four natives—Cíbolans—who made signs of peace, indicating that next day food would be sent the white strangers. Cárdenas acted promptly—and like a Spaniard. He seized two of the party as hostages and told the other two through an interpreter to return to their city and inform their people that Coronado was coming in the name of the king, to "aid and defend them."

Undoubtedly this message created some little astonishment in the home pueblo. Cíbola had gotten along very well thus far without "aid" and had never needed anyone to "defend" it. Defend from what?

Detaining the hostages was bad policy. It could not fail to arouse fear among the Indians, and perhaps resentment as well. When Coronado caught up with Cárdenas, he talked to the prisoners through interpreters. He told them not to be alarmed—by this time they probably were frightened to death—and gave them "paternosters and some little cloaks." The paternosters were probably strings of beads resembling rosaries, or they may have been actual prayers. In either case the hostages should have been grateful, for they had a unique distinction. Henceforth their people would receive nothing for compensation, unless sword blows and larceny can be accounted gifts.

On the following day, seeing some Indians near a lake, Coronado sent Pedro de Tovar and Melchior Díaz to bring them into camp. The Spaniards were mounted, the Indians on foot. Three of the natives were rounded up before the general, while the others took advantage of marshy ground to escape and carry back to their pueblo this fresh news of what happened to an Indian when he encountered the terrible bearded strangers.

As for the three confronted by Coronado, there was some display of the cross, and also, very likely, some even more convincing flourishing of swords, as the general illuminated those ignorant savages with the information that they must become Christians and submit peacefully to the will of His Majesty Charles V. He added that if they did so they would not be harmed. Benighted as they were, the savages had no difficulty understanding the collateral implication: if they did *not* do so, something unpleasant was likely to happen to them.

Meantime Cárdenas was sent forward with the vanguard to occupy a pass ahead which was narrow and rocky enough to afford a chance for ambuscade. The maneuver reveals that the Spaniards had some inkling that there were resentments against them. This may have gone back to the time of the unfortunate Estevan, but it is likely that the recent acts of Coronado's men were chiefly responsible.

Cárdenas found some Indians in the pass. He offered them presents, gave them a cross, and bade them go home and tell their people the Spaniards were on a "peaceful errand." The natives, however, seemed strangely skeptical, and that night a party of them stole up, shouted a hullabaloo of war cries, and discharged arrows among the Spaniards on the outpost. It created such panic among the younger members of

Cárdenas' party that Castañeda later wrote that the greenhorns were so excited that they tried to put the saddles on their horses hind side before. The veterans, however, saved the situation. At their charge the Indians fled. No casualties on either side resulted from the midnight brush.

Next day Coronado came up. Though neither he nor Cárdenas knew it, the pass was within three air-line miles of Cíbola itself—the Zuñi pueblo of Hawikuh. Coronado gave the *"Adelante,"* and the column took up its march along the twisting canyon of Zuñi River. They saw smoke signals in various directions and had glimpses of Indian watchers who stayed at an extreme distance, and climbed like mountain goats, so there was no chance to come near them.

All at once someone caught sight of Hawikuh ahead.

A closer look. The moment of great, enormous disappointment.

So *that* was their goal—Cíbola, the city which Fray Marcos had described in such glowing terms . . . "larger than the City of Mexico" . . . with jewels on its doors and women wearing belts of gold. . . .

And what they saw was a squalid little Indian pueblo "all crumpled together"!

Now at last the accumulated resentment against Fray Marcos burst forth. As Castañeda wrote, "Such were the curses that some . . . hurled at Fray Marcos, that I pray God to protect him from them."

Perhaps the sickest man in the whole column was its leader. Coronado had his personal fortune and his reputation invested in this venture. At one fell blow both seemed lost.

But the pueblo was there, before him, and he had certain orders to carry out. He must make the natives acknowledge Spanish authority as the first step, and extend to them the priceless benefits of the true religion as the second. The third step, which, under ordinary circumstances, would have been to rob them, seemed unhappily futile in consideration of the obvious poverty of the place.

About two hundred Zuñi warriors came out and ranged themselves before the pueblo, while others looked down from the *azoteas* (terraces). The outer defenders made a ceremonial line, probably of colored meal as is the pueblo custom, beyond which they warned the invaders not to advance.

But Cárdenas rode forward with a "peace deputation" including Fray Luis, Fray Daniel, Bermejo the notary (lawyer), and a small escort.

Fray Marcos did not go with this advance party. Either he thought there was with it already enough spiritual artillery, or he may have considered that those yelling savages looked ugly, and even a provincial of the Franciscan order had tender ribs when a stone-headed arrow came into them.

According to the Spanish custom, Bermejo the notary addressed the natives through an interpreter, informing them that they now were subjects of the king who lived beyond the sea, and that the Spaniards had come not to harm them but to defend them.

The Indians found this hard to digest. The process by which they suddenly became "subjects" of a monarch of whom they had never before heard seemed obscure to them.

When, therefore, Cárdenas advanced beyond the deadline, a shower of arrows greeted him and his men. The Zuñis never were notable archers, and their volley did no serious harm. One arrow wounded the horse ridden by Bermejo, another entered a chink in the notary's armor but did not hurt him, and a third skewered the cassock of Fray Luis, without cutting his skin.

At this Coronado, in his gilded armor, moved forward with his men. The Zuñis were not unduly impressed. Still playing out the role Mendoza had enjoined upon him, he held his men in check and continued making peace signs. His hesitation, however, was only taken by the Indians as an indication of timidity, and they rushed forward "almost to the heels of our horses to shoot their arrows," as he later reported to the viceroy.

That was going too far. Spanish patience, never long-suffering, was exhausted. No doubt Coronado felt relief at being freed from his unaccustomed role, when he gave the *Santiago*—the order to charge.

Out came swords, flashing in the desert sunlight, and with a rush the soldiers began a slashing attack. Between twelve and twenty of the natives were slain, and the rest fled up the ladders into the pueblo or scampered across the plain.

At last Spain had returned to the normal in dealing with the Indians —that is, to cutting throats. There was no question as to the Spanish courage, once the fight started. The men were, furthermore, encouraged by gnawing stomachs and the prospect of getting at some food behind those walls. Coronado, with perhaps eighty cavaliers and thirty footmen, was outside the walls. Two to four hundred yelling enemies were within. But the few besiegers had never a thought of retreating. Instead they began to look for ways to capture the pueblo.

And now still another discrepancy in Fray Marcos' account of Cíbola appeared, making it more evident that he had never actually laid eyes on the place. He had described "cities guarded with gates." But Hawikuh was a communal structure like most of its kind, with no gate whereby entrance could be made. Its stories receded terrace-like, each above the other, until at its center it was six floors high. And the lower story had no doors, no apertures of any kind, ladders being used to reach its roof, whence it was entered by trap doors, and other ladders mounting thence to the higher *azoteas*.

As Coronado's men studied the pueblo, Fray Marcos came puffing forward from his position in the rear. He had, it appears, been having rather a thin time, what with the uncomplimentary remarks concerning his reverend self with which his ears burned, and he was out of sorts. When Coronado spoke to him, evidently to receive the permission of the Church for what was going to ensue, Fray Marcos said, "Take your shields and go after them."

He did not, as did Fray Juan de Padilla later on, lead the charge. Fray Marcos was, as has been said, a timid man, but he was not backward when it came to sending others forward to fight.

Coronado accepted the permission of the Church, and deployed part of his men around the pueblo to cut off any who tried to escape, after which he prepared with the rest of the cavaliers to charge the walls.

Of course they found no way to enter the place, although they rode all the way around it, and had to fall back under a shower of arrows.

Next Coronado dismounted his cavaliers and sent them forward on foot, under cover of the fire of his arquebusiers and crossbowmen. The Zuñis were well protected, and the crossbow quarrels and primitive musket balls did little damage to them.

At one place, however, the Indians had neglected to draw up a ladder, and there Coronado, at the head of his men-at-arms, sought to climb the wall. With rolling rocks and bounding boulders from above the Indians defended this point. Coronado, conspicuous in his gilded armor, was an especial target. Twice he was felled by stones, and at last was stunned by a boulder which all but smashed in his helmet.

In the dust and trampling fury, Cárdenas and Alvarado fought over their fallen chief, covering his body with their shields until he could be carried to the rear. The captain general suffered several bruises and wounds, including an arrow in one foot and at least a mild brain concussion, for he lay unconscious for a time in the tent which was raised for his shelter.

Meantime Cárdenas, Tovar, Alvarado and Pablo de Magosa, their blood rather heated than cooled by the mishap to their commander, carried on the attack with the usual Spanish impetuosity. Under a shower of stones and arrows they grimly led their men in a climb to the *azotea* of the first-floor apartments, losing seven by bruises or wounds in doing it.

The Zuñis saw the battle was lost. They surrendered to Cárdenas, beseeching him to harm them no more, as they wished to leave the pueblo.

Cárdenas told them they could remain if they wished, but they preferred the room of these ferocious strangers to their company, and fled at once to their stronghold on the high mesa Taaiyalone, which towered at some distance away, to which before the battle they had moved their women, children, old men, and much of their property and provisions.

Yet the Spaniards discovered enough food in the captured pueblo to fill their bellies. One of them later recounted that "we found there something we prized more than gold or silver; namely, plentiful maize and beans, turkeys larger than those . . . in New Spain, and salt better and whiter than any I have ever seen in my whole life."

They ate their first full meal in weeks, then rested and slept. Coronado, limping and presumably with a headache, was about next day to inspect the pueblo his men had captured. He renamed Hawikuh, calling it Granada, in honor of Viceroy Mendoza, who came from that Spanish city.

But he wrote a doleful account of it to his superior: "It now remains for me to tell about the Seven Cities, the kingdom and province of which the father provincial [Fray Marcos] gave your lordship an account. To make a long story short, I can assure you he has not told the truth in a single thing he said, for everything is the very opposite of what he related except to the name of the cities and the large stone houses."

Coronado had discovered no gold. No silver. No pearls. Two "points" —possibly arrowheads—of "emerald" were found, but lost. These probably were not emerald at all, which does not exist in the area, but some lesser green stone, such as malachite or nephrite. At any rate they disappeared, and Coronado could not even send so small a token as they were to his friend and partner the viceroy.

CHAPTER FOUR

Divers Futile Discoveries

THE enormity of his failure was evident to Coronado, but he had no intention of turning back at present. Once the Spanish grasp was laid on anything, it held that thing tenaciously, and certain forms and rituals must be gone through, to render this *tierra paz.*

With a commendable return of conscience, Coronado ordered all prisoners who had fallen into the hands of his men, especially the women and children, to be well treated. Meantime he carried on negotiations with the head men of the pueblo, and through them with the other nearby pueblos. Envoys approached the Spanish camp cautiously, old men bearing timid gifts, consisting of "ragged blankets and some turquoises"—probably the best they had.

To these Coronado repeated that they should henceforth consider themselves subjects of the king of Spain, and that they must become Christians, bringing in their families and children to be baptized. The old men promised to obey, but as soon as they were out of arm's reach they showed a notable lack of zeal for the new religion, and it was days before any of them returned. Actually the captain general had touched on a very marked characteristic of the Pueblo Indians: they were tenacious, and still are, concerning their ancient beliefs and customs. Out of this was destined to come much trouble later for the Spaniards who settled in this country.

Time now to take full stock of the situation. After the first shock of disappointment over the barren findings in the Zuñi country, Coronado began to consider if there might not be better things a little farther on. Perhaps the reported gold of Cíbola—disgustingly notable by its absence—might actually exist in some other "kingdom," a word the Spaniards persisted in applying to various Indian countries, although among the Indians within the present borders of the United States no such thing as a kingdom was known. Government in the pueblos was by the old men and the priesthood. There were also chiefs or *caciques*, sometimes called by the Spaniards *capitáns*, who had a very loose authority, pithily summed up by Juan de Oñate half a century later: "In their government they are free, for although they have some petty captains, they obey them badly and in very few things."

Coronado's conclusions were obvious. He must investigate the lands farther on for treasure as well as information. Furthermore, there was this to consider: the people themselves might be a form of wealth.

In the Americas the Spaniards had evolved a pleasant and profitable (to themselves) institution called the *encomienda*. The sense of the word is a recommendation, a commission or a patronage. But this euphemism did not interfere in the slightest degree with its real meaning, which was slavery. By the terms of this system, "pacified" territory was divided into estates and given to the chief *conquistadores*. The people dwelling on those lands at the same time were "recommended" to the care of the new owners and made tributary to them, which included the right of their masters to force them to labor for them.

It was all very legal, with the agreement of everyone save the unfortunate natives who were its victims.

To do justice to the Spanish government, and to some of the truly humanitarian religionists, like the great bishops, Las Casas and Zumárraga, it was intended to make this overlordship as gentle as possible. *Encomienderos* were enjoined to behave toward their serfs as kind fathers rather than merciless taskmasters, teaching their wards the arts of civilization, instructing them in Christian doctrine, watching over and guiding them, and protecting them from injuries and undue burdens.

But Spain was far away, the natives close at hand, and the colonists eager to get rich quickly. The father-protector role was quickly disregarded; the "arts of civilization" were taught under the stinging lash of the slave whip; and the overlords took it for granted that the "injuries and undue burdens" from which they must protect their vassals were those that might be imposed by outsiders, never themselves. It must be admitted that the doctrines of the Christian Catholic religion were sedulously taught to the natives, particularly the virtues of humbleness and long-suffering, and the beauty of contemplating the hereafter as a heavenly reward for the labors, pains and unhappiness of this transitory existence.

Sometimes the natives accepted this new state, sometimes they resisted. But the results were about the same in either case. If they resisted, they were murdered at once, or at once put into chained slavery. If they accepted, the bonds of serfdom were wound about them more slowly and tenderly, but with equal strength. They died off so rapidly in some districts, such as the Antilles, that to replenish their labor ranks regular slave-hunting expeditions were organized, one of which was responsible for the discovery of New Spain itself.

Indians who lived in pueblos and tilled the soil were naturally more valuable for *encomiendas* than wild nomadic tribes, who were hard to catch and harder to keep. The Pueblo Indians were accustomed to the discipline of labor and were comparatively mild and tractable by temperament; usually fighting only in self-defense, and then none too efficiently, as Coronado's capture of Hawikuh had demonstrated. With this thought it is easy to comprehend the eagerness of the Spaniards to explore further the territories and peoples of Cíbola.

First, Coronado dispatched Tovar with twenty soldiers and Fray Juan de Padilla, the fighting Franciscan who had been a soldier, to the land of the Moquis (Hopis), which was reported west of Cíbola.

While he waited for the return of this expedition, the captain general made a full written report to the viceroy and sent it southward by Juan Gallego and a small escort. Melchior Díaz accompanied this party, with orders to establish a base camp on the Sonora River as a connecting link between Cíbola and New Spain, and instructions to scout westward to see if he could find out what had happened to Alarcón and the naval expedition up the Gulf of California.

One other went with these. Fray Marcos de Niza took advantage of the escort to return to the capital. He was a very unhappy man. A good many in the army, including Coronado, blamed him for their unfortunate situation, and uncomplimentary remarks embittered his life. Of his departure Castañeda wrote:

"Fray Marcos did not consider it safe to remain at Cíbola, since his report had proved false in every particular. For they had not found the kingdoms he had told about, neither populous cities, nor the wealth of gold and precious stones that had been proclaimed, nor brocades, nor other things that had been told from the pulpits."

Shortly after his return to New Spain, Fray Marcos was paralyzed by a stroke and later died in obscurity.

Meantime Tovar marched westward with Zuñi guides to the Hopi pueblos, which were similar to those of Cíbola. His arrival was after nightfall, so the Spaniards concealed themselves, being able to hear the people of the pueblo on the mesa talking to each other, unconscious of the peril that crouched near them.

With the coming of dawn the Spanish party was discovered, and the Hopis, recovering from their surprise, swarmed out to give battle.

Tovar went through the customary mummery. Sending forward his interpreters, he called on the Hopis through them to render obedience to God and the king. This utterance, to the Spanish mind, legalized anything that followed, for by it the natives were considered to have been swept into the capacious arms of Spain, and whatever they did in the way of resistance could be regarded as rebellious—a nice point of legality, but the Spaniards always were careful in such matters.

The Hopis showed little disposition to accede to this new definition of their status. They drew the customary line of colored meal over which the invaders were not to pass, and when some of the Spaniards did so, one of the Indians grew so "impudent" that he struck a horse ridden by a *caballero* with a club.

Only twenty against many were the Spaniards, but Fray Juan de Padilla, who had never forgotten his soldiery training, exclaimed to Tovar, "To tell the truth, I don't know for what we came here!"

The benison of the Church being given in this manner, Tovar shouted the *Santiago,* and the horsemen charged, the fighting friar among them. Several of the contumacious natives lost their lives or were captured, and the rest were routed.

It was enough. The Hopis sent down gifts from the pueblo and begged for peace. Representatives from the six other pueblos of the people hurried in soon after with more presents—a little cotton cloth, tanned skins, maize, piñon nuts and a few turquoises—and surrendered also.

Having thus "pacified" the Hopis, and lacking authority to go beyond, Tovar returned to Coronado, arriving about three weeks after he had left. He could give his general no encouragement as to gold and precious stones, but he did have one piece of information picked up in his tour of two hundred and fifty miles. Farther west there was a great river. From reports it was navigable. It might be the long-sought way to the western sea.

Presented thus with another chance to save his expedition, Coronado immediately dispatched Cárdenas, with twenty-five horsemen, to discover the river and claim it for His Most Catholic Majesty. It was not, of course, realized that this was the same river—the Colorado—which already had been discovered and claimed two or three times at or near its mouth: by Ulloa, Cortés' explorer; by Alarcón, who was supposed to support Coronado; and by Díaz, who reached it a little later overland from the Sonora Valley.

After twenty days of rough travel Cárdenas found his river. Indeed, he found something that has caused people to gasp with awe throughout all these centuries since—the Grand Canyon of the Colorado. What those first white men must have said and thought as they gazed down into that stupendous mile-deep gash in the earth, with its multicolored splendor of rocky crags and pinnacles, is not of record. But Cárdenas, who was told by his Indian guides that the river, looking no more than a silver trickle far below, was "half a league"—a mile and a half—across, spent three days trying to find a way down to it. On the final day Captain Melgosa, Juan Galeras and "another companion"—possibly an Indian guide, since he remained nameless— tried to climb down the terrific walls to the river. Late in the afternoon they clambered back to the top, exhausted, having been less than a third of the way down. But they had visual proof of the immensity of the canyon. Some rocks, jutting out from the wall, had been estimated by those looking from the top of the gorge as "about the height of a man." The climbers reported those rocks were "taller than the highest tower of Seville"—and the perspective grew in proportion.

But scenery, however awe-inspiring and sublime, was not what Cárdenas sought. His men were thirsty and hungry, and after following the brink of the mighty *barranca* for a distance, he returned to Coronado, more interested in a salt spring he discovered than in the greatest canyon in all the world.

One more thread needs to be tied. Melchior Díaz, that brave and loyal soldier, going south with the party of Gallego and Fray Marcos, encountered the main body of the army, led by Arellano, toiling northward to join Coronado. He commandeered from it a detachment, established his camp on the Sonora River, naming it San Gerónimo, and leaving as its temporary *alcalde* Diego de Alcaraz, marched west with twenty-five Spaniards, some Indian servants, a herd of sheep for provisions, and a greyhound, to look for Alarcón.

In due time he reached the Colorado, discovered a message left by Alarcón to the effect that the navigator had been there and gone back, and found the natives hostile, especially the Yumas, among whom were noticed some gigantic men of great strength. Here, as always, the Spanish leaven had begun to work, and while he made ready to cross the river, Díaz suspected a hostile plot among the natives. At once he had one of the Indians seized and examined under torture, whereupon the prisoner confessed that his people were planning to wait until part of the Spaniards were on the far shore, another part in the middle of the river crossing, and the rest on their own side, whereupon they would attack the divided force on both banks of the river.

The captive was killed and his body secretly sunk with heavy weights in the river, so that the Yumas would not know that he had turned informer. When the Indians made their attack the Spaniards were ready. Stone-headed arrows and primitive war clubs proved inferior to arquebuses, steel swords, and lances wielded from the backs of horses by armored men. Leaden balls shook the hostile array, the lancers and swordsmen raged among them, and the Yumas took to their heels, leaving their dead behind.

Crossing the Colorado after this battle, Díaz advanced perhaps into what is now the Imperial Valley of California, in the vicinity where the Salton Sea was formed long afterward. And there the captain, who had survived so many armed clashes with enemies, was fatally injured in a singular accident. The greyhound which had accompanied the expedition began to chase the sheep. Díaz, pursuing the dog, threw his lance at it. He missed the animal, but the lance struck in the ground in such a manner that he, being unable to stop his horse, impaled himself on it, the shaft penetrating his groin and bursting his bladder.

For twenty days his sorrowing followers bore him homeward, suffering. But he died before they reached the first Spanish outpost, and was buried in the desert. By courier Coronado received word that he had lost one of his best.

Having decided by now that the west was profitless—and it is ironic that the Spaniards, with their lust for gold, overlooked the very land where it was most plentiful, California—Coronado began thinking of the prospects eastward. He could not give up without exhausting every possible lead, for his fortune was invested in this expedition, and Mendoza had in it an even greater sum. Perhaps the viceroy's interests were a greater consideration to the young general than his own, for the wrath of a superior was not to be taken lightly in the Spanish realms.

Word had come of another "kingdom" called Ácucu, or Ácus—a fair enough rendition of Áko, the Indian name for Ácoma, as we know the pueblo today. Should he investigate it, or was it only another of Fray Marcos' chimeras?

While he hesitated, the decision was made for him. One day a small deputation of natives arrived in the Spanish camp at Hawikuh, saying that they were from a distant place called Cicuye—Coronado's Spanish tongue and pen found it impossible to pronounce or spell an Indian word like Tshiquite. It was the name, as it turned out, of the principal one of a populous group of pueblos, later known as Pecos, located in the upper valley of the Pecos River.

Heading the deputation were two chiefs, one of whom, because he had a mustache—probably of a few thin hairs as do some Pueblo Indians today—was called Bigotes (Whiskers) by the Spaniards. The other, an older man, they simply called Cacique, or chief.

Bigotes, tall and impressive, was the spokesman. He said that his people had heard of "strange, bold men"—the Spaniards—and wanted to make friends. Evidently the reports of the actions of Coronado's men were somewhat alarming, carried by runners from the Zuñi villages who had no need to exaggerate the facts in the case.

To Coronado, Bigotes offered gifts—dressed skins, headpieces, shields and other handwork, which the general "received with affection." It was the kind of affection with which the tiger gazes upon the plump and innocent lamb.

Something was given the visitors in return: beads and little bells. And they were provided with lodgings. Though the circumstances is not reported, one can presume that the "lodgings" had a lock and key on the outside, and perhaps armed sentinels, for the Spaniards wanted to question these men and would not like to see them get away.

Next day the questioning began and Coronado learned much. First, there were settled regions to the east. Second, there were "cattle," immense herds of them. One of the Indians had a buffalo "painted"— perhaps tattooed—on his body, and from this epidermal representation the Spaniards gained an idea of the humped beasts of the plains. It corroborated one of Cabeza de Vaca's stories and fanned the dying embers of a hope that perhaps gold might still be discovered. Cabeza de Vaca had told also of populous cities and fertile valleys, of turquoises and emeralds, and finally of "many signs of gold, antimony, copper and other metals." Enough to make one drool. Perhaps to the *east* was the true El Dorado!

Coronado acted with promptitude. Detaching another of his bold captains, Hernando de Alvarado, who with Cárdenas had saved the general's life at the storming of Hawikuh, he organized yet another exploring expedition. Alvarado was a brother of the famous Pedro de Alvarado, the Tonatiuh of the Mexican and Guatemalan conquests, and he had the family bravery, ferocity in battle, and also the family hunger for gold or any other wealth.

Taking as guides Bigotes and his companions, the party of twenty or more horsemen, with four crossbowmen and the indefatigable Fray Juan de Padilla on foot, set out August 19, 1540. Marching eastward, they saw several abandoned pueblos, and after crossing the *malpais* of jagged black volcanic slag, they beheld Ácoma, the famous "City in the Sky," of which Bandelier was one day to write, "No other town in the earth is so nobly perched. The only foreign hints of it are the Königstein, in Saxony; and (perhaps) the Gwalior, in the Deccan."

Alvarado's own description, while not so poetic, covered the situation: "The pueblo was one of the strongest ever seen, because the city is built on a very high rock. The ascent was so difficult that we repented of climbing to the top."

These natives were friendly, gave the Spaniards the usual gifts, and seemed anxious—with every good reason—to see them on their way. Provisioned by Ácoma, Alvarado proceeded and presently came upon Tiguex (*Ti-wesh,* the Indian name), a collection of pueblos near the present site of Bernalillo, on the Rio Grande, which the Spaniards named the Nuestra Señora. Reports concerning the Spaniards and their methods were getting wide dissemination in pueblo land, and representatives from twelve pueblos promptly visited Alvarado's camp with gifts and an eager plea for peace.

In turn, Alvarado visited the twelve pueblos, and probably went through the usual formula for claiming them for Spain. We know that he erected several crosses, no doubt under Fray Juan's direction; and the natives, eager to co-operate, promptly decorated these sacred symbols with feathers, powders and "even the cotton garments they wore." One wonders what the good Friar Padilla thought as he watched the stark symbols of his faith receive these garish embellishments.

Presently the Spaniards passed on up the river, visiting a pueblo they called Braba—the famous Taos of today, favorite of tourists and artists. Thence, turning southward, they came to Pecos, or Cicuye, home of Bigotes and his companions. The Spaniards were feasted, and serenaded with drumming and primitive fife playing. Pecos was a highly strategic point, lying in the pass through the Sangre de Cristo Mountains through which east-and-west trade, hunting and war parties passed between the pueblo country and the great plains.

CHAPTER FIVE

Enter the Second Liar

AT PECOS, Alvarado rested a few days, but he still had to see the "cattle" described by Bigotes. When he was ready to travel again, however, Bigotes begged off, saying he already had been absent too long from his pueblo. As a substitute he offered two "slaves" who knew the buffalo plains.

One of these, probably because he wore some sort of a turban on his head, the Spaniards named El Turco (the Turk) "because he looked like one." For the present Alvarado saw nothing particularly remarkable in El Turco, who was from a distant country called Harahay—since identified as the land of the Pawnees. But had the Spanish captain known it, he stood in the presence of the second of the great creative liars who were to exert such influence on Coronado, Fray Marcos being the first.

The other slave was named Isopete. He was from Quivira, since established as the region of the Wichita Indians in Kansas. The latter called themselves Kirikurus, and Quivira was about as close as the Spanish could get to such native tongue twisters.

A word here about slaves and slavery. Though slavery was widely practiced not only among the civilized Aztecs and other peoples of Mexico but in the Pacific Northwest, there is considerable doubt that El Turco and Isopete were slaves in the Spanish concept of the word, or that slavery in its real sense existed among either the Pueblo or the Plains Indians at this time. It remained for the white man to give the red man the true conception of the institution, and the natives learned rapidly, but at this time they were innocent in the matter.

Inveterate slave drivers themselves, the Spaniards assumed that what they saw was slavery, but it was something quite different. In the constant intertribal wars of the Indians frequent population losses occurred. To compensate for these losses the system of capture and adoption had become virtually universal. Though, after a battle, some prisoners frequently were put to death by torture or otherwise, when the savage passions of the victors had been glutted the rest of the prisoners often were taken into the tribe, being expected to assume the place of lost husbands, wives or children.

Adopted, even against his will, the prisoner had a status very different from that of a slave. The latter had no rights whatever, while the former, within the fabric of personal relations and character, was theoretically on an equal footing with his captors. In the later Indian wars white women and girls often were captured by raiding war parties, and these, in spite of their own dismay and horror, were almost without exception taken as squaws by the warriors, and in very many cases had children by them. White men, being less easily handled, usually were slain. White children, often were brought up in the wild tribes and became Indians to all intents and purposes. The case of Cynthia Ann Parker, to which later reference will be made, is one in point.

Accustomed to this system of capture and adoption, captive squaws made little objection to becoming wives of warriors who had taken them prisoner or perhaps bought them, their children were treated as equal to any in the adopting tribe, and captive warriors also accepted the status placed upon them, particularly since in many tribes one who was captured was disowned and ceased to have any connection with his own people.

El Turco and Isopete, taken prisoner by Bigotes himself, probably were undergoing the preliminary probationary period which would have ended in their marrying into and becoming members of the Pecos tribe. But at the time of Alvarado's arrival they seem to have been newly captive and both desired to return to their homes, a motive which would have an important bearing on the future.

With these two as guides, Alvarado rode west until he reached a river—probably the Canadian. Shortly he saw herds of buffalo, and an astounded man was he.

"The cattle . . . are the most monstrous beasts ever seen or read about. . . . There are such multitudes of them that I do not know what to compare them with unless it be the fish of the sea. . . . Their meat is as good as that of the cattle of Castile, and some said it was even better."

The Spaniards held the first white man's buffalo hunt on the continent. "We availed ourselves of them, although with danger to the horses at first, until we gained experience." Also, "The bulls are large and fierce, although they do not attack very often. But they have

wicked horns and they charge and thrust savagely. They killed several
of our horses and wounded many others."

The nemesis of the bison—the buffalo-running horse—had arrived,
and would, eventually, come into common use in every Plains tribe.

Just at this time El Turco created his first sensation.

"By signs, and in the Mexican tongue, of which he knew a little,"
he told Alvarado that he should turn northeast, because in that direction lay a country called Quivira, which possessed gold, silver and
fabrics, and was "abundant and fruitful in everything."

Alvarado stopped right there, forgot about buffalo hunting, and
began to question his guide. Obviously El Turco was a savage of more
than ordinary intelligence and close observation. He had marked the
affection of the Spaniards for the yellow metal, of which he probably
saw samples in rings, brooches and even bracelets, for the grandees
were not above wearing such ornaments. He could not have hit upon
a more magical formula to attract and rivet interest on himself.

It should be remarked here that El Turco did not use the word
"gold." What he said, evidently, was *ha-kwi-chis*, the word for "metal,"
in the language of the Harahays and Quiviras—Pawnees and Wichitas
—who are closely allied in language and blood. In the transliteration
the Spaniards spelled this *acochis*, and the term came to be regarded
as meaning gold, and by misinterpretation was even applied to the
country of Quivira itself.

El Turco could have had no actual experience with gold, and his
observation of any metal must have been confined to occasional copper
trinkets traded down from the Lake Superior region where mines
were worked and primitive metallurgy, chiefly the pounding of raw
ingots into the shapes desired, was practiced. Cabeza de Vaca had
seen evidence of this when Dorantes, of his party, came into possession
of a rattle made of copper, carved like a human face. But El Turco
was not going to permit a free-wheeling imagination to be curbed
by limited personal experience. His next step was characteristic.

Perhaps he had a grudge against Bigotes, his captor. He now proceeded to say that Bigotes was well acquainted with Quivira, and
owned a gold bracelet from there. To give this an air of veracity, he
added, as if it were an afterthought, that he himself had brought the
trinket down from his own country, but it had been appropriated from
him.

There is little question that he hoped by this story to induce Alvarado to turn northeast toward his homeland, perhaps expecting to
escape there from the Spaniards. But he wrought too well. To a
Spaniard, distant gold was never as attractive as known gold, even in

small quantity. Instead of going forward, Alvarado ordered a counter-march. He was going to see Bigotes about that bracelet. It was, further-more, his duty to report the interesting new development to his commander.

With disappointment and misgivings El Turco saw this turn of af-fairs. On the way back to Pecos he tried to hedge his story by caution-ing Alvarado not to mention the gold bracelet to Bigotes, for fear the Pecos people would kill him for telling.

Alvarado, however, believed in the direct method. As soon as he saw Bigotes and Cacique, he demanded from them the bracelet. Their astonishment should have convinced anyone but a Spaniard. They "denied in all possible ways that they had any such ornament. In fact, El Turco was lying."

But good Spanish custom presumed everyone guilty until proved innocent. Alvarado invited the chiefs to his tent, where he had them overpowered and put in chains. He took the precaution also of plac-ing El Turco under guard. Somebody was lying here, and the captain meant to learn who it was.

Up to now the Pecos people had shown the Spaniards nothing but friendship and hospitality, but at this flagrant and inexcusable breach of good faith the men of the pueblos swarmed out angrily, shooting arrows and yelling that Alvarado had broken his word and violated his faith.

Their demonstration failed to ruffle the war-hardened Spaniards and the arrows seem to have injured nobody.

Shortly after, El Turco managed to slip away from his guards. To Alvarado this was worse than hostile arrows and epithets. Accusing Bigotes and Cacique of aiding the prisoner's flight, he told them he would never release them until El Turco was returned.

That brought action. Cacique was allowed to go to his people while Bigotes was detained, and the slippery El Turco was captured and brought back. Thereupon Alvarado clapped Cacique back in irons, and the pueblos hummed again with hostility.

Again El Turco disappeared, and so did Isopete. But threats to the chiefs once more brought them back, which leads to a suspicion that Alvarado was not so wrong about the complicity, or at least knowledge, of Bigotes and Cacique concerning these "evasive tactics."

Eventually the Spaniards marched back with their four prisoners to Tiguex, where they awaited the arrival of Coronado and the main army. Alvarado had added greatly to the knowledge of the geography of the Southwest and its peoples. He also had erected some bitter enmities.

Arellano had by this time reached Hawikuh with the main army, and Coronado sent Cárdenas to establish winter quarters at Tiguex, then moved with the rest of his men eastward from Zuñi land.

Cárdenas, arriving at Tiguex, where there were twelve pueblos, six on each side of the river, made his preparations in the cool Spanish manner. Selecting the pueblo he considered best fitted as barracks for the army, he notified its inhabitants that they would have to move out and find room with their friends in the other pueblos during the winter. The population of the pueblo on which he visited this honor— the southernmost of the group, called Alcanfor—vacated as ordered, although not without unhappy complaints. This unhappiness would have been greater had the Indians known what was to befall them when these dangerous white strangers came to live in such perilous proximity to them.

Cold weather was setting in, for fall was well advanced. A snow-storm had swept Arellano's column just before it reached Hawikuh, and the Indian auxiliaries, who were from the warm regions of New Spain, suffered so severely that some had to be carried on horseback to Coronado's camp. That the army find warm quarters was imperative, and Coronado must have been greatly relieved when, on reaching Tiguex, he found that the forehanded Cárdenas had provided a whole pueblo—warm and dry, though perhaps a bit smelly—by moving the owners out.

This was most welcome. But the real excitement was furnished by Alvarado, who with his prisoners and his story of gold also awaited his leader.

Brought before Coronado, El Turco threw aside the coyness he had been displaying since he had been in the company of Bigotes and Cacique. Again he told of the land of gold and gems, Quivira. Coronado must have listened with the open mouth and eager eyes of the self-convinced.

Such an audience stimulated El Turco, and his imagination, sufficiently active heretofore, embarked on flights that displayed a touch of genius. In that golden land, he told Coronado, a river flowed with fish "big as horses," on the waters of which a vast number of canoes floated, with sails, and more than twenty oarsmen on each side.

Some of the huge catfish of the Mississippi-Missouri river system have been known to reach a length of six feet and a weight of 250 pounds, but the comparison in size to horses reveals the scorn of El Turco for a mere trifle like fact. The "vast number" of canoes is another peg for appraising the wonderful store of falsehood in El Turco's system. The chief river flowing through Quivira was the Arkansas, which for most of the year runs nearly dry, and even in times of freshet was crossed by "bull boats"—coraclelike affairs made of green buffalo hides stretched over a basketlike frame of willows—or at most by crude rafts or dugouts. But El Turco's canoes had twenty "oarsmen" on each side—and *sails!* Where did he get that conception? Had some story reached his country of the winged ships of white explorers on distant seacoasts? Or was it sheer inspiration?

But there were further marvels. The "nobles," he told Coronado, rode seated under canopies in the sterns of these gargantuan canoes, and at the prows of the craft were "golden eagles."

Good, very good. But the master touch was still to follow. The lord of that land was named Tatarrax, and this potentate, said El Turco, took his *siesta*—that invariable Spanish custom seems to have struck the narrator quite forcibly—under a tree from which hung many golden bells, the musical tinkling of which lulled him pleasantly to slumber. One must pause to marvel at the powers of invention that could think that one up, since El Turco had never seen gold in his life, nor indeed any of the things he recounted. As another of his little afterthoughts, it was later said, he added that the "common table service of everybody" was generally of "wrought silver," and the "pitchers, dishes, and bowls were made of gold."

How well he understood his listeners! Where a few golden bells and even golden-eagle figureheads might not be enough to tempt them to make the perilous march northward, mention of such plenitude of gold and silver that it was used even in "common table service" was irresistible to them. *Table service*—in a land where food was eaten out of a pot on the earthen floor, and where no such article as a table was known.

The Spaniards swallowed the whole story "because of his straight-forward manner in telling . . . and also because, when they showed him ornaments made of tin, he smelled them and said they were not gold, for he knew gold and silver very well, and cared little for other metals."

That bland, innocent expression—one pictures it to oneself. And the Spaniards, beguiled, believing absolutely because they so wanted to believe, accepting every fabrication. The enormous capacity of the Spaniards to believe they heard *what they wanted to hear* must be taken into account. Could it be that in their self-deception they unconsciously invented the whole story of the "table service"and put it into El Turco's mouth, by asking him questions so that all he had to do was corroborate their hopes?

In any case, El Turco achieved what he wanted: he made himself the hero of the army, so that for a time the men ascribed to him almost supernatural powers. In so doing he also brought about the downfall of Bigotes. Completely deluded by El Turco, the Spaniards decided that Bigotes was deceiving them when he continued to deny that he had the golden bracelet of which El Turco had told.

Coronado assigned Fray Juan de Padilla and Alvarado to "put the question" to the chief. This was the first step of the process worked out by the Spanish Inquisition, which was operated by the Dominican monks in Spain, but in the New World was under the Franciscans, of whom Padilla was a member. The Inquisition's system, which had been so successful, was: first, the "question" was put by the religious; then, if the one questioned proved obdurate, he was delivered over to the "secular arm."

Fray Padilla reported that Bigotes "denied everything." He was thereupon delivered over to the secular arm, taken to an open field, and some fierce hounds belonging to Captain Tovar were set on him to terrorize him into confessing where he had hidden the gold bracelet. Old Cacique also was subjected to the tearing teeth of the beasts.

In spite of his wounds Bigotes stuck to his denial and so did Cacique. Thereafter the two of them, together with El Turco and Isopete, were kept imprisoned for the remainder of the winter. Already the Spaniards had found something new to divert them.

Spanish "kindness" to the natives had by this time been prolonged beyond all precedent. It had been broken only by such melees as those at Hawikuh and the Hopi pueblo, and Alvarado's high hand at Pecos. But remembering Mendoza's pious injunctions, Coronado held off real Spanish oppression, such as was practiced elsewhere. Something was due to explode.

Even before Coronado arrived at Tiguex, an incident occurred which was an indication of the future. A young grandee in Cárdenas' command, Juan de Villegas, saw a pretty woman at the pueblo of Arenal six miles upstream from Alcanfor, where the Spaniards were quartered. Calling her husband down to hold his horse, Villegas climbed into the pueblo above and ravished the woman. When her husband later angrily reported it to Cárdenas, although the offender was identified he was not punished because he was a brother of a high official in New Spain.

This rape, combined with the dog baiting of the Pecos chiefs, thoroughly alarmed and antagonized the Indians of Tiguex. But more trouble was coming their way. Coronado's army needed food and clothing. Detachments marched to the eleven pueblos occupied by Indians to obtain three hundred cloaks of skin or cotton. Their methods were brusque. When a mantle was given them, if the giver wore one that was better, the superior garment was torn off him and taken away. Turkeys, maize and other provisions were requisitioned in a similar manner. The Indians were furious. Once when a soldier attempted to seize a garment he was beaten with hoes and thrust inside a house. His Spanish comrades rescued him and arrested the Indians responsible, but when they were taken before Cárdenas, that captain ordered them freed.

"What do you expect, señores?" he said. "Has not the captain general ordered that if an Indian gives a Spaniard a blow in the face he must turn the other cheek?"

The sarcasm indicated the temper of both soldiers and their officers, which had a low boiling point at best. An overt act was certain to come. One day a Mexican Indian horse herd, wounded, staggered into camp with word that the natives of Tiguex had attacked the horse guard, killed one man, and driven off the horses.

Cárdenas, who was army master, acted with exemplary promptitude. With a force of mounted men he rode hard on the trail of the stolen herd. Ominous signs multiplied. The pueblo nearest Alcanfor, the one called Alameda, was deserted. Farther along, near Arenal, where the rape of the Indian woman had occurred, two or three dead horses were found, killed by arrows. The trail led across the Rio Grande, which was forded, and on the other side twenty-five more arrow-riddled carcasses were found, including seven mules belonging to Cárdenas himself.

Most of the living horses were rounded up and started back to camp. But on the way, passing Arenal, the Spaniards discovered a corral of palisades, in which some of the still missing horses were being chased around, "as in a bull ring," the natives shooting arrows at the animals. Cárdenas remonstrated but was greeted with hoots and jeers. He thereupon returned to Coronado to report.

Coronado called a council of war. It was agreed by all the captains, and also the friars, that the "rebellion"—for now it was regarded as such—should be put down by force of arms.

Not all the army had yet arrived at Tiguex, but Coronado decided to attack with the men he had. Spanish indignation was hottest toward the pueblo called Arenal, because of the horse episode. If there was one thing a Spaniard could love, it was a horse. To slaughter horses indiscriminately and cruelly was revolting—especially to do it by running them around "as in a bull ring," without even a bull! The difference between having a horse disemboweled on a bull's horns and having him killed with arrows, which may appear tenuous to some, was very real and apparent to a Spaniard. The first was sport; the second, desecration.

To Cárdenas, who personally had lost seven mules, Coronado gave the task of capturing and punishing Arenal, and the discoverer of the Grand Canyon accepted the assignment gladly. First the usual cere-

monial: the natives were notified of "the evil they had done" and
called upon to state their grievances and render obedience, whereupon they would be pardoned for their "rebellion." Since the natives
had so many grievances, ranging from the rape of the woman down
through robbery to mere insult, they did not bother to state them, and
since they correctly mistrusted the Spaniards they replied to Cárdenas
with yells and jeers.

The captain thereupon sent mounted lancers to surround the pueblo
and cut off escape and with his main force began the assault. Now
grew the roar of gunfire, the shouts, the dust and smoke, the flash of
arms and whizzing of arrows. With their invariable courage the Spaniards stormed against the walls, but though the arquebuses and crossbows were superior to the native bows, so that many warriors died on
the terraces, the Indians defended the pueblo with such tenacity and
courage that it was several hours before the Spaniards at last mounted
the *azoteas,* during which time they lost a good many men, killed and
wounded.

Though the terraces were now in Spanish hands, Arenal still held
out. Driven from their *azoteas,* the warriors shut themselves, with
their women and children, inside the pueblo and defied their foes.
Night descended and snow began to fall, adding to the discomfort of
the attackers on the terraces. As lean Spanish shanks shivered in the
chill wind, hot Spanish wrath kindled against the stubborn defenders.

Cárdenas sent his wounded to Alcanfor, with a report of progress
to Coronado, and received back a message ordering him to continue
the battle until victory was won. Such an injunction was not needed
by Cárdenas. He had Arenal by the throat and he wanted blood—
plenty of it.

At dawn the battle was resumed, with more losses on each side, and
it began to look like a stalemate. But Cárdenas, looking the place over,
hit on a scheme to force out the defenders where his men could get
at them. With bars and axes he directed his men to break into the
lower story of the pueblo, which was used only for storage, and
within it he caused "heavy smudge fires to be built," which soon filled
the entire upper pueblo with smoke. The suffocating defenders stood it
as long as they could, then begged to surrender. Captains Melgosa
and Lopez accepted the surrender on a promise of mercy.

But Cárdenas was not a party to the promise. His orders from Coronado were "not to take anyone alive, in order to impose a punishment
that would intimidate the others." Accordingly, having gathered two
hundred prisoners together, he caused two hundred stakes to be
driven in the ground and faggots gathered to burn his captives to death.

Seeing the preparations, the terrified Indians made a last futile effort to break away. In their despairing struggle, without weapons, about a hundred died by the sword and thus at least gained an easy death. Some managed to escape and carry word of this further breach of faith to the other pueblos. The rest, about thirty, perished agonizingly, lashed to the stakes and consumed by the flames.

Among those who watched this horror were Bigotes, Cacique, El Turco and Isopete, who were sent over from Alcanfor to "witness the penalty inflicted . . . in order that they might spread the news among their people in their new land."

Cárdenas marched his men back to Alcanfor, where Coronado "approved what he had done" and gave him hearty embraces. Later Coronado was to say that Cárdenas acted without his knowledge in burning the natives, but the sending over of Bigotes and the others to witness the penalty, and the embraces and approval of Cárdenas on his return, make this almost impossible to believe.

In spite of the terrible punishment of Arenal, the people of Tiguex were by no means subdued. Perhaps in desperation, but certainly with valor, most of their warriors withdrew to a large pueblo called Moho, of which the *cacique* was Juan Alemán (John the German), so called by the Spaniards because to their eyes at least he had a Teutonic look.

Once more were taken the usual steps whereby Spanish consciences were eased: the pueblo was called on to render obedience, cease its "rebellious ways," and accept pardon for its "misdeeds" on penalty of war.

But Juan Alemán and his people of Moho had knowledge of the kind of "pardon" the Spaniards gave. Still stank in the air the smoke of charred Arenal, and there were the ghastly ashes where thirty Indians died at the stake.

Followed by thirty men, Cárdenas rode around the walls to reconnoiter. Looking up, he saw Juan Alemán, who smiled at him and invited him to come up on the *azotea* to exchange embraces of friendship. With amazing foolhardiness the captain accepted.

Leaving his weapons behind, he climbed a ladder let down for him. All at once Juan Alemán seized him about the arms with a bear hug that rendered him helpless, some of the Indians rained blows on his helmet that stunned him, and they began to carry him into the pueblo. They blamed him for the cruelties at Arenal, and perhaps intended to torture him to death in retribution.

But pueblo doors are narrow. Cárdenas recovered his senses enough to brace himself as they tried to get him through, until his companions could rush to his rescue. In the brief fight that followed, while the captain was being brought away, several Spaniards were wounded.

Cárdenas himself had an arrow through one of his legs, besides an aching head.

Coronado and the main army now moved up to the assault. Remembering their stratagem at Arenal, the Spaniards first tried to break into the lower story of Moho to smoke the inmates out. Now they discovered why this pueblo had been chosen for defense. Beneath the outer coat of stone and adobe its walls were made of trunks of trees, interwoven with poles, so strong that they could not be penetrated by battering rams, crowbars or fire.

The Spaniards looked grimly up. Nothing for it but to carry the place by assault.

In all the world existed no better fighting men than the Spanish soldiers, and Coronado's men were fully worthy of their great military tradition. Yet now, for the first time, they were to meet defeat.

Placing ladders against the walls, they fought their way upward, against desperate resistance, battling for every inch they gained. When they cleared a foothold on the first terrace, reinforcements hurried up the ladders, and the fight continued, story after story.

Everywhere the Indians resisted fiercely. From the upper *azoteas* they hurled down stones and boulders, stretching out many a Spaniard. With the stones came showers of poisoned arrows, made deadly with rattlesnake venom. Some men, wounded by these arrows, died in agony; others were left with scars for the remainder of their days.

Yet, rage as they might, clambering from one *azotea* to another, showering sword blows on every yelling Indian in sight, and storming savagely at the doors which were defended as savagely from within, the Spaniards could not subdue the pueblo. At length they were forced to fall back sullenly, carrying their dead and wounded with them.

Coronado's men had received very rough handling and the hospital list was large—nearly one hundred casualties. The general decided to set siege to the place.

For fifty days it continued, with many assaults made and repulsed, in one of which Captain Francisco de Ovando was dragged inside the pueblo and put to death. Cold weather set in, snows were frequent, and in the siege lines the Spaniards shivered and sniffled and there was much sickness.

But if conditions were bad for the besiegers they were desperate in the pueblo. In the middle of March the defenders of Moho sent out their women and children, begging the Spaniards to be merciful to them. This the Spaniards promised to do, and kept their promise by at once ushering these unfortunates into a life of slavery.

Two weeks later the men in the pueblo made their bid for freedom— a night sortie and flight. Cavaliers sprang to horse and pursued in the gloom. Swords flailed among the fugitives, and the trail was bloody with dead. A few were captured and became slaves. Those who escaped sprang into the icy flood of the Rio Grande and by swimming reached the other side.

So passed the winter. The Spaniards were kept warm (part of the time) by their exertions at the long siege and final reduction of Moho. To the most censorious eye the "pacification" of Tiguex was complete. All twelve pueblos were destroyed or partly destroyed, everything of value taken from them, and every person found in or near them—although almost all had fled to the mountains—was killed or placed in slavery.

Spain, civilization and Christianity had left a sufficiently bad stench throughout the pueblo country. It was time for Coronado to extend his efforts at pacification and conversion to fresh territories, and as the weather moderated he made his plans to do so.

CHAPTER SIX

The Llano Estacado

WHILE the siege of Moho was in progress, El Turco, under guard at Alcanfor, kept his wits and tongue busy, and by design or by chance took a cunning psychological method of whetting Spanish curiosity concerning the fabulous "kingdom" of Quivira, by letting drop fresh hints at nicely spaced intervals.

His river, on which canoes with sails had plied, now became a great lake, and he added *golden* oarlocks to the craft which carried the ruler himself. Furthermore, there was so much gold that not only horses but *wagons* could be loaded with it.

A remarkable savage, El Turco. How could he conceive of "golden oarlocks," since at best he could have seen nothing but wooden paddles, used in the common Indian way and dispensing with oarlocks, golden or otherwise? How could he speak of wagons, when his eyes never had rested on a wheeled vehicle, since all the Coronado baggage came on pack animals or men's backs?

Probably he heard these things in chance bits of conversation, eagerly waited until other references gave him an inkling of what they were, and then, at the right moment, dropped them casually into his stories, with his usual aureous adjectives.

There was more along this line. The monarch of Quivira was mighty, and served by many people in a great house. He was carried to war by his subjects in a splendid litter. These touches were so reminiscent of Montezuma, from whom the *conquistadores* had extorted great wealth, that it made a Spaniard believe, even if he had not yearned to do so.

El Turco became increasingly generous in details. The lord of Quivira, it appeared, had hounds which he kept muzzled, except when he unleashed them to tear his enemies to pieces. Perhaps the dog baiting of Bigotes and Cacique inspired this touch, but to the Spaniards who were well acquainted with dog baiting it added a convincing note. At judicious intervals El Turco now began to supply details as to the trade, customs and garb of the people of Quivira. Some of these, to more skeptical listeners, might have sounded overstated, but no Spaniard choked over a single statement. They swallowed all, and waited for more.

Now, in El Turco's accounts, a new country appeared. This was Harahay—his own land, as they were to learn, in what is now western Nebraska. It was, said El Turco, even richer than Quivira, and beyond it lay still another land, called Guaes, equally wealthy. In Harahay, went on El Turco, the ruler was bearded, gray-haired, rich (of course), and a man who—oh, now came the shrewdest touch of all—"prayed from a book of hours, worshiping a woman, Queen of Heaven."

Prayer books, and the Virgin Mary! The Spaniards could not doubt that they were hearing of a Christian country. According to one chronicler, this news "greatly cheered and encouraged the army." There were, however, a few skeptics, "who took it to be false, and a stratagem of the friars." What is this distrust of the holy fathers—and by Spaniards? Evidently the Inquisition was very remote from Tiguex, for such statements came perilously close to the mortal sin of heresy.

But even those who discounted the theory that Harahay was a Christian land had no doubt of the riches of the country. It was what they wanted to hear. It may be that the dissenters voiced their skepticism because they did not wish to think they were embarking on an expedition to rob a Christian nation. It was so much more easeful to the conscience to be despoiling and slaying unbelievers.

So El Turco slyly kept his auditors bemused, leading them by gradual ways into swallowing steeper and still steeper falsehoods. The man's genius is evident. Had he told the whole of his wonders right at first, even Spanish gullibility would have been overstrained. But now, with at least the main points of his story fully accepted, he had achieved the first part of his plans.

On April 23, 1541, a year and two months from when he set forth with such glorious hopes from Compostela, Coronado broke his winter camp at Tiguex and set forth with his entire army—fifteen hundred persons, including the Mexican Indian auxiliaries and the recently captured Pueblo Indians, now serving as *tamanes,* or porters, together with a thousand horses, five hundred cattle, and five thousand sheep. El Turco and Isopete were the guides. Cacique had been permitted to return to Pecos, but Bigotes still marched in manacles.

The captain general had been advised by his council not to take this whole unwieldy force, but lead instead a smaller flying column for exploration. El Turco, however, had told his stories too well. The "king" of Harahay, to say nothing of the "emperor" of Quivira, had been impressed on Coronado's mind as rulers with formidable powers. If fighting became necessary he wanted sufficient force to handle the job. Vivid was the recollection of the still recent wars fought by Cortés and Pizarro.

At Pecos the army tarried only long enough to enjoin upon its people "the obligation of loyalty," to gather some provisions, and to restore Bigotes belatedly to his own. The man who had come to the Spaniards as an envoy of good will had some most unhappy experiences as a reward for his effort, and could show the scars of the teeth of the hounds which were set upon him. He had no reason to love the Spaniards, nor did he.

Certain of the Pecos chiefs, perhaps Bigotes among them, managed to hold a secret conference with El Turco. They wanted above everything to rid themselves of the dangerous company of the Spaniards, and what was plotted was nothing less than to lead the entire army out on the pathless plains, and there lose it to starve to death or die from thirst.

Soon thereafter, with vast new hope, the army set forth on paths which became progressively more unknown. Following the general route Alvarado previously had taken, it reached and climbed the great escarpment of the *Llano Estacado*—the Staked Plains. Of the many theories for that name, one is that Coronado's army had to place stakes at various points to find its way back—which is not verified by the records. It is more logical to take the adjective *estacado* at its usual meaning, "palisaded," or "stockaded." Those remarkable escarpments, rising from the lower plains on both the Texas and New Mexico sides, must have resembled to the Spaniards at a distance a huge stockaded wall, like the Palisades of the Hudson, which would account for the name *Llano Estacado* for the tableland.

With his own eyes Coronado now beheld the buffalo herds, and was in turn astonished by the immensity of the sea of animal life. "I found so many cattle," he wrote, "that it would seem impossible to estimate their number for . . . there was not a single day until my return that I lost sight of them."

Castañeda, the chronicler, had a gift for description: "At first there was not a horse that did not run away on seeing them. . . . Their faces are short and narrow between the eyes, the forehead two spans wide. Their eyes bulge out on the side, so that when they run they can see anyone who follows them. They are bearded like large goats, and when they run they carry their heads low, their beards touching the ground. From the middle of the body toward the rear they are covered with very fine woolly hair like that of choice sheep, and from the belly forward they have thick hair like the mane of a wild lion. They have a hump larger than that of a camel, and their horns, which barely show through the hair, are short and thick. . . . They have a short tail with a small bunch of hair at the end, and when they run they carry it erect like a scorpion."

One man, who had read Marco Polo's account of his journey to Cathay in the thirteenth century, called attention to the fact that Marco Polo in Asia encountered crook-backed cattle with long wool (yaks). Could it be they now were in Asia? Perhaps this might be Tibet, or the Gobi!

Presently, following scratches in the sod, such as would be "made by dragging lances," they came upon a camp of Indians. The scratches had been made by travois poles, dragged on the backs of dogs which, since the horse had not been introduced, were the only beasts of burden the savages possessed. Here the Spaniards saw *tipis*, the characteristic skin lodges of the plains.

The people they had discovered they called Querechos, nomadic hunters hanging on the edges of the buffalo herds, from which they took all the necessities of life. Coronado described them as "gentle . . . not cruel, faithful in their friendship, and skilled in the use of signs."

Yet these undoubtedly were the forerunners of that tameless, lean and deadly people who were to be known for their one outstanding trait—*Apache* (*Enemy*). What Coronado encountered was an evidence of a great dislocation in peoples and cultures. The Apaches were part of the Athabascan stock, which included the Navajos, and which had comparatively recently marched down from the snowy north, until its bands were scattered from the Black Hills to the Rio Grande. They might have remained on the plains had it not been for unseen forces in the making to the north. A migration of Shoshonean peoples from the higher plateaus of the Rocky Mountains was under way. It would one day encounter the Sioux, numerous and mighty warriors, and the impact would drive the Shoshoneans—including the Shoshoni proper, the Snakes, the Bannocks and the Utes—back into their mountains. But one branch of the Shoshonean stock, a numerous, wily, lethal division

called the Comanches, would be forced southward. Outnumbering and
forever inimical to the Tinde, as the Apache-Navajos called themselves,
they would by degrees drive them south, and still south, until at last
they forced them out into the desert and mountain country of Arizona,
New Mexico and western Texas, where they would make history.
There, in some manner, from the very ferocity of their surroundings,
the Apaches would attain deadliness and malice beyond all other
American Indians.

Out of this would come much disaster. But Coronado, remarking on
the gentleness and kindness of the Querechos, had no inkling of their
fierce potentialities. He talked with the people of this camp, and later
with a second camp he encountered on the Canadian River, and heard
from them vague accounts of a great river to the east, along which were
"rich settlements."

Here must be taken into consideration the Querecho estimate of
what was "rich." Wearing buffalo skins, transporting their few belong-
ings by dogback, and carrying primitive weapons, almost anything
exceeding their own state might have appeared to them as magnificence. Later some said that El Turco told the Querechos to give this
story. But one wonders if perhaps the Indians might not have been
repeating some rumor of the Mississippi River, along which stood the
semicivilized Natchez and Quapaw villages, which De Soto, now far
out on his expedition from Florida, was destined to encounter.

Whatever its inspiration, the story was enough to cause Coronado to
change his plans. Encouraged by the continued mendacities of El
Turco—although Isopete now was protesting that his fellow captive was
lying—the army turned southward and presently was swallowed in the
vast expanse of grass and sky.

"Here the guides lost their bearings," wrote Castañeda, "because
there is nowhere a stone, a hill, a tree, or a bush, or anything of the sort.
But there are many excellent pastures of fine grass."

One man, going out with a hunting party, wandered away and was
never heard from again, being unable to find camp in the trackless
waste.

Fortunately it was spring, the rains were frequent, and there was
plenty of surface water, which gathers in pools on those plains, so that
thirst did not destroy Coronado's people. The buffalo herds furnished
sufficient meat, so they could exist. In this lay the failure of the plan
which El Turco had been commissioned by the Pecos chiefs to carry
out—to lose the army in the *Llano Estacado* and let it perish.

Suddenly, in their wanderings, they came upon one of those vast
barrancas that gash the eastern escarpment of the Staked Plains. This
probably was Tulé Canyon, and here they met another band of Indians,

the Teyas, "enemies of the Querechos." Interesting to note is the fact that the so-called Teyas or Texas were not that at all. Their real name was Hasinai, and the word *teyas* (spelled also *texas*) meant "friends." It was their form of greeting, as one might say, "Hello, friend." Misunderstanding this, the Spaniards supposed it was their tribal name, and so it has come down, and given the state of Texas its name.

One of the Texas Indians, blind and bearded, by signs told of having encountered four others like these Spaniards years before—the Cabeza de Vaca party. And the simple Indians gathered a heap of buffalo robes, expecting them to be blessed by the white strangers, as had been done by those four on the previous occasion. But Coronado's men appropriated the robes, even squabbling among themselves over the choicest ones, whereat the Texas women, and even some of the men, "wept." Yet they showed no enmity at the highhanded behavior. This was a wandering hunting party, such as sedentary tribes sometimes sent out, for the Hasinai lived in villages and maintained an important cultivation of various crops in eastern Texas, as De Soto and La Salle both would discover.

CHAPTER SEVEN

Quivira, and the End of Hope

THE *barranca* created new concern and discussion among the Spanish leaders, and Isopete and El Turco were hotly questioned. For some time Isopete had been trying fruitlessly to convince the Spaniards that his colleague was misleading them. But they, and most particularly Coronado, over whom El Turco seemed to hold an influence almost hypnotic, refused to accept his statements.

The change in terrain, however, and information from the Texas Indians, who told them the truth about the area to the east, suddenly made Isopete's words important. His actions lent point to this. At the edge of the *barranca* he threw himself on the ground "in desperation," saying he would rather have his head cut off than go any farther in the present direction, because it was not the way to Quivira.

Confronted with the now deeply fixed suspicion of the scowling Spaniards, El Turco at last lost his nerve, broke down, and confessed that he had led them astray, even saying he had lied about the wonders of Quivira, the houses of which were "only grass." He was put in irons while Coronado decided what to do with him.

The army now turned north until it reached a second *barranca*, greater than the first, "which extended a league from bank to bank," with a stream flowing at its bottom. It was the Palo Duro Canyon, now a Texas state park, and one of the wonders of the plains. Descending into it, Coronado had his army camp along the little stream, which is now called Prairie Dog Town Creek, and arrived at a great decision. Clearly, from what the Hasinai had told him, and from what Isopete said—for now that young Indian was the one who was believed—the journey to Quivira was impossible for the full army. Coronado decided to take a few picked men, seek the shadowy land of Quivira, and send the bulk of his force back.

Arellano, who had done such a fine job of bringing the army up from Culiacán, was again given command over it and responsibility for its safety. It should be said now that again he accomplished the almost miraculous, extricated himself and his soldiers, with the cumbersome and undisciplined horde of camp followers from the pathless *Llano Estacado*, and led them back without loss to Tiguex, where they went into quarters in the pueblo they formerly occupied, awaiting the return of the captain general.

Coronado, his gilded armor now somewhat tarnished, took thirty horsemen, half a dozen foot soldiers, some Indian servants and horse wranglers, and Fray Juan de Padilla with two lay brothers of the Franciscan order, and marched north. In this chosen group rode Alvarado, Juan de Zaldívar, the former lieutenant of Díaz, Diego Lopez, and Juan Zaramillo, who wrote the account of this part of the expedition. Isopete was chief guide. El Turco, in deep disgrace, was forced to march with irons on his wrists. He and Isopete now were sworn enemies. The latter had received a promise from Coronado that as his reward for leading them to Quivira he would be given his freedom there.

Traveling "by the needle" of a compass, Coronado and his party rode north for many days, crossing the Texas and Oklahoma Panhandle areas, into what is now Kansas, and waded the shallow waters of the Arkansas River at about where Ford, Kansas, now stands, naming that river, incidentally, the St. Peter and St. Paul, upon whose feast day, June 29, 1541, he reached it. Isopete recognized the stream—he was practically home!

Three days later, marching down the left bank of the river, they encountered the first Quivirans, a hunting party out for buffalo. These would have bolted, but Isopete ran after them, shouting to them in their own tongue, and brought them to the Spaniards, whose horses they viewed with deep misgivings. They said their main town was three or four days farther downstream. Isopete's story was verified. El Turco sank into still deeper humiliation. Coronado's hopes rose.

Perhaps, after all, there *was* some truth to the golden promise. He even began to think more kindly of El Turco, one of whose lies—that about prayer books and the Virgin Mary—had struck deep. Coronado began to wonder if he might not encounter "Christians from the wrecked fleets of Florida," and sat down to write a solemn letter "to the governor of Harahay and Quivira." It was dispatched by Isopete, who might have taken the occasion to disappear forever. Instead he returned, having presented the letter, as ordered, to the uncomprehending savage to whom it was addressed.

With his men and the Indian hunting party, Coronado continued on down the river, and encountered the first villages in the vicinity of what is now Lyons, Kansas.

Quivira! At last!

And with the sight, utter, bitter disappointment. The sick extinction of the last feeble flicker of hope in Coronado's breast.

These were savages, living in straw houses, tattooed and barbarous. They were, if anything, less civilized, and incidentally possessed less of value, than the Pueblo Indians. Failure, irrevocable failure for the expedition into which so much treasure, blood and labor had been poured, was finally pronounced as by a voice of doom.

Crushed though he was, Coronado went through the usual formula of claiming the land, and according to his report to the king of Spain, the natives "gave allegiance to your majesty and placed themselves under your royal authority." By this hocus-pocus he added another "province" to the Spanish Crown, at least on paper; although it was never occupied by Spaniards.

For twenty-five days Coronado remained in Quivira, visiting or receiving descriptions of twenty-five towns of beehive-shaped grass houses. He reached the vicinity of Lindsborg, Kansas, and perhaps went farther; and even interviewed Tatarrax, the "monarch" whom El Turco had so glitteringly described. He was as disappointing as the country, being an aging chief, "huge, with body and limbs in proportion," whose only wealth consisted of a copper ornament at his neck— not worth the trouble of filching. He had a bodyguard of two hundred warriors armed with bows. Incidentally, the word *tatarrax* proved to be simply the Wichita title meaning "head man," so it was not even this dignitary's real name.

No gold. No precious stones. Only a beautiful prairie country teeming with game and containing uncivilized tribes. The end of the trail for Coronado. At a council of war with his *caballeros* it was decided to go back, find the main army, and return with it to this Quivira, further to explore and occupy it. But nobody, in any likelihood, really believed this stout determination would ever be carried out.

Now El Turco made his last effort. He attempted to stir up the Wichitas to attack Coronado's party, urging them in particular to kill the horses, for without them the Spaniards would be helpless. The treachery was reported to Coronado by Isopete.

It was time to deal with El Turco. Diego Lopez was instructed to "put the question" to him. In what manner it was put we do not know, but the Spaniards were expert in gaining confessions. El Turco told the whole story, how he had tried to lead the army out on the *Llano Estacado* to its death, how all his tales of the "glories" of Quivira were fabrications to cause Coronado to overreach himself. He laid the blame on Bigotes, who, he said, had not forgotten having the dogs set on him.

Terrified now, he attempted another lie, to the effect that the really rich lands lay farther on, and that he had led the Spaniards by way of Quivira merely to get his wife, who was there, and take her along.

It was no use. That night, by order of Coronado, El Turco was executed. He was held immovable by the arms while a soldier "from behind put a rope around El Turco's neck, twisted it with a garotte, and choked him to death."

Gloomily the Spaniards began their return march.

And here is a most interesting circumstance. All the time Coronado was struggling northeast from Compostela, De Soto was fighting his way northwest from Florida. There was no communication between the rival expeditions; neither knew where the other was. De Soto had the advantage of a head start, but when Coronado began his march from Compostela, his rival in the race for the fabled riches of Cíbola was only breaking camp at Apalache, near modern Tallahassee, Florida.

At about the time Coronado was fighting the Tiguex war, De Soto was engaged in bloody battles with the Indians at Mobile Bay. Near the end of April 1541, when Coronado began his last march to Quivira, De Soto was discovering the Mississippi River. Building boats or barges—after massacring some Indians who visited him on a friendly mission—and still chasing the phantasm of gold, he reached a village called Coluca, in what is now Arkansas, on the banks of the very Arkansas River, farther up on which Coronado was encamped at the time. On that date, early in August, the expeditions were less than three hundred miles apart, although they did not know it. What if they had learned of each other and made a junction? History might have been strangely changed.

From that time they receded from each other. De Soto, continuing southward, met his death and was buried under the rushing waters of the great river he had discovered. Coronado made good at least one promise by giving the honest Isopete his freedom, and began the long, discouraging march toward Tiguex.

Guided by Wichita Indians, he returned by a more direct route than he came, and not far from Pecos was met by Arellano and a covering detachment. So discouraged was the captain general that he did not even turn aside to exterminate Bigotes, who thus at last escaped the Spaniards. That chief, however, figured later—*in absentia,* of course— in Coronado's trial.

The Quivira explorers accompanied Arellano to Tiguex, where the army spent the ensuing winter, and because by now all the natives had been successfully estranged, the men nearly died from cold and starvation.

A final disaster capped all others. Taking exercise on horseback, December 27, 1541, Coronado engaged in a race with Rodrigo Maldonado. His saddle girth broke, he was thrown in front of Maldonado's horse, and was struck in the head by a hoof. For a time it was thought he would die, but though he eventually survived, he was never the old Coronado again. The injury to his head completed what his terrible disappointments had begun—from then on he was a sick man, feeble both mentally and physically.

Although some in the army desired to return to Quivira, it was by now apparent to all but the most self-illusory that the treasure hopes were all dreams. Cíbola and Quivira were equally barren. In April 1542, Coronado gave the order by which all Spaniards were to march back to Compostela, incurring enmity from some, including the virago Señora Francisca de Hozes and her henpecked husband, Alonso Sánchez, by so doing.

With the exception of three friars, all returned to New Spain. The friars were Juan de Padilla, Luis de Escalona and Juan de la Cruz. Of these, Escalona chose the Pecos pueblos for his field. There he was left, and there he died, for no word was ever heard from him.

La Cruz remained at Tiguex. The Franciscan records note that "it is to be understood that he died a martyr." In other words, he probably was killed by the Tiguex Indians.

Padilla turned his steps northward, to be missionary to the Quivirans. He was killed while on a journey to bring his gospel to the Gaus (Kaws or Kansas Indians).

Returning to New Spain, Coronado put down a revolt of the Indians in the Sonora Valley, then reported to Mendoza, who sent him back to Nueva Galicia as governor. But his troubles were not ended. Malcontents in his expedition, including the termagant, Francisca de Hozes, lodged complaints against him which brought about what amounted to a trial.

One charge was that he had committed "great cruelties upon the natives of the land" through which he passed. Another was that he had been guilty, more or less directly, of what amounted to peculations of government funds—a strange charge against a man who spent such huge sums as he had, out of his own—or rather his wife's—pocket, for the Crown, receiving nothing in return for it.

Other complaints were that he gambled—what Spanish gentleman didn't? And that he was responsible for burning the captives at Tiguex and setting the dogs on Bigotes and Cacique.

Señora Francisca de Hozes and her subservient husband were principal witnesses against him. Poor Coronado was a broken man, never having fully recovered from his head injury, and was feeble and halting in his answers when interrogated. Nevertheless, the royal *audiencia* exonerated him and dismissed every charge against him.

But his career was ended. No longer capable of governing, he was relieved of his post. Sometime in 1554 he died, an embittered man when he went to his grave.

Yet he was more successful than he knew. He had recorded the features of topography, described the peoples, and assayed the resources of the Southwest in a manner remarkably full and intelligent. No explorer of the continent did more than he to acquaint the world with the interior of what is now the United States.

BOOK 2

Trial and
Terror
in
New Mexico

Tierra Paz, *after Coronado*

FOR some decades after the return of Coronado's expedition, no Spaniard interested himself in the wilderness north of New Spain.

Several matters occupied the government, of which one was a serious and bloody rebellion, called the Mixtón War, which broke out in Coronado's own province of Nueva Galicia. As this was *tierra paz,* the Spaniards were both wounded at the ingratitude of the natives, who thus showed their lack of appreciation for the beauties of Spanish civilization and Catholic Christianity, and astounded at their ability to rise in arms and resist. In the Mixtón War two Spanish armies were defeated, with the death of Pedro de Alvarado, the famous Tonatiuh, who commanded one of them; and the rebels were beaten at last by Viceroy Mendoza himself, with a large army from the capital. It is said that he put ten thousand of the revolters in chains and sold them as slaves to reimburse himself for 30,000 pesos he had spent out of his own pocket in subduing them.

All this happened far below the present borders of the United States, but it illustrates the fact that *tierra paz* was not always so pacified after all, and prepares one for what happened later in the American Southwest.

Another event of far-reaching importance was the discovery of rich silver mines in Nueva Galicia. Other metals, including gold, copper, mercury, iron and tin, were likewise found. Royal treasuries were established at such places as Compostela by the monarch across the sea, who, though laggard enough in giving financial aid to his pioneering explorers and *conquistadores,* was wonderfully prompt in setting up agencies whereby his royal fifth of their winnings could be collected.

This eagerness for treasure and the grasping proclivities of the Spanish Crown were evidences of mighty influences in Europe which would have profound effects on the American colonies not only of

Spain but of other nations. Charles V, son of Joanna the insane daughter of Ferdinand and Isabella, as king of Spain ruled over the greatest realm the world has ever known, including theoretically almost all of the two Americas, a large part of Europe, much of Africa, and some of the richest Pacific islands. Yet, though his reign outwardly was the very climax of Spain's splendor, it actually was the beginning of the nation's deterioration and breakdown into a minor power.

Reasons for this were many, but two were most important. Charles was not only king of Spain but emperor of the Holy Roman Empire and head of the House of Hapsburg. Throughout his reign he was preoccupied with European politics and the internal Hapsburg policies, which were of no interest to Spain and hardly understood by most in that nation. Complicating this was the wildfire spread of the Protestant Reformation. Only two years before Charles ascended the throne, Martin Luther had nailed his ninety-five theses to the door of the church in Wittenberg. The Spanish king considered himself the defender of the Catholic Church, and Spain its chief stronghold.

These were the reasons for the intense royal preoccupation with mines and other sources of quick revenue in the Americas. To his interests outside of Spain and the costly wars they engendered, as well as to his personal extravagances, Charles dedicated the vast stream of Spanish bullion which flowed from the New World into his coffers in the 1540s and 1550s, literally squandering that immense treasure. As a result, by the time of his strange abdication in 1556, Spain was invisibly sliding down the ladder toward impotence, which would be graphically underlined by the defeat of the Grand Armada by the English in the following reign.

As to the territories north of New Spain, even had the mining fever and Indian wars not diverted attention from them, Coronado's report was so discouraging as to make understandable the dearth of interest in them for a full generation.

But fate had touched the land of the pueblos: the first ripple of civilization had lapped into it, and there is about the spread of civilization an inevitability like the rise of a tide.

In New Spain something less resounding than the mines of gold and silver, but in its consequences more far-reaching, was taking place which one day would carry civilization resistlessly northward with it. Spanish colonists never took to ordinary agriculture as did the English, who soon were to establish their first settlements on the Atlantic seaboard; but by instinct and background they were natural stock raisers. As early as 1521 the first small shipment of cattle—six heifers and a young bull—was landed in New Spain by Gregorio de Villalobos. Other cattle followed them. Horses, of course, came with the first *conquista-dores,* and sheep and swine were early importations.

The cattle and horse herds grew and spread. New *ranchos* sprang up and *rancheros,* seeking grazing lands, pushed farther and farther north. The Indians, though they died in the mines, proved to be apt *vaqueros* and thrived at stock raising. Cortés himself became a cattle-man; his estate was significantly called Cuernavaca (Cow's Horn), and he is said to have used the first cattle brand in America, three Christian crosses on the flank.

When Coronado marched, the frontier of New Spain extended in a rough semicircle from Culiacán on the Gulf of California to Pánuco (Tampico) on the Gulf of Mexico. But led by stockmen seeking new range, and also by mining prospectors and missionaries, to say nothing of slave hunters, the line of settlement pushed forward until in 1580 Santa Barbara was established on the Conchos River, a tributary of the Rio Grande, and thus, at last, a base was provided from which the great drainage basin of that stream could be thoroughly explored.

Three bold friars made the first effort—Fray Agustín Rodríguez, Fray Francisco Lopez and Fray Juan de Santa María. On June 5, 1581, roughly forty years after the Coronado expedition, they set forth from Santa Barbara, accompanied by nine soldiers and sixteen Indian serv-ants. Following the Conchos to its confluence with the Rio Grande, they went up the latter stream for many leagues, through a partly populated Indian country at first, then desert, until they reached Tiguex, which had been rebuilt and reoccupied after the departure of Coronado.

From there Fray Juan de Santa María, against advice, set out alone to return to Santa Barbara and report the discoveries. He was killed on the way by Indians of the Tano pueblos, then on the Rio Grande, but now, like many of the tribes encountered by the early Spaniards, extinct.

The rest of the party went west to Ácoma and Zuñi. Returning, the two remaining friars, Rodríguez and Lopez, were left at Tiguex, the soldiers going back to Santa Barbara. Sometime, probably soon after, both friars were murdered by the Indians, who had never forgotten the Spanish occupation. Years later a partly effaced painting was dis-covered in one of the pueblos depicting their martyrdom.

When the soldiers returned to Santa Barbara, they reported the land as having considerable population, and—more important—they "dis-covered in the said country eleven mine prospects, all having great veins of silver . . . and also a very rich saline containing a great quan-tity of granulated salt of good quality." To which the deponents added, with the curiously combined piety and greed of the day, "We are ready . . . to go and settle and save so many souls which the devil holds captive, by teaching and instructing them. . . . There are reports of much more wherein God our Lord may be served, and the royal crown increased, as regards both vassals and royal fifths . . . for the land abounds in [mines] as also in forests, pastures, and water."

The fate of the friars was not, at this time, known. But the report of the soldiers naturally aroused the cupidity of every Spaniard, and rumors concerning the deaths of the padres drifted down, creating anxiety and thus providing a double motive for further exploration.

With the sanction of the viceroy, Antonio de Espejo, a colonist of some wealth, with a self-financed expedition backed by the Franciscans, left Santa Barbara November 10, 1582. He was accompanied by Fray Bernardino Beltrán, fourteen or fifteen soldiers, and the usual train of Indian servants.

The Franciscans were concerned over the fate of their missionary brethren, so Espejo marched up the Rio Grande to Tiguex, discovering there indubitable evidence that Fray Lopez and Fray Rodríguez had been killed. Thence he turned east to the Pecos River, where the death of Fray Santa María was verified.

This part of the expedition's duty accomplished, Espejo extended his exploration north to Jémez pueblo, and thence west to Ácoma and Zuñi. At the latter point he left about half his party with Fray Beltrán and, taking nine companions, continued north and west seeking a lake of gold (*laguna de oro*) which the Indians had reported in that direction. They found no such lake, but Espejo did find evidence of rich mines in what is now western Arizona, and brought back ores to prove it.

The party returned to Santa Barbara without loss. Espejo had made a daring exploration, but unfortunately his report of it is chiefly interesting for its exaggerations—the population of every pueblo he visited was doubled or trebled. But he had found the *minas de plata* reported previously by the soldiers of Fray Rodríguez' party and, filled with great notions, he asked the viceroy for a license to explore further and take possession of the lands he had been through.

He lacked the proper connections, but his report stirred such excitement that a rash of more influential applicants sprang into being, so that the Conde de Coruña, who was then viceroy, had difficulty making up his mind who was to receive the coveted license for colonization.

Some even took the bit in their teeth and made illegal northern *entradas*. There was Gaspar Castaño de Sosa, lieutenant governor of Nuevo León, who in 1590 took the entire population of a mining camp which existed at what is now Monclova, formed it into a "colony," and marched with 170 persons of both sexes northward. He went far enough up the Pecos River to "capture"—again—the much-harried Cicuye pueblo; carried Spanish fire and conquest westward through Tiguex and the Keresan and Tewan towns; and arrived at the most northerly of them, Taos, where Captain Juan Morlette, with a force of soldiers dispatched by the angry viceroy, caught up with him and put an end to his career of rapine (without license) by placing him in irons and conducting him back to New Spain, his "colony" following disconsolately.

Three years later another *contra bando* (illegal expedition) set out under Francisco Leyva de Bonilla and Antonio Gutiérrez de Humana. This was strictly a treasure-hunting foray, with no colonizing pretensions.

It would be fascinating to know the full story of treachery, murder and disaster that befell that expedition, only hinted at in the accounts of it, which are of the vaguest and sketchiest nature, depending on accounts by Josephe, an Indian auxiliary, and Alonzo Sánchez (no connection with him of Coronado's army), who survived and remained with the Indians, his version being brought back to New Spain years afterward by one who saw and conversed with him.

The little known concerning it is as follows: After spending about a year among the pueblos, with their principal headquarters near San Ildefonso, the freebooters started northeast toward Quivira, which in the years since Coronado seemed to have regained some of its stature as a legendary place of wealth. Eventually they reached a large settlement of Wichita Indians on the Arkansas and, passing through it, traveled to another large stream farther north—perhaps the Platte River in Nebraska.

Before they reached this river, however, jealousy and hate between the commanders reached an explosive stage, and Humana murdered Bonilla. At this, six of the Indian auxiliaries, including Josephe, deserted and fled homeward. Only Josephe ever reached New Spain again. He knew for certain that one of his companions was killed, and the other four disappeared. He himself was captured by the Apaches and kept for a year, finally escaping to one of the pueblos, where Oñate found him and got his story.

Having failed to discover anything resembling gold, Humana, with what was left of his party after the desertion of the six, started southwest. On the way they camped on a plain where there was much dry grass. Indians set fire to the grass just before dawn and under cover of the smoke rushed the camp. Humana and all with him were killed, except for Alonso Sánchez and a mulatto girl. The girl became an Indian warrior's squaw and Sánchez lived among the Indians, eventually becoming something of a chief among them. He told his story to someone who took it back to New Spain, though he himself never returned.

The miracle of these private expeditions is that *any* of them ever returned. And they combine to illustrate the extraordinary courage and endurance, as well as the extraordinary greed, of the Spaniards. The greed, of course, inspired the courage, but one cannot but wonder at and admire the prodigious journeys and perils undergone by those old fortune hunters, who apparently thought no more of it than if it had been the ordinary course of their lives.

The Rodríguez party of three friars and nine soldiers, with some Indian servants, traversed twelve hundred miles of wilderness, going and coming, and though the three friars managed to lose their lives, the rest of the party returned safely.

Espejo, with a friar and fourteen or fifteen soldiers, plus the usual Indian camp servants and the *wife and three children* of one of the soldiers, traversed paths virtually unknown in the desert and mountain country for more than eighteen hundred miles and got back without losing a single member of his little force.

Sosa, with 170 persons of both sexes, waged a private campaign in the pueblo country. How many of his people died is not recorded, but after his arrest most of them returned safely to New Spain.

Bonilla and Humana, with another small force, including at least one woman—the mulatto girl—and presumably others, traveled even beyond the limits of the Coronado expedition, to the Platte River, and except for dissension and treachery among themselves, might have returned safely also.

When the difficulties of the country are considered, the great stretches of unknown blank geography, and finally the savage peoples to be encountered, one is amazed that any of these ever got back.

One answer, of course, is that, misused though they already had been, the Indians of the Southwest had not yet been sufficiently badgered, bullied, enslaved, tortured and murdered to make them instantly hostile to anyone who had a white skin. Another is that the Apaches had not yet arrived in the desert country, although they were at its borders; nor had they yet acquired that tribal ferocity which was to make them deadliest of all warrior peoples fighting the white man. Had Mangus Colorado and his Mimbreño Apaches been present at the time of these wanderings they would without much question have ambushed, harried, trapped and slain those Spanish parties. The Pueblo Indians were different—a sedentary people, living good-humored, working lives, asking only to be let alone. They sought no trouble, and they had to be prodigiously mishandled before they would revolt against their oppressors.

CHAPTER TWO

Moses of the American Wilderness

ALL these ill-planned and illegally attempted private expeditions at length brought about an officially approved colonizing effort for New Mexico, and with it the second phase in its history. On September 21, 1595, the coveted contract for the "exploration, pacification, and conquest" of the area was awarded by the viceroy to Juan de Oñate, who began at once to make ready for his great enterprise.

By all accounts he was an arresting figure, this Oñate, being haughty beyond ordinary Spanish haughtiness, fearless beyond ordinary Spanish fearlessness, demanding, ruthless, single-minded, and domineering, yet at the same time whole-souled in his thought and care for his colony, and not entirely lacking in the quality of self-sacrifice.

He was in 1595 about forty-seven years old, and had illustrious parentage. His father, Cristóbal de Oñate, was a hero of the Mixtón War, succeeded Coronado as governor of Nueva Galicia, and through discovery of mines in Zacatecas became one of the richest men in America. Juan's mother, Doña Cathalina de Salazar, was a daughter of the royal factor, Gonzalo de Salazar.

Juan de Oñate himself, as soon as he was old enough to become a soldier, won renown. His services on the northern frontier included "bloody encounters with the Chichimecs, and the discovery of the rich mines of Zichú, Charcas, and San Luis Potosí, which he peopled with Spaniards." His wife was Isabel Tolosa, a granddaughter of Cortés and a great-granddaughter of Montezuma. From both sides of his family he was, therefore, wealthy and the project he was to undertake was enough to tax immense wealth.

In preparing for that project he was not modest in his demands for himself. These included that he should be governor as well as captain general of the territories to be occupied; that he should be permitted to take thirty leagues of land as an *encomienda*, including all the "vassals" thereon; that he should receive a salary of 8000 ducats and exemption from the crown tax for working any mines found; that the government should furnish arms and ammunition for his army; that he should be given a hereditary title of nobility; that his colony should receive a loan of 20,000 pesos; that his officers should receive estates and Indian "vassals"; that for his spiritual fortification he should have six friars and the fitting churchly accouterments; and, finally, that he should be given "instructions" for the *forcible* conversion of the heathen, and—perhaps even more important—the collection of "tribute" from them.

Disappointments awaited him, and how much of this was granted is not clear. A new viceroy took office and modified his contract. The loan, it is certain, was cut down to either 4000 or 6000 pesos. He probably was given all he asked that did not cost the Crown anything, such as the title of nobility, the *encomienda*—since he would carve that out for himself—and the governorship and captain-generalship of the proposed province, though with hardly the salary he requested.

Nevertheless, with his commission in hand at last, Oñate financed out of his own pocket an expedition of 400 men, of whom 130 were accompanied by their families, for now permanent settlement at last was to be made by the Spaniards. In the train were eighty-three wagons, the first wheeled vehicles to enter the area, and seven thousand cattle, the first permanent herd for a country which later would be part of the great cattle empire.

Oñate's son Cristóbal accompanied the train with the rank of lieutenant governor and captain general—at the ripe old age of ten years. Among the chief officers were two brothers, Juan and Vicente Zaldívar, nephews of Oñate, who were destined to figure in a bloody story of massacre and revenge.

Another officer was Captain Gaspar de Villagrá, who played an important role in a rather remarkable way. He was the author of an epic poem, *Historia de la Nueva México,* with the usual plenitude of preliminary dedications and preludes, and no less than thirty cantos.

The first lines of this extraordinary work, published just eleven years after Oñate's *entrada,* are as follows in translation:

> *Of arms I sing and of the man heroic;*
> *The being, valor, prudence, and high effort*
> *Of him whose endless, never-tiring patience,*
> *Over an ocean of annoyance stretching,*
> *Despite the fangs of foul, envenomed envy,*
> *Brave deeds of prowess ever is achieving. . . .*

Which sufficiently indicates that his literary model was Virgil and his epic inspired by the *Aeneid.* But where the Latin poet dealt in mythology and legend, the Spaniard wrote of facts and actual persons from his knowledge. The result is that his work is far the best account of Oñate's adventures. As Hubert Howe Bancroft wrote, "Of all the

territories of America—or of the world, so far as my knowledge goes—
New Mexico alone may point to a poem as the original authority for
its early annals."

Oñate did not begin his journey without the usual delays due to
politics, the inevitable red tape of the viceroy's court, and the jealousy
of other would-be *empresarios*. It was February 7, 1598, before he
actually left Santa Barbara, since the Conde de Monterey had succeeded the Conde de Santiago as viceroy and felt he had to go over
the whole matter again before he gave Oñate final approval.

Once given authority to proceed, Oñate struck out at once. Instead
of following the Conchos to the Rio Grande, as had his predecessors,
he took a route reported by his scouting parties which afforded a good
road for wagons straight north to the Rio Grande. Without serious mis-
adventure they reached that river about twenty-five miles below present-day El Paso, Texas, where Oñate went through the long and ver-
bose ceremony of claiming, for God, the king and himself, New Mexico
"and all adjoining provinces."

The territory had been claimed a good many times before: by Fray
Marcos, Coronado, Rodríguez, Espejo and others. But there were two
important differences now. First, it was given an official name—New
Mexico. And it was thus named, incidentally, long before Mexico, the
nation. At that time, and for almost three hundred years thereafter—
until the Mexican Revolution—Mexico was officially called New Spain.
Second, this proclamation of the claims of Spain was to be implemented for the first time. The territory was to be occupied, conquered
and settled in earnest by Spanish colonists.

The ceremony completed, Oñate marched up the stream twenty-five
miles and on May 4 reached a ford which he named El Paso del Norte
—the site of El Paso today. He was all business. Crossing his people,
he let them follow at a leisurely pace while he took sixty armed horsemen northward to "pacify the land."

The land seemed pacific enough. Passing several pueblos on his way
up the Rio Grande, he at last reached two which fitted his purpose.
They were occupied by Tewa Indians, closely related. On the west
bank of the river was Yugeuinnge. Across the stream was Caypa.

At once Oñate conferred upon these pueblos some unasked honors.
Unlike Coronado, he was not one to try to twist his tongue around
outlandish Indian names. So he renamed the pueblos. Caypa he called
San Juan. Yugeuinnge, on the other side of the river, he named San
Francisco de los Españoles. A year later the latter title was changed
again, this time to San Gabriel. Now a good Spaniard had no difficulty
with pronunciations, and the policy thus initiated proved so practical
that it was later extended to most of the pueblos in New Mexico.

At the same time a still greater (and even more unsought) honor was given the Tewas. One of their pueblos, Yugeuinnge, was made the headquarters of the Spanish colonists. To facilitate this, the inhabitants were "requested" to vacate their homes and fields. Without resistance the mild people did so, and in spite of some overcrowding, their generous friends of Caypa, across the river, received them into their houses.

When the main body of colonists arrived, Oñate began the construction of an irrigation ditch, and fifteen hundred of the Indians were given the privilege of sweating and toiling on this work—without pay, of course.

Yet the governor defended them from undue mistreatment. Writing to the viceroy the following March, he said, "The Devil, who has ever tried to make good his great loss occasioned by our coming, plotted, as is his wont, exciting a rebellion among more than forty-five soldiers and captains, who, under pretext of not finding immediately whole plates of silver lying on the ground, and offended because I would not permit them to maltreat these natives, either in their persons or in their goods, became disgusted with the country, or to be exact, with me, and endeavored to form a gang in order to flee to New Spain, as they proclaimed, although judging from what has since come to light their intention was directed more to stealing slaves and clothing and to other acts of effrontery not permitted."

He arrested two captains and a soldier, and would have garroted them as ringleaders, but spared them on the pleadings of the friars and the entire army. Later, four men stole horses and fled south. The horse theft weighed more on Oñate's mind than the desertion. He sent messengers south and authorities arrested the men. They were beheaded.

For a Spaniard of his time, Oñate began with excellent intentions. Except for being forcibly evicted from their homes, and being required to labor on his irrigation ditch and other works the natives were not to be "maltreated." There was another requirement. They were to be converted to the Holy Catholic Church—*forcibly*, if need be. A chapel was built at San Gabriel, and the eight friars with the expedition were assigned to the surrounding pueblos, beginning their missionary work at once.

With his colony a going concern, although autumn was approaching and cold weather threatened, Oñate turned his attention to searching for treasure, absence of which, as noted, already had caused discontent. At Picuris, one of the pueblos north of San Juan, was found the Indian, Josephe, survivor of the Humana expedition. His report of the river (the Platte) reached by that fated troop, and rumors of a salt lake (perhaps Utah's Great Salt Lake), had restimulated speculation about the fabled Strait of Anian. Perhaps Josephe's river and the great salt lake were one and the same—an arm of the sea extending across America and affording the long-sought passage from Spain to Asia!

One of the Zaldívar brothers, Vicente, was army master. He, with sixty men, was sent eastward toward the plains. They established two missionaries at Pecos, went out into the buffalo country, tried to capture a buffalo alive (and failed), got a good supply of hides and meat, and encountered a wandering band of those Indians, called Querechos by Coronado, who, first and last, were to add considerably to the excitement of life in the Southwest.

It was Oñate who first gave the name Apache to these Indians. It is a Zuñi word and signifies "Enemy." The name was obviously so excellent both in meaning and sound that it stuck. Although Oñate wrote of the Apaches "they are a people whom I have compelled to render obedience to His Majesty," he did not know how far he was wrong.

The main wave of the Apache-Navajo migration had now reached the Southwest. Behind them came the still more numerous Comanches, pushing them ever southward, until they turned for living room into the desert country. Very soon they would be found as far west as Arizona. And from the time of this first Spanish colony until the present day, when still "unpacified" remnants of their tribes wander in the Sierra Madre of Mexico, they have lived up to that name of Enemy, the Ishmaels of the desert, their hands against everyone, and everyone's hand against them.

At first, however, there were no Apache hostilities. It was one of the pueblos which first punctured Oñate's assumption that New Mexico was *tierra paz*.

While Vicente de Zaldívar was on the plains, Oñate took another force of men and, leaving orders with Juan, Vicente's brother, to follow him as soon as the latter returned from the buffalo hunt, started southwest to look over the salines and mines which had been reported by Espejo. The captain general regarded his nephews, the Zaldívar brothers, with affection which they merited, being the most trustworthy and enterprising of his captains.

Arriving at Ácoma, on its towering mesa, October 23, Oñate demanded the formal *obediencia* of that pueblo. One of the *caciques*, Zutucapan, had recently been to San Juan, however, and witnessed the operations of the Spaniards across the river. He did not like what he saw, and now, standing on the rooftops, he harangued his people, urging them not to yield to the Spaniards. Other head men did not agree with him and, believing the invaders invincible, counseled against resistance. The *obediencia* was at least technically tendered.

Nevertheless, Zutucapan continued his opposition secretly, and with twelve other men who shared his feelings made a plot to lure Oñate into an *estufa*—one of the underground ceremonial chambers of the pueblos—and there kill him. Being pressed for time, Oñate declined the invitation to enter the *estufa* and thereby preserved his life. Without even knowing how near death he had been, he proceeded on his march.

Reaching Zuñi, he confirmed Espejo's account of fine salt deposits, and marched on to the Hopi towns, from which he sent Captain Marcos Farfán with a detachment to locate the mines. The captain succeeded in discovering rich veins, probably on the river now called the Bill Williams Fork, staked out claims, and brought back a full report.

Meantime, in November, when his brother returned to San Gabriel, Juan de Zaldívar, with thirty men, set out after Oñate as ordered. The captain was unaware of the plot against his leader at Ácoma, or indeed of the hostility of that pueblo. Zutucapan, the chief who foresaw only misery for his people under the yoke of Spain, had by this time fully convinced them that they should defy the invaders, relying on the apparently impregnable nature of their fortress-town.

Quite unconscious of danger, Zaldívar approached the mesa. A deputation of Indians descended with gifts, and he and his men were permitted to climb to the pueblo above. Next day, when members of the Spanish party were wandering about in groups, scattered in the pueblo and on the plain below, the shrill enemy yell suddenly sounded, and without any warning Zutucapan, wielding a huge club, headed a charge of his warriors on the visitors.

Unable to get together, the Spaniards fought—like Spaniards. No higher praise can be given them. In single combats they performed prodigies of desperate valor. But the odds were too great. For three hours the unequal fight continued, the Spaniards falling one by one.

It was Zutucapan's great club which at last dashed out Zaldívar's brains and laid him dead. That ended the battle. Five Spaniards who had thus far survived leaped from the towering mesa to the plain. The place is still shown, and when one looks at those cliffs, three hundred and fifty feet high, it is hard to believe that of the five only one was killed. The other four, bounding and rolling to the plain below, bleeding and injured, yet lived.

These four, with three others who escaped the massacre by a less spectacular climb to the plain, joined the horse guard which had been left under the command of Captain Tabora. That officer at once rode to overtake Oñate, while messengers were sent to warn padres at other pueblos, in the event this attack was part of a general conspiracy,

which it proved not to be. What was left of the command returned to
San Gabriel with the dread news of disaster.

In the midst of the mourning by the families and friends of the dead
men, just after the funeral rites had been held, Tabora appeared, saying he had been unable to find Oñate. To get word to the governor
was imperative. Captain Alférez Casas, with three men, volunteered
to locate him. They succeeded, and Oñate, gathering in his various
scouting parties, hurried back to his colony.

Now took place one of those curious ceremonials so dear to the
Spanish heart. Before Juan Gutiérrez Bocanegra, the *alcalde,* formal
proceedings were brought against the "rebels"—*in absentia,* of course.
It was standard Spanish legal practice, with a rich and powerful set
of precedents provided by the Inquisition. Presence of a culprit,
whether heretic, Jew, Moor or other offender, was by no means necessary at a trial before the Holy Office. Many were found guilty and
sentenced to be burned at the stake or otherwise punished, who were
at the time far beyond the reach of the Inquisitors. One of the excellent
results of such a pronouncement of guilt was that the property of the
condemned could be seized at once, the money going to the receiver
of the Holy Office, and from him very often to the royal treasury, to
pay for the wars in which Spain was always being involved.

In the proceedings before Bocanegra, every formality was observed.
All the friars present gave written opinions, in which they pronounced
the Ácoma people rebels, laid down the rights of victors over those
they vanquished in a "just war," and gave the projected punitive expedition against the pueblo the solemn blessing of Holy Church.

Thereupon Oñate turned to that fierce and sun-browned captain,
Vicente de Zaldívar—who probably had been begging to lead the force
to avenge his brother's death—and told him to take seventy picked
men and march at once.

In record time the fire-breathing Zaldívar reached Ácoma, where
the people appeared in crowds on the summit of the mesa, full of
defiance, shouting down taunts, and some "dancing stark naked" as
"an insult"—or so the Spaniards took it, though in view of what we
know of Indians we may assume that these were warriors stripping
for battle, perhaps to the breechclout, a common Indian custom, and
intended not to insult the foe so much as to give the warrior freedom
in his movements.

With all formality Zaldívar first summoned the leaders to come down
from the mesa, surrender, and answer for the murders they had done.
The summons, understandably, was rejected.

Now Zaldívar kissed the cross hilt of his sword, gave the *Santiago,*
and led the assault on the rock.

As a feat of arms, the battle Zaldívar fought has scarcely been equaled in the annals of war. With seventy men, he had to scale a cliff-girt mesa which could be surmounted only by a precarious path cut in the rock, and by rickety ladders at one place, and that in the face of the furious resistance of three thousand savages, of whom perhaps not less than a thousand might be regarded as warriors, although women and even children could roll rocks down as well as men.

Every advantage of arms and armor, to be sure, was with the Spaniards. And they were picked men, all trained to the last degree in the profession of war, which is the dealing of death. Yet even so, to carry that mesa would have seemed an impossibility.

Under a beating cloud of arrows, Zaldívar sent most of his force against the side of the mesa where the ladders and footholds led up, thus concentrating there the resisting warriors. Meantime, twelve men, especially selected for their ability as athletes and fighters, began slowly to climb the cliffs at another place, clinging to depressions and projections in the naked face of rock, until at last they managed to reach the top and scramble on the level mesa.

At once their presence was discovered and the Ácoma warriors swarmed to drive them over the cliff. But as soldiers the Spaniards were unbeatable. The twelve, with fiery play of steel swords, held off the rush of the counter attack, while others climbed steadily up the precipice behind to reinforce them.

As the Aztecs had discovered when they confronted Cortés, the Ácomans now found that in single combat none of them could match their steel-clad enemies. Moment by moment the Spanish force on the rock grew and the foothold widened. Now they began forcing the defenders back.

Zutucapan's chance for successful resistance was ended, yet he kept up the fight for three days. The rocks were slippery with the blood of his best warriors as room by room the Spaniards carried the houses of the pueblo. But at last the leader was slain, and Zaldívar's men swept over the mesa, cutting down men, women and children in a massacre such as even the Spaniards rarely perpetrated. Many Indians, in despair, sprang over the cliffs to spatter in death below. In the end a pitiful remnant—600 of 3000—were permitted to surrender under their venerable chief, Chumpo, who was a hundred and twenty years old and had from the first opposed Zutucapan's warlike policy.

These were allowed to descend to the cactus plains below where they made their homes as best they could, while the city in the sky was systematically destroyed. It was long before the pueblo was rebuilt and the mesa occupied again.

To the viceroy, Oñate reported of this, "As punishment for its

[Ácoma's] crime and its treason against His Majesty, to whom it had already rendered submission by a public instrument, and as a warning to the rest, I razed and burned it completely."

It was pretty clear that the Pueblo Indians had better learn to read Spanish as rapidly as possible, so they would be able to comprehend legal "public instruments" in the future.

Ácoma's fate quelled other symptoms of revolt in the pueblo country for a long time, and Oñate was able to enumerate "the great increase which the royal crown and rents of His Majesty have and will have in this land," in part as follows, in his report to the viceroy:

First, the great wealth which the mines have begun to reveal and the great number of them in this land, whence proceed the royal fifths and profits. Second, the certainty of the proximity of the South Sea, whose trade with Piru [Peru], New Spain, and China is not to be depreciated, for it will give birth in time to advantageous and continuous duties. Third, the increase of vassals and tributes, which will increase not only the rents, but his renown and dominion as well, (if it be possible that for our king these can increase). Fourth, the wealth of abundant salines . . . mountains of brimstone . . . I will not mention the founding of so many republics [sic], the many offices, their quittances, vacancies, provisions, etc., the wealth of the wool and hides of buffalo, and many other things. . . .

Decidedly Oñate knew how to appeal to the viceroy and the monarch above him. He was seeking confirmation of his titles.

While he waited, he was not idle. In the spring he had Vicente de Zaldívar out again, this time trying to reach the South Sea (Pacific). Zaldívar had trouble with the Jumanos, whom Oñate personally punished, then continued his journey until he reached impassable mountains at a place said to be three days from the ocean.

He turned back but Oñate himself later made it.

Next, in June 1601, the governor embarked on one of his most ambitious explorations. With two friars and more than seventy men, he set out to rediscover the country visited by Humana. Josephe, the Indian who had been with Humana, was the chief guide. Through what are now New Mexico, the Texas and Oklahoma Panhandles, and Kansas he marched, encountering at last a band of Escansaques (Cansa or Kansas) Indians.

These savages received him with friendliness. They knew of the destruction of the Humana party, telling Oñate it had been committed by an enemy tribe living farther north, and accompanied the Spaniards on their march. At the Arkansas River, the Indians camped while Oñate went upstream. Next day he encountered the enemies of the

Kansas—the Quiviras, or Wichita Indians, near the present site of Wichita, Kansas—from his description—the confluence of the Arkansas and Little Arkansas rivers, always a favorite dwelling place of the tribe.

The Wichitas were hostile, tossing dirt in the air and shouting war cries. But presently they quieted and permitted the Spaniards to camp near their village. From them Oñate derived the information that it was they who had wiped out the Humana party. With them still was the mulatto woman who had escaped the massacre, but who had been "injured by the fire" with which the Humana camp was overwhelmed.

Time now for the apparently inevitable treachery to take place. The chief of the Wichitas was "called Catarax"—another Spanish twisting of Coronado's "Tatarrax," which was simply a Wichita title, signifying head man. When Catarax came to the river to converse with the Spaniards, Oñate had soldiers seize him from behind and "put irons on him."

But the Wichitas had stratagems also. "Making a feint of an attack, while the Spaniards were getting their arms, they took care to carry off the prisoner bodily, ironed as he was."

The hornet's nest had been stirred up and the Spaniards had to get out of Quiviran territory. Oñate ordered a retreat.

But when they encountered the Kansas farther down the Arkansas, a new difficulty arose. Believing that the Spaniards had been friendly with their enemies, the Wichitas, the Kansas suddenly attacked the advance party of a dozen riders under Zaldívar, driving them back with a shower of arrows which killed one horse and wounded two of the *caballeros*.

A serious situation. The Spaniards were faced, according to their own estimates (perhaps somewhat exaggerated), by fifteen hundred enemies, who formed "in a semicircle." Against these Oñate had only seventy men. But they were some of the finest battle-hardened veterans of the New World.

It was a challenge the Spaniards could not fail to answer. With their customary grim bravery, the horsemen charged their enemies, probably expecting to scatter them rather quickly. But these were not Pueblo Indians. The Kansas warriors neither scattered nor fled. Though the steel-clad Spaniards, on their rearing steeds, raged among them, killing many, the savages fought for more than two hours, "with the greatest courage, although at their own cost, for they proved the valor of the Spanish nation," as Oñate later reported.

By the end of that time many of the Spaniards were wounded and the enemy had not retreated an inch. Things looked bad, and Oñate felt it was time to disentangle his force and withdraw.

"Seeing the great barbarity of our enemies, and that many of them were dead, and that they were not to be frightened, and would not turn their backs, [he] ordered his men to retreat."

First, however, he freed some Indian women whom the soldiers had taken forcibly either from the Wichita or Kansas camps. The command, evidently, was beginning to get a little out of hand in the matter of women, having been a long time away from home. He kept, however, "some boys, upon the request of the religious, in order to instruct them in the matters of our Holy Catholic Faith." And also, probably, to make slaves of them. One of these was a captive of the Kansas, a Tancoa (Tonkawa), whom the Spaniards named Miguel, and who was glad to go with them to "furnish information of this land."

With their few human trophies the Spaniards retreated, leaving the field to the valorous Kansas warriors. It was the first significant defeat suffered by a white force within the Southwest, the massacres of the Humana and Juan de Zaldívar parties involving only a few individuals.

Oñate returned directly to New Mexico. Thence he made another expedition, which took him to the Colorado River and down that stream to the Gulf of California, the arm of the "South Sea" he sought. On the way he paused at a looming rock, between Ácoma and Zuñi, and did something that gives today a feeling almost of personal acquaintance with him when one sees, incised on the face of what is now called Inscription Rock, his inscription translated thus:

"Passed by here the officer Don Juan de Oñate to the discovery of the sea of the south on the 16th of April, year 1606."

It is the first and oldest of the Inscription Rock names and messages. Many others later added their notations. But Juan de Oñate's brief announcement, almost as clear and perfect as the day he wrote it, is of greater interest than any other, unless perhaps that of Vargas, made many years later.

The hard-riding, energetic *adelantado* had re-explored the whole territory first covered by Coronado. But what was more important, he had established a permanent colony in New Mexico. It is true that during his absence most of his colonists attempted to desert, including many of the friars, who charged Oñate with tyranny, falsehood and general unfitness to govern.

One padre did not desert. Juan de Escalona, *comisario general* of the religious, stuck it out at San Gabriel with the ever faithful Alférez Casas and the few colonists who stayed with their lands. He wrote a letter excusing the desertion of those who went south, on the ground that there was nothing to eat, the crops having failed, but he ended with the stout assertion that it seemed a pity to abandon New Mexico, after such efforts, expense and something of success.

As a footnote to this he criticized Oñate for systematically sacking the nearer Indian pueblos, taking, as he said, the whole reserve store of six years' crops saved by the natives against a possible year of famine, such as this one turned out to be; and forcing them to eke out a miserable existence on the wild seeds which they found. This is interesting in view of Oñate's pious criticism of the fomenters of the earlier revolt, in which he called himself the protector of the Indians, for which reason—so he said—his men became discontented with him.

The governor acted promptly to cut off the desertion. The inevitable Zaldívar was sent riding furiously southward with a detachment of soldiers, armed with writs charging the recalcitrant colonists with being traitors and in some cases condemning individuals to death. Zaldívar overtook the deserters, rounded up most of them, and "acting with great cruelty"—according to the complaints of the friars, who appear to have lost their missionary fervor in the raw and uncivilized land of New Mexico—sent them packing back to San Gabriel under guard.

Zaldívar continued on, visited the viceroy at the City of Mexico, and took ship for Spain, where he presented Oñate's request for confirmation of titles and authority at the royal court, and succeeded in obtaining the grant from Philip III, who had followed to the throne his father, Philip II—he of the Grand Armada disaster—in 1598. Few finer lieutenants than Don Vicente de Zaldívar are revealed by history.

The royal grant, however, lasted only a few years. In 1605, Oñate was obliged to ask for reinforcements. Only twenty-four soldiers and two missionaries were sent: aid so far from being sufficient that for the next three years New Mexico's fate hung in the balance.

Apparently for the purpose of bluffing the viceroy into sending more help, Oñate resigned his governorship in August 1607. The viceroy called his bluff and accepted the resignation, but ordered him to remain in the province.

Presently his successor arrived, Pedro de Peralta, who in 1609 abandoned the San Gabriel site and moved the colony south to a more favorable place where a new city was founded under the florid title La Villa Real de la Santa Fé de San Francisco (The Royal City of the Holy Faith of St. Francis). Quickly and mercifully this unwieldy caravan of a name was shortened to Santa Fe. On the basis of this date, Santa Fe, New Mexico, today claims to be the oldest capital—though not the oldest city—in the United States. The change of location was highly beneficial and assured the permanence of the colony.

Discredited, Oñate returned to New Spain, where he was tried on charges of misrepresenting the value of New Mexico, mistreatment of the colonists, soldiers and Indians, and disobedience to the orders of the viceroy. He was found guilty of some of the charges in 1614, fined 6000 ducats, and sentenced to perpetual banishment from New Mexico, and from the City of Mexico for four years. In 1622 he appealed against the judgment, but though he had support of the Council of the Indies, he failed to obtain the king's pardon. Perhaps he was more successful later, for in 1624 he was in Spain trying to obtain a position in New Spain or the Philippines. Though in this he was unsuccessful, he was entrusted with the visitation of mines in Spain. That year, or the next, he died.

Oñate had done enough to insure his place in history. At one step he had advanced Spanish civilization hundreds of miles northward, and by establishing his colony confirmed the Spanish Crown in its title to an area comprising what are today New Mexico, Arizona and western Texas, with a good claim on Colorado, Nevada, eastern Texas, Oklahoma and even Kansas—an immensity of mountains, rivers, fertile valleys, deserts, plains and varied peoples, greater in extent than Spain and all her European possessions combined. Spanish civilization and the Spanish Catholic religion were well launched on the second phase of their assault on the Southwest.

CHAPTER THREE

The Heathen and the Holy Office

I T H A S been sometimes said that the French were preeminent in winning and holding the friendship of the American Indians but were not stable as a colonizing nation; that the English were superior to all in creating something like a replica of their home civilization and hence were the greatest colonists; and that the Spaniards were chiefly interested in treasure and what could be wrung from the natives, and therefore lacked the essential qualities for true colonial achievement.

Yet how is one to consider the fact that today the Spanish tongue is spoken from the Rio Grande to Tierra del Fuego, save for Brazil and the Guianas; that the Catholic faith is almost universal among these Spanish-speaking peoples; that Spanish customs and laws obtain, even modifying land titles and statutes in our own Southwest; and that in spite of long American occupation, more landmarks, streams, mountain ranges and towns in the Southwest bear Spanish than American names? The truth is that in their own way the Spaniards were remarkable colonizers.

The first *conquistadores*, it is true, were concerned chiefly with precious metal. After the conquest of Cortés, some of the world's greatest silver lodes were discovered in New Spain, and other ores also, including gold. Even today Mexico is one of the richest, if not the very richest, countries in the world in metals of many different kinds.

Spanish adventurers going north of the present Mexican border looked first for treasure in the possession of natives, from whom it might easily be wrested; and later for mines of gold or silver, when it was found the natives had nothing of the kind.

When Juan de Oñate was starting out on his colonizing expedition into New Mexico, an old friar named Diego prophesied as follows: "By the life of Fray Diego there are great riches in the remote parts of New Mexico; but by the life of Fray Diego it is not for the present settler that God holds them in reserve."

The prophecy was a true one. At that time Arizona was part of New Mexico. It was more than a generation before the Spaniards occupied the country sufficiently to work the mines they discovered. Most of these later were abandoned because of the ever present lurking menace of the Apache Indians, and it was not until the American era that the Southwest's mines were fully developed. Josiah Gregg recorded, early in the nineteenth century, the multitude of stories concerning fabulous mines discovered, worked and lost by the early Spaniards; and J. Frank Dobie has traced out some of these traditions in two fascinating books. The Indians, it appears, once they discovered what an irresistible magnet gold was to the white man, took care to obliterate all traces of mine workings so that they were hard to find, once they were lost.

The second factor in Spanish occupation was not so spectacular as gold seeking but in the end more important. Unequaled as breeders and raisers of stock, the *rancheros,* seeking more and ever more range land, spread over the unoccupied country. According to the conclusions of one Texas historian, there were cattle grazing north of the Rio Grande in Texas by the fall of 1583. Whether or not this conclusion is justified, Oñate certainly established the livestock industry in New Mexico in 1598.

The third, and perhaps greatest, force of Spanish expansion was the priesthood and the Catholic Church. From the beginning every expedition that set forth to rob, murder and enslave was well upholstered with holy padres as chaplains, to give their blessings to these outrages. Padre Olmedo was with Cortés and played an important part in the conquest of Mexico. Padre Vicente de Valverde was with Pizarro in Peru, and had a key role in the treachery by which the Inca, Atahualpa, was seized and later basely murdered.

There has been a disposition on the part of some writers to sanctify all padres and what they did, because they were priests of the Church.

But this is simply ridiculous, and does a disservice to history. Padres were human like other men. Some were weak and some strong; there were brave and cowardly ones among them; kindly and devoted ones, and some who were harsh and cruel, even venal.

Fray Marcos de Niza was a good and kind man, though he was inclined to stretch the facts, and had a well-developed interest in protecting his own skin. Fray Juan de Padilla could be fierce in battle, but he was a dedicated and fearless winner of souls. Fray Rodríguez and his two companions were true martyrs who did not shun the prospect of death when they sought to carry their gospel to the pueblos. Most Franciscan fathers, indeed, who went forward on the frontiers were courageous in the extreme, ever willing to sacrifice their lives for their beliefs and their missionary vocation.

It must be admitted that they were bigoted and intolerant, and to them there could be only one side to any question if it involved even the most attenuated hint of doctrine. But this was by no means an attitude confined to Spaniards, or to Catholics, in that era. It was an age of stark and uncompromising intolerance. Both the Roman and Protestant hierarchies were governed by the same principle of jurisdiction—the criminality of heresies. Whoever believed wrongly—that is, otherwise than the Holy Office of the Catholics, or, say, the Venerable Consistory of the Calvinists—believed nothing. And he who believed nothing thereby committed the crime of treason to God and deserved capital punishment. Persecution hence became a sacred duty, an act agreeable to God, and the greater the intolerance, the greater the value.

Those Franciscan fathers who carried the cross into the Southwest at this time—the Jesuit period was yet to come—were in very many cases, indeed in most cases, the true friends and protectors, according to their own lights, of the Indians over whom they took spiritual command.

But they labored under one grave disadvantage: they were the officers of the Spanish Inquisition. In Spain itself this distinction, with all its vast powers and terrors, was held by the Dominican monks. But the Franciscans were such pre-eminent missionaries in the Americas that they were made the administrators of the Inquisition in the New World.

Lord Acton's truism, that all power corrupts, and absolute power corrupts absolutely, had its exemplification here. Perhaps there never has been in the world a power more terrible than this of the Holy Office, which overrode even that of the throne, operated under a sinister cloak of secrecy whereby witnesses against the accused were not known to him or any but the Inquisitors, could invade the private life of anyone, and had no scruples in its methods of extorting "confessions." Its self-authorized interpretations of orthodoxy, its use of torture, and its almost invariable conviction of those it tried, which always meant confiscation of the victim's property, in most cases imprisonment, and in thousands of instances death—often by the agony of fire—made it a terror to everyone in Spain during its long tenure. And it spread its tentacles very rapidly to Spain's possessions.

By 1524, three years after the conquest, the Holy Office was beginning its work in the City of Mexico, and on November 2, 1571, it was permanently established there, its jurisdiction extending from the Isthmus of Panama to the extreme northern limits of Spanish occupation. The Inquisitorial tribunal took cognizance not only of heresy but of such offenses as blasphemy, sorcery or witchcraft (in which the holy fathers fervently believed), perjury, idolatry, forgery, bigamy and piracy; and exercised a censorship of books whereby it burned all which came under its condemnation, and forbade, on severest pains, anyone's reading such volumes as escaped the fire.

Under the Franciscans in the New World, the Inquisition never went to the excesses that it did under the Dominicans in Spain. Usually it was content to punish those it convicted by fines, flogging, confiscation or imprisonment. Yet numbers suffered the death penalty also, as will be seen, and its career was sufficiently maleficent.

As officers of the Inquisition, the Franciscan friars possessed awesome power. Differences of policy in the treatment of Indians, which set the friars at odds with governors and other officials, often sent the latter to stand trial before the Holy Office in the City of Mexico. One such trial, of a highly important official, had bearings on the history not only of New Mexico but of Spain, all America, in fact the world.

It must be understood that the establishment of missions on the frontiers was dual in policy, with a dual object. It was encouraged and aided by the Spanish Crown for very excellent reasons of a military nature, as well as being promoted by the Church for conversion of the heathen. Traveling through the Southwest, from California to eastern Texas, one cannot but be struck today by the fortresslike character of many missions. That is exactly what they were—military strongholds. Many of them had perhaps a prison function also, for within those walls were kept the *reducidos*—the "reduced ones"—a felicitous name by which Indian converts, when thoroughly cowed, were called.

The followers of St. Francis believed in the beauty and dignity of labor. It must be confessed that most of their Indian converts had difficulty in discerning either the beauty or the dignity, but the Franciscans had another tenet—discipline. And the Indians found that this second rule insured their compliance with the first.

Toil was enjoined, then exacted. Indian backs bent under burdens, and Indian brows dripped with sweat to build the great rambling missions with their churches, dormitories, convents, priest-houses, walls and barracks for soldiers, as well as their irrigation systems and tilled fields. Lives of the *reducidos* were sternly regulated. Each day was divided into periods for prayer, study and work. A double motive existed for bringing more heathen into the fold, for each new convert meant not only a soul saved but also a new laborer in the fields or building gangs, it being held, evidently, that in order to free his soul an Indian's body must first be enslaved.

At night the *reducidos* were locked up in the compound, from which they could not venture except by express permission from the father superior. To insure strict morality, unmarried men were herded together and confined each night in a special building assigned to them, while unmarried women and girls were shut up similarly in the convent-dormitory of the mission.

When Indians wearied of sweating for the padres and ran away to join their friends of the wilds, they were pursued by mounted soldiers and usually recaptured. Brought back, they were publicly flogged, to teach other Indians what happened to those whose faith was weak. Such punishments invariably were meted out by the soldiers, although ordered by the padres, since the latter, though believing the discipline was necessary, did not wish the resentment of the Indians to be turned against themselves.

And such ironhanded discipline *was* necessary, not only to save Indian souls from hell-fire but because the missions were at least as importantly agencies of the Crown as of the Church. Much of their support came from the government and it was well understood that they served the government's purpose as permanent citadels of Spanish power. Almost always soldiers garrisoned them—either in the mission itself or in a *presidio* erected nearby—and on occasion of attacks by hostile Indians their walls, loopholed for gunfire, were havens not only for the missionaries and their charges but for white settlers living in the vicinity.

In the pueblos this classic form of Spanish mission was varied, for the very good reason that those natives were sedentary rather than nomadic, and did not need confinement to keep them from wandering away. A church usually was built in the pueblo itself, and the missionaries, trusting in the mild and tractable character of the Pueblo Indians, in most cases dispensed with military guards, a fact which accounts for the numbers of friars slain in the pueblo troubles of the first century of Spanish occupation of New Mexico.

The missionaries were looked upon not only as apostles and civilizers but among the outlying tribes as explorers and diplomatic agents. They counteracted foreign influence, such as that of the French, and sometimes kept Indians from warlike incursions on the settlements.

The period following Oñate's establishment of his colony was one of sporadic activity. Spain was sagging, though her American colonies still retained much of their vigor. Quivira had lost its charm for the Spanish ear. And trouble was brewing. First, the infiltration of the Southwest by the Apaches was well under way. Before the end of Oñate's regime a band of those deadly warriors, led by a chief named Quima (or Quinia), occupied the mountainous regions west of Taos. They were afterward visited by a missionary expedition led by Fray Estevan de Perea, and "since it was the first expedition to that bellicose nation of warriors, Don Francisco de Sylva, governor of these provinces, went along, escorting them with twenty soldiers."

"That bellicose nation of warriors," it seems, already had earned its fearsome name. On this occasion, however, it offered no enmity to the white men. That would come later, and terribly.

Of more immediate portent was a growing sullenness among the Pueblo Indians. Padre Alonso Benavides, who went to New Mexico as *custodio* in 1621, bringing with him a reinforcement of twenty-seven friars, reported in a memorial to the Spanish king that among the pueblos there were 63,500 converts. This seems somewhat strange in view of the fact that even by the Spanish count there were less than 30,000 natives in the pueblos of record in 1680—just before the revolt, when they were presumably at top numbers. Many sincere converts, without question, were made by the early missionaries. But there were many others not so sincere, and large numbers, while outwardly observing the Catholic form, clung tenaciously to their ancient rites and the creed of their ancestors.

When the padres discovered evidences of this, they were zealous to punish it. And a deep-seated resentment against the priests began to show as early as February 1632, when two friars, Padres Arvide and Letrado, together with two soldiers who accompanied them, were murdered by five Zuñis—ostensible converts—whom they took along as companions on a visit to a wild tribe called the Zipias, somewhere beyond the Zuñi country.

The following year Padre Porras was poisoned by the Hopis, and from then on mission work among those people led a precarious existence.

A curious charge was made against the padres in 1640–42—that they were so determined to hold temporal as well as spiritual authority that they encouraged a revolt in those years, in which Governor Luis Rosas was stabbed and died from his wound. But the "revolt"—if one really

threatened—seems to have been among the Spanish and Mexican settlers, rather than among the Indians.

In the rule of Governor Arguello, about 1645, *apostasy* among the
natives grew so prevalent that forty Indians who refused to give up
their faith were flogged and hanged. There was a brief uprising among
the pueblos as a result, but it was easily put down by the military.

Still later the people of Jémez pueblo conspired with some Apaches
and killed a Spaniard named Naranjo. In reprisal, twenty-nine Indians
were hanged and many more imprisoned—for the *crime of idolatry*.
Jémez subsided, for a time.

Other incidents, some mere plots which were discovered before they
could bear fruit, others involving a few Spanish deaths here and there,
occurred over the years. Meantime tension mounted and grew between
Spanish officialdom and the religious. Each accused the other of cruelties and injustices toward the natives, while the former also charged
the latter with creating unrest by forcing their religion down the
throats of the Indians.

The contempt of the priesthood for the Spanish laity at this time
was expressed by Padre Gerónimo de Zárate Salmerón: "They are
content if they have a good crop of tobacco to smoke, caring for no
more riches, apparently under a vow of poverty, which is saying much
for men who in their thirst for gold would enter hell itself to get it."

In the controversies the priests had the advantage because, through
their connection with the Holy Office, and their recording of events in
their annals and correspondence, they usually had the last say. So unpleasant were their relations with Governor Bernardo Lopez de
Mendizabal that the Franciscans threatened to leave the New Mexican
field in 1660. This became unnecessary, for in 1661 the viceroy, under
pressure from the Holy Office and the prelacy, sent Diego Dioniso de
Peñalosa Briceño to succeed him—which meant also to arrest and investigate him.

In Diego Peñalosa the Southwest acquired another of its remarkable
figures, and an important, though indirect, mover of history. He was
born in Lima, Peru, about 1622, the son of Alonso de Peñalosa, a
Spaniard. By every contemporary account, Diego was a man of uncom-
monly handsome face and figure, an elegant manner, a dashing way
of wearing always splendid clothes, and unlimited assurance. He was
a thorough adventurer and fortune hunter—called an *embustero* (im-
postor) by his foes, who were not few. And he possessed an unfettered
imagination which scorned the prosaic and pedestrian limitations of
truth, ambitions equally unfettered, and a wonderful ability to change
political colors like a chameleon according to his surroundings.

In his early thirties, about 1654, he appeared in New Spain and held a series of high military and political offices, until in 1661, apparently by sheer magnetism of personality, he induced the viceroy to appoint him governor of New Mexico.

Yet even one so nimble-footed as Peñalosa fell foul of the Inquisition. He arrested his predecessor, Mendizabal, according to orders, but exceeded his instructions and seized Mendizabal's property—ostensibly for the Crown, but perhaps for himself. In either case the Holy Office was offended, for it had issued a writ not only for the arrest of Mendizabal but for the attachment of his property for its own benefit. Padre Posadas, *comisario* of the Inquisition in New Mexico, denounced the governor for this, and in the quarrel Peñalosa had the effrontery to imprison the officer of the Holy Office. Very quickly he realized the enormity of this act, freed Posadas, and made full apology. But though the Inquisition now had Mendizabal, his wife and four lesser officials to fine and chastise, it was unforgiving and unforgetting toward the rash new governor.

Peñalosa used his time at first to good effect in the inspection of his province, visiting the pueblos, missions and outposts, founding two new settlements, and traveling as far west as the Hopi pueblos. In other words, he was a better than average governor.

From the Indians he heard of the great "kingdoms" of Teguayo and Quivira, and also of Texas, with such glittering reports of their wealth that he determined to outfit an expedition to visit them. He never had a chance to do so, however, for in 1664 he made one further mistake which sealed his fate in Spanish colonial government—he quarreled again with the friars.

It appears that he sought to stop exploitation of the Indians by ordering that they be not employed in spinning and weaving cotton *mantas* without the governor's license. Perhaps this was done with an eye to some possible revenue for himself or the Crown, rather than a pure reform—one must look for hidden motives in almost every act of Spanish administrators of that day. But whatever the motive, the decree struck at one of the leading industries of the friars in New Mexico, who marketed, for the glory and benefit of their order and the Church, the *mantas* which their spiritual charges wove.

Peñalosa's term as governor was ending, and he was not reappointed. Returning to the City of Mexico, he was arrested, thrown into prison, and the dread Inquisition filed a formal complaint against him.

From 1665 to 1666 Peñalosa, the flamboyant and proud, lay in a cell without being brought to trial. To the Inquisitors other men's time meant nothing, since the Holy Office itself was self-perpetuating and seemed to be everlasting. When at length Peñalosa was permitted to leave his dungeon and go before the tribunal for trial, among the offenses charged against him was one of "talking against the Holy Office"—which, to the Inquisition, was a thing bordering on blasphemy.

A ruinous fine was placed upon him, and in February 1668 he was deprived of all right to hold political or military offices, exiled forever from New Spain and the West Indies, and sentenced to march barefoot through the streets of the capital, carrying the green candle of penitence in expiation of his crime.

The contemporary account says that Peñalosa, in his penitential march, attracted attention everywhere by his "handsome face, proud bearing, and rich clothing." Shortly after his punishment Peñalosa disappeared from the Spanish realms.

Had it known, the Holy Office made a mistake by merely confiscating Peñalosa's worldly goods and sending him on that humiliating march after letting him lie in prison more than two years. To permit a proud man, whose pride has been mortally wounded, to continue to live and brood is to court trouble. It would have been wiser, perhaps, from its own standpoint and that of Spain's interests, had the Inquisition gone further and executed him.

CHAPTER FOUR

Blood in the Pueblos

A N O M I N O U S cloud of disaster began to gather in New Mexico in 1672. That year a wave of fierce nomads from the desert attacked, overwhelmed and destroyed the old Zuñi town of Hawikuh, where first Coronado had encountered the people of the pueblos. Padre Pedro de Ayala and many of its inhabitants were killed, and the structure was so devastated that it was never reoccupied.

The desert nomads were Navajos, and the fact that they made the attack as a separate and independent war effort indicates that by this time they had broken away for good from their kinfolk, the Apaches, and taken a separate identity of their own. They had been spoken of as Apaches de Navajo as early as 1629, the name being derived from a ruined and deserted Tewa pueblo west of Zuñi, and signifying something like "tilled land." When this branch of the Apache stock made the area in which that ruin stood their hunting grounds, the name was given them by extension. They were not ground tillers, but they had a kind of racial genius of their own, and through the years would diverge further and further from the true Apaches.

In that same year, 1672, the Apaches sacked several pueblos farther east, one of them Tabira, since come to be called Gran Quivira, the ruins of which can still be seen near the town of that name. There has long been a legend that the padres, fleeing for their lives at the time of this raid, hid their sacred vessels and other treasures under the walls, and the grounds about the ruined stone church have been honeycombed with pits and shafts by successive generations of treasure hunters; though nobody ever found the hidden articles, so far as is known, if indeed they actually existed.

Significantly, the forays of the Apaches and Navajos came from the *west*—what is now Arizona. That meant that those savages had by this time discovered the population vacuum in the desert and mountain country and established themselves there, so adapting themselves to their harsh surroundings that they became the most terrible and efficient of desert raiders.

By 1676 Apache warfare was a serious menace to the whole colonial enterprise of New Mexico. At that time the defensive force in the province was so small that only five soldiers could be spared for each station outside of Santa Fe, and even these were short in horses and equipment. They could not hope to cope with the Apaches, who continued to destroy towns and churches.

In 1677 Fray Francisco de Ayeta, the *custodio*, sent to the viceroy an urgent plea for reinforcements. But red tape delayed the start of the relief expedition until 1679. By the time it reached the border it was already too late to avert the disaster which had been in the making.

Naturally the unrest of the Pueblo Indians was increased by the bloody activities of the Apaches. They had been promised protection, and received none.

But their grievance was even deeper than this. Then, as now, the pueblo peoples were more strongly attached to their primitive faith than any other American Indians. In part this was because they had a complicated, interesting and sometimes beautiful religion, well worked out, with a pantheon of gods and a native theology not only mystical but almost metaphysical in its nature and reasoning. To this day, in spite of everything the Church has been able to do, the peoples of Hopi, Zuñi, Ácoma, Isleta, Taos and elsewhere continue to observe their native ceremonials—the snake dance of the Hopis, the *kachina* representation of savage gods, the nightlong sessions in *estufas* or *kivas,* the curious *chongo* chase of the Isletas, the telling over of their hero tales and their mythology, in every pueblo.

Most Pueblo Indians today are nominally Catholic. But often there is but a patina of Christianity overlaying the material of pagan beliefs. Having learned a severe lesson, the Church is content to permit native practices to continue, as not being harmful, so long as the necessary obligations of baptism, confirmation, confession, mass, marriage and burial are carried out.

But that is since 1680. Before that time the rigid suppression by the priests of the native mysteries precipitated a great explosion.

Of course the Spanish authorities also were at fault. Certainly the natives had every reason to hate them, being forced to render implicit obedience to them, and required to pay heavy tribute to them not only of pueblo products but in personal labor and service. Yet the revolt of 1680 was largely on religious grounds, and the fanaticism and intolerance of the priests was at the bottom of it.

Virulent in disciplining natives who strayed from the Catholic observances, the friars used their authority, rooted in the Holy Office, to cause secular officials to punish recalcitrants severely. For thirty years before the outbreak of 1680 there had been floggings, imprisonment, enslavement, even executions, when the crimes were considered by the reverend fathers sufficiently serious to merit those penalties.

One case is illustrative. In 1675 the superior of the convent at San Ildefonso pueblo, Fray Andrés Duran, charged the Indians with *bewitching* not only himself but also his brother, his sister-in-law and an Indian interpreter. The record is not clear on just the nature of this exertion of the powers of Satan on the holy father.

Forty-seven natives were arrested, and all, surprisingly, pleaded guilty. Evidently all were medicine men, and fully believed in their own powers—a belief which, equally evidently, Fray Duran fully shared with them. Of these, forty-three were sentenced to be whipped and sold into slavery, and four to be executed. Of the four, one was hanged in Nambe pueblo, a second in San Felipe, a third in Jémez, and the fourth hanged himself.

This Southwestern witchcraft episode, incidentally, occurred just seventeen years before the Salem witchcraft episode of 1692, in New England.

A crowd of Indians marched to the governor's *palacio* in Santa Fe to demand of Governor Juan F. Treviño release of the surviving prisoners. They offered ransom, but with it a threat, saying if the captives were not freed they would kill every Spaniard they could, and flee to the mountains, risking annihilation by the Apaches rather than see their medicine men enslaved. Some of the prisoners were released; perhaps all.

A leading figure in this episode was a medicine man of San Juan pueblo named Popé, of whom the Spaniards made note as an Indian to be watched, and who justified that attention by achieving great and sinister prominence later.

The wounds suffered by the Indians continued to fester. Never did the friars relax their opposition to the native rites. Indians were hanged for the heinous crimes of *sorcery* and *communing with the devil*—in other words, practicing their time-honored religion. In many cases, it is true, there were collateral charges that the persons condemned had conspired against the Spaniards, which provided the technical crime of treason as a further reason for executing them.

Yet in spite of these stern measures there remained old men in every village, the primitive priesthood, who were skilled in the ceremonies, dances and other observances of their religion, and who secretly passed on their knowledge to the younger people. Those aged medicine men were listed by the Spaniards as "sorcerers," and since sorcery was a recognized partnership with the Foul Fiend, the extreme penalty could be invoked against anyone found guilty of it. Fully aware of their danger, the pueblo priesthood continued to teach their beliefs and rites, though some were arrested and punished; and perhaps exerted the stronger influence because of the peril in which they lived, so that they became the hard core of the great trouble soon to come.

After the San Ildefonso episode, Popé left his home at San Juan and moved to Taos, which, being far to the north, provided him a rather remote place for his work. There he began quietly to preach the doctrine that all Spaniards should be rooted out and driven from New Mexico, and the old pueblo ways of life restored. Like all Indian "prophets" who have arisen from time to time, he claimed some sort of communication with the spirit world, and hence supernatural power.

In later years these claims of Popé were to be interpreted by the friars as proof that he was in league with the Devil—a most convenient interpretation, for when suits were afterward brought against the missionaries as chief causes of the revolt, the assertion that Satan himself was in the conspiracy against the holy fathers was enough to cause all the actions to be dropped in terror, since their prosecutors knew that, should they continue them, they would be classed, by inference, as in league with the spirit of evil also.

Gradually Popé became the center of a wide conspiracy. He planned nothing less than a united revolt by all the pueblos to exterminate or drive from the country every one of the twenty-four hundred Spanish colonists, officials, soldiers and priests who lived within it. Chief among his lieutenants were Catiti of Santo Domingo, Luis Tupatu of Picuris, and Jaca of Taos. With enthusiasm the pueblos took up the plot. Swift runners, carrying curiously knotted cords as a primitive calendar, went to every Indian town, save those in the lower Rio

Grande Valley, notifying them of the date for the simultaneous uprising—August 13, 1680.

The conspiracy was as well planned as any ever made by American Indians. Every precaution was taken to keep it secret. No woman was permitted to know about it, and Popé with his own hand slew his son-in-law on a mere suspicion of treachery.

In spite of this an Indian neophyte at San Lazaro revealed the plot to Fray Bernal, and a like confession was received at Pecos by Fray Velasco. The friars hastened to communicate their news to Governor Antonio Otermin, and that official at once made every possible effort to save the scattered settlements.

Messengers galloped south to those below San Felipe, instructing them to flee down the Rio Grande toward Guadalupe, near El Paso del Norte, where they might find protection. The colonists in the north were instructed to leave their homes and possessions at once and start for Santa Fe, where the only considerable body of soldiers in the province was stationed.

By the time Popé realized that his careful plans had been betrayed, his only hope for success was to strike immediately. He therefore ordered the revolt to start three days ahead of schedule, on August 10.

It had been impossible for Otermin's messengers to reach all the outlying haciendas and settlements in time to evacuate the people. Rising all together, the pueblo warriors in one bloody sweep slew more than four hundred Spaniards, including many women and children and twenty-one friars, and destroying every mission church together with the holy furnishings.

The hatred of the Indians was directed in particular against the padres, and there were brutalities. One padre, bound naked on the back of a hog, was paraded with blows and yells through Jémez, and afterward killed. Padre Juan de Jesús, of the same pueblo, was murdered as he knelt embracing a crucifix. At Ácoma, Fray Maldonado and two other friars were tied together and marched naked through the pueblo, jeered at and abused until, by predicting the downfall of their tormenters in three years' time, they provoked the Indians to make an end of them with clubs and stones. At Zuñi three padres were shot by the servant of one of them, who was forced to do the deed. One Zuñi padre was spared, the Indians later saying he saved his life by abjuring his faith. But this is to be doubted. More probably he was away from the pueblo at the time and made his escape. Whatever criticism may be made of the Spanish friars, they never lacked the courage to die for their faith.

Eleven padres escaped, eight to the south, and only three to Santa Fe itself—Gómez de la Caena, Francisco Farfán and Andrés Duran.

The last-named was the central figure in the San Ildefonso "witch-craft" charges of 1675. Could the San Ildefonsans have caught him they might have invented a special way for him to die.

As usual, the escapes of the friars were accompanied by miracles. A story in the Jesuit archives, written in 1754, relates how a Franciscan friar carried with him to New Spain a headless image of the Virgin, called Nuestra Señora de la Macana. The name came from an episode during the revolt of 1680, when a pueblo chief raised his *macana*—a sort of hatchet—and struck off the head of the image. Thereupon, according to the pious tale, blood flowed from the wound and the *Devil* hanged the impious wretch from a tree.

In this case, the "Devil" probably wore the boots and morion of a Spanish officer, but whatever the circumstances, the headless image was venerated in New Spain for a long time thereafter.

Of the non-clerical population, the Indians killed all they found without mercy, and without regard to age, friendship, station or sex, except for a few of the most beautiful women and girls who were kept as captives, the usual Indian custom in war, dictated by the necessity of replenishing the tribal population. At least three Spanish women, later recovered from the Indians, when Vargas reconquered New Mexico, are known to have borne children thus to Indian fathers during their captivity. How many others experienced a like fate will never be known.

Of the 1950 settlers who escaped massacre, about 1000 collected in Santa Fe, the remainder fleeing southward. One small resolute group rallied at La Cañada under their *alcalde,* Luis Quintana, and fought their way to the capital. Counting noses, Governor Otermin found that in this rabble of fugitives were only 155 men he considered trustworthy to bear arms.

Those days were filled with terror. Santa Fe had not yet been directly attacked, but missing friends were mourned as dead—or worse. Reports and counterreports told of new disasters, overwhelming numbers of enemies marching toward the capital, and the savagery of the foe.

Otermin did his best to organize his defenses in this welter of confusion. The refugees and all the fighting men were drawn into the plaza surrounded by the official buildings, including the governor's *palacio.* Every available weapon was issued, and men who were unaccustomed to firearms were instructed in handling them. Scouts were kept out to watch for the approaching enemy.

These brought in word, August 14, that a war party of five hundred Indians was coming from the direction of Pecos on the southwest. Next morning the enemy was in the outskirts of Santa Fe.

At first no shots were fired. An envoy from the Indians boldly entered the fortified plaza and conferred with Otermin. He offered the choice of two crosses—one red, signifying war, the other white, signifying surrender. If the white were accepted the Spaniards would be permitted to evacuate and march back to New Spain; if the red, they would die to the last man.

"We have killed God and Santa María," he said, "and the king must yield too."

Otermin refused to accept either cross. Instead, as soon as the envoy departed, he began an attack on the Indians in the outskirts of the town, hoping to drive them out before reinforcements arrived. Through the day desultory fighting went on in the streets, but the Indians still held part of the suburbs when toward nightfall a great cloud of warriors was seen coming from the north—the fighting men of Taos, Picuris, San Ildefonso, San Juan, Tesuque, Santa Clara and other pueblos. Otermin estimated at least three thousand new enemies were in view and hurriedly withdrew his men to the inner stronghold of the plaza.

That night the beleaguered Spanish watchers saw the skies black with tumbling clouds of smoke, on which leaping flames were ruddily reflected, as the Indians looted and burned the town. The church and convent were destroyed by fire, the water supply of the plaza cut off by diverting water from the ditch which flowed through it, and no man could enter or leave the defenses without being fired upon.

Days passed. Within their little fortification the refugees listened to yells of triumph and insults shouted from without. Arrows came over the walls. No direct assault was made, but thirst began to do its work and the stench of decaying bodies outside the walls grew intolerable.

In desperation Otermin on the twentieth mustered all men capable of bearing arms, chose a hundred whom he thought could best be depended on in great danger, and with this handful, invoking "the sweet name of María," he rode out against the besiegers.

With that bravery for which their nation has always been noted, the Spaniards hurled themselves against the overwhelming numbers of their enemies with such fury that they drove the Indians back. There was an element of surprise, but it was sheer cold courage that accounted in the last analysis for the success of the devoted handful. The arquebuses took their toll and Spanish men-at-arms on horseback plunged among the natives with sword and lance. Five Spaniards were killed and the governor and many others wounded in the furious fighting, but they slew more than three hundred of the Indians and marched back to the plaza with forty-five prisoners.

That evening the captives were questioned. When all possible information had been gained from them, they were taken out and shot in the plaza. Otermin had learned enough to convince him that evacuation was his only recourse. That night he decided to cut his way through the besieging lines and march south to New Spain, taking with him every one of the refugees and abandoning all of New Mexico.

Drums ruffled and commands were shouted within the plaza the morning of the next day, the twenty-first. The Indians surrounding the place suddenly saw the Spaniards issue forth, burdened, lengthening their column, hurrying without any attempt to keep step. Women, children and non-combatants marched in the center, mothers carrying babies and toddlers clinging to their hands, the old and weak stumbling and aiding themselves with staffs. Before and on either side of this column strode armed men, while Otermin rode back and forth anxiously shepherding the movement.

A tense moment as the Spaniards came out from their defenses. Would the Indians attack? Spanish hands fiercely gripped musket butts or sword hilts at the sight of the enemy, gathering thickly on high places to watch the exodus.

But not a movement was made by the foe. Perhaps the bloody lesson taught them the day before by Otermin and his hundred fighting men had left the Indians without appetite for further combat. Or perhaps since the Spaniards were evacuating Santa Fe the warriors were simply content to let them go.

In any case the maneuver was unexpectedly easy. On foot, each person carrying his own baggage—for there were barely enough horses for the wounded and sick—the colonists trailed southward. A few days later they reached Isleta, on the Rio Grande, just below El Paso del Norte.

On the way they had seen continual evidence of the fury of the Indians. At Santo Domingo they buried the bodies of three friars and five other Spaniards. San Felipe and Sandia were destroyed, all vestiges of Christianity in particular being wiped out, although the inhabitants had escaped southward at the start of the revolt. Haciendas were burned everywhere, their occupants slain or fled.

Popé, the pueblo dreamer, had terribly and effectively rooted the Spaniards out of New Mexico. For a full decade and more the Pueblo Indians were to be free, to follow their own religious bents, hunt and raise crops as before the white man came, rebuild their houses, and return to the familiar existence of old. For that period the farthest northern outposts of Spain would be the settlements of Isleta, Guadalupe and a small *presidio* at the site of what is now Juárez, on the Rio Grande at the border of New Spain.

Having ejected the white men, Popé set out to accomplish the rest of his dream: to restore his people to their pristine condition. Dressed in ceremonial garb, including a headdress with bull's horns on it, he traveled from pueblo to pueblo, sprinkling the people with sacred meal as a primitive blessing, and overseeing his program.

Every trace of Christianity and Spanish life was to be eradicated. Those who had been baptized were "cleansed" of that rite, by washing with water and soapweed. It was forbidden to utter the names Jesús and María. Baptismal names were dropped in favor of Indian names. *Estufas* were reopened for native ceremonials. Every word of the Spanish language was abandoned for native dialects. New crops introduced by the Spaniards, such as wheat and various fruits, even if valuable, were no longer grown, and only the old crops—maize, squash, beans and so on—were cultivated. Old customs governing marriage and divorce were reinstituted and, according to Spanish records, there was a considerable shifting around of husbands and wives; the inflexible canons of the Church being discarded for the easy Pueblo plan, whereby divorce was the wife's prerogative: she was given the power to dismiss her husband at will, whereupon he returned to the home of his parents, after which each was free to marry again.

At first Popé's commands were obeyed enthusiastically. The Indians made a festival out of destroying churches and Christian relics, holding noisy processions, dances, and making offerings to native deities, the very things the padres had most severely punished.

But presently, from the role of teacher and guide, Popé assumed that of despot. Heavy tribute was exacted by him from each pueblo; persons who disobeyed him were punished, sometimes by death; and he began to display an unadmirable interest in women—when he saw one who appealed to his fancy, he took her whether she would or no, and regardless of the rights of her husband or family, either for himself or for one of his *capitáns*.

Now, as if by a curse, a prolonged drought set in and crops failed. Creeks and even rivers ceased to flow, and for the first time in memory the Rio Grande ran dry. Hunger stalked through the pueblos.

Those old foes, the Apaches, began again to raid and pillage from the south and west. And to make things worse, a new scourge evidenced itself: the Utes of the mountains, a branch of the Shoshonean people, found that the Spanish guardians of the pueblos were gone and began to make incursions against the towns to the north.

It was in this era that many pueblos were abandoned or their populations exterminated. Sites of others were changed. Ácoma, which after the Zaldívar conquest had existed on the plain, moved back to the top of its mesa. The Tompiro pueblos east of the Rio Grande were wiped out. A whole half of the population of the Tano pueblos migrated bodily westward and joined the Hopis, at Oraibi. Other dislocations took place, partly because of attacks of hostile wild tribes, partly in fear of Spanish reprisals, partly through destruction by Spanish raiding forces from New Spain, and partly because of a civil war which presently sprang up among the pueblos themselves.

In 1680 Spanish official figures on pueblo populations, excluding those of the lower Rio Grande and the western Hopis, gave a total of 29,250 people, with twenty-nine active pueblos. A census made later, after the reconquest, showed the population had shrunk to 9296, and the active pueblos to twenty-two, of which several had been established at new sites since the beginning of the rebellion.

Popé's tyranny, coupled with these various disasters and jealousy among the leaders, brought on wars among the pueblos. The Keresan, Taos and Pecos pueblos fought against the Tewas and Tanos, and it was during this trouble that the Tanos migrated westward.

Popé was deposed and Luis Tupatu of Picuris elected governor. But in 1688 Popé again headed the pueblo confederation. He died two years later and Tupatu once more took command. How much the death of the "prophet" had to do with the success of Vargas' reconquest in 1692 is open to speculation. Certainly, in spite of his weaknesses, Popé was the driving central force of his people during his life. Since he did not live to witness the destruction of his dream of independence, he perhaps died happy.

After Popé's death in 1690 many of the Pueblo Indians were sick of their condition. Perhaps some began to wonder if they had not made a mistake in offending the Christian God. In that year a strange, grim rite took place—the sacrifice of a virgin to the rain gods. It is the only known instance of human sacrifice among the pueblo people, although the practice was common south of the Mexican border among the Aztecs, and occurred occasionally among a few tribes in the United States, notably the Skidi Pawnees, the Iroquois, the Natchez and the Haidas. It so happened that this isolated blood rite of the pueblos was followed by rains, breaking the long drought so that water once more flowed in the Rio Grande, and "confirming them in their stubborn, insolent apostasy," as the padres expressed it. Yet even with rain falling matters were not so favorable as to make the pueblos enthusiastic over their liberty.

The Spaniards, meantime, made desultory efforts to regain their foothold in New Mexico. Spurred by the friars, who kept hoping that the natives, "prompted to revolt and apostasy by the Devil and a few sorcerers," might repent of their evil ways, Otermin with 146 soldiers and 112 Indian allies invaded the province in the summer of 1681. He found all the southern pueblos abandoned and pillaged—probably by the Apaches—and destroyed what was left of them. But when he learned that a great war party was coming south to fight him, led by Catiti, an elderly chief who had been one of Popé's chief lieutenants, the governor decided his army was inadequate to meet the combined strength of the Indians and hastily retired to New Spain.

Next year Otermin was replaced by Garbaceo de Cruzate y Gongora, who came to the rather empty governorship armed with a royal *cédula* charging him to make every effort to recover the lost territory, with—as a thrifty proviso—*the least possible expense.*

Cruzate was energetic. In his two terms of office he made fifteen campaigns, marching once as far north as Sia pueblo on the Jémez River, about sixteen miles from Bernalillo, where the Keresan Indians were fortified. The place was not well calculated for defense and in a daylong battle the Spaniards captured the pueblo and slaughtered six hundred of its inhabitants, the battle and massacre being the bloodiest of the rebellion. More than seventy captives were driven back to Isleta, where Cruzate weeded out the old and infirm, had them shot to get rid of them, and sold the young and able-bodied into slavery.

Sia never recovered from that terrible day. It still stands, its population far smaller than at that time, wringing a hard living from an infertile soil and perhaps dreaming of a better time, before the white man came.

CHAPTER FIVE

Vargas, the Avenger

FOR his memorable punishment of Sia, Cruzate might have remained governor, had it not been for the slowness of communication with Spain. He reported his success and two years later, in 1691, received in reply a royal *cédula,* which approved his actions and gave official favor to his enslaving the captives, except their children.

But in the meantime a new governor had been appointed—Diego de Vargas Zapata y Luján Ponce de León. The *cédula* commending

Cruzate contained an instruction to the viceroy that if Vargas had not already taken possession of the office Cruzate was to be retained as governor and Vargas mollified with "another good position."

Vargas' appointment, however, was dated six months earlier than the *cédula* and he already had taken over the office. There was nothing for the viceroy to do but permit matters to stand as they were. As it turned out it was the best thing he could have done anyway, for Diego de Vargas proved to be the most capable, brave and far-sighted leader New Mexico had seen since Oñate, even excelling that founder of the colony in many respects, particularly as a fighting man.

Irresolution, delays and timidity disappeared when Vargas took over the administration. He intended to reconquer New Mexico, and his plans were all-inclusive. Where even Cruzate had been content with an invasion and single victory, Vargas would be satisfied with nothing less than complete subjugation of all the pueblos and re-founding of the colony with Spanish settlers.

Yet he was fully aware of the difficulties he faced and the wide range of decisions and actions necessary. He must be bold to fool-hardiness one day, cautious to the appearance of timidity the next; furious and merciless on occasion, gentle and even wheedling on another; a keeper of his own council who must never permit his men to know what fears, hesitations or doubts he might himself suffer; an inspiration always to his followers; and a constant thinker and planner, even while he swung his sword in battle or took part in the most violent actions.

If ever there was a one-man task, the reconquest of New Mexico as Vargas undertook it was that. A Spaniard of Spaniards, he was nearly fifty years old when he became governor, with some military training and administrative experience. His will leads one to believe that he liked fine articles of clothing, silverware and jewelry, and that he was considerate of his family, servants and debtors. He was married and before he began his reconquest a power of attorney was executed whereby his wife, Juana de Vargas Ponce de León, was given control over extensive properties in Spain and Mexico, as protection for her in case of his death. Little is known of her beyond this, and she may shortly have died. But Vargas was gifted with remarkable virility, and had an eye for a pretty face and a way with women. At his death he left at least three surviving children, all of them illegitimate.

He assumed office in 1691, but his first months were devoted to restoring order along the lower Rio Grande where some of the Indians, notably the Suma and Manso, had caught the spirit of rebellion from the north and were giving trouble. By August 1692, Vargas had taught them a severe lesson and the survivors were gathered in two pueblos on the river, properly guarded by soldiers and padres.

Only then did Vargas turn to the north. In his impatience he did not even wait for reinforcements that were on their way, but started up the Rio Grande August 21, with only sixty soldiers and a hundred Indian allies. Later he was reinforced by fifty more soldiers, but even then his force was appallingly weak.

Rapidity of movement and boldness of execution had to be the key-notes of his operations in the rebellious country. Passing the southern pueblos, all of which were deserted, Vargas suddenly appeared before Santa Fe after dark on September 13. It was occupied by Tano Indians who had moved over in a body from their Galisteo pueblo, twenty-two miles to the south, and were living in the buildings of the villa, including the governor's *palacio* and the other *casas reales* around the plaza.

In the revolt the Tanos had been active and murderous. They killed not only their resident padre but also Fray Juan Bernal, the august *custodio* of New Mexico, and the missionaries from San Marcos and Pecos, who were coming to give warning. With these priests the Tanos slew also numerous colonists. Warlike as they were, however, they were completely surprised by Vargas' rapid march and sudden arrival.

In the night gloom the Spanish advance came upon walls which suddenly swarmed with warriors who heard the trampling of horses and the clink of armor. Since the Spaniards left, the Indians had built quite extensive fortifications, with walls and towers, to make Santa Fe stronger.

There followed, in the darkness, a curious colloquy, shouted back and forth. First, Vargas informed the Indians that he was the Spanish governor who had come to rule New Mexico again. The Indians—evidently to gain time—replied by expressing doubt that the newcomers were Spaniards, saying they must be Apache or Pecos warriors in disguise. As proof they were Spaniards, the Tano defenders demanded that the soldiers fire an arquebus in the air. This was done.

Vargas next called out to the Indians that if they would postpone hostilities until dawn they could see the emblem of the Holy Virgin on his banner. In reply the Tanos told him to sound the trumpets in Spanish fashion. The captain general not only complied with his bugles but had his drums join in also.

This was pretty good proof, and the Indians, who usually managed to see quite well even at night, could hardly have doubted who the newcomers were. Actually they were delaying things as long as possible while within the walls workers were furiously busy, building up their defenses by filling openings "with many *morillos* and rocks, as well as *metates*." The latter were concave stones used by Indian women to grind corn, and some of them weighed as much as a hundred pounds.

All this activity Vargas could hear and he understood perfectly what was taking place. Yet he hoped to get Santa Fe peacefully, and calmly continued to assure the Indians of his wish to avoid conflict and his willingness to pardon all of them for past offenses.

No fighting occurred during the night. At dawn Vargas, on horse-back, with the Virgin standard flying, continued his overtures, swear-ing on a rosary that the Indians would receive a general pardon if they surrendered peacefully. The natives said dubiously that they feared treachery, and mentioned an episode during the previous Span-ish occupation, when a band of Apaches surrendered only to be mas-sacred. To this Vargas replied that the Apaches were enemies of both the Pueblo Indians and the Spaniards—which, while it did not answer the doubt expressed, appeared to have its effect.

Next the Tanos raised a sore point. They were afraid, they said, that if they accepted the pardon and surrendered they would be com-pelled to rebuild churches and houses, "and to be whipped if they refused, as they had been before." Vargas gave them assurances on this matter, which were not very well carried out, it must be confessed.

The governor of the town was Josephe, but the war captain was Antonio Bolsas. The latter now suggested that the insurrection had been "caused by the Devil," and those guilty were now dead or had been only boys when the outbreak occurred. As a plea of extenuation this had a favorable sound and Vargas renewed his assurances.

There was another tense delay and hesitation. Vargas remained cool. Some Indians who had been working in the distant maize fields and camped out the night before appeared. Dispatching a detachment under Roque de Madrid, his second in command, Vargas prevented their joining their people in the fortified plaza. Though no blows were struck, Madrid captured several of these newcomers. One of them was a subchief named Domingo. It was a fortunate catch, for Domingo became a sort of intermediary between Spaniards and Tanos in the negotiations that followed.

At last Vargas, seeing the negotiations at a stalemate, ordered the water supply of the fortification cut off. This was easily done, as it had been when the Indians besieged Otermin years before. A small ditch from the Santa Fe River supplied the convent, inner plaza and other places, running along the south façade of the *palacio*. This was diverted and the Indians were without water.

After that the Tanos grew less defiant. They proposed that the padres with Vargas should enter the fortifications, after which the

Indians would come forth. Two of the priests bravely volunteered to go, but Vargas refused to permit it.

"These rebels are treacherous and can commit cruelty on you, Reverend Fathers, taking from you even your lives," he said. "It is not just of me to place you in such danger or grant you this *entrada*."

Domingo, promising to return, entered the fort and made every effort to bring his people to surrender, but they refused. True to his promise, he returned and told Vargas the defenders were making all preparations to resist.

Time for parleying was over, and time for action had come. Vargas issued ammunition and rations to his men, disposed his forces at strategic points, brought forward his artillery—a large field piece called the *pedrero grande de bronza,* and a small one called the *pieza de bronza*—and gave an ultimatum: if the Indians did not surrender in one hour, "they would be destroyed with fire and great slaughter."

With that the Tanos surrendered. Slowly they ventured from their walls, the women and girls first. Over and over Vargas assured them that they would be pardoned and all would be well.

Next day they were gathered together, and Vargas went through the usual lengthy Spanish formality of taking possession of the province, with all its pueblos and peoples, for the king and God. Thereafter the Indians listened to the singing of the *Te Deum Laudamus* and a long sermon delivered by Fray Francisco Corvera through an interpreter, after which absolution for their apostasy was pronounced over them. Following this, children who had been born since the revolt were presented for baptism and Santa Fe was again—for the time being—a loyal Spanish villa.

The victory was bloodless and in the following weeks pueblo after pueblo made submission. Vargas nearly wore himself and his men out making *visitas* to these, and lecturing them on their misdeeds, for which he pardoned them, and their new duties of loyalty.

Farthest west were the Hopis, who also were the least inclined to accept Spanish rule. Late in December, in spite of the severe cold, Vargas and his little army reached those distant mesa dwellers.

When the defiant Hopis came forward, shaking weapons and throwing dust in the Spanish soldiers' eyes while they screamed their war cries, Vargas suddenly rose in his stirrups and thundered out this threatening denunciation:

"Ah, Indians, ah, you dogs of the worst breed that the sun warms! Do you think that my tolerance is owing to fear of your numbers and arms? Pity is what I have had for you in not killing you, for by a single threat on my part, you would all perish! What is this, anyway? With whom do I speak? Do you still keep your weapons in your hands when you see me angered? . . . Kneel, kneel at once before I consume you all with the fires of my indignation!"

Awe-struck, the natives complied, surrendering their weapons and kneeling in worship of the Virgin Mary. The incident gives a glimpse of a different Vargas. He could be patient and long-suffering beyond the power of most men, as he had shown, but when it was necessary he could be a roaring lion also.

The Hopis were the last of the Pueblo Indians to be subjected, and Vargas led his men back to Santa Fe. It was probably on the return that he paused at Inscription Rock and left the following notation, which can still be read in his clear Spanish script:

"Here was the General Don Diego de Vargas, who conquered for our Holy Faith and for the Royal Crown all the New Mexico, at his own expense, year of 1692."

In the whole campaign the only bloodshed was in encounters with the ever warlike Apaches, who thrice attacked Vargas on his marches, drove off some of his horses, and wounded a soldier. But on the third attack an Apache was made prisoner. He was shot, though not before he was exhorted and baptized by a priest.

Vargas had achieved a brilliant conquest, but the work was only begun. He marched back to El Paso del Norte, where news of his achievement caused rejoicing all over New Spain, including a devout service of thanksgiving at the cathedral in the City of Mexico, attended by the viceroy and his civil magistrates.

The next months were devoted by the governor to gathering soldiers and settlers to the number of eight hundred, including seventeen friars under Fray Salvador de San Antonio, who had been appointed *padre custodio,* and on October 13, 1693, he was once more marching north with them. In his few months of absence the Pueblo Indians, who had seemed so thoroughly cowed when Vargas left New Mexico, appeared to have repented of their easy surrender. Signs of trouble were noted, such as pueblos suddenly vacated and smoke signals in the mountains, but Vargas, his troops and colonists carrying Oñate's original banner, reached Santa Fe December 15 without encountering actual hostilities.

There, however, they discovered that the Tanos had changed their whole attitude and become so hostile that the Spaniards camped outside the town to avoid conflict while once more the governor tried to reason the Indians into peaceful submission.

It was a season of bitter cold and the colonists, not properly prepared for camping in such weather, suffered greatly, particularly the women and children. On the tenth day of Vargas' parleys to gain peaceful entrance into the town, a petition was brought him by the settlers, saying that twenty-two children had died from lack of sufficient shelter, and urging that force be used to eject the Tanos from the buildings in Santa Fe and return them to their own pueblo of Galisteo.

Vargas knew he must act. Daily the attitude of the Indians grew more defiant. At first they had given some corn, but this now ceased. They refused to furnish timbers for the construction of a church, and instead offered the use of an old *estufa*—a place where, exclaimed the scandalized padres, heathen worship had been conducted!—saying it was good enough for divine services until warm weather came.

After calling a council of war, Vargas ordered the natives to quit town. At once the fortifications were buzzing with preparations for war. On December 28 the Tanos closed the entrance to the plaza, yelling that "El Demonio could do more for them than God or María" —a blasphemy of which the padres took indignant notice—and that all the Christians would be killed.

Vargas later wrote, "I exhorted them with great kindness and love, I expressed my regret at their rebelling, and at their hardened and vindictive minds."

This hardly sounds like him. The fiery denunciation of the Hopis is more in keeping when battle actually confronted him. But one had to be careful in what was reported to the viceroy; and particularly to the tender-minded priests of New Spain, who were safe and comfortable in their parishes, and prone to criticize "injustices" toward Indians—if they were Indians in some remote province and not Indians working for some nearby wealthy Spanish *haciendado*.

Whatever he really said, Vargas was answered with jeers. At once he formed his army into two divisions and gave the *Santiago*.

Right up to the foot of the walls the Spanish fought, while arrows, stones and boiling water were hurled down upon them. The roar of battle grew and mounted, smoke rose, shouts and musket reports created tumult. At times the guns of the soldiers cleared the tops of the parapets, but from embrasures missiles continued to fly. Repeated attempts were made to scale the towers with ladders, but the men were hurled down by stones and wounded by arrows.

Late in the afternoon Vargas ordered the main gate broken down with axes and battering rams. It proved too strong, so the captain general had combustibles placed against it, which were set on fire in spite of the rain of arrows from the walls.

Flaming, the gate fell open. "We recognized that half the battle was won," said Vargas later.

Before the soldiers could rush in, however, a body of warriors was seen coming over the hills to the north. They were from the Tewa pueblos—Tesuque, Nambe, San Ildefonso and Santa Clara. Vargas paused in his attack on the town to direct his cavalry and some of his Indian allies against them. Twice the hostile Tewa array was charged. Six warriors were killed and after the second charge they retreated.

By that time night had fallen. In the darkness Vargas made the rounds, disposing his men to prevent a possible sortie of the besieged Indians. Some of the Spaniards occupied an old *estufa,* which they converted into a sort of fort, breaking holes in the roof from which they could shoot. Others worked their way around the walls, feeling for a weak place in the fortifications.

About four o'clock in the morning an unguarded section of the defenses was found. A ladder was placed and in the darkness a long line of Spaniards climbed cautiously upward. Once on the walls they quickly took possession of all the defenses surrounding the plaza, and at dawn the Indians found themselves at the mercy of their attackers. At once they surrendered.

The royal standard was unfurled over the *palacio* and over the main entrance to the plaza a cross was raised. Soldiers went about herding natives out of cellars and other hiding places. Josephe, the governor, was found dead. He had committed suicide after his wrist was broken by a shot during the fighting. Another Indian also hanged himself in despair.

Sixty-nine warriors, including Antonio Bolsas the war captain, stood with arms bound listening to their fate. An image of the Virgin had been found, smashed by a club. This, together with the shout from the walls that "El Demonio can do more for us than God or María," constituted sufficient blasphemy, sacrilege and heresy, according to the friars, to warrant the death penalty. It seems odd to condemn men for sacrilege when they really were to die for the crime of armed resistance, but the Spanish conscience was full of interesting inconsistencies and had to be salved, and in the end the same result was achieved.

Bolsas and his companions were shot. But first they were forced to listen to the usual lengthy sermon—delivered by Fray Juan de Alpuente—and receive absolution from the friars as they stood in sullen silence, so that their souls, as soon as the arquebus balls released them from their bodies, could wing their way to heaven. The Spaniards always were quite careful about such matters, when convenient.

Once more Santa Fe was a royal provincial city. The colonists moved into the buildings, grateful for their shelter. It was not necessary, however, for the Tano survivors—mostly women and children and numbering about four hundred—to return to the deserted Galisteo pueblo. Arrangements had been made for them to remain at Santa Fe. They were all distributed among the colonists as slaves.

All this was accomplished on December 30. That day and the next were spent gathering into sacks all the store of maize, beans, vetch and lentils which had been thriftily hoarded by the Indians, for the use of the Spaniards.

So ended the year 1693.

CHAPTER SIX

"By Blood and Fire"

JANUARY 1694 opened bleak and gloomy. Not only did the weather continue cold and disagreeable, but an epidemic carried off sixty of the newly made Tano slaves and presumably some of the colonists. An atmosphere of constant peril prevailed. Though the Spaniards held Santa Fe, their jurisdiction ended almost at the limits of the villa.

In those dark days one man, and one alone, never feared or faltered. Vargas, on whose shoulders rested all responsibility, was always cheerful, always confident, always active, lifting the spirits of those about him by his courage and faith.

Even in cold weather and flying snow he began a series of marches so numerous and crisscrossed that it would require too much space to follow them all. Pueblos awoke to find the hard-riding governor and his horsemen at their gates when they had not dreamed he was within many miles. Many of these gave assurances of obedience and friendship after the invariable peace talks he made. A few, however, did not give in so easily.

Chief of these were the Tewas of San Ildefonso, the Jémez of the pueblo that bears their name, and the Keresans of Cochiti. A reconnaissance up the Rio Grande revealed that the inhabitants of Tesuque, Nambe, Santa Clara and San Ildefonso—all related tribally—had deserted their pueblos and fortified themselves on a grim volcanic height called by the natives Tunyo, and in modern times Black Butte. Vargas conferred with these Indians, who promised to return to their pueblos, but this, as it appeared later, was only to gain time to further strengthen their position.

To the west the Cochiti grew bolder and began stealing livestock from the settlers at an alarming rate. One aspect of the situation was strategically serious. The Keresans of Cochiti and the Tewas of San Ildefonso, with their allies, were at war with each other. But if they forgot their mutual hostility they might, by joining forces, erect a powerful confederacy from which the worst effects might be anticipated.

Characteristically, Vargas, rather than waiting for the danger to come to him, went out to meet it. Ignoring the San Ildefonso rebels, he marched April 12 on the Cochiti with ninety soldiers and a hundred Indian allies, chiefly from the pueblos of Santa Ana and San Felipe, which remained friendly to the Spaniards.

The Cochiti had abandoned their pueblo in the valley and were occupying a high rock called the Portrero Viejo, on which they always took refuge when threatened by enemies. It was an ugly position to attack, but Vargas had it thoroughly scouted, and Bartolomé de Ojeda, the Santa Ana chief, informed the captain general that assault was feasible at a place where the Cochiti usually brought their stock down to water.

Dispositions were made, the *Santiago* given, and up the rocky slope swarmed the Spaniards and their allies, with a steady fire of arquebuses to which the Cochiti replied with arrows and boulders rolled down the declivity. There were some firearms among the Cochiti—captured in the revolt of 1680—but no ammunition.

In the brisk little battle seven of the defenders were killed and four of the attackers wounded before the top of the mesa was gained. One Cochiti was burned to death in a house which the Indian allies set afire, and thirteen men were captured. These thirteen were shot, first being preached at and shriven.

Most of the warriors, however, escaped with considerable celerity down the unguarded sides of the rock, leaving their women and children, together with seventy horses and nine hundred head of "young cattle," of which four hundred were identified by their brands as belonging to Santa Fe settlers.

After the victory, Ojeda and the other Indian allies returned to their pueblos, leaving Vargas somewhat shorthanded with regard to herding his captured animals and guarding his prisoners. From the Cochiti who had escaped came presently a message promising peace and begging him to return their women and children, to which he replied that he would release the captives as soon as the tribe returned to its old pueblo in the valley.

His bargaining power in this respect was somewhat diminished, however, on the return march to Santa Fe, when he was waylaid in a defile by the Cochiti. Though he beat off the enemy in a sharp fight in which two of his men were killed, most of the captives took advantage of the confusion to dive into the brush and escape. Vargas nevertheless received the promise of the Cochiti to return to their valley pueblo, whereupon he released the remainder of his captives and returned to the capital.

The Cochiti kept their promise. But the release of the prisoners was ill received by the colonists, who coveted them as slaves. They were glad enough, on the other hand, to get the livestock which he distributed among them.

Now the captain general could turn his attention to San Ildefonso, which he found a somewhat tougher foe. The pueblo had a long record of trouble with the Spaniards. It was there that the medicine men were accused of "bewitching" Fray Duran, and the resultant hangings, floggings and imprisonment had much to do with touching off the revolt of 1680, in which the San Ildefonsans murdered their missionaries, Frayes Luis de Morales and Antonio Sánchez de Piro, and many colonists. Since Vargas' first *entrada* they had never fully accepted his authority.

He found them fortified in the heights of one of the finest natural fortresses on this continent—Tunyo, or Black Butte. It is a forbidding volcanic upthrust, with sheer cliffs about most of its circumference and a difficult path leading to its heights. Traditionally this mountain was the home of the thunder gods worshiped by the Indians.

After a little skirmishing in which he captured forty-eight horses but lost two men, Vargas decided he could not hope to carry the fortress with the eighty-one soldiers he had with him and returned to Santa Fe. A second attempt on the San Ildefonso Gibraltar, May 24, was no more successful. Obviously the rebels would be difficult to subdue, and their resistance was dangerous because it was a living incitement to other disaffected pueblos.

Vargas was not well, paying the penalty for his great labors, and June passed with the San Ildefonsans still defiant on their volcanic mesa. The governor recovered his health somewhat in July, but still he left the rebellious Indians alone, by-passing them when he marched north and ascended the Rio Grande to a point perhaps near the Colorado border.

The pueblos had complained of Ute raiding, and there he had his first taste of combat with the Utes. It was not pleasant. Just before dawn of July 12, with shrill whoops and a whizzing of arrows, the mountain Indians swept down on his camp. In a brief flurry of fighting he lost six men, and though he repulsed the Utes he forever afterward had thorough respect for that fighting tribe. Before he returned to his capital he spent some time treating with them and received a temporary agreement of peace. On the way back to Santa Fe he once more reconnoitered Tunyo, from the top of which San Ildefonso warriors shouted down their defiance at him.

Vargas, however, had something else to occupy him. Jémez Indians, hostile toward Sia and Cochiti, had ambushed some of the friendly natives and killed them. So the captain general could not rest. Hardly pausing in the capital long enough to refit and revictual his soldiers, he set out for Jémez to restore peace.

What followed was a repetition of the Cochiti battle. The Jémez had barricaded themselves on a mesa, but the Spaniards in two columns, led respectively by Eusebio de Vargas, the governor's brother, and Antonio Jorge, captain of artillery, swept up the slope and captured the mesa. Twenty-five or thirty of the defenders were killed and seven warriors hurled themselves off the mesa cliff to die rather than fall in the hands of the Spaniards.

Six captured men and one captured *woman* were preached over and baptized by Fray Alpuente, who seemed to accompany these expeditions for the specific purpose of preparing the souls of the doomed so that they might be ushered into the hereafter with proper sanctification, and they were then shot by Antonio Jorge's firing squad. Why that one woman was shot is not explained. Other women, together with children of all ages, to the number of 372, were taken prisoner.

Vargas expressed pious joy: "Giving thanks to His Divine Majesty, and to His Most Holy Mother for such a happy outcome, the Apostle Santiago having acquired the position of patron of the armies and universal mediator of the kingdoms of Spain, on the eve of his glorious day, for without doubt he inspired this most happy victory with his patronage."

Thereupon he turned to plundering the pueblo. A wounded Keresan chief was captured, his leg crippled by a bullet and his right shoulder and arm black and blue. He had hidden in the rocks until thirst forced him to surrender. The Spaniards gave him water and questioned him. He told them the inhabitants of Santo Domingo had fled to the hills with the Jémez and, since he seemed to know where they had hidden their food supplies, his life for the time being was spared.

Not so fortunate was a Jémez spy (scout), seventy-two years old, who was taken prisoner next day. Since he could add little to the fund of useful knowledge, Vargas ordered Fray Alpuente to "prepare" him to be shot by Antonio Jorge and three soldiers, which was accomplished efficiently, both as to sermon and baptism, and as to the firing squad.

As it turned out, the Keresan chief had only a short respite. He pointed out the Santo Domingo corn barns, but they were empty, the grain having been carried off. At this he received his sermon, his absolution and his bullets from Jorge's arquebusiers.

Leaving Jémez pueblo in flames "as a punishment and warning that by blood and fire triumph has been acquired over those who were rebellious to divine and humane majesties," Vargas returned to Santa Fe. Having added many living men to the dead, the Spaniards halted on the way back to dig up a man already dead—Fray Juan de Jesús, who had been killed at Jémez in 1680. The sacred bones were carried to the capital and entombed in the chapel August 11, with ceremonies far more impressive than those by which the poor captured natives were sent into the hereafter.

Jémez envoys appeared August 26, imploring mercy, and got it on the promise to return to their pueblo and send half their warriors to help in the campaign Vargas projected against the San Ildefonsans.

The new assault on Tunyo mesa began September 4. The valorous defenders met the Spaniards hand to hand and drove them back with a loss of eleven men. But where Vargas could not defeat them in battle he brought them to their knees by destroying their maize fields. When they asked for peace he granted it on the usual condition—that they return to their pueblo.

A curious quarrel now occurred between the governor and his own people. Since Jémez warriors had fought faithfully against San Ildefonso, Vargas freed their women and children, who had been brought captive to Santa Fe. The Spanish colonists, who had taken them as slaves, bitterly complained of this.

To make matters worse, forty-five Tano slaves captured in the fall of Santa Fe ran away. Their owners made loud representations, whereat Vargas sent word to the surrounding chiefs that the fugitives must be captured and restored. His order was complied with promptly, and so pleased was he by the evidence of respect and obedience that he freed the forty-five escapees and promised freedom to the others in the colony.

All this made for good relations with the natives, but the settlers, deprived of their human livestock, were furious.

That November a new *custodio*—and agent of the Inquisition—came to New Mexico, in the person of Fray Francisco de Vargas. Though the names of the chief padre and the governor were similar, they were at odds from the beginning.

Some new colonists who arrived were established by the governor in a villa of their own at a site previously chosen by Oñate north of Santa Fe, but abandoned in the revolt of 1680. The full name of this village deserves distinction even among unwieldy Spanish names: *La Villa Nueva de Santa Cruz de los Españoles Mexicanos del Rey Nuestro Señor Don Carlos Segundo* (The New Town of the Holy Cross of the Spanish Mexicans of the King Our Master, Don Charles the Second).

It was sufficiently imposing to have staggered a city the size of London, but the little hamlet of seventy families took it in stride, being accustomed to resounding verbiage, and soon cut it down to a comfortable Santa Cruz.

Vargas deserved a rest but he did not get it. In the late spring of 1696, the last year of his term as governor, Fray Vargas, the *custodio*, waited on him, with a report and a request. Missionary padres, stationed in various outer pueblos, said the *custodio*, believed themselves in danger. Indians were sullen, and there had been some suspicious acts and minor insubordinations. The padres wished military protection.

Governor Vargas took little stock in the reports. A spark of rebellion among the pueblos after the chastising he had given them? Incredible. With a thin edge of sarcasm he told Fray Vargas that any missionaries who were afraid might return to Santa Fe.

That touched the pride of the padres, who, whatever their faults, could hardly be accused of cowardice. They stayed at their posts.

For once the governor was wrong. The storm the friars feared broke in sudden fury, June 4, when eight pueblos—Taos, Picuris, Tesuque, Nambe, San Ildefonso, Santo Domingo, San Cristóbal and Jémez—rose all at once by a plan evidently concerted, and in a flurry of bloodshed murdered five missionaries and twenty-one other Spaniards, then fled to the mountains.

Two of the padres suffered especially cruel deaths. Fray Antonio Moreno of Nambe was visiting Fray Francisco Corvera, the resident of San Ildefonso. The two priests were shut up in the church, which was set on fire, and they miserably burned to death.

Fray Francisco Alonso Ximénes de Cisneros, of Cochiti, escaped to San Felipe, from which he sent a message by an Indian to Vargas, giving first news of the outbreak.

Vargas was aghast. Now, when it was too late, he realized that he had been careless and hasty in dismissing the warnings of the padres, whose blood, and that of others, might now be said to be on his hands.

Already terrified refugees were pouring in, some of them wounded and almost naked, and the wide extent of the revolt was beginning to be realized. The colony was terrified. Was 1680 to be repeated? Were the outlying settlements all doomed, Santa Fe itself, perhaps, to be the grave of the settlers, who would be besieged in it?

From Santa Cruz came a group of refugees shepherded by Juan de Archuleta, who had come to New Mexico as head muleteer for Vargas' army, and had just performed a journey of remarkable bravery.

When first he learned of the uprising, Archuleta left his home and rode to San Juan, where he rescued Fray Blas Navarro and sent him, with Mathias Lobatto, a soldier, and the sacred vessels of the church, back to Santa Cruz. From San Juan, in spite of the deadly danger, he continued on to San Ildefonso. It was deserted, the church and convent burned, and Archuleta found the bodies of the two friars who had been put to death there. Thence he went to Nambe, discovering the convent and church looted and the holy vessels all gone. Lying unclothed at the door of the church lay the bodies of Juan Cortés, a prominent settler, with those of his daughter Juana and her husband José Sánchez, and Andrés Baca. Cortés' wife and another daughter, it was later learned, had been taken as slaves by the *cacique* of the pueblo, and two boys, his sons, shared the same fate. With this information and sure knowledge that the Indians had taken to the mountains, probably Tunyo again, Archuleta completed his daring ride, returned to Santa Cruz, and brought his refugees and news to Santa Fe.

Those were sleepless nights and bitter days for Vargas. His mistake in not believing the *custodio* weighed on him. He drilled men, organized defenses, and sent out forces to relieve threatened settlements. Presently he learned that some of the pueblos had not joined the revolt. Pecos, for example, not only was loyal but was sending one hundred warriors with Roque de Madrid, who had ridden there, to help the Spaniards. San Felipe, Santa Ana and the southern pueblos had refused to take part in the uprising. This was some reassurance, and Vargas prepared to deal with the rebellion in the north.

He made a quick reconnaissance, going as far upriver as San Ildefonso, where he caught an Indian. Fray Alpuente was on the job to see that the captive's soul went heavenward as he was shot.

Bartolomé de Ojeda, that war captain of Santa Ana, similarly scouted swiftly westward, reporting many signal smokes and signs of enemy activity.

Felipe, *cacique* of Pecos, arrived with his warriors and some prisoners they had taken. These included some influential men of Jémez and Tesuque, and although their guilt as fomenters of the revolt was manifest, Felipe advised Vargas not to hang them because it might further inflame the hostile Indians. Thereupon Vargas suggested that Felipe and his warriors handle the task.

At this Felipe took his men and the prisoners into an *estufa* and asked the latter what they thought of the revolt. When they upheld it, saying the Spaniards were "of different blood," Felipe raised a baton and cried, "Here, for the king!" His followers at once seized and hanged four of the captives. Evidently the ubiquitous Fray Alpuente was not present on this occasion to perform his grim task.

Four other prisoners were "questioned" in the secret rooms of the guardhouse by Luis Granillo, a veteran of the province. His methods are not recorded, although there is a casual reference to a "knotted rope." He "persuaded" the four Indians to give full particulars, naming the pueblos taking part in the revolt and other pertinent matters. Following this testimony, which gave Vargas a full picture of what he had to face, the prisoners were given three hours to be "confessed and prepared"—no doubt by the excellent Fray Alpuente—and then shot by chosen soldiers "until they die naturally," which means they were not tortured to death.

By the end of July Vargas felt that all the settlements were fairly secure and the friendly pueblos protected. Now, sword and firebrand in hand, he raged across New Mexico, punishing.

Twice he struck hostile forces and scattered them, killing forty men. He assaulted Ácoma August 8, and although he was unable to reach the summit he captured the *cacique* of the pueblo and five warriors. The five common warriors were preached at, confessed, and shot, but the *cacique* was released to go back and admonish his people. Taos surrendered October 8, and even San Ildefonso's people, on their impregnable Tunyo, treated for peace. By November 24, Vargas reported to the viceroy that only Ácoma, the Hopis and perhaps Santo Domingo and Cochiti were not fully pacified. These soon gave in. Many of their people had died in the mountains or joined the Apaches, and their crops had been devastated.

Last to submit were the distant Hopis. In 1700 that sturdy people sent ambassadors to make peace and propose that each "nation"— Spanish and Hopi—"be allowed to retain its own religion." No such agreement could be made by the Spaniards, of course, but differences were adjusted. The Hopis then as now remained the freest and most individualistic of all the pueblo peoples.

Vargas' term as governor ended in 1696. He had done an almost unbelievable job in reconquering and repopulating New Mexico; fighting two savage wars; thoroughly exploring the province; building churches and towns; and establishing this farthest appanage of Spain on a firm basis at an incredible expenditure of strength, energy and resolution, to say nothing of money from his own pocket.

For all this he received the usual reward the Spanish Crown gave to its great servants. He asked for reappointment, but his petition, owing to delays in New Spain, did not reach the king until 1699. Meantime Captain Pedro Rodríguez Cubero got in a petition first (and 2000 pesos) and was given the office.

With his loss of power trouble gathered about Vargas. The *cabildo*, governing body of the colonists—who so often fled to the captain general for protection, and looked to him to house, victual and watch over them—dug up old grudges now. He was charged with depriving the settlers of slaves he had previously given them, in order to return the prisoners to the Indians at the conclusion of peace; with embezzling large sums of money belonging to the colony; with provoking by the shooting of the Tano captives and other oppressive acts the hostilities of 1694 and 1696; and with driving families out of the colony by his dictatorial ways.

There was some truth in these charges; but Vargas in his entire governorship was forced to maintain a sort of martial law, while the money he was accused of "embezzling" went to conduct needful military operations.

Cubero, the new governor, arriving at Santa Fe, found Vargas protesting Cubero's appointment to the viceroy and exhibiting reluctance to admit his successor's authority. Personal enmity sprang into being between the two men, while the *cabildo*, forgetting all gratitude, renewed its charges against Vargas. Since Cubero held a commission as *juez de residencia* as well as governor, he arrested and imprisoned the former governor. In chains Vargas was brought before the successor who hated him and who conducted the trial and questioned the witnesses as well as judging the case. Vargas was found guilty, all his property was confiscated, an additional fine of four thousand pesos was imposed on him for "court costs," and he was remanded to prison, where he lay for three years in such close confinement that few even of his family were allowed to see him.

Now occurred an episode which it is pleasant to record because it was so unusual. Fray Francisco de Vargas, the *custodio*, had his differences with Diego de Vargas, the governor. The Franciscans, indeed, charged the deposed official with having caused many of their most unhappy misadventures, particularly the massacre of 1696. Yet Fray Vargas believed in justice, and he was seeing a brave man mistreated when he should instead have been rewarded. On his own responsibility, the *custodio* made the long journey to the City of Mexico, and by his arguments obtained from the viceroy an order to release the prisoner, under bond, and allow him to defend himself in the courts of New Spain.

Again the long journey by the *padre custodio*, this time northward with the documents. But a hitch occurred. The proud Vargas refused the terms offered, saying that to give bonds was degrading to a man of his rank and services. He preferred to remain in his cell.

Meantime the slow workings of the governmental machinery of Spain creaked on. At last the king received Vargas' petition, together with a full report of his achievements. At once Charles II announced his royal appreciation of the services of Vargas, conferred on him the rank and title of Marqués de la Nava de Brazinas, and ordered him reappointed governor of New Mexico, either at the end of Cubero's administration in 1702 or when the office became vacant if it did so before that time.

All this, together with the viceroy's order for Vargas' instant release, reached Santa Fe in July 1700. Now the situation was vastly changed. The *cabildo,* in the light of the royal *cédula,* made all haste to drop its accusations. Vargas was quickly and fully exonerated by the viceroy, his property was restored and his fine remitted, and his reappointment as governor made valid.

Cubero, who had done little in his administration aside from prosecuting and imprisoning Vargas, departed hurriedly from New Mexico at the conclusion of his term. It would not have been healthy to remain. Vargas hated him bitterly, felt his honor had been affronted, was an expert swordsman, and the *code duello* was well recognized in Spanish countries.

Once more Vargas was lord of New Mexico, justified and triumphant, with the title of *marqués.* But he did not live long to enjoy his restoration to royal favor. His health was ruined, as much by his three years in a prison cell as by his many campaigns and constant exertions. Leading his troops against Apache raiders, he was suddenly stricken ill in the Sandia Mountains, April 2, 1704.

They carried him to Bernalillo, where he died, April 14. Like a good Spaniard and Catholic, he made his peace with God before his death, and left a will. Most of his property was divided among his three children—two sons and a daughter, all born of love affairs out of wedlock —but he reserved sufficient to reward his closest and most faithful associates, and gave his old Negro slave, Andrés, his liberty. He was buried at Santa Fe, in the parish church, the savior of New Mexico as Oñate was its father.

CHAPTER SEVEN

English Sea Rovers and Spanish Jesuits

WHILE Vargas was waging his wars to regain New Mexico, events on the other side of the world were vastly affecting the American frontier of the Spanish Empire. The "Invincible Armada" had been destroyed in the English channel by an English fleet in 1588, marking the beginning of the downward cycle of Spain. Useless wars and the fanatical and horrifying Inquisition destroyed the nation's agricultural economy and drove out of the country the best commercial and administrative minds. In one single period of twenty-five years—from 1500 to 1525—the Spanish Inquisition accused 348,907 persons of heresy or other sacerdotal crimes, condemned 28,540 to death, actually burned 12,000 at the stake in the dreadful *autos-da-fé*, and imprisoned and impoverished almost all the others. The rack, the red-hot iron, the iron boot, the iron maiden and other ingenious forms of torment were still in vogue in 1700, and some of them persisted in the proceedings of the Holy Office as late as 1820, when at last the Inquisition was abolished in Spain. It was then thought that torture, officially approved by a so-called civilized government, was forever ended. But that was before Mussolini, Hitler and Stalin came to establish new records and devise new abominations in human misery and torment.

Even though Spain lost her pre-eminence in Europe, however, her colonies in America still gave her vast and apparently inexhaustible resources and powers. With the belief that ever beyond the horizon lay new Golcondas of wealth, Spain's policy was to push her frontiers unceasingly northward and ever northward until she occupied the whole of the American continent for her king and faith.

A further spur to this was the activity of English freebooters like Sir Francis Drake, who in his ship the *Golden Hind,* and with a few other small vessels, operated off the west coast of the Americas in 1577–79, looted Valparaiso and Santiago, captured the Manila galleon, the *Nuestra Señora de la Concepción,* with her fabulous cargo of silver and gold headed for New Spain, and then circumnavigated the globe after first touching on the coast of California and claiming it with due pomp for England's Queen Elizabeth I. Drake's exploit made Spain realize the vulnerability of her Pacific flank.

At the same time buccaneers and pirates grew so numerous, ferocious and bold in the Caribbean Sea that they made it unsafe for any Spanish sail to navigate its waters unless accompanied by what amounted to a veritable war fleet. If anything were needed to prove the decadence of Spain even in the Americas, it was the series of terrible raids led by Henry Morgan, the Welsh freebooter, and his "gentleman adventurers"—the worst offscourings of the ocean world. Morgan sacked Puerto Bello in Panama in 1668; Maracaibo in Venezuela in 1669; and crowned his evil exploits by sailing to the Isthmus of Panama, leaving his ships, crossing to the Pacific side, and there pillaging and destroying the City of Panama amid scenes of murder, torture, rape and fire as terrible as any the Spaniards themselves had ever engaged in during their conquests.

These events brought about a flurry of activities in New Spain. It was necessary to consolidate the western territories, and the Church led the way. Under the inspired leadership of Padre Eusebio Francisco Kino, beginning in 1683 while the pueblo revolt in New Mexico was at its peak, the great gap in geography from Lower California to the entire Gila River valley in present-day Arizona—that area known as Pimería Alta—was explored and mapped.

Geographically Padre Kino's travels were important, and spiritually the missions he established in the area were magnificent. But historically his contribution was perhaps less mighty, because the territories his unexampled energy and single-minded devotion opened up were too arid and too lacking in resources to play a great part in the Spanish dream.

Yet he deserves special attention, if only because he seems the type-perfect missionary zealot of the Spanish era.

Actually Kino was not a Spaniard. He was a Tyrolese Swiss, born near Trent in 1644. When he was twenty-one years old he became a novitiate in the Society of Jesus, and so distinguished himself in his studies at Freiburg and Ingolstadt that he might have won fame as a scholar in Europe. Instead, as the result of a serious illness when he was twenty-five years old, from which he recovered, as he believed, because of the intervention in his behalf of St. Francis Xavier, he chose to become a missionary to the heathen.

No portrait of Kino exists, nor even a physical description of him, except what can be conjectured from his characteristics as noted by his contemporaries. He was an ascetic in the absolute sense, taking his food without salt, and with mixtures of herbs "which made it more distasteful." He neither smoked nor took snuff, as did many religious of his day. The only wine he ever tasted was when he celebrated mass, and he slept always on the floor, on mats or horse blankets, refusing to take a bed. At times he appears to have submitted to flagellations, to further curb his flesh, and when he fell sick with fever he tried no remedy for six days, except to celebrate mass and then retire to his horse blankets again. When it was necessary to reprimand a sinner he could grow "choleric," but otherwise he was mild and meek, never appearing to resent abuse, which was sometimes directed at him. In saying the mass he invariably wept. As Fray Luis Velarde wrote of him, "he was merciful to others, but cruel to himself."

From this, one gleans a picture of a man lean from self-deprivation, but with the fire of his holy cause burning in his eyes. We have, however, nothing further as to height, features, color of hair or eyes, or other physical characteristics.

His self-denial, which might have weakened other men, did not seem to do so with him. At times he was energetic almost to the point of ferocity, and he was never idle except when seriously ill. Herbert E. Bolton, who has made the best study of him, records that at the age of fifty-one Padre Kino made a fifteen-hundred-mile horseback ride, from his frontier mission to the City of Mexico, in fifty-three days, including stops necessary to say mass and confer with other priests.

Another instance of his endurance as a horseman occurred in 1700, when Padre Kino was fifty-six years old, an age when many men begin at least to think of slowing down. On the morning of May 3 that year, when he was about to say mass at sunrise, at Tumacacori in southern Arizona, he was given an urgent message begging him to hurry to San Ignacio, in Sonora, to save from execution an Indian whom the soldiers had imprisoned and were going to put to death next day. Padre Kino said his mass, wrote a letter to one of the military officers, and clambered on his horse. By midnight he was in Imuris, a way station, and by dawn the following day reached San Ignacio, a distance of seventy miles. Thereupon he again said mass, and saved the prisoner from execution.

His courage was as great as his endurance. When the Pimas revolted in 1695, and killed Padre Saeta and others, he refused to flee from them, but calmly waited for them to come and kill him. The Indians respected him too greatly to lift a weapon against him, and as soon as the revolt was suppressed he went on with his work. Often he was warned of danger from the Indians but he continued to go out among his spiritual children in complete indifference to signs of murderous hostility. One has a mental picture of a lean, black-robed figure with brilliant, almost hypnotic gaze, moving among the savages as if he were in a cage of wild beasts, subduing them by the force of his personality and his will.

But it was something greater than this. Padre Kino was so genuinely the friend of the Indians, so completely sincere, so humble and long-suffering, that he impressed even those children of the wilderness who had come to hate all white men but him. Among them he lived out his life and died in 1711, when he was sixty-seven years old, at Magdalena, one of the missions he had founded, collapsing while dedicating a new chapel consecrated to his beloved St. Francis Xavier.

"His deathbed, as his bed had always been, consisted of two calf-skins for a mattress, two blankets such as the Indians use for covers, and a pack-saddle for a pillow."

Unhappily, Padre Kino's final years were filled with heartache. Spain, faced with multiple dangers in its colonies, withdrew support from the missions in remote Arizona, so that they starved for funds, their chapels and churches fell into disrepair, and their missionaries were called away. This was the sponge filled with bitterness which was his to taste as he passed on to the heaven in which he so fervently believed. It was not given him to know that two decades after his death his work would be revived, or that he would become known as the greatest of the missionaries of the Southwest.

Meantime there was another, far wider arena of struggle developing, in which a Spaniard, as unlike Padre Kino as it is possible to be, played a part.

Diego de Peñalosa's punishment and humiliation by the Holy Office, as previously recounted, sent him out of the Spanish realms burning with bitterness and anger. He took ship and touched at the Canary Islands, presently appearing in London. On this voyage, or perhaps before it, he must have visited Santo Domingo also, for sometime during this period he became well acquainted with the French *boucaniers* of that island—the buccaneers of the Caribbean—and especially their leader, a pirate named Grammont, striking up a friendship with that freebooter.

In London he lived an embittered life for a time, maintaining himself by selling to the British information concerning the defenses of the West Indies and New Spain. But presently his old flair for ingratiating himself with the powerful stood him in good stead. He made himself so agreeable in the dissolute court of Charles II, and especially to the profligate and immoral Duke of York, afterward James II, that when a formal request was made by the Spanish ambassador for Peñalosa's arrest and delivery to Spain the king rejected it.

But France, not England, was at this time the great power of Europe. Inevitably, Peñalosa arrived in Paris about 1671. He was impressed by the splendor and authority of the French monarchy under Louis XIV, and readily understood the ambition of the *Grand Monarque* for fame, for the increase of his territories, and for extension of his already great power, since they found an echo in Peñalosa's own character. They might, the Spaniard considered, be turned to his own advantage; not only to enable him to avenge his wrongs, but to achieve a vast plan he undoubtedly had formed already.

But how might a discredited Spanish official—however splendid in appearance and courtly in address—obtain recognition from the greatest ruler of the time? Peñalosa, a man of many resources, believed he knew a way. He turned author.

What he produced was one of the prime literary hoaxes of history, entitled, *Freytas, Relación del descubrimiento del país y ciudad Quivira, echo por D. Diego Dioniso de Peñalosa* (Freytas, Account of the Discovery of the Country and City of Quivira, Made by Don Diego Dioniso de Peñalosa). The author of the work with this imposing title was supposed to be a friar, Nicholas de Freytas, but if such a person actually existed, he had nothing to do with the document. Peñalosa knew that his "exploits" would be much better glorified by another than himself, but he, without much question, was the real author. It was in the form of an ostensible copy of a report *to the Spanish court* of an expedition supposedly made by Peñalosa into the fabled land of Quivira.

Whatever else Peñalosa had done in New Mexico, he managed to saturate himself with the legends of the great treasure-filled "kingdoms"—over the horizon somewhere—which filled the province when he governed it. With that background, and taking the records of Juan de Oñate's expedition of 1601—to which as governor of New Mexico he had access—as a skeleton for his narrative, he made himself the hero of an almost identical exploration, which, however, he covered with superabundant exaggerations and trappings of his own invention. It need hardly be added that he made no such expedition, or one faintly resembling it.

He told of battles with the Indians, in one of which, with only eighty soldiers, he coolly slew three thousand of the enemy; gave mouthwatering descriptions of the richness of the land and the grandeur and prosperity of Quivira, which was pictured as a vast center of population, with regular streets extending for leagues in every direction and lined with buildings of three or four stories, made of masonry in which lived a civilized and prosperous population; and referred casually to "rich gold mines" farther north, which were *known also to the English*. In the last statement the suggestion was implicit that the king of Spain had full knowledge of those riches, through this report, and since another rival, England, also might be moving toward it, France would do well to act speedily to head them off.

This literary fantasy Peñalosa allowed to be seen by the French minister of the admiralty. The minister soon called it to the attention of Louis. Very quickly Peñalosa found himself well received at court, and on good terms with Colbert, Seignelay and other important ministers, which was the end toward which he had been working.

It gave him the opportunity to address several written memorials to the French government, of which the most important was dated January 18, 1682, and contained the following extraordinary proposals:

If the French government would finance him, he would establish at the mouth of the Rio Bravo (Rio Grande) a colony, composed of "filibusters from the Island of Santo Domingo," which was then a French possession. With these bold fighters and forayers he would "on the first occasion of a war with Spain"—and wars with Spain were almost annual occurrences in that era—set forth and conquer Nueva

Viscaya, the northwest province of New Spain, which contained some of the richest gold and silver mines in the world.

Meantime, as he awaited the "occasion of a war," he would not be idle. He would begin "an important trade with the tribes of natives," which he would wrest from the Spaniards because the latter had to transport their merchandise at great cost three hundred leagues overland from Vera Cruz. The "colony" also would raise herds of cattle, and by cultivating the fertile soil raise great crops of all kinds of grain, fruits and fabric plants. Finally, Peñalosa said, it was a practical certainty that the interior (of Texas) was immensely rich in precious metals, which his "colony" would explore and discover, both enriching itself and providing the coffers of the king of France with great revenues by payment of duties "after the manner of the Spaniards."

The great central objective was, however, the conquest of Nueva Viscaya, which he assured the French ministry could easily be accomplished, winning a vast territory containing wonderful mines, such as those in Zacatecas and Chihuahua. As a final footnote, he pointed out that he was sure of success by populating his "colony" with the filibusters, because those people were "inured to war, and accustomed to hardships and a similar climate."

The recent exploits of Morgan, the ravager of the Spanish cities of the Caribbean—for which he was knighted by the English king—still rang through the world. That buccaneers were inured to war there could be no question, and that they had the hardihood to survive any climate—even that of hell—seemed equally without a doubt.

The proposal Peñalosa thus made sounded so ambitious yet plausible that it aroused great interest in the French ministry. But it took time to come to a decision on a project so vast, and before a final answer was ready, something happened to complicate matters for Peñalosa.

BOOK *3*

France
on the
Frontier

La Salle's Forlorn Hope

RENÉ ROBERT CAVELIER, Sieur de La Salle, the greatest of the French explorers, had caught a vision of the scope of America when as a young man he went to Canada to seek his fortune. He first discovered and navigated most of the length of the Ohio and Illinois rivers, and finally in 1682, at the very time when the Pueblo Indians of New Mexico were in revolt, descended the Mississippi River to its mouth and took possession of the river and its entire immense drainage, in the name of the king of France, calling it *Louisiana* in honor of Louis XIV.

But laying claim to this continental area—which extended from the Rocky Mountains to the Alleghenies, and from Canada to eastern Texas, comprising two thirds of what is now the United States—and actually winning control over it were two very different matters. Drake had "claimed" California for England in 1579—without notable results for Elizabeth's domain. As a matter of fact the Mississippi and its valley already had been "claimed"—and for Spain—by De Soto, who was buried beneath the river's waters. De Soto called the stream the Espíritu Santo, a favorite title with the Spaniards. La Salle called it the Colbert, after the great French minister. Neither of these names was more than transitory. The Indian title for the mighty torrent, *Misi Sipi,* sometimes poetically translated "Father of Waters," but actually meaning, in the Algonquin tongue, "Great River," superseded them both.

La Salle was not awed by the magnitude of his enterprise. He reascended the river, and in 1683, while Peñalosa's proposal was being studied by the French ministry, he arrived in Paris filled with enthusiastic plans for a great exploring and trading enterprise which would capture and hold control of the Mississippi basin for France.

As was perhaps natural, the proposals of La Salle, a Frenchman and a very famous one, took precedence over those of Peñalosa, a

Spaniard and a somewhat discredited one. Nevertheless it is pretty certain that Peñalosa's grandiose scheme, plus his imaginative account of the riches of the west, and his bold plan for moving over into the territory of New Spain, did much to crystallize the decision of the French king and his ministers in La Salle's behalf. They had been convinced of the glittering possibilities before La Salle appeared.

Peñalosa must have seen that he was being shunted aside, but he made another effort, presenting a second plan which now took into consideration La Salle and his proposals. He suggested that the French government support *both La Salle and himself* in a joint operation. The two expeditions would co-operate, La Salle colonizing the mouth of the Mississippi while Peñalosa took over as his base Pánuco, where modern Tampico stands.

This memorial was dated January 1684. Peñalosa proposed to gather from a thousand to twelve hundred French buccaneers from Santo Domingo and named as his lieutenant their chief, Grammont, "a bold fellow whom they willingly obey." Then with these he would descend on Pánuco, capture and rob it, strengthen it with new fortifications, and then march west into Nueva Viscaya, which he said was without any fortress and defended only by five hundred "enervated Spaniards." Should the viceroy send reinforcements, Peñalosa's buccaneers, he asserted, would be aided by the natives, "who would rise against their tyrannical Spanish masters." Victory would be assured for the invaders, the rich mines and cities would fall to them, and a large territory gained for France. Peñalosa's reward was to be the governorship of all territories seized, with Grammont his lieutenant governor.

It was a wildly ambitious scheme, but there had been others more wild which had succeeded in the New World. That Peñalosa and La Salle knew each other and perhaps discussed together their projects, there can be no doubt. References are made to Peñalosa by Beaujeu, La Salle's associate, in his reports and there is indication that when La Salle sailed Peñalosa was expected to follow and sustain him.

La Salle's own plan, in fact, was interestingly similar to the prior suggestions of the Spaniard; so much so that his familiarity with them is evident. He proposed to return to America, not by way of Canada, but by the Gulf of Mexico—Peñalosa's plan—and to the mouth of the Mississippi, which Peñalosa had suggested. He urged that "great benefits" could be expected from a fort and colony at the mouth of that river: first, the usual pious hopes that "the cause of God may be advanced by preaching the gospel to the Indian tribes"; and second—and more immediately interesting and practical—that "great conquests may be effected for the glory of the king, by seizure of provinces

rich in silver mines, and defended only by a few indolent and enervated Spaniards."

The last words are almost an echo of the Peñalosa memorial.

La Salle asked for two vessels and two hundred men, with their
arms, munitions, pay and maintenance. Going further, he borrowed
another leaf from Peñalosa's book, by saying he would pick up fifty
buccaneers at Santo Domingo to augment his force, and once in
America would rally the Indian tribes to form of them an army for
the invasion of Nueva Viscaya, which, by an error of geography, he
assumed to be no more than forty or fifty leagues from the river
Seignelay—the Red River.

La Salle's plan was accepted, he was given the commission, and
there was such enthusiasm for his scheme that the king doubled his
number of requested ships to four.

As for Peñalosa, something happened—just what is not known. The
fickle favor of the French monarch turned from him. When La Salle
sailed on July 24, 1684, with letters patent to "rule over the country
which will be subject anew to our dominion in North America, from
Fort St. Louis on the Illinois River, into Nueva Viscaya," the Spaniard
who first proposed the plan and had done so much to mature it was
left behind. Three years later, in 1687, Diego de Peñalosa died in
Paris. He was about sixty-five years old, and embittered and disap-
pointed. But he had helped set on foot a movement that limited forever the Spanish dream of northern expansion, save for a brief, forty-
year period of European politics in the next century.

La Salle sailed with four vessels, two of them listed as frigates, the
Joly of thirty-six guns and the *Belle* of six, and two storeships, the
Aimable and the *St. François*. No regular troops could be spared, so
agents were sent to Rochelle and Rochefort to gather recruits by
impressment, a method then in vogue among all European nations.
As was to be expected, they got a hundred men who were described
as "the scum of the French towns." To these were added thirty "gentleman adventurers," some of whom had financial investments in the
expedition; a number of mechanics and laborers; several families of
colonists; three Récollet (Franciscan) friars and three Sulpician
priests, including La Salle's brother, Abbé Jean Cavelier; and finally
"a number of girls seeking husbands," whom they presumably looked
forward to finding in the New World. Altogether more than three
hundred persons embarked on the expedition.

The voyage was known to be dangerous, not only because Spain
had forbidden any other nation to sail the waters of the Gulf of Mexico, but because another of the periodic wars had broken out, and

Spanish ships were on the lookout for French prizes anywhere and at any time.

Commanding the actual navigation of the vessels, but otherwise under La Salle's orders, was Captain Sieur de Beaujeu, of the French royal navy. From the first this arrangement was bad. Beaujeu, of the hereditary nobility and a professional navy man, looked down on La Salle, who was of the untitled nobles with burgher blood in his veins, and a landlubber civilian.

On the other hand, La Salle was cold and appeared, at least, to be haughty and domineering. He was born René Robert Cavelier, of a well-to-do mercantile family, in 1643. Educated in a Jesuit school, where he showed remarkable abilities, he took the preliminary steps toward entering that order; but before 1666 something occurred to make him leave it, and thereafter he had for the Jesuits as deep distrust and dislike as before he had admiration. The law of France deprived from inheriting from relatives one who, having entered religious orders, afterward withdrew; and when his father died, the young man received nothing and was practically penniless, looking about for some way to mend his fortune.

At this time his elder brother, Abbé Jean Cavelier, was a priest of St. Sulpice, stationed in Canada. Scraping together what funds he could, the young man sailed for that distant French colony.

Almost from the day of his arrival he distinguished himself there. A restless nature, coupled with intrepid courage and inflexible purpose, and implemented by an imagination capable of embracing vast schemes, made him an explorer—the greatest France ever produced. Followed his Canadian and Mississippi discoveries.

In his lonely years on the frontier he acquired mannerisms and habits that gave him a reputation for harshness, haughtiness and self-will. Interestingly, we have his self-analysis, written by him to Abbé Bernou, a friend in France, defending himself from a charge of harshness, of which one paragraph reads:

If I am wanting in expansiveness and show of feeling towards those with whom I associate, it is only through a timidity which is natural to me, and which has made me leave various employments, where without it I could have succeeded. But as I judged myself ill-fitted for them on account of this defect, I have chosen a life more suited to my solitary disposition; which, nevertheless, does not make me harsh to my people, though, joined to a life among savages, it makes me, perhaps, less polished and complaisant than the atmosphere of Paris requires. I well believe that there is self-love in this; and that, knowing how little accustomed I am to a more polite life, the fear of making mistakes makes me more reserved than I like to be. So I rarely expose myself to conversation with those in whose company I am afraid of making blunders, and can hardly help making them. . . . It is a defect of which I shall never rid myself, as long as I live, often as it spites me against myself, and often as I quarrel with myself about it.

There, in his own words, is the inner soul of the man. Proud, he was yet shy. He found it difficult to express himself in the mincing ways of the French court, and had a morbid fear of being laughed at. However courageous and farsighted he was, the same painful timidity caused him, even in the forests, to draw into himself, and by way of compensation assume a manner far more arbitrary, cold and aloof than he perhaps really wished. Because of this he rarely aroused enthusiasm among his followers, distrusted the motives of others, and took none into his confidence. It is a picture of an unhappy man, without humor, unsmiling, and too devoted to his purposes to have time for pleasure or relaxation, yet daring, enduring and ambitious beyond almost anyone of his day.

From the first the expedition seemed dogged by misfortune. The commanders, Beaujeu and La Salle, were constantly at cross-purposes. There was a false start, a quarrel because La Salle refused to sanction a stop at the Canary Islands—for the excellent reason that he feared word of his design might reach the Spaniards—and when they reached Santo Domingo, although they had agreed to stop at Port de Paix, capital of the island, Beaujeu ran by it and anchored instead at Petit Goave, on the other side of the island.

La Salle was angry, but there were fifty sick persons aboard and he was one of them, and a layover was necessary. The *Joly,* moreover, had lost touch with the other ships. Two of these, the *Belle* and the *Aimable,* appeared shortly, but the *St. François* did not arrive. She had been captured by Spanish cruisers. With her the expedition lost tools, provisions and other needed supplies; but more important, the captured members of the crew were forced to disclose the expedition's plans, and thus Spain was apprised of La Salle's project before he even reached the mainland.

The soldiers and sick were landed on the island, where the former, the "scum of the French cities," proved as disorderly as might have been anticipated. "The air of this place is bad," wrote Henri Joutel, La Salle's best lieutenant, "so are the fruits; and there are plenty of women who are worse than either."

Another writer said that the soldiers and crew members "gave themselves up to every dissipation and vice, and thereby contracted loathsome diseases which eventually carried them to their graves." In these wallowings in vice they were joined by some of the gentleman adventurers. We have a specific instance of a rakehell noble, the Marquis de la Sablonnière, who suffered from the effects of his Santo Domingo excesses later.

La Salle was prostrated by fever, possibly typhoid. While walking with Joutel one day he had a sudden seizure and was half carried by the latter to a house which had been rented by the Duhaut brothers. Remember that name. The elder Duhaut had money invested in the colonial enterprise, and future events would prove him one of the worst scoundrels in the history of early America.

In that house La Salle passed through stages of his fever which made him delirious at times, so that his friends despaired of his life. Abbé Cavelier, his brother, attended him; as did Joutel.

The latter, though a comparatively young man, had for sixteen years served in the French regular army. He was a native of Rouen, his father being a gardener to La Salle's uncle, for which reason he joined the expedition. Of all La Salle's followers he was the best.

When at last La Salle recovered enough to proceed, the alley-rat soldiers and sailors were brought back to the ships, and in November the voyage was continued. Now they entered the Gulf of Mexico— forbidden to foreign sail by Spain—and coasted along the shores of Cuba in constant danger of encountering enemy ships. Rounding Cuba's western point, Cape San Antonio, they took a northeasterly course, which they thought would bring them to the mouth of the Mississippi, and sailed for several days without sighting a ship of any kind.

Unfortunately, La Salle did not have an accurate reckoning of the delta of the great river, and the course taken caused the little fleet to miss it, so that when a landfall finally was made it was on the coast of Texas, far to the west. There were unhappy periods of inde- cision and dispute with Beaujeu, while La Salle tried to decide whether he was east or west of his goal, but he finally turned westward, past Galveston Bay, and entered Matagorda Bay in January, 1685, under the belief that it was one of the mouths of the Mississippi.

La Salle was mistaken by more than four hundred miles. It was the greatest error he ever made, and it was to prove tragically fateful. Still quarreling with Beaujeu, he and some of his men went ashore in boats, and the *Aimable*, with its supplies, was ordered to navigate the strait and land its cargo.

Now occurred a sinister incident. As he stood on shore watching his supply ship attempting to negotiate the uncharted reefs and bars of the harbor, La Salle heard outcries, and some of his men came running to him in terror. They had been cutting down a tree to make a dugout canoe when suddenly a party of savages leaped out of the bushes,

seized some of them, and carried them off. Among the prisoners was
the Marquis de la Sablonnière, who, though dissolute and already
rotten with his disease, was a noble, and therefore one of the officers
of the expedition.

La Salle had dealt with Indians before, and knew the necessity of
promptness and firmness. With a party of armed men he set out in
pursuit.

Well that he did so, for the captors of his people were the ferocious
Karankawas, sometimes called Kronks, who inhabited the Texas coast
from modern Corpus Christi to Galveston. Of all North American
Indians these were possibly the most unpleasant, being addicted to
the practice of *living* cannibalism. When they had a captive, or captives, it was their custom to engage in a *mitote*, or dance of death,
with the most agonizing torments for their helpless victims.

As described by Fray Solis, in his *Diary* of 1768, a *mitote* began
with "music"—tapping on diminutive drums made by stretching skins
over tortoise shells or gourds, and blowing on high-pitched long cane
pipes. Whereupon, to quote Fray Solis' bloodcurdlingly fascinating
account, "The music is accompanied by unnatural and dreadful
shrieks. The dancers make gestures and grimaces, wriggle their bodies
in a strange fashion. . . . They drive a stake into the ground. They
then kindle a huge fire and bind to the stake the victim whom they
are going to *make dance*, or whom they are going to sacrifice. All of
them gather together and as soon as the discordant notes . . . are heard
they begin to dance and jump around the fire. . . . Dancing and
leaping, and with sharp knives in their hands, they draw near the
victim, cut off a piece of his flesh, come to the fire and half-roast it,
and then within sight of the victim himself, devour it ravenously. . . .
In this way they go on tearing the victim to pieces until he dies. . . .
They cut off the skull and, with the hair still clinging to it, place it on
a stick so as to carry it in triumph in the dance. . . ."

La Salle surprised the Indians in their camp before they had harmed
the prisoners. By coincidence, as he rushed into the village a distant
boom of a cannon was heard. The Karankawas groveled on the ground
at this apparent "stamping" by the white leader, and made no effort
either to fight La Salle or detain his men. With their rescued comrades
the French returned hurriedly to the coast.

In their absence disaster had occurred. That booming of cannon,
as it turned out, was a distress signal from the *Aimable*, which, badly
handled, had struck a reef and foundered. Her cargo, so necessary
to the colony, was almost entirely lost. La Salle, realizing that because
of the calamity he was perilously short of supplies and provisions,
salvaged what he could from the *Aimable*, then did his best to make

secure his colonists who had landed, by setting up a camp, building crude huts with timbers from the wrecked ship, and throwing up about it entrenchments.

The location was terribly unhealthy. Wrote Minet, a member of the party, "They were all sick with nausea and dysentery. Five or six died every day, in consequence of brackish water and bad food. There was no grass, but plenty of rushes and plenty of oysters. There was nothing to make ovens, so that they had to eat flour saved from the wreck, boiled into messes of porridge with this brackish water. Along the shore were quantities of uprooted trees and rotten logs, thrown up by the sea and the lagoon."

Another quarrel with Beaujeu, and that haughty captain sailed away in his *Joly,* some of the colonists going with him, including the Minet who left the above record, and who, on his return to France, was arrested and imprisoned for a time, for deserting La Salle.

Adding to the gloom, the Karankawas were dangerously hostile from the first. Once the savages set fire to the sedge, to burn out the colonists. They failed in the effort, but La Salle, to avert future danger, made his men cut down all the herbage around the camp and carry it away. Yet the thievish savages hung around and managed to steal a number of blankets and other articles.

Discovering the loss, La Salle sent an armed party, led by his nephew, a hotheaded young man named Moranget, who was impolitic, reckless, and a creator of internal enmities which would one day bring disaster. On this occasion he marched, sword in hand, into an Indian camp, the natives fleeing. It may not have been the right camp, for none of the stolen articles was discovered. Nevertheless, Moranget seized several canoes, as "pay for the stolen goods," and with them started back, paddling through the lagoon toward the French camp.

Night overtook them, and the party landed, made a fire, and posted a sentry. The latter promptly went to sleep, and the Karankawas crept up unseen, arousing the white men with war cries and a volley of arrows. Two of the party, Oris and Desloges, were killed. Moranget's arm was skewered by an arrow, and another man, Gayen, was badly wounded. Moranget was no coward. He fired his gun at the enemy, others followed his example, and the Karankawas, unaccustomed to firearms, fled. Next day the survivors of the party returned to La Salle, having succeeded in further inflaming the Indians against them.

To La Salle the prospect must have seemed forlorn. He was alone with his handful of people, on an inhospitable and unhealthy coast, without exact knowledge of where he was, surrounded by furtive but deadly savage foes, and with his only means of escape cut off by the departure of the large frigate, the *Joly*. The *Belle* remained, but she was too small to carry a tenth of the stranded colonists. Besides La Salle, his nephews Moranget and Cavelier—the latter a beardless lad— together with the priests and friars, the soldier Joutel, the Sieur le Gros, the Sieur Barbier, and the debauched Sablonnière, "whose patrimony was his sword," were the persons in authority. Under these were the so-called "soldiers," without discipline or valor; the colonists and artisans with their wives and children; and the poor young girls who had come to America "seeking husbands."

Fortunately food was plentiful. In his journal Joutel noted that there were infinite numbers of "beeves [buffalo], wild goats [prong-horns], rabbits, turkeys, bustards [prairie chickens], geese, swans . . . and many other sorts of fowl to eat." There also were fish, of which catfish were the favorites of the party.

La Salle, after exploring the vicinity, was forced to make to himself the alarming admission that he had missed the Mississippi's mouth and was he knew not where. At camp, things went from bad to worse. Sickness and death increased and the Indians prowled about so that it was dangerous to venture forth. Two men disappeared and were never heard from again. They may have been victims of a *mitote*. The Sieur le Gros, while shooting snipe, was bitten by a rattlesnake and died. A group of malcontents tried to desert, but were caught by Joutel and brought back, and their ringleader hanged. Out of this grew a plot to kill Joutel, but it was betrayed and the plotters punished.

Once a ship under full sail was seen off the coast. The colonists had a chill of fear. Without question it was a Spaniard searching for them, since their plans were known through the loss of the *St. François*. But it did not sight them and passed on, stately under its lofty canvas.

After that La Salle moved his camp to a more remote—and healthier —place inland, up one of the rivers. This site long was surmised to be on the Lavaca River, but a few years ago Professor Herbert E. Bolton, of the University of California, following an ancient map, discovered on the Garcitas River, about five miles above its mouth, relics and evidences which seem conclusive in fixing the second position of the colony there.

First necessity was a fort, and La Salle set about building it. He had to drive his men at the work, especially many of his formerly roistering soldiers and gay young blades of Paris, who were suffering from the malady they had acquired by their indiscretions in Santo Domingo. Some of these died, and it was charged that their deaths were hastened because the commander forced them to labor at cutting logs and dragging them from a wood two miles away for the palisades and cabins of the fort, which he named St. Louis, as a compliment to the king.

With construction well started, La Salle decided to see if he could not find the Mississippi, which he still did not think was any great distance off. In his original plan, he had made arrangements to have a subordinate expedition come down that river from Canada, led by Henri de Tonty, his one faithful friend and lieutenant, to reinforce him at the delta. Hoping to find Tonty, La Salle left the fort under the command of Joutel and started up the coast.

With him went his brother, Abbé Cavelier, and fifty men including the elder Duhaut and two brothers named Liotot, the elder of whom was a surgeon. Sometime, probably on this expedition, the younger Liotot was lost. He was never found, and the surgeon, blaming La Salle, nursed a fatal grudge against him for it.

At the fort Joutel continued the work of constructing a chapel and other buildings, and of directing hunting parties to bring in food. Sometimes he had difficulty maintaining discipline. On the other hand, we have a glimpse of romance from his diary:

"When Sieur Barbier went out hunting, I commonly sent with him some women and maids, to help the hunters to dress and dry the flesh; but being informed that he used to slip aside from the company with a young maid he had a kindness for, and which gave occasion to some well grounded railleries; the said Barbier being told I was acquainted with the affair, came and spoke to me in private, desiring leave to marry the young woman. I made some difficulty of it at first, advising him to stay until Monsieur La Salle returned; but at last, considering that they might have anticipated upon matrimony, I took the advice of the Récollet fathers, and of Monsieur Chedeville, the priest, and allowed them to marry. Monsieur le Marquis de la Sablonnière followed this example, asking the same liberty, being in love with a young maid, which I absolutely refused and forbid them seeing one another."

So one of the hopeful girls from France found herself a husband. That Sablonnière was refused marriage to the second, Joutel officially said, was due to the fact that the marquis was of higher blood than the girl, which he thought unfitting. But perhaps Joutel acted also out of consideration for the girl herself, for Sablonnière was an odious libertine, and so rotten with the disease he had acquired in Santo Domingo that shortly after this it disabled him from walking. So lacking in responsibility was he that he had to be kept on a short allowance, for he habitually bargained away everything given to him. To permit even a peasant girl to go to the arms of this titled monster must have been more than the sturdy soldier, Joutel, could stomach.

Barbier and his "maid" evidently did "anticipate on matrimony" as

Joutel surmised, for she soon was seen to be pregnant, and out of this rose a controversy. The king of France traditionally granted certain privileges to a first-born child in any of his American colonies. Anticipating an early arrival, Barbier and his young wife claimed these privileges for their expected offspring. This was disputed by the "Widow" Talon, who had borne a child on the voyage from France. A miscarriage by Barbier's wife, however, removed the immediate cause of argument.

As for Madame Talon, it seems she was not a widow at all. One of the colonists, Pierre Talon, presumably was this woman's husband. He had gone with one of La Salle's earlier expeditions and failed to return. Either he deserted or was lost and presumed dead. The "widow" with her four children, three boys and a girl, remained with the colony. She did not live to learn that her husband—if he was her husband as seems most probable—survived, but her children were destined to have adventures which would be remembered.

One day those in Fort St. Louis heard a call. It proved to be Duhaut, who was perhaps "the greatest villain of the company." He had deserted La Salle and made his way back to the fort. With him he brought bad news. The *Belle,* the only ship left to the colony, while coasting the shore, was tied up one night, its crew sleeping on the land. In the darkness Karankawas, or some other hostile Indians, crept up on them and killed every man. La Salle found their bodies. The *Belle,* evidently set adrift, was lost. It seemed the final disaster for the colony.

CHAPTER TWO

Murder of a Great Man

WEEKS later La Salle, with only part of his expedition, returned. He had reached a river which he *thought* might be the Mississippi, built there a stockade, and left in it several of his men. It is improbable that he actually reached the Mississippi. The river may have been the Brazos, or even the Sabine. What happened to that little fort and garrison he left is one of the mysteries of time, as is the true location of the stockade. Nobody ever saw it again, though Frenchmen encountered later among the Indians may have been survivors from it.

All recognized now that the situation was desperate. As the difficulties and dangers increased, La Salle, knowing that some of the men hated him because of their discontent and the rigorous punishments he had meted out, grew more harsh, dogmatic and seclusive. Yet he spent all his time thinking for them. His was the responsibility, his alone, and the burden of it was terrible.

If the colony were not to perish he must do something without delay. Believing that by now Tonty, if he had come down the Mississippi, must have returned to the Illinois country, La Salle decided on a desperate expedient, one that only an extremity could have dictated. He would take an expedition, somehow find the Mississippi, and ascend that long and treacherous flood, hoping to make contact with his friend and lieutenant and return with succor for his unfortunate people. It meant peril and exertion beyond computation, a terrible journey of not less than fifteen hundred miles through uncharted wilderness, with every hardship, and filled with danger of death from accident, sickness or savage foes, for many or all of his party.

Every bit of his greatness of resolution and ability to command must have been required to get some of the men to go with him, but on January 7, 1687, taking with him almost every man who could travel, and leaving the fort in command of Barbier, the bridegroom, he began his grim northward march.

With him, this time, went Joutel. Also in the party were his brother, Abbé Cavelier; his nephews, Moranget and Cavelier; Abbé Douay; Duhaut the elder and Liotot, who both hated him; Hiens, a buccaneer of German nativity, who was probably picked up at Santo Domingo, and who had all the brutal qualities of his piratical fraternity of crime; the Sieur de Marle; Teissier, a "pilot"; the eldest of the Talon boys, called the "Orphan" Talon; another boy named Barthélemey; Saget, La Salle's personal servant; Nika, a brave Shawnee hunter and warrior, who twice had crossed the ocean with La Salle, and now was with him in this distant Texas land, far from his lake and forest home in Canada; and Jean L'Archevêque, the personal servant or lackey of Duhaut.

Remember that last name—L'Archevêque. Hardly more than a youth, but with a lackey's simper and fawning manner, and the absence of honesty and loyalty of so many of his ilk, yet plausible and with a sharp mind for gaining advantages for himself withal, he will appear in strange places and guises as this history unfolds.

There were a few others besides these, but the entire party was small in numbers as for weeks it struggled north and east along the coast, seeking the Mississippi, which Joutel called "the fatal river."

Moranget, the scornful and hot-tempered, was a constant trouble-maker, arousing resentments against not only himself but his uncle by his overbearing ways at a time when men's tempers were short at best. Duhaut, a man of good birth but treacherous instincts, and Liotot, the surgeon, both already hated La Salle mortally, partly because of the commander's sternness, partly because of the loss of Liotot's brother, but chiefly because each had put money into the colony, and now believed their investments lost. Even before this expedition began Duhaut had been plotting with other malcontents at Fort St. Louis against La Salle.

When, therefore, the party camped on March 15 near the Brazos River, probably at its confluence with the Navasota, an explosive situation existed, of which La Salle appears to have been unaware. He was near a place where on a previous expedition he had left a cache of corn, and he ordered some of the men to go thither and get the grain. This group consisted of Duhaut, Liotot, Hiens, Teissier, L'Archevêque, Saget and the Shawnee hunter, Nika.

They found the cache but the contents were spoiled. As they began to return from the fruitless errand, however, Nika killed two buffalo. So they camped there to butcher and prepare the meat, sending Saget to La Salle for two horses, which he had obtained from the Indians, to transport it.

Saget was back next day with the needed horses, bringing with him Moranget and De Marle. By this time the meat was cut up and in the process of being smoked on scaffolds. All might have gone well but the officious Moranget, seeing that Duhaut and the others had set aside for themselves marrowbones and other delicacies—to which, by hunters' custom, they had a right—flew into a rage, abused and threatened them, and ended by appropriating all the meat.

That causeless tantrum precipitated murder.

Liotot, who detested La Salle, also hated Moranget, for a different reason. When the latter was wounded in the arm by an Indian arrow, as has been recounted, it was the surgeon who treated him so that he recovered quickly. Instead of being grateful, Moranget had, since that time, only been offensively abusive.

That night Liotot, Duhaut, Hiens and L'Archevêque conspired to kill Moranget, even though if they did so they must also murder Nika and Saget, who had done the conspirators no harm. The latter two were attached to La Salle, and the callous-minded plotters seemed to feel no compunctions in the matter. Teissier and De Marle were for the moment not involved.

Waiting until their victims were asleep, the murderers crept up on them. While Duhaut and Hiens stood ready with their guns to finish the work if necessary, Liotot struck each of the three sleeping men a blow on the head with an ax.

Saget and Nika died instantly. But Moranget, receiving a glancing stroke, sat up with a gasp, half stunned and speechless.

De Marle had been aroused by the noise and the murderers forced him to take the ax and finish Moranget, so that he too would be compromised.

Now the fat was in the fire. La Salle must be dealt with. The only course for the conspirators was to murder their commander also. They prepared accordingly.

Meantime, in the main camp, La Salle was worrying over the absence for a second night of his foraging party. Early next morning he set out with Abbé Douay and an Indian guide to find his men. He seemed to have a premonition of death, for the abbé later recorded that he spoke on the way of "matters of piety, grace and predestination," and was "overwhelmed with a profound sadness, for which he himself could not account."

After a time, noting two "eagles" (more probably buzzards) circling in the air, he judged that they were attracted by carcasses of animals, and that Duhaut's camp was near. He fired his gun, then his pistol, as signals and headed in that direction.

Unaware of the murders of the previous night, or that his own death had been decided upon, La Salle approached a stream—probably the Navasota—and saw the lackey, L'Archevêque, standing in plain sight. What he did not see were the dark crouching forms of Liotot and Duhaut, who were hidden among the reeds. L'Archevêque was to act as a decoy to draw La Salle into shooting range of the assassins.

The lackey knew admirably how to do this. He began by playing on La Salle's known impatience with impudence of any kind. With his hat cocked on his head and a voice of studied insolence he replied to his commander's query about his nephew that Moranget was "strolling about somewhere." The manner and words of the valet were exasperating to the last degree to a man who expected deferential behavior from such a servant.

Lifting his voice, La Salle angrily rebuked him, whereat L'Archevêque's attitude became more insolent, his words more insulting, purposely to infuriate his chief. At this La Salle strode forward angrily to chastise him; and L'Archevêque, carrying out his role, retreated toward the ambush where his friends lay.

Suddenly two shots rang out from the reeds. La Salle, with a bullet in his brain, fell dead. He was stricken down in his prime, for he was only forty-three years old.

Leaping from their concealment, the murderers first assured the panic-stricken Abbé Douay that they would not harm him, then insulted the corpse of their slain leader by stripping it of all clothes and casting it into the bushes to be devoured by buzzards and wild animals.

Perhaps they felt triumph over their bloody act. But had they known it their murder of their great leader was the death knell not only of the colony *but of every one of themselves*. The events that followed, and the deaths of the murderers one by one, seem almost to have the inevitability of Greek classical tragedy.

Abbé Douay fled terrified back to the main camp. When he stammered out his news, Joutel, Abbé Cavelier and the others feared they would meet the same fate as La Salle. But when Duhaut and his gang arrived some time later they seemed satisfied for the time with the blood they had shed and did not harm the survivors.

These numbered six: Joutel, Abbés Cavelier and Douay, and three boys, young Cavelier, Barthélemey, and "the Orphan Talon." Joutel credited L'Archevêque with interceding for them.

Duhaut and Liotot seized all of La Salle's money and personal effects for themselves. By so doing they earned the wrath of Hiens, an individual so redoubtable that it was a mistake to anger him. The old buccaneer must have sailed with English freebooters—very likely under Morgan himself—for he was sometimes called *Gemme Anglais,* or "English Jem." Accustomed to the code of those rascals of the sea, which called for an equal division of all booty, he was furious when Duhaut and Liotot excluded him from any part of La Salle's property, on the ground that they had put money into the expedition and were therefore entitled to what they could get before anyone else. For the time being, however, Hiens nursed his anger and did nothing.

The murderers and their virtual prisoners traveled together from the Brazos until they crossed the Trinity on a boat of rawhides near the villages of the friendly Hasinai (Caddo) Indians whom the Spaniards called the Texas. When Hiens, Liotot, Teissier and Joutel went to those villages to buy corn, they were well received and even provided with young women as temporary wives—at least Joutel was. He said that she came as she was told, and seated herself at his side, "but as my mind was full of other cares and anxieties, I said nothing to the poor girl. She waited for a little time; and then, finding that I did not speak a word, she went away."

The others, if a like courtesy was extended to them, which is probable, possibly acted with less abstraction, or perhaps less consideration.

In the village they discovered a young Frenchman, probably Pierre Muesnier, a native of Provence, who had deserted La Salle on his previous expedition and was now living among the Indians as a member of the tribe. The French always had a singular ability to adopt Indian ways and this man was as much of a savage in appearance as the natives themselves, painting his face, clad in breechclout and moccasins, wearing feathers in his long hair, and already almost forgetting his mother tongue. Through him they also came into contact with two other deserters, Ruter and Grollet, who had taken to Indian life quite as completely as he. It is possible that these men were survivors from the tiny stockade La Salle left behind him in this part of the country on his first journey to seek the Mississippi.

With all the corn and beans they needed, the party returned to camp. Shortly, Hiens went back to the village to purchase horses—and it is an illustration of the rapid spread of horse-owning among the tribes that here, in 1687, on the far coast of Texas, La Salle had obtained horses and the Indians seemed to have enough of them to sell more to Hiens.

While at the village Hiens learned that Duhaut and Liotot were planning a quick march to the Mississippi and thence to Canada. Swearing a great oath that his accomplices would never leave without dividing the spoil taken from the murdered La Salle, the buccaneer hurried back to camp with Ruter, Grollet and twenty Indian warriors.

He found Duhaut and Liotot practicing at a target with bows and arrows. At once an angry argument broke out among the three, Hiens announcing he had decided to stay with the Indians and demanding his share of the loot. Duhaut refused to give him anything.

"You're a scoundrel!" Hiens exclaimed. "You killed my master!"

With that he drew a pistol from his belt and shot Duhaut. The latter staggered a few paces, then fell dead.

At the same moment Ruter fired his gun at Liotot and brought the surgeon to the ground, dying, with three buckshot in him.

Turning now to Joutel, who with the priests and the boys believing they would be next to die, Hiens called to them not to be alarmed, and added that he had only revenged the death of La Salle—a singular claim, inasmuch as he was in the plot to kill the leader, even though he did not fire the fatal shots. It did not prevent his appropriating all the murdered commander's goods and money which Duhaut and Liotot had taken, and Joutel later related, "we had the mortification and chagrin of seeing this scoundrel walking about the camp in a scarlet coat laced with gold, which had belonged to the late Monsieur La Salle, and which he had seized upon, as also upon all the rest of his property."

Liotot lived long enough to make his confession to one of the priests, after which Ruter killed him "by exploding a pistol loaded with a blank charge of powder against his head." Bullets, evidently, were scarcer than gunpowder.

L'Archevêque, the lackey, would have been murdered also, had he not been away from camp at the time, for he had been given a small share of the La Salle spoils. At the pleading of the priests Hiens spared him.

Still trembling for their lives, De Marle and Teissier sought spiritual consolation from Abbé Cavelier; and La Salle's brother, after he assured himself that neither had participated willingly in the murders, absolved them of guilt.

Now Hiens, the bloody swashbuckler, looked his miserable prisoners over, for a time regarding them with glowering suspicion, undecided whether or not he would kill them all. Eventually, however, he allowed them to go.

The survivors, eight all told—Joutel, Teissier, De Marle, the two priests and the three boys—left the Indian villages, traveled wearily for two months, during which De Marle lost his life while bathing in a stream, and eventually reached the confluence of the Arkansas and Mississippi rivers, where near the Quapaw villages Tonty had built a fort.

Tonty had returned to the Illinois, but the small garrison aided the refugees, some of them accompanying the party when it paddled up the Mississippi in canoes. Not until they at last reached France itself did the survivors reveal the end of La Salle. This secrecy, it has been charged, was enjoined upon the other members of the party by the Abbé Cavelier, so that he could obtain possession of his dead brother's property before anyone else set forth a claim to it.

CHAPTER THREE

The Lost Colony of Fort St. Louis

So seven survivors of La Salle's expedition finally reached France. But what happened to those left behind on the flat Texas coast in Fort St. Louis?

Originally, after the *Joly* left them, there were 180 persons in La Salle's settlement. But so greatly had the colony been depleted by deaths, desertions and other causes that when the commander started north on his fatal journey Barbier, in command at the fort, had with him only about twenty men, most of them sick or disabled, besides the women and children. Among the men who did not go with La Salle was the abominable Marquis de la Sablonnière, now helpless and unable to walk because of his disease.

As soon as the refugees appeared in Canada, the brave Italian captain, who was La Salle's friend and faithful lieutenant, determined to try to reach the colony. Abbé Cavelier and the others had kept secret La Salle's death, so Tonty probably hoped to see his chief when, with five Frenchmen, a Shawnee warrior and two Indian slaves, he descended the Mississippi and made a heroic effort to travel overland to Fort St. Louis in the fall of 1689.

On the Red River he visited a Hasinai village and was told that Hiens and the other renegades were at another village "eighty leagues distant"—perhaps on the Neches River. In spite of the growing perils of the way, Tonty struck out for that village, to interview those men, though all of his party, except one Frenchman and the Shawnee, refused to accompany him farther.

Henri de Tonty was none of your powerful bushrangers. He was a member of a Neapolitan banking family, his father having devised the *tontine,* one of the earliest forms of life insurance. Early in life he was cadeted to the French army and after a good battle record was recommended to La Salle as an aide in his explorations, since which time he had been in America.

He was described as slight of stature and further handicapped by the loss of a hand, incurred in one of the battles he fought while in the French army. As a substitute he had an iron hand made and wore it, developing surprising dexterity in using it, and even at times employing it as a weapon. Because of this the Indians called him "Iron Hand," and regarded him with some awe as having magical powers.

Slight of physique though he was, the little Italian did not comprehend the meaning of fear. So with only two companions he plunged into the wilderness, and after a weary journey reached the distant Indian village he sought. No white men were there when he arrived, but he learned the fate of Hiens, one of the conspirators in La Salle's murder. In a quarrel over some loot he had been shot and killed by Ruter. The Indians shortly after killed Ruter in turn.

Of the other renegades, including L'Archevêque, nothing was known, and Tonty, unable to proceed because he lost his ammunition at a river crossing, regretfully took the back trail, having learned from the Indians that his friend La Salle was dead. He reached the Illinois country once more in September 1690.

Had Tonty reached the colony, the exact location of which he did not even know, he would have been too late to save its people or more than look upon the ruins of the fort La Salle had built. It was the Spaniards who later pieced together the story of what happened at Fort St. Louis.

Spain, as noted, was not ignorant of La Salle's effort to plant a bit of France on the Texas coast. As early as 1684 they were corresponding about it in official circles, and a ship, evidently searching for the colony, was sighted in the first days after the landing. This ship probably was one commanded by Captain Castro, which was wrecked at Espíritu Santo Bay (Matagorda Harbor). Its failure to return perhaps accounted for the delay thereafter in seeking the French colony, although the Pueblo Revolt in New Mexico greatly occupied the attention of New Spain in this period.

Not until 1686 was a land expedition sent to find and deal with the interloping French. That year and the next military forces under Juan Enrique Barroto and Andrés Pérez made their way up the Texas coast from the Rio Grande. They discovered the wreck of a ship—probably the *Belle*—and from it took four pieces of artillery and three painted *fleurs de lis*, as evidence that the French expedition had perished. But they did not locate the fort, which was some miles inland.

The viceroy was not satisfied with the evidence, and further expeditions probed the unknown country. The appearance at a Spanish settlement in Coahuila of a Frenchman known as Juan Enrique, a deserter from La Salle, with a matted beard and a fantastic garb of skins, spurred more determined action.

With more than a hundred soldiers, Padre Damian Masanet as chaplain, and the French deserter as guide, Governor Alonso de León of Coahuila marched from Monclova to Matagorda Bay. As an exploration this journey was of some importance, for after leaving the Rio Grande, León crossed *and named* the Nueces, Hondo, Medina and Guadalupe rivers, which names they retain to this day. On April 22, 1689, he stood at last on the site of the French colony.

What León found was a ruin. The fort, as he reported, consisted of six small houses within a palisade, and a larger house, all constructed of logs or of timbers from a ship (the *Aimable*). In the yard were "eight small guns of four or six pounds," some of them yet on their carriages. Litter and wreckage told the dreadful story of massacre and looting. Chests and caskets of the colonists had been torn open and the ground and the floors of the buildings strewn with their contents. Costly books with rich bindings had been thrown out to be blown and rotted by wind and rain. Guns, with gunstocks broken, some utensils, also rendered useless, and smashed furniture lay among the debris.

Outside the palisade were found three skeletons, picked clean by birds and beasts. One was identified as that of a woman. It was clear that the French colony had been liquidated. Padre Masanet busied himself setting fire to the empty buildings.

León, however, was not entirely satisfied. He rounded up some of the natives—Karankawas—verified from them the fact of the massacre, and also learned that some white people were still living, scattered among the tribes. With this to go on he marched northeast until he reached the Colorado, where he discovered Pierre Talon and Pierre Muesnier, living with the Indians. Talon did not know the massacre had occurred or what had happened to his family, including his "widow." Both he and Muesnier refused to return with the Spaniards, and since the Indians backed them up, León allowed them to remain.

Learning, however, of two more Frenchmen farther north, at the Brazos villages of the Hasinai, he caused them to be brought to him. They proved to be L'Archevêque, the last survivor of those involved in the murder of La Salle; and Grollet, the surviving member of the renegades who supported Hiens in the killing of Duhaut and Liotot. This pair told León that they had visited Fort St. Louis after the massacre and buried fourteen bodies near the palisade. The governor put them in irons and took them back to New Spain, where they were put in prison. L'Archevêque is said to have spent some time in a dungeon in Spain itself.

Next year León was back in Texas, with a stronger force of soldiers and several priests, to establish a mission. On the Trinity River a church was constructed in the short space of three days, and dedicated with holy fanfare to impress the Indians who witnessed it. This first mission—and hence first military post—of Spain in eastern Texas was called San Francisco de los Tejas. It was located about forty-five miles southwest of the present city of Nacogdoches, and three padres and a detachment of soldiers were left in it when León returned by way of Fort St. Louis to Monclova.

Of especial interest in this expedition—or another at about the same time—was the rescue of two white boys. They were the children of the "Widow" Talon, and now at last the massacre at Fort St. Louis was described by eyewitnesses. The story was one of despair, misfortune and mistakes.

Shortly after La Salle's departure, smallpox broke out among the colonists, carrying off a good part of the few remaining in the fort. Barbier now commanded only a handful, mostly women and children, including the poor young girls who came to the New World "seeking husbands." The latter compel one's sympathy. One of them, by a bold intrigue which tarnished her reputation, won the love of Barbier himself, to whom she was married, thus achieving her ambition. A second almost got herself a husband—such as he was—but Joutel refused to let her marry Sablonnière for reasons already discussed. What happened to the others in the marital line the record does not reveal, but it seems the husband market was bad—a poor girl had to take one of the disease-rotted soldiers or go without. Their fears, hopelessness and bitter disappointment can be imagined. But even in despair they hardly counted on the extremely dreadful fate awaiting them.

Knowing his helplessness, Barbier sought to make friends with the savages in hope they might spare him and his people. The hope was vain; indeed, it made easier the annihilation of the colony.

One morning five Indians—Karankawas—approached the fort as if to barter. Barbier caused the gates to be opened and the visitors made welcome. No sooner was this done than a band of warriors who had concealed themselves nearby leaped from their hiding place and bounded into the stockade. There was a horrible whooping, a flurry of axes and knives, and it was over.

According to the Talon boys, the whole colony perished—Barbier, his few remaining men, his wife and the other women. Even the children were slaughtered, save for the three of the "Widow" Talon; after which the two boys and the girl were carried away to the camp of the Indians.

This childish account was not entirely accurate. Not all the women were killed. At least one was rescued by a later León expedition and there is room to believe that more of them, the younger and prettier ones, were spared. How many of the little "maids" who "sought for husbands" in the New World found them—or a barbarian substitute for them—in the persons of savage overlords, and lived out their lives in skin or reed huts, bearing Indian children and finally dying unheard from, can never be known. It was not a unique fate. White women on the frontier experienced it more times than can be recorded in the centuries of Indian warfare.

We know only that León heard of "other persons of white blood," living as captives among Indians in the hinterland beyond his reach. Since, in a massacre, adult white men almost never were spared, many of these survivors almost surely were women, by that time becoming unhappily accustomed to their new barbaric life as squaws; and children, being brought up as members of the tribes.

The Mission San Francisco de los Tejas had a life almost as short as Fort St. Louis. Although a subsidiary mission was established near it, the work did not prosper. An epidemic decimated the surrounding tribes, the Indians were restive and refused to live in the communities ordained by the missionaries, livestock was lost or stolen, and the soldiers grew arrogant and unmanageable.

In a few months the mission was abandoned, and from this time, for twenty years and more, neither Spain nor France made any effort to occupy eastern Texas.

Distant events meantime had their impact on the American wilderness. The War of the Spanish Succession was fought, in which Prince Eugene of Savoy and the English Duke of Marlborough made military reputations in mighty battles like Blenheim, Oudenarde and Malplaquet. The Treaty of Utrecht which concluded the war created many changes in territorial possessions in America.

Spain was firmly established in Pensacola and the Florida peninsula. France, forced to cede Newfoundland, Nova Scotia and the Hudson Bay Territory to England, while still holding New France (Quebec), compensated by establishing a line of posts down the Mississippi and placing settlements at Biloxi and Mobile Bay under D'Iberville, solidly confirming the French possession of Louisiana.

CHAPTER FOUR

The Ubiquitous Jean L'Archevêque

E VEN had La Salle not planted his colony on Matagorda Bay the aggressive policy of France would have been sufficiently alarming to the Spaniards. No Europeans were as daring and clever as traders, as restlessly enterprising as explorers, or as well able to get along with the Indians, as the French.

Before the Pueblo Revolt of 1680, Frenchmen were roaming over great areas of the West, their major interest the fur trade, on which New France had a virtual monopoly. In 1678, Father Hennepin's map of the regions west of the Mississippi correctly placed the Pawnee villages, showing full acquaintance with that tribe. Shortly thereafter— or perhaps before—Canadian traders were among the Osages and Missouris, moving on a free and friendly basis.

Vargas, in 1695, reported to the viceroy news of Europeans to the north within territory at least considered to be Spanish. A party of Chipayne Apaches (probably Mescaleros) visited Picuris pueblo and described a battle in which white, blond men destroyed a party of Conejero Apaches (Jicarillas). It was one of the numberless fights between Indian war parties and bands of traders and trappers which occurred endlessly on the plains, and of which no official record ever was made.

The following year Luis Gramillo, an Apache, gave positive evidence that many Frenchmen were advancing toward the *Llano Estacado,* and later the same year it was reported that white men "came to the banks of a lake to make war on the Quiviras." At this news Vargas requested two additional pieces of artillery, but he was just being replaced and about to begin his long imprisonment, and the request was forgotten.

Even more disconcerting information came in 1697. Thus far the officials of New Mexico had only hearsay evidence, but now Navajos, who made a long trading journey to Quivira, stated positively that they had fought Pawnees *and French,* who were allies. The Navajos brought back some spoils, including captive children. It is not clear whether the latter were Indian, white or half-breed, but in any case when the Spaniards refused to ransom them the Navajos beheaded them. When Charles II of Spain heard of this he was so horrified that he ordered royal funds to be used thereafter to save such unfortunates from similar atrocities.

Next time the Navajos met the French and Pawnees they suffered a great defeat. But they avenged themselves by a raid in 1698, in which they destroyed three Pawnee *rancherías* and a "fortified place"— possibly three temporary hunting camps and a permanent village of earth houses, such as the Pawnees built. The raiders appeared at a Spanish fair in New Mexico with prisoners, "jewels," carbines, cannons (!), powder flasks, *gamellas* (bowls or platters), sword belts, waistcoats, shoes and small brass pots. To this indubitable evidence of the presence of white men in the Pawnee country they added their own words, praising the bravery of the French, their shooting ability and their quick support of their Pawnee allies when the latter were defeated.

By this time the vestiges of La Salle's fort in east Texas had been found, and the testimony of survivors among the Indians proved the definite effort to found a colony—unsuccessful but indicating the determination of France. All these accumulating reports caused acute concern. Accustomed to thinking in terms of continents, Spanish statesmen saw that a new frontier of hostilities might be in the process of creation, with their ever vigilant rivals and enemies, the French, endangering not only their plan and hope, never ceasing, of further expansion to the north and west but the very safety of their existing colonies.

Meanwhile the rulers of New Mexico had their hands full of troubles at home. Some of the Pueblo Indians, fleeing from their villages, had to be pursued and brought back. Even more serious, the western Apaches began an endless war which lasted almost without interruption until the last part of the nineteenth century, their raiding parties growing so bold that they stole livestock and sometimes took scalps almost within sight of Spanish towns, making military action against them continuously necessary.

The Apaches to the north and east, however, remained friendly toward the Spaniards. This was demonstrated when, early in July 1706, Juan de Ulibarri led an expedition north to a *ranchería* of Apaches (probably Jicarillas) called El Quartelejo, to rescue some Picuris Indians who had fled to that place and been made prisoners. With him Ulibarri took twenty soldiers, a hundred Indian auxiliaries and twelve settlers.

One of the settlers is of more than passing interest. Jean L'Archevêque, the lackey of Duhaut, who acted as decoy, with his impudent and insulting manner leading La Salle into close range of the guns of his murderers, was the last living member of that conspiracy. He was imprisoned by León and probably sent to Spain in 1689.

Of the next few years of his life there is no record. But in 1706 he was listed as a prominent settler and captain, in Ulibarri's expedition to El Quartelejo. He now called himself Juan de Archevêque, though the name sometimes was spelled Archeuêque and Archibêque in the Spanish records. By 1701 he had become a property holder in Santa Fe, and the document recording the transfer to "Juan de Archibêque, a soldier," still lies in the archives of the U. S. Surveyor General's office in Santa Fe.

In the records there is still another link with the La Salle episode. A document called by the Spaniards a *diligencia matrimonial*—an investigation made on the petition of parties applying for a license to marry—dated 1699, reveals that such a petition was made by Pedro Muesnier. This was the Muesnier who deserted La Salle and with Talon lived with the Indians. The document was signed not only by Archevêque but by "Santiago Groslee." This last, it has been shown, was the sailor Grollet, now living as a citizen in New Mexico, who was involved, although perhaps indirectly, in the deaths of Duhaut, Liotot and Hiens.

Going back a little further, there is record that Archevêque—who now has definitely dropped the "L" from before his name—became a member of the garrison of the *presidio* of Santa Fe in 1696, and the following year married a Mexican woman, the widow of Tomás de Ytta, who was murdered in 1694 near Zacatecas. She died and he married again, though the name of his second wife is lost. By his two wives Archevêque had two children, but he by no means confined his procreative activities to the marriage bed, for at the time of his death he had *four* surviving children of whom two were illegitimate.

By 1706, when the Ulibarri expedition took place, Archevêque was out of the army and, besides owning property in Santa Fe, was a successful trader. The former lackey who accompanied the expedition as a volunteer not only bore now the title of captain but enjoyed the luxury of having a lackey of his own—quite a rise in the world for a man who had played an odious role in the murder of La Salle, lived for years as a savage among the Indians, and later was an inmate of a Spanish cell.

With his force Ulibarri marched north, his chief scout being Captain José Naranjo, who had served with distinction under Vargas. He encountered Apaches here and there east of the Rocky Mountains, finding them all friendly, though they warned him of their kinsmen, who were hostile. Crossing the Arkansas River, he turned east to the El Quartelejo country, which was located probably on Beaver Creek, in Scott County, western Kansas. Ruins of a pueblo exist there and archaeologists believe it was built either by Taos Indians who fled from New Mexico in the great revolt, or by the Picuris whom Ulibarri was seeking to rescue. The Apaches did not go in for such construction.

Ulibarri found Apaches there, another footnote on how recent is Apache occupancy of the Southwest. In that year, 1706, Apaches of various bands—Quartelejos, Ochos, Rio Colorados, Penxayes, Fleches de Palo, Lemitas and Nemantinas, whose identity under those names has been lost—were scattered all along the plains and foothills east of the Rocky Mountains, and the band in western Kansas was only one of them. Less than a century later not an Apache would be found in this area—they would have drifted into the arid mountains and plains of the Southwest under the relentless pressure of the Comanches.

At El Quartelejo, Ulibarri had no difficulty in obtaining the release of the Picuris. He brought back to New Mexico, as he piously reported, "sixty-two persons, small and grown, of the Picuris who were living as apostates, slaves of the devil, and as captives of the Apaches."

He also brought back something else: newer and more direct information about the French to the north. Pawnees and French had raided El Quartelejo. Apache warriors had overtaken a white man *and a woman,* in a grove beside a small stream, and killed them both. They told Ulibarri that because the man was bald they did not scalp him, but the woman provided them with an excellent scalp.

One wonders about her. Was she a white woman? It is possible that she was of native blood, either a half-breed or full-blooded Indian woman, the wife or mistress of a French *coureur de bois.* Yet the existence of genuine white women in that country at the time seemed well established by later Indian testimony, although no Spaniard could say he ever actually saw one of them. The circumstance gave at least the appearance of a colonizing project, since traders, French or otherwise, were not in the habit of taking white women with them on temporary expeditions.

The Quartelejos showed Ulibarri some articles captured from the Pawnees: firearms, clothing, small short swords, two French iron axes, "and a foot of a gilded silver chalice which they sold [to the Spaniards] for two yards of sackcloth." One of the guns was identified by Archevêque as of French manufacture.

With this information and his Picuris, Ulibarri returned to Santa Fe, learning on the way that the Jicarilla Apaches were at war with the Utes and Comanches, who were beginning to push out on the plains from the mountains. In the ensuing years the Spanish soldiery was increasingly busy with the marauding Apaches, Utes and Comanches, who struck swiftly and then led the slower-moving white men on fruitless chases through the mountains.

One of these expeditions, led by Governor Antonio de Valverde Cosino, encountered some friendly Apaches in eastern Colorado, among whom was a man suffering from a gunshot wound. Asked how he got it, he told Valverde that his people recently had been attacked by French, Pawnees and Jumanos, and driven south out of their hunting grounds. He added, as Valverde reported, "that the French had lately established two other settlements up the river [Jesús María, now called the South Platte]: that they were confederated with the Pawnees and Jumanos to whom they had given firearms which, as he showed, they fired on forked sticks."

The "two settlements" may have been traders' camps, or the French may have been living with the Pawnees in their permanent villages, since the Platte and its branches were the center of the Pawnee country. The "Jumanos" probably were Wichitas, who were related to the Pawnees and were sometimes confused in Spanish writings with the Jumanos on the Rio Grande.

But the Apache had more to say: "Among the French there are beautiful white women." He made motions to show that they wore their hair tied together on top of the head.

This was convincing, since the Apache could have no other knowledge of Frenchwomen's style of hairdress, which differed radically from the Spanish and Indian women's, except by personal observation or firsthand description by one who had seen them. To Valverde this could only mean permanent colonizing. In his report to the viceroy, he said, "The purposes of the enemy [French] appear accordingly to penetrate little by little inland. This country is very suitable for doing this because of its abundant meat, game, streams, and plains."

He concluded by asking for reinforcements, but not with much air of hope that he would receive them, then mentioned Juan de Archevêque, saying, "He is today married, with some means of supporting himself honestly, and a very good servant to His Majesty. He accompanied me on this journey as a settler and as an interpreter of the tongue of his nation; he is ready for all that one may command of him in the royal service."

The French valet and murder accomplice was becoming respectable. Evidently he had changed his nationality as neatly as ever he changed his master's coats in the lackey days, for now he was perfectly willing to serve against his former countrymen and king, as scout and interpreter, tasks for which he was well fitted.

The Marqués de Valero, then viceroy, was much concerned by Valverde's reports of French activities. He sent the governor an order to establish an outpost at El Quartelejo. This the governor and his council of war thought too risky. Instead Valverde dispatched an expeditionary force, led by his lieutenant general, Pedro de Villasur, and consisting of forty soldiers and seventy Indian allies, "to make reconnaissance of the settlements which they say those of the French nation have established."

It was a highly important movement, but Villasur was the worst possible choice for so important a command. He was a political appointee, with some previous governmental service in Nueva Viscaya, but inexperienced, careless and cocksure. Second in command was Captain Tomás Olguin, commander of the *presidio*, "who, in the opinion of all in the kingdom, was reputed to be its best soldier." Villasur had with him as chief scouts Naranjo and Archevêque—the former lackey accompanied by his own lackey now, Santiago Giraville. With the expedition also went Captain Christóval de la Serna, a settler who had a "servant"—actually a slave—named Sistaca, a Pawnee who had been carried off from his village on the Platte in his childhood by the Apaches and sold to the Spaniards. He was baptized under the Christian name Francis, but his surname remained Sistaca, and it was thought he might be useful as an interpreter, for he could speak the Pawnee tongue.

In Europe the War of Devolution had ended, and Philip of Anjou, grandson of Louis XIV, had ascended the throne of Spain as Philip V, the first Bourbon king of that country, quieting objections of other powers by some territorial trades. But though Europe momentarily had no war on its hands, it was different on the frontiers of the New World.

When Villasur set forth in June or early July 1720, his expedition was fully equipped for fighting, trading or converting. The men were well armed and well mounted, with a change of horses for each. Pack mules carried baize, knives, sombreros and other articles of exchange; together with silver platters, cups, spoons, forks, a candlestick and an inkhorn, the private service of Villasur, who believed in traveling in style. Fray Minguez had everything for setting up a chapel, and his arguments were well rehearsed, in case he had the opportunity for rescuing a few heathen brands from the burning.

CHAPTER FIVE

A Tiny Battle of Large Consequence

NORTH to El Quartelejo marched Villasur, then turned northwest until he struck the South Platte, called by the Spanish Rio Jesús María, possibly a little east of where Greeley, Colorado, is today. He followed that stream until he approached its juncture with the North Platte—which he named the Rio San Lorenzo —in what is now western Nebraska. Crossing the South Platte, he followed the northern branch downstream a few miles to near the site of present-day North Platte, at the confluence of the rivers. He was some three hundred leagues from Santa Fe.

At this point Naranjo, who had been scouting ahead, reported that he had seen a band of Pawnees doing a war dance. Villasur should have realized not only that his presence was known to the Indians but that they were making hostile preparations, and his actions thereafter, in the presence of such danger, seem the more inept for that reason.

First, he decided to send Serna's Pawnee, Sistaca, forward to "win the confidence of the Pawnees"—a fatuous plan at best. Sistaca told Villasur that he remembered that the village from which he was taken was on the south bank of the river. At that, Villasur crossed his command to the north bank, below the fork, where there was an island of considerable length.

After the crossing Sistaca rode away. The slave was attired in at least semicivilized garb, for he wore a hat.

Late in the day he came galloping back, much alarmed. He said he had found the village, as he remembered it, on the south bank of the stream—it really was on the long island—and dismounted, calling across to the people and making signs of friendship and peace. But his garb was against him. The Pawnees could not believe that a man wearing a Spanish sombrero was one of them. They began fording the stream toward him, shaking tomahawks threateningly and with bows and arrows ready to shoot. Sistaca confessed that when they approached "within a stone's throw" he became frightened, mounted, and "made signs with his hat as if he were calling people behind him." The ruse halted the savages long enough so that he made his escape and returned to Villasur. But for the white man's clothing which caused the Pawnees to threaten him before he could prove his identity, Villasur might never have seen him again, as later events strongly indicated.

The command camped and resumed the march next day, arriving before nightfall at the point across the stream from the Pawnee town. Very likely it resembled later Pawnee villages—a collection of earth lodges, looking superficially like large mounds, but well braced with timbers and solid within, and each capable of accommodating twenty or more people in its living quarters.

The Pawnees were great warriors, raiding as far south as New Mexico and fighting constantly against the Apaches, Comanches and sometimes Wichitas to the south, and against the Sioux and Cheyennes to the north. But they were a step ahead of simple nomad culture, for they dwelt in settled communities, erected earth houses, and cultivated in the river valleys crops of maize, pumpkins and beans, which they supplemented with meat brought in by their hunters from the herds of deer, antelope and buffalo which roamed their country.

The warriors were distinctive in appearance. They shaved their heads, except for a narrow ridge of hair which was worn roached from the forehead to the scalplock. The scalplock itself, allowed to grow long, was stiffened with paint and grease, so that it stood erect and curved like a horn. It was from this that the tribal name was derived, for Pawnee is a corruption of *pariki*, meaning a horn, and refers to the stiff and curving scalplock. Frequently a strip of deerskin or cloth was bound about the head like a turban. El Turco, the deluder of Coronado, was a Pawnee and was called El Turco, very likely, because he affected this turbanlike headdress, so that, to the Spaniards, he resembled the turban-wearing Turks, who just then were the terrors of Europe.

There may not have been at the moment Frenchmen in the village at which Villasur gazed across the river, but there is no question that there were French in the immediate vicinity. Villasur had information from the Indians of at least two French "pueblos," where white men wore red clothing, had many guns, including small guns (pistols) which they carried hanging from their belts, and lived in "strong round houses, which hold four persons," on the roofs of which were large "arquebuses," which were perhaps small swivel guns. The presence of white women among them had been noted, and indicated a permanence to the settlements. That the French had won the friendship and loyalty of the Pawnees, as they almost always succeeded amazingly in doing with Indian tribes, Villasur soon discovered.

At the sight of the Spanish column across the stream twenty-five or thirty of the Pawnees came from their earth mound lodges to the edge of the water and shouted across. Foolishly, Villasur sent his only interpreter, Sistaca, over with presents. The slave had learned his lesson. Discarding his Spanish garments, he swam or forded the stream stark naked. He did not return. Undoubtedly, naked and particularly without that damning hat, he established his identity as a Pawnee and was received back by his people, for which he probably was most grateful since he could hardly have any strong desire to return to Spanish slavery again.

He did come to the edge of the river and call across that the Pawnees would not let him return—as good an excuse as any—but that they were well disposed. He said also that he knew nothing of any "Spaniards" among them—the word "Spaniard," in New Mexico, meaning any white man.

As to this he may have been lying, under instructions; for next day some of the Indians visited the Spanish camp and by signs indicated there was a white man in their village. A French trading post or fort may have been quite near.

Having lost his interpreter, Villasur tried another expedient, and here Archevêque entered the picture. He alone could speak or write French. Under the direction of Villasur, who was by now convinced of the presence of French in the immediate neighborhood, he wrote a letter in that language. It was given to one of the visiting Pawnees to deliver.

In due time a "reply" was brought back—so illegibly written that Archevêque could not read it, but on a piece of old *paper*. Since the Indians owned no such commodity, here was further proof of the near presence of white men. With the reply the Indians brought a *linen* flag, another evidence of white men.

A second letter was given the Indians, this time written with "ink and quills" in the Spanish language, under the supposition that Archevêque's letter had been misunderstood. Now came a wait of two days, with no sign of a reply. Villasur grew uneasy, fearing trickery, and at the end of the second day withdrew upstream, recrossed the North Platte above the confluence, and camped there. His retreat was hastened by a sinister circumstance. While some of the New Mexican Indian allies were bathing in the stream, a band of Pawnees rushed them. Most of them escaped, but one was carried off, a captive.

Villasur's new camp site was objected to by Captain Olguin, an experienced soldier, who urged that the retreat be continued until they were farther out of reach of the Pawnees. To this Villasur replied with an insulting suggestion that Olguin was afraid. Thereat the latter closed his mouth and made the camp as ordered—at a place which even the inexperienced wrongheadedness of Villasur should have seen was bad, since it was in "very thick grass higher than the stature of a man," a perfect place for the Indians to make a stealthly attack.

Tents were pitched and the commander retired, to have supper on his silver service, giving orders that if "anything remarkable" took place he was to be notified. The horses were turned loose, under herders, to graze. Sentries were posted—Indian sentries, who, as it turned out, were not too assiduous in their duty.

During the night noises were heard and reported to the corporals of the guard: a sound as of numerous people swimming or fording the river, a dog barking near at hand and indicating the presence of some-one whom the animal had followed, and other slight alarms. The corporals, in awe of their commander, who probably disliked having his sleep broken, did not think the reports important enough to arouse him.

Villasur was up at dawn and ordered the horse herd brought in. His officers—probably Olguin and Naranjo, and even Archevêque—told him it was an Indian custom to attack at daybreak, and he was ready. But no attack came. The high grass all about the camp was breathlessly quiet.

An hour after sunrise Villasur ordered that the horses which had been under saddle all night be relieved and fresh horses saddled. This was good horse mastership, but by poor organization all the saddle changes were made at once.

At that moment, when hardly a single horse was ready for service, the Pawnee battle yell was heard, and the attack began.

So perfect was the timing that the Spaniards later attributed it to their erstwhile slave, Sistaca. Governor Valverde, reporting to the vice-roy, wrote, "These scoundrels [the enemy], in order to take advantage of their dastardly purpose, remained in hiding until after the sun had come up, giving time to our people to lessen their precaution, some being engaged in catching horses, others gathering utensils, and all busy. It is thought that the advice of this situation may have come from the Pawnee Indian [Sistaca] who, disloyal, had remained in the enemy camp. Only with that warning could they have attacked at such a time and caught them [the Spaniards] afoot."

In other words the Spaniards felt that the Pawnees in some measure broke the rules of Indian war with their delayed-action attack. But whatever they thought of it, the strategy was excellent.

At the first rush of the enemy, who leaped from the tall grass on every side, filling the air with noise and dust, the horse herd stampeded. Ten men, who were already mounted, set off after them and thus escaped the general slaughter.

Around the confused and scattered Spaniards swept the Pawnees—and French also, presumably, for the discharge of musketry was heavy and the Pawnees at that time had few firearms. Official Spanish reports later stated that Frenchmen were present, and probably directed the attack.

Arrows flew in glinting clouds and bullets found their marks. At the first volley Jean L'Archevêque, now Juan Archevêque, the valet-turned-soldier, was killed. And thus, on the far plains of Nebraska, the last of the conspirators who murdered La Salle met a violent death such as had marked every one of the others.

Villasur and his personal servant were slain before the commander's tent. Dust and smoke filled the air so that at times men could hardly see each other, with continuous gunfire and war whoops creating a tumult. Minute by minute the toll of Spanish dead increased. In the din and confusion the surviving defenders somehow staggered into a group, where they defended themselves as well as they could against the overwhelming numbers of enemies pressing murderously about them.

At this point the ten men who had been trying to round up the stampeded horses returned to the battlefield. A quick look must have revealed to them the hopelessness of the situation and, had they at once retreated, saving themselves, nobody could have blamed them. But these were Spaniards, with the flawless courage which is the Spaniard's great flaming virtue.

Without a moment's hesitation the corporal in command, whose name was not recorded, led his handful of horsemen in a fierce little charge right into the ring of savages surrounding Villasur's few remaining men. The unnamed corporal and one of his men were killed, but the others broke the ring, making a momentary opening by which, as they cut their way out again, seven of their comrades escaped.

Those rescued from the Pawnee-French death circle, together with some few others who had not been caught in it, fled from the battlefield. The enemy did not pursue them. Governor Valverde said to the viceroy that the Pawnees had suffered such severe losses that they wanted no more fighting, but it is more likely that the savages all wished to be in at the extermination of the last Spaniards within their ring, and the looting which followed.

When the fugitives, many days later, reached El Quartelejo—where the Apaches received them kindly—noses were counted and it was found that fifty-seven of Villasur's men were dead or missing. These included Villasur himself, Fray Juan Minguez the chaplain, Archevêque, Captain Olguin, Serna, who had owned the Pawnee slave Sistaca, the fine scout Naranjo, and other officers, soldiers, servants and Indian allies making up the total.

Almost all of these were certainly dead. Missing, but not dead, was Sistaca, who probably took up his life with the Pawnees where it had been interrupted when as a child he was carried off into slavery. Of

Villasur's command sixty-three found their way back to New Mexico, and of these only fourteen were Spaniards.

The battle at the forks of the Platte has been called a purely Indian attack, an assumption based chiefly on the statements of Felix Martínez, who had been deposed as governor by the appointment of Valverde, and who, nursing a grudge against the latter for that reason, sought to show everything he did in the worst light. Although Martínez was not within hundreds of miles of the battlefield, he asserted in the most dogmatic and positive manner that the French did not participate in the battle, "because if they had been French, they would not have killed so many, but would have managed to take them prisoners."

A marginal note on this declaration, made by Juan de Olivan Revolledo, judge of the royal *audiencia,* says, "Bad inference: The French would not only have made them prisoners if they could have, but they would have killed them as surely as they were killed, so that the Spaniards could not seize and dislodge them from that spot, since they came furtively, hiding themselves as much as they could from the Spaniards."

This seems a logical enough dissent to Martínez' statement, when the activities of the French in conjunction with the Indians of the eastern seaboard are considered, including such massacres of the English as those at Fort Duquesne, Oswego and Fort William Henry.

As against the Martínez assertion, Valverde, who was removed from office because of the Villasur disaster, said positively there were Frenchmen in the battle, basing his statement on the testimony of survivors he questioned. There were, he said, "two hundred soldiers using arquebuses, with an endless number of Pawnee Indians as their allies." This evidently is an exaggeration.

Yet Ensign-Corporal Bartolomé Garduno, one of the survivors of the battle, swore in an affidavit before a royal scrivener that from his own knowledge there were French with the Indians. Spanish officials at the time accepted that Frenchmen participated in the attack, perhaps directed it, and it is so written in many official communications, including a strong representation by Revolledo that the "event reveals a flagrant act of breaking the truce, of which Your Excellency [the viceroy] will be pleased to give an account to His Majesty."

Villasur's defeat was a small battle, judging by the numbers engaged. Fifty-seven men were lost by the Spaniards out of a total of 120, in an engagement where the enemy numbered perhaps 500—this is the estimate of Phelipe Tamariz, the only eyewitness who gave testimony on this point. But the results and consequences of that early morning flare of death and bloodshed on the Platte were out of all proportion to the numbers of men involved.

Out on the Nebraska plains, at an extreme distance from the European capitals—it was more than five thousand miles from Madrid by the sea route and the roads of New Spain, and not much less from Paris by the ocean and routes through New France—the outer tentacles of two great empires met. For a moment the tentacles clutched, parted bleeding, and those of Spain recoiled.

Villasur's defeat put an end to the Spanish dream of northward expansion. The project of the *persidio* at El Quartelejo was abandoned. Instead of extending to western Kansas and eastern Colorado, Spanish rule was at one stroke limited to New Mexico. In its final effects on continents and peoples, the bloody little struggle near the Pawnee villages equaled in importance many a far greater conflict in which a thousand times the numbers of men were involved.

Yet though the victory was with the French and their allies, and by it the high-water mark of Spanish expansion in that direction was repelled, a circumstance now occurred which prevented the former from following up their advantage and expanding in their own right. This was the appearance, at this very time, of a new force on the Southwest plains—the savage Comanche nation.

CHAPTER SIX

Tawny Cossacks of the Plains

AT THE time of Villasur's disaster there were Apache bands ranging far north of New Mexico. El Quartelejo, in Kansas, was one of their centers, and a band called the Paloma Apaches hunted in Colorado as far north as the latitude of Denver in 1727. Yet fifty years later there was not an Apache on the plains north of the Staked Plains. Almost all of them had retreated into the Texas Big Bend country or the deserts and mountains of New Mexico and Arizona.

The reason for this was the sudden expansion—almost explosion—of the Comanches out on the plains. And the reason for the Comanche expansion was the horse.

Before the Spaniards came, the only beast of burden known to the North American Indians was the dog. But shortly thereafter the horse began to change the whole culture of the wild tribes, particularly of the plains.

The first horses stolen from the Spaniards by the Indians probably were taken as meat animals. Apaches, in particular, never were horse-back Indians in the sense the plains warriors were, and always looked on their horses as potential food. They used them for riding, but frequently the terrain in which they operated was unfavorable for horses. Furthermore, the Apaches always preferred to fight on foot, whereas the plains tribes preferred to fight mounted. Yet the horse, plus the bite of the desert sun and heat, made the Apache one of the greatest enemy warriors.

As for the plains tribes, a people which moves on foot necessarily has a range somewhat limited. The arrival of horses and the acquiring of them by the Indians caused a change in their mode of life greater in proportion than the development of modern speedy types of locomotion have made in America in the last half century. Almost overnight the range of a tribe increased from perhaps one or two hundred miles to seven, eight hundred, sometimes more than a thousand miles. Hunting, particularly in the buffalo country, became infinitely easier and more productive; and more time, consequently, was left for the congenial occupation of warfare.

Among all the Indian tribes of North America, none surpassed the Comanches in the knowledge and use of the horse, so that even such great horseback Indians as the Pawnees later became spoke of the Comanches as *"the* Horse Indians." As soon as the Comanches became acquainted with horses, they began to acquire them. There was some trading, but the Comanches had better, cheaper and quicker methods than trade. Colonel Richard I. Dodge, writing of Indian ways in warfare, said, "Where all are such magnificent thieves [of horses], it is difficult to decide which of the plains tribes deserves the palm for stealing. The Indians themselves give it to the Comanches. . . . For crawling into a camp, cutting hopples and lariat ropes, and getting off undiscovered with the animals, they are unsurpassed and unsurpassable."

Possession of a few horses enabled the Comanches quickly to steal more. Within a few years their raids were running off horses from Spanish and Mexican settlements by the hundreds, sometimes as many as fifteen hundred in a single swooping rush. According to J. Frank Dobie, in *The Mustangs,* the Comanches, at the height of their power, boasted that "the only reason they allowed Spaniards and Mexicans to remain in New Mexico, Texas, and Northern Mexico was to raise horses for them."

From a mountain tribe which was closely associated with its near relatives, the Utes, when first it was noted by the archivists, the Comanches suddenly became mounted killers and raiders, who were well and unfavorably known from the Arkansas River to Durango, deep in Mexico. They occupied most of the Southwest plains, letting a few other tribes, such as the Kiowas, Lipans and Caddos, exist by sufferance or by alliance. It was these Cossacklike riders who for a time filled the vacuum between the French outposts and those of the Spaniards, and prevented any further outspreading by either.

Although during this period the French could not handily come at them, the menace of those northern European intruders continually alarmed the governors of New Mexico. In a report to Viceroy Casa Fuerte, April 20, 1727, Governor Juan Domingo Bustamente said that Apaches asserted that the French had moved into El Quartelejo, adding, "The Apaches lie a great deal, but one can neither believe everything nor can he afford to neglect anything. I report this rumor in order not to be guilty of an omission."

A little later a captive Comanche woman was brought by the Apaches to Bustamente, to whom she said, through an interpreter, that she had with her own eyes seen the French. "She specifies the manner of their dress, which she says is of white cloth, some wearing red coats, hats with a small band of silver, and having equipment of tents and much provision of arms. Asked the manner which they had of preparing and cooking what was necessary to sustain them, she answered that they carry kettles of copper in which they prepare their fare of meat, and bread, and jugs in which according to our understanding, they prepare chocolate. She says that on the . . . Rio de Chinali [perhaps the Arkansas], a short distance from El Quartelejo, is an inlet where they had established and built some walled houses, and that is where there is found the greatest number of them. She says that these white people are stationed outside that place where they protect those who go in and out, for according to the information she gave, they are colonizing in those regions."

The "manner of dress" she described sounded like regular soldiery, French uniforms at the time having much red, and the officers frequently being attired completely in white. But this post, if it was established, must soon have been abandoned, for the French made no permanent settlement in Kansas.

The report, indeed, probably was an echo of the Bourgmont expedition of three years before. That the French had accurate knowledge of Spanish doings was evidenced when, in 1722, two years after the defeat of Villasur, Governor Bienville, of Louisiana, ordered steps taken to secure the Missouri Valley. Accordingly, Etienne Venyard, Sieur de Bourgmont, who once had commanded Detroit, was sent west with an expeditionary force from the Illinois country. He established Fort Orléans above the mouth of the Grand River, on the Missouri, late in 1723. The following year he went up the Missouri to the villages of the

Otos and Iowas south of the Platte. Thence he cut southwest to the Kaw River, which he followed until he could go overland to the great bend of the Arkansas River, which he pursued upstream until he reached the Padoucas (Comanches) in western Kansas.

Bourgmont may have reached the El Quartelejo area in 1724, and made there a temporary fortified post, which the Comanche woman reported three years later to Bustamente. He succeeded in bringing about temporary peace between the Comanches, on the one hand, and the Missouris, Osages, Kansas, Otos and Iowas on the other, and promised to send traders to the Comanches.

The promise, however, was not fulfilled. Shortly afterward Fort Orléans was abandoned and destroyed, and the constant wars of the Sacs and Foxes—the only Algonquin Indians ever to hold enmity against the French—closed the lower Missouri to trade or travel for years. Bourgmont's expedition was the last official French thrust toward New Mexico for a considerable time.

The first French actually to reach Santa Fe were the Mallet brothers, Pierre and Paul, who, with a trading party, driving pack horses, explored a route from the mouth of the Platte to New Mexico in 1739. They came peacefully, with goods, and were allowed to trade and depart, returning to the Platte a year later. Their success in penetrating the Comanche country aroused great interest among the French, but thereafter New Mexico was closed to private expeditions. In 1748, at which time El Quartelejo was officially reported by Governor Codallos as having disappeared as an Apache stronghold, with no Apaches north of New Mexico, thirty-three Frenchmen were rumored to be among the Jicarillas. But next year the Pierre Satren party was stopped in Santa Fe; another party in 1750 was arrested and sent to Sonora; and nine men led by Jean Chapuis, coming from the Illinois country, were thrown into prison where they lay for several months, after which they were sent all the way across the ocean to Spain.

Clearly, French efforts to communicate with New Mexico were to be discouraged.

In spite of this, French traders—and none were more adept at trading than the French—knew that rich profits could be made by barter with the New Mexico settlements, to say nothing of the Indian tribes intervening, if only some formula could be reached by which pack trains could travel back and forth without being molested, either by savages or by stuffy Spanish officers. They devoted much thought and speculation to the problem.

CHAPTER SEVEN

St. Denis, the Unabashed

IF THE French were cut off from the north, they were active in east Texas, and posed a constant threat to Spanish territorial claims there. Strong French colonies by this time existed near the mouth of the Mississippi, where New Orleans was established in 1718, and at Biloxi and Mobile; and posts had been built and garrisoned up and down the Mississippi itself. While France, England and Spain were fighting wars and disputing the possession of the Atlantic seaboard, French and Spaniards were closely watching each other on the borders of the Southwest.

As early as 1713, Antoine de la Mothe, Sieur de Cadillac, governor of Louisiana, sent an adventurer named Louis Juchereau de St. Denis, with twenty-four Canadians, up the Red River to build a French fort.

It is worth while to pause a moment and examine this St. Denis, for he was another of those gaudy figures the Southwest seemed to be producing continually. Born in Canada, near Quebec, in 1676, at the time of this expedition he was in his late thirties. At the age of twenty-two he joined D'Iberville's expedition that founded the permanent settlements in Louisiana, and he had been up the Red River twice before 1713. He was, therefore, a veteran of the lower French colonial administration.

There is little in the records to complete a picture of him, save that he had a fondness for fine clothes and a kind of taste which made him wear handsomely even a frontier garb of buckskins. Evidently his face and figure were such as to attract a second glance anywhere; and he possessed the ability to be at one time impressive in appearance, to win the respect of men of consequence or savage Indians, and at another to display the charm, gaiety and gallantry which made the ladies love him. With these qualities went an eloquent tongue, courage to the point of recklessness, an adroit mind, and the trait of personality which never undervalues itself, even to a trace, perhaps, of braggadocio.

St. Denis made this journey of 1713 up the Red River as the result of a letter written by a Spanish priest, Padre Hidalgo, asking the French to assist him in financing a mission among the Hasinais. In the interests of his mission—though later he was stigmatized for it as disloyal by some Spaniards—the good father suggested the value to the

French of opening up at the same time trade relations with the Indians in question.

The letter came exactly at the right moment. The year before, 1712, the French government, desiring to rid itself of the expense of running the colony, had given to Antoine Crozat, a wealthy merchant, full commercial control over Louisiana. Cadillac was Crozat's governor, and Crozat regarded Louisiana purely as a commercial enterprise, caring little for France's claims to Texas. To use the words of Lester G. Bugbee, a Texas historian, "If the trade of Louisiana could be increased by winking at the Spanish occupation of Texas, Crozat's governor was ready to be seized with impenetrable blindness in that direction."

So St. Denis went up the river, and at a favorable spot on its banks built a stockade. In the vicinity were the villages of the Natchitoches Indians, and this was the beginning of the present city of Natchitoches.

Leaving half his men and much of his goods in this fort, St. Denis next struck southwest, evidently to communicate with Padre Hidalgo. He did not find the priest, who had returned to New Spain, but for some time he traded with the Texas Indians (Hasinai), and fought and won a battle for them with the Lipan Apaches.

Thus far St. Denis had followed orders, but now he embarked on a course of his own. The Texas Indians wished to present a petition to the Spanish officials of Coahuila for the return of Padre Hidalgo, who had been compelled to leave them for lack of funds. To St. Denis this seemed a beautiful opportunity for a certain business he had in mind. The French of Louisiana then, and later, were wonderfully inspired smugglers, and the venturesome officer wished to survey the routes and perhaps make some contacts for this kind of trade.

Sending his men back to Natchitoches, therefore, he traveled with the delegation of Texas Indians under their chief, Bernardino, to San Juan Bautista, a military outpost below the Rio Grande.

The unannounced arrival of a Frenchman at his *presidio* was a startling surprise to the Spanish commandant, a veteran named Captain Diego Ramón. But the captain had no orders specifically covering the situation, and the visitor was handsome, with beautiful manners, and appeared anything but hostile. One couldn't help liking him, even if he was a devilish *Francés*.

So Captain Ramón treated St. Denis with all courtesy, invited him to be a guest at his own house—and sent a message hurrying to Governor Anaya at Parral for instructions. Meantime St. Denis occupied himself with such entertainment as the *presidio* afforded. And presently became aware of the charms of a lovely girl, Manuela Sánchez Ramón, the commandant's granddaughter.

No Frenchman willingly resists the allurements of the opposite sex, and St. Denis was French to his finger tips. There were difficulties, including the Spanish custom of the duenna; but it was said that in this case the duenna, a widowed daughter of Captain Ramón, and therefore an aunt of the girl, was a matchmaker at heart and frequently turned her back or nodded in supposed slumber while she was supposed to keep an eye on the couple. So St. Denis wooed the fair Manuela, won her, and one day proposed to the captain, her grandfather, that he be given permission to marry her.

While the veteran was digesting this request and wondering what problems would ensue if he gave his consent for the marriage of his granddaughter to a stranger and a Frenchman—though an undeniably attractive one—Gaspar de Anaya, governor of Coahuila, arrived in person. According to the best account, the governor also was a suitor for the hand of the charming Manuela. As soon as he heard that St. Denis was Manuela's accepted suitor, Anaya had the Frenchman arrested and thrown into prison.

Thereupon the governor first offered to release St. Denis, if he would renounce Manuela. Naturally the Frenchman refused, "with scorn." He was clapped back in jail.

Next Anaya attempted to renew his suit to the lady in contention, "with fervor." She did not respond to the fervor, so he attempted a threat. Either she should marry him, he told her—by a messenger—or he would put her lover to death, presumably as a French spy.

The lady, according to the chronicle, replied—by the same messenger who brought her the ultimatum—that if Anaya executed St. Denis, "by my hand or that of a trusted friend, a dagger shall be planted in his cowardly heart."

One hopes the dainty Manuela did not use such flamboyant language, and the words are probably apocryphal, although their sense is not. Her threat appeared to have effect. Instead of being executed, St. Denis was sent under guard to the City of Mexico, for judgment by the Duque de Linares, the ruling viceroy. Still protesting his desire and intention to marry the beautiful señorita, the prisoner rode away with his guard, arriving at the capital in June 1715.

He had been a prisoner six months before at last Linares got around to interviewing him. But then St. Denis' powers of persuasion went beautifully into play. He made a sworn statement of his journey and motives for penetrating into New Spain (not forgetting its religious bearing as an embassy to gain a Spanish padre for the Indians) which the viceroy read with something like approval.

Two interviews with Linares were held, and St. Denis made some startling proposals. It appears that the love affair in San Juan Bautista had altered even a patriotic Frenchman's viewpoints. He now displayed a desire to advance the cause of Spain, which could at least be explained by his romantic attachment to Captain Ramón's grand-daughter. First, he advocated that Spain occupy Texas, "painting the country in glowing colors"; and then he offered to enter the Spanish service himself.

In making these proposals, it must be remembered that St. Denis was acting more as the agent for Cadillac—and hence the financier Crozat—than for the king of France. Crozat desired Spanish settlements near Louisiana for the purposes of trade, so St. Denis was acting according to that policy when he suggested that Spain move into the Texas country. On the other hand, St. Denis did not mention his own pet plan, which seems to have been the establishment from his post at Natchitoches of a lucrative personal smuggling enterprise, dealing with frontier Spanish outposts.

The plausible French adventurer even suggested—without any authority from his government—that, to put an end to rivalries between France and Spain, the Mississippi River should be fixed as the boundary between their colonial possessions, and Spanish posts established on the west banks of that great stream.

Naturally a visitor so genial and engaging, so filled with grand notions, and so favorable to Spain, won the hearts of the Spaniards. Very shortly, in February 1716, St. Denis was riding northward again, this time bearing a commission from the Spanish government, in company with a Spanish military force under Captain Domingo Ramón, son of the commandant at San Juan Bautista, and uncle of the señorita on whom St. Denis had set his heart.

When they arrived at the Rio Grande outpost there was a reunion between the handsome Frenchman and the charming Spanish girl, which no doubt was all that a romancer's pen might desire; and conditions now being quite different, Captain Ramón, the commandant, was graciously pleased to give permission for the nuptials between St. Denis and Manuela. One presumes there was quite a little social flurry at the *presidio* when the union was solemnized, and that among those not invited to attend the ceremony and the celebration afterward was Gaspar de Anaya, the spurned suitor and governor of Coahuila, who had made trouble for the couple.

After perhaps a suitable interval for a honeymoon, St. Denis was on the march again, with the younger Ramón. With them, north into Texas, went twenty-five cavalrymen, twelve padres, and other persons including seven women and two children, the whole party numbering seventy-five. The official errand of the expedition was to establish Spanish mission-forts on the upper seaboard of Texas.

Romance was not lacking on the trek north, for when camp was made on the Nueces River, May 2, it was enlivened by the wedding of José Galindo, a soldier, to Ann Guera, the sole unmarried woman in the party, with whom Galindo had fallen in love on the march. Nor were difficulties absent. At one place eighty-three horses were lost by drowning; at another a swollen river kept them from crossing for days. But late in June they reached the Hasinai villages.

St. Denis and Ramón made a treaty of peace with the friendly Texas Indians there, and established four missions in the section, one of which, Nuestra Señora de Guadalupe, was at a village of the Nacogdoches Indians and was the beginning of the present city of Nacogdoches. There also was erected a *presidio,* which was garrisoned, and from that day until the Texas revolution of 1836, Nacogdoches and Natchitoches, of oddly similar name, confronted each other as frontier sentinels, often hostile.

After this business was finished, St. Denis and Ramón, who seemed to be the best of friends as well as now relatives by marriage, paid a visit to French territories, going all the way to Mobile, where with supreme self-confidence St. Denis appears to have told Governor Cadillac much or all he had done. That official said he was "charmed" with the success of the mission, although it involved tacit abandonment of French claims west of the Red River. Privately, however, Cadillac recorded his suspicion that St. Denis "was not very zealous in the service of the king [of France]."

At first the governor refused his subordinate's request for goods with which to re-enter Texas for trade. But Louisiana at that time was a commercial enterprise rather than a governmental colony, and Cadillac was Crozat's governor, rather than the king's. Crozat's warehouses were bulging with goods, and an outlet was needed. So in October 1716 the ban was lifted and merchandise advanced to the amount of sixty thousand livres.

With many loads of goods, St. Denis and Ramón once more plunged into Texas. No official sanction had been given such a trading venture, and Spanish laws forbade a foreigner even entering New Spain, while any goods introduced unlawfully were subject to seizure. Nevertheless St. Denis, no doubt depending on his marital alliance, cheerfully set forth on his illegal mission. Significantly, the goods, which belonged to Crozat, were made to appear as St. Denis' property, so that he really was engaged in a smuggling enterprise.

After a winter spent among the Texas Indians, St. Denis, eager to see his wife, arrived at San Juan Bautista the following March. For a brief period all was joy, but then the spectacular Frenchman found himself in trouble again. A letter written by him to the French authorities in Louisiana had been intercepted, in which he urged that France establish a military post at Espíritu Santo—Matagorda Bay, where La Salle had attempted his colony. This was deep in territory the Spaniards considered their own, and which they had occupied with missions and forts St. Denis himself had helped erect. It had leaked out, furthermore, that the goods St. Denis had brought really were Crozat's, which made him still more a figure of suspicion.

There is, indeed, little reason now to believe other than that the ebullient Frenchman was a man of many purposes and loyalties. By his marriage with the Spanish girl, he seems to have felt some allegiance to Spain, whereby he fostered and led the occupation of eastern Texas and the establishment of the outposts there. On the other hand, his French blood kept him also to a degree loyal to his own king, so that he kept the French informed of what was going on and advised counter movements against Spain. Meantime, he had still a third loyalty —to himself—and had never given up his scheme of smuggling as a way to wealth.

What made matters worse, the Duque de Linares, St. Denis' friend, had been succeeded as viceroy by the Marqués de Valero, who was far from friendly toward the French, while Martín de Alarcón, very zealous to carry out his superior's policies, had supplanted Anaya as governor of Coahuila. Priestly jealousy complicated matters, through the influence of Padre Olivarez, who had considerable influence in high circles and is represented as envious of the friars who founded the missions in Texas under the protection of St. Denis.

So once more St. Denis found himself under arrest, his goods seized. Leaving behind him his weeping wife, he rode under guard to the City of Mexico to answer charges.

Nothing, however, could completely abash the man. After two months in prison, he obtained a hearing and set forth his case so well that Valero released him, though ordering him to remain within the limits of the capital while instructions were asked from Spain. In due time a royal *cédula* came, directing that the troublesome Frenchman be sent to Guatemala, where he would be out of harm's way.

St. Denis was wrathful at this order. He did not care for Guatemala and had no intention of going there. Only the briefest mention is made of what next must have been a very flamboyant adventure. He "took forcibly" a horse from a Spaniard and escaped from the City of Mexico. What happened on the long ride north, with soldiers in pursuit, and just how he took that horse, one would very much like to know. But he reached San Juan Bautista ahead of all his pursuers.

It was evident now that Spanish territory was unhealthy for him. He stopped at San Juan Bautista, we are told, to "clandestinely visit his wife in the garden of the fort," and when he rode on, the pretty

Manuela, evidently a lady of typical frontier resolution, was riding with him.

Together they made their way through the Indian country and arrived safely in Louisiana, April 2, 1719, whereupon Governor Cadillac promptly reinstated St. Denis in command at Natchitoches.

Whatever his motives, St. Denis always set events moving in his wake. Among the mission-*presidios* he helped establish with the younger Ramón, was San Antonio de Valero, on the site of which afterward was built another mission, known to history as the Alamo, which all good Texans consider the cradle of Texas liberty. Owing to the excitement caused by the second *entrada* and escape of the spectacular foreigner, the Texas country was incorporated into the jurisdiction of Coahuila, and Governor Alarcón, entering his new territories, established near the Alamo mission a strong *presidio,* which he called San Antonio de Béxar, and which became a buttress of Spanish power in Texas.

Hostilities broke out between France and Spain and a force of Indians and French—led, according to the Spaniards, by the indefatigable St. Denis—captured the frontier mission of San Miguel de los Adaes. The friar in charge proved nimble enough to escape and carried warnings to the other missions on the frontier, which were at once abandoned, the missionaries and soldiers retreating to Béxar.

French ships began coasting the Texas shore, probing for settlements. One of these, the *Maréchal d'Estrés,* thirty-six guns, carrying a large contingent of soldiers and a crowd of convicts for labor in the colonies, was lost near Galveston Bay. Five officers, including the Sieur Semiars de Bellisle, a knight of the Order of St. Louis, had landed before the disaster. They tried to make their way inland, and in two months of wandering hopelessly lost, four of them died, one by one, of starvation, only Bellisle surviving.

When near his end, he was found by three Indians who took him to their village. These were Attacapas, living in southwestern Louisiana. Their name is interesting, being derived from the Choctaw words *hatak* (man) and *apa* (eats)—hence, man-eaters or cannibals. They had many of the disgusting habits of the Karankawas. Although they did not eat Bellisle—perhaps he was too lean from starvation to make a good meal—they kept him prisoner for eighteen months, and on one occasion he was fed human flesh, which he ate not knowing what it was. On discovering what he had swallowed, he *"vomit ce qu'il avoit mangé"* as the old record has it.

A fortunate accident secured his release. He had kept his papers in a tin box, which of course was taken from him. One of the Attacapas, trading with the French, appeared one day at Natchitoches with the box. Attracted by an article so extraordinary in the hands of a savage, St. Denis requisitioned it, discovered from the papers within the name of the owner, and on questioning the Indian learned that Bellisle was a prisoner among them. St. Denis never hesitated when action was indicated. With a force of soldiers he promptly descended on the Attacapa village and rescued the unhappy Bellisle. The latter reached Biloxi safely April 5, 1721, his adventures having been not the least interesting of those recorded of the Texas coast.

Governor Alarcón of Coahuila having resigned, his successor, the Marqués San Miguel de Aguayo, received orders from the viceroy to "reconquer" Texas, which for the time being was called Nuevas Filipinas. Obediently the governor set forth with a strong expedition of five hundred men and sixty-six hundred horses to reoccupy the lost territories. When he reached Béxar, in February 1721, Captain García, the commandant there, gave him disquieting reports of hostile demonstrations by the French and Indians, under that *diablo*, St. Denis. It was said that the French commandant had summoned a grand council of all the tribes in the Red River Valley, and the Spaniards, having witnessed the almost miraculous manner in which he induced the Texas tribes to agree to peace, easily believed that he would with equal facility incite them to war.

Much worried, Aguayo, after detaching an expedition to establish a post on the disputed Espíritu Santo Bay, sent García north to reconnoiter. At the Brazos River García observed signal smokes arising in many directions and, assuming that it meant the gathering of the tribes, hurried back with his report.

It confirmed Aguayo's apprehensions. There, somewhere to the north, was St. Denis—St. Denis the resourceful, the enigmatic, the enterprising, the daring, the quondam friend but now foe, whose name had become almost a legend in New Spain. But Aguayo was courageous. After pursuing and defeating some marauding Indians who appeared in the vicinity of San Antonio de Béxar—the first scouting band of the Comanche horde that was just over the horizon—he resolutely marched north to the Rio Neches, across which he built a bridge, "thirty-two *varas* in length and four wide, at the cost of six days' labor."

At this juncture a messenger arrived with a surprising message. It was from St. Denis himself—and that French *embustero* was requesting a safe-conduct, saying he wished to come and confer with Aguayo in person!

The governor turned this over in his mind. What did the rascal have up his sleeve? At last, not seeing where he could lose anything by it, he gave the promised safeguards.

Shortly, on July 31, St. Denis arrived at the Spanish camp. In what manner the Frenchman made his appearance is not described, but it is safe to say that he was garbed, as always when possible, in eye-filling grandeur, and that his escort, of French and Indians, was equipped and mounted in a style fitting for such a personage as he was.

Aguayo, at first very much on his guard and suspicious of St. Denis, found the charm and manners of his guest irresistible, as had many a Spaniard before him. In almost no time it was as if they were old friends. The Frenchman actually welcomed the governor to the country, assured him that he had no intention of opposing the occupation, and they parted with mutual embraces, smiles, compliments and assurances that the new truce between them would be observed.

What St. Denis gained by the conference was security for the French foothold at Natchitoches. At this period the French colonies were weak and the garrison small, so that he almost invariably had to use Indian allies in his frequent military expeditions. He could never have opposed by arms such a force as Aguayo commanded.

Returning to Natchitoches, he went to Mobile to render a full account of the movements of the Spaniards and his own achievement to the French governor. At this time, or shortly thereafter, he was made a knight of the Order of St. Louis as a reward for his adroit services.

Aguayo, probably wondering why he had so quickly promised no aggression against the French outposts, felt himself bound by his promises. That man St. Denis was practically irresistible!

The governor re-etablished the missions and posts in the Trinity-Sabine country, and near San Miguel de los Adaes built a strong *presidio* called Pilar, garrisoning it with a hundred soldiers, of whom thirty-six had with them their families, and mounting in it thirty-six fieldpieces. Then he returned to Coahuila.

Though in the following years there were alternate periods of tension and friendliness between Pilar and Natchitoches, not more than thirty miles apart, the one on the Sabine, the other on the Red River, by this establishment the Sabine was fixed as the eastward limit of Spanish influence, the Red as the westward boundary of the French, and the territory between as a sort of neutral ground, the final ownership of which was not settled until the young American nation took full possession of it.

As for the engaging adventurer, St. Denis, he was commandant at Natchitoches for a quarter of a century, visiting Spanish outposts frequently and conducting, it appears, a very profitable smuggling trade with impunity because of his influence with the Indians.

He was a fiery figure in the great Natchez uprising which began in 1729 and lasted for three years, first holding Natchitoches during a siege by the hostiles, then leading a force which punished them so terribly that the Natchez as a tribe practically ceased to exist.

Thereafter St. Denis and Natchitoches were left in peace, though he was a constant thorn in the side of the Spanish government. He died June 11, 1744, and was buried at his fort, after thirty years of almost continual command. When news of his decease reached the Conde de Fuenclara, then viceroy of New Spain, the latter is said to have exclaimed, "St. Denis is dead, thank God! Now we can breathe easier!"

Which fervent tribute is a sufficient epitaph for the man who more than any other established the general boundaries of Louisiana and Texas.

CHAPTER EIGHT

The Massacre at San Saba

ALTHOUGH the rough outlines of the Spanish Southwest were established, the apparently illimitable expanses of the interior plains of Texas remained to be defined. Audacious French traders were in those areas first, making friends with the Indians and buying their peltries and slaves. The Spanish effort was slower and, characteristically, aimed at permanence. It took the usual form of building mission-*presidios* and settlements.

Indian troubles in Texas increased. About 1730 a band of five hundred Apaches, probably Lipans, fought a battle with soldiers near San Antonio de Béxar, killed two of them and wounded thirteen, drove the rest back into the *presidio*, and ran off sixty head of cattle. Juan Bustillo y Cevallos, the commandant, pursued the Indians, surprised them at a river—possibly the San Saba—and defeated them, claiming that he killed two hundred, although the official historian of the time, Padre Juan Agustín Morfi, called this report "exaggerated."

There were other, smaller raids. All these Apache depredations were part of a great turbulence in the interior plains, where the Comanches, now made terrible by the horse, were spreading their fierce bands and driving other tribes before them. Some time after the Bustillo battle, the Lipans came to the padres at Béxar, asked help in recovering the women and children the Spaniards had captured from them, begged for peace, and even petitioned that a mission be established among them.

It happened to be another of those frequent periods of bickering between the priests and Spanish officials. The latter sometimes demanded that Indian *reducidos* of the missions be "loaned" to them, to labor for the officials' advantage—proof of the slave quality of the Indian status. The padres, naturally, resisted this, feeling the work of the Indians belonged to the Church.

In spite of these difficulties, the enthusiasm for the conversion of the Apaches, aroused by the pleas of the Lipans, was great, and in April 1757, a military force under Colonel Diego Ortiz de Parrilla, with five priests headed by Padre Alonso Giraldo Terreros, marched from Béxar for the San Saba River, a branch of the Colorado, in the country of the Apaches. On that stream a *presidio* was at once erected, and named San Luis de las Amarillas. Four and half miles distant, also on the river, was built the mission.

Selection of this site seems to have had a triple purpose. Not only was it a military outpost, extending Spanish authority, and a religious center for the conversion of the heathen Apaches, but there is a persisting story, best told by J. Frank Dobie in his *Coronado's Children,* that a rich silver mine was found there, or in the vicinity. The discovery was made by Bernardo de Miranda, lieutenant general of the province, in February 1756, a year before the establishment of the *presidio* and mission, but his report and the samples of ore he brought were later lost.

Nevertheless, tradition insists that the *presidio* and mission were placed on the San Saba to protect miners of the area as much as for any other reason; also, that considerable silver in bars was freighted down through Béxar during the short life of the *presidio.*

If the Spaniards actually got a mine to operating there, it was about the only satisfaction they derived from the San Saba enterprise. Though the Lipans seemed friendly, they displayed remarkable reluctance toward congregating within the confines of the mission and submitting to the regimen of work which the friars wished to impose upon them. These were no meek, sedentary Indians. They were hunters and warriors, and they only wanted the *presidio* and a mission as buttresses against the Comanches, who were beginning to press fiercely against them in the northwest. Of this pressure the Spaniards were as yet ignorant, or did not understand its full meaning, although at least one Comanche raid extended as far south as Béxar in 1743, and by this time the tribe had a most evil reputation in New Mexico.

Learning of the Spanish outpost among their enemies, the Lipans, the Comanches at once classed the Spaniards as enemies also. Like a distant and unseen thundercloud, the menace of their war preparations began to gather on the far plains.

As early as July 1757, less than three months after the *presidio* was established, warning came from the Lipans that a vaguely terrible trouble might be expected from the unmapped interior where the Comanches were gathering. All the Spanish outposts were alerted, and there was such alarm that military commanders did not feel able to send any more help to San Saba, which was left to defend itself as it might in its exposed position.

But after the scare, nothing happened. Summer ended, fall came, winter passed. And no sign of the Comanches. Everyone relaxed.

Had the Spaniards known the Comanches as well then as they came to know them later, they would instead have braced themselves for a shock when the grass grew green the following spring. For Comanche war movements now were conditioned by their horses, and spring, with rich, tender grasses, was the time of all times for raids and assaults.

It was March 2, 1758, when a swooping rush of mounted Indians drove off sixty-two horses from a pasture right between the mission and *presidio*. Colonel Parrilla sent fifteen cavalrymen after them, but the detachment returned without the horses and with the alarming report that there were so many tracks and other signs in the country that it was evident a large number of Indians were near—perhaps concealed in the breaks along the river. It was the very first intimation of the near presence of those outland enemies who were so dreaded.

Parrilla strengthened his guards, and when the hostile demonstration did not at once take place, he got word to the padres at the mission to come in to the fort. They did not do so. Still no attack came, and on March 15 the colonel personally visited the mission with an escort and tried to persuade Padre Terreros to bring his people and sacred articles to the *presidio*.

The padre, however, seemed not to comprehend the acuteness of the danger. He agreed to come to the fort, but postponed his start until the next day. From first to last he acted as if he could not credit the presence of an enormously vindictive and deadly foe in the vicinity.

Perhaps he counted on the defenses of the mission, if necessity arose. It was quite strong, consisting of several log buildings, including the church, and surrounded by a high log palisade with only one gate, which was protected by two swivel guns. A garrison of seventeen soldiers was stationed in the mission enclosure, besides priests, their servants and such friendly Indians as lived there. Actually the mission was a strong little fort and, but for the incredible folly of Padre Terreros, might have stood off any but the heaviest of Indian attacks.

Soon after daylight of the sixteenth—the day Padre Terreros had reluctantly agreed to retire to the *presidio*—while mass was being said, loud yells and the discharge of firearms were heard outside. A big band of Comanches had appeared before the mission and thus announced their arrival.

On the palisades the soldiers stood to arms, but the Comanches, approaching without apparent fear, made signs of peace. Among them a corporal of the guard recognized, or thought he recognized, some Indians whom he had met before and believed to be friendly. He went to Padre Terreros—who had come, somewhat hastily perhaps, from mass—and gave his opinion that no attack was intended.

Announcing that he would confer with the Indians himself, the padre ascended the parapet, accompanied by another priest, Padre Molina. By this time more than two thousand Comanches, all mounted and many of them carrying guns which they had obtained from French traders, were riding back and forth before the walls. At the sight Padre Molina expressed surprise and alarm, but Terreros spoke from the parapet to the chief who appeared to be leading the marauders, rather weakly expressing his belief in their friendly protestations.

At that, throwing themselves from their horses' backs, several of the Comanches went to the gate and lifted the bars. Because of the head padre's helpless inaction, the soldiers did not try to prevent it. In another moment the stockaded enclosure was full of savages, all armed, and hideous in their red and black war paint, their coverings of wild beast skins, and their headdresses of horns, antlers and eagle plumes.

At first the Indians extended their hands, feigning friendship. The padres, who by this time must have had some inkling of the dreadful mistake they had made, brought out gifts of tobacco and other articles, hoping to placate the enemy to whom they had delivered themselves.

By putting off the massacre at the mission which they had so well planned, the cunning Comanches hoped also to gain entrance into the *presidio,* and at their demand Terreros gave them a message to Colonel Parrilla. Bearing this message, a large body of warriors set off for the fort, four and a half miles away, at the full speed of their horses.

Some time prior to this an Indian servant of the mission, who understood only too well the deadly meaning of the Comanche actions and the folly of the priests, had slipped away and reached the *presidio,* telling Parrilla what was happening. At once the colonel called his men to their stations and dispatched a detachment of soldiers to the aid of the mission.

It happened that the rescue column encountered the very party of Comanches which was coming from the mission with the message from Padre Terreros. The sight of the soldiers was too much for the Indians. All pretense of friendship was thrown off, and the wild warriors, whooping, charged. It was over in a few minutes. The Spaniards fought like Spaniards and killed some of their enemies, but they were ridden down, shot or lanced, and every man of them killed, except for José Vásquez, who, though grievously wounded, in some manner escaped and later made his way to the mission.

Meantime, at the mission itself, matters grew graver every moment. The gifts the padres offered them only stimulated the rapacity of the Comanches, who presently, not satisfied with these, began to help themselves. Then the interior of the stockade became a scene of frightening confusion, with savages forcing their way into storehouses and cabins of the residents to seize whatever they fancied.

In the midst of this riot the war party which had been sent to the *presidio* returned, carrying scalps. Its warriors were furious because they had lost some of their number in wiping out the soldiers.

Yelling, the Comanches now showed their true enmity. They laid hands on the trembling Padre Terreros, forced him to mount a horse, and began to lead him on the animal out of the enclosure. Perhaps torture was intended for him. If so he was spared, for firing began and at the gate he was killed by a bullet.

Everywhere the enclosure became a slaughter pen. Most of the soldiers were shot down at once. Padre Santiestevan was killed and his head severed from his body. Servants and friendly Indians gasped out their lives in their own blood.

Padre Molina managed to lead a handful of people into the log house where their murdered *padre presidente* had resided. Fortunately for these, the Indians had become so preoccupied with pillaging that though one fired through an opening in the log walls, wounding Padre Molina, most of them, wildly whooping and leaping, devoted themselves to breaking open buildings and dragging forth everything their savage cupidity desired, while others began setting fire to the palisade and its houses.

The log house in which Padre Molina and his few refugees had taken refuge was soon in flames. As long as they could stand it they remained, but when the place soon became a crackling pyre they were forced from it. Scorched and gasping, they opened the door and bolted for the church.

The Comanches were too busy looting to stop them. A few guns were discharged toward them at random, but they gained the church, which, being of greener logs, did not burn down, though part of it was on fire. Evidently the Indians thought the flames would finish their work, for they did not molest the survivors in the burning church and presently withdrew from the mission, which was in flames, taking with them everything they considered to be of value.

Somehow Padre Molina and his little group managed to control the fire in the church, and after midnight they crept out of the burning mission into the woods along the river. Eventually all of them reached the *presidio*.

By the nineteenth Parrilla's scouts reported that the Comanches had left the neighborhood. His force was much reduced by the cutting off of the detachment by the Indians and by the deaths of the soldiers in the mission, but he took a column and reconnoitered. The mission was in ashes. The bodies of Padres Terreros and Santiestevan were found and buried in the mission cemetery, and the other dead likewise disposed of, after which Parrilla retreated to the *presidio*.

There is no exact record of the number of soldiers and friendly Indians killed in the massacre, but the only survivors were those who found refuge with Padre Molina in the church, among whom was the wounded soldier José Vásquez.

For Spain the disaster was a stunning setback, spelling the end of Spanish enterprise to the north of Béxar. Parrilla, it is true, led an expedition of five hundred soldiers and volunteers against the savages in August 1759, and surprised one camp, killing fifty-five of its people. But soon after he encountered a force of savages from several federated tribes, which he estimated as numbering six thousand—and displaying a French flag, according to his report—at the Tawehash villages on the Red River. Fighting from behind breastworks, the Indians defeated Parrilla, who lost his pack train and two cannon and retreated with such precipitation that years later Bonilla wrote of it, "And the memory of this event remains today on the Taovayases [Tawehash] frontier as a disgrace to the Spaniards."

Parrilla was court-martialed in Mexico, and after the defeat of the Spaniards the hostile tribes, particularly the Comanches, became a continual peril in spite of periodic and temporarily successful efforts to make peace with them.

San Saba was abandoned together with other frontier missions and posts on the upper San Antonio River and elsewhere. By 1763 the Spanish tide, which once had leaped almost across Texas, had ebbed to a weak collection of settlements, missions and *presidios* along the coast and in the southern part of the province.

Limited north of New Mexico by Villasur's disaster, on the Texas littoral by the eccentric activities of St. Denis, and toward the central plains by the Comanches and other hostile Indians, Spain henceforth would forever be on the defensive, never on the offensive, gradually receding, fighting a long-continued but already doomed struggle to keep what she had, until at last she would lose every possession of the magnificent empire she once held in the New World.

BOOK 4

The
Travail
of Texas

CHAPTER ONE

American Rifles and Filibusters

T H A T year, 1763, when the Spanish tide ebbed in the
Southwest, also marked the end of the Seven Years'
War. A thin-faced, cold-eyed Prussian soldier, Frederick the Great,
won durable military fame in that war by his battles against the united
strength of Russia, France and Austria: and a British statesman, William Pitt, who planned in terms of continents and human races, destroyed the power of France on the seas and in her colonies. In India,
Clive won control of the subcontinent for England; American colonials
and British regulars fought the bloody French and Indian War, which
was climaxed by Wolfe's defeat of Montcalm, the fall of Quebec and
the passing forever of New France, henceforth called Canada, into
British hands; and the English navy swept the seas so that France
ceased to exist as a major naval power.

Out of this maelstrom of world conflict Spain might have gained
much had she simply remained out of it and waited to pick up the
pieces. But Charles III foolishly entered into the celebrated *pacte de
famille*, in which all Bourbon rulers, including those of Italy and Spain,
joined France in an alliance against Britain. The Spanish king soon
rued his blunder. The magnificent English sea dogs devoted themselves
to Spanish ships and colonies with such annoying assiduity that by the
end of the war they had seized Cuba, the Philippines, Minorca and
Florida; had almost swept Spanish commerce from the seven seas; and
had even made a landing on the Texas coast, although this project was
soon abandoned.

Yet Spain came unexpectedly well out of the Treaty of Paris, which
ended the Seven Years' War. With Canada lost, France felt that Louisiana was untenably isolated between the British and Spanish possessions. It had never been profitable and about it still clung the malo-
dorous memory of John Law's "Mississippi Bubble." Rather than let it
fall into Britain's hands, Louis XV of France made a gift of the "Island

of New Orleans" and all French territories lying west of the Mississippi to his cousin, Charles III of Spain, while at the same time ceding all territories east of the Mississippi to England. There were numerous territorial adjustments, including confirmation of Spain in the possession once more of Florida, Cuba and the Philippines. But France's disposal of her continental territories affected most directly and importantly the Southwest.

Thus France, which had for generations been Spain's great adversary in America, stepped forever from the arena. And because of French hatred of Britain, Spain discovered herself possessing—on paper at least—the very territories from which France had so long held her back. And facing, incidentally, across the Mississippi a far more aggressive threat in the restless Anglo-Americans.

That threat became increasingly acute when, twelve years after the Treaty of Paris, the American colonists began their War for Independence, winning it in 1783. And shortly after that Europe once more went into eruption. Out of the French Revolution and the Reign of Terror stepped an undersized young artillery officer who, with the famous "whiff of grapeshot," ended mob rule in Paris and went on to become Emperor Napoleon I of the French, and possibly the supreme military genius of all time.

In this explosive situation the Spanish rulers, as usual, blundered. Charles IV, "stupid to the point of imbecility," and subservient to his strong-minded and sexually unvirtuous wife, Maria Luisa of Parma, and her paramour, Manuel de Godoy, at first attempted to aid the old regime in France. But when the French revolutionary army came swarming over the Pyrenees he quickly reversed himself and signed a treaty of peace; and when Napoleon came to supreme power, the Spanish king—under some pressure—secretly ceded Louisiana back to France, on October 1, 1800.

To the people of the Southwest these events seemed distant and vague, although their eventual effects were climactic. Settlers were more concerned with their local problems, not the least of which had to do with the Indians. The record of the last half of the eighteenth century is spiked with Comanche forays on missions and settlements in Texas, and with depredations of Apaches, Navajos and Utes in New Mexico, in which towns and *ranchos* were scourged and many Indian pueblos decimated, destroyed or abandoned.

Yet during this period one Spanish official of energy and daring, Juan Bautista de Anza, first demonstrated a feasible land route from Sonora across the desert to California, and then, in 1775, led a colony of 244 persons over that route to San Gabriel mission near present-day Pasadena, California, and thence north to San Francisco Bay, where he established in 1776 the *presidio* and mission which were the foundations of the city of San Francisco. From that date the true history of California as a whole began, and coincident as it is with the opening of the American War for Independence, it serves as a yardstick whereby the comparatively recent settlement of California can be compared to that of the Southwest, of which California is an offshoot.

Leaving his colony and returning to New Mexico, Anza was appointed governor of the latter province in 1777, and personally recorded one episode which is worth recounting as illustrating the destruction of some of the pueblo peoples.

Sturdiest of all the mesa dwellers were the Hopis, who never fully accepted Spanish authority after the revolt of 1680. In their communal houses, perched on cliffs in their harshly eroded country, they kept at bay the Apaches and Navajos and preserved toward the Spaniards an attitude of peace, dignified and aloof, so long as the Spaniards did not approach too closely.

A few *visitas* were made to them by padres, and on each occasion the friars were well received but had singularly few results insofar as conversions to the Catholic faith or loyalty to the Spanish Crown were concerned. On one such *visita,* about 1774, Padre Silvestre Velez de Escalante counted 7494 people living in seven pueblos on three separate mesas, the largest of which was Oraibi; and reported that though the Hopis were "well disposed" their chiefs would not give up their authority, keeping from submission to Spain and the Church not only their own people but the Cosninas (Havasupai) as well. In his enthusiasm for the good work the holy father proposed that a Spanish army be sent to reduce the Hopis, by fire and sword, to a meekness which would make conversion attractive to them.

This was not necessary, for an even more baleful evil than Spanish soldiery shortly made its appearance in Hopi land.

"*Viva la viruela!*" had shouted Cortés' men when smallpox, brought to Mexico by one of their own number, began to rage through the valley of Tenochtitlán, leaving the dead by thousands and making Spanish conquest infinitely easier. And *la viruela,* the loathsome disease to which the Spanish tongue gave so beautiful a name, suddenly struck down the Hopi towns where Spanish arms and Spanish priests had proved so ineffective. Through the seven pueblos smallpox swept with dreadful mortality. To the pestilence was added famine. No rain fell in three years and the Apache and Navajo raids never ceased. Where Padre Escalante found 7494 souls in 1774, there survived only 798 in 1780. And where Hopis once herded 30,000 sheep only 300 remained, while in all seven pueblos were but five horses and not one head of cattle.

Yet when Governor Anza, in that terrible year of 1780, visited the Hopis with a military expedition and offered them a load of provisions to relieve immediate wants, the chief at Oraibi proudly declined the gift on the ground that "he had nothing to offer in return." He added that he and his people did not care to hear any preaching by Anza's padres because, since his nation seemed doomed to perish, the few remaining were resolved to die in their own faith. Yet, if any of his people wished to go with the Spaniards and become Christians, he would not hinder them.

Of the 798 Hopis existing so miserably, only thirty families accepted the Spanish food and the Spanish religion. These were taken along by Anza when he withdrew, and were settled near the present Laguna, New Mexico. The Hopis dropped into the limbo of obscurity after that. Yet somehow they managed to survive. And they kept their customs and beliefs, too. Today there are about 2500 of them, still living on their mesas, the essential pattern and structure of their life changed comparatively little.

Meanwhile, more important events, historically speaking, were taking place toward the east. No sooner had Napoleon secured title to Louisiana (with the solemn promise not to alienate it except back to Spain herself) than he turned about and sold the great territory to the United States. At this time Louisiana included the entire western watershed of the Mississippi, bounded roughly by the Red River on the south, the Rocky Mountain continental divide on the west, the indefinite Canadian boundary on the north, the Mississippi itself on the east; and including also the "Island of New Orleans," a strip of land extending east of the Mississippi to the Pearl River, in what is now southern Louisiana.

The young Republic thus acquired at an expenditure of $15,000,000 —which Napoleon needed for his new war with Britain—more than 1,000,000 square miles of territory and 90,000 inhabitants. The historic transaction was completed late in 1803, and President Thomas Jefferson sent William C. C. Claiborne and General James Wilkinson to take over the new territory as governors, Claiborne of the south and Wilkinson of the north division.

So, by a stroke of a pen, almost, the Spanish-Mexican settlers, who had been occupied with Indian difficulties and with bickerings between the Franciscans and Jesuits over jurisdiction, suddenly found themselves cheek by jowl with far bigger trouble on their northwest border.

While Spain held Louisiana, commerce with the American settlers had been forbidden by law. Spanish officials deemed it dangerous to permit a flood of the aggressive, formidable Americans to enter their

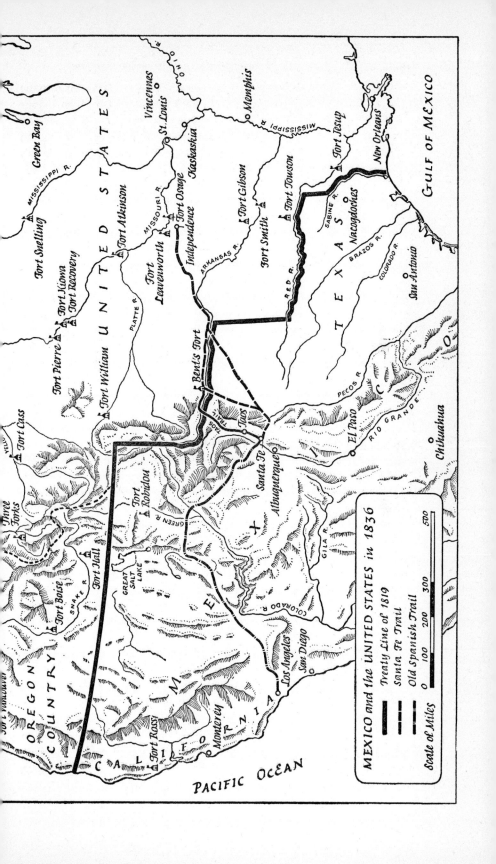

MEXICO and the UNITED STATES in 1836

Treaty Line of 1819
Santa Fe Trail
Old Spanish Trail

Scale of Miles
0   100   200   300   500

territory, but it was like trying to turn back a tidal wave. Each year larger numbers of flatboatmen from upriver clamored for unrestricted commerce in New Orleans, while a smuggling industry of wide proportions sprang up. So great was the irritation created that Kentucky, Tennessee and Illinois frontiersmen made open threats to march in an army and take over New Orleans by force.

With the Louisiana Purchase this long-pent flood was loosed. The sturdy young United States still was unfilled and unformed, and had no idea what its eventual frontiers would be. But down the Mississippi floated the cargo craft of the American settlers—flatboats, arks, broadhorns, even rafts—with crews of boatmen, long-haired, bearded, fierce, outlandish and often brutal; frontiersmen accustomed to every danger and hardship, uneducated and uncivilized, yet carrying in them the immense vitality of a new people. And overland came the wagons, with families—a tide which swept over and occupied Louisiana, changing its ways, its tempo of life, the very character of its population.

Land-hungry settlers even began looking over into Texas, and from the very first a cause of quarrel existed—a boundary argument. The United States said that the Sabine River was the boundary of its new acquisition. Spain insisted that the line was along the Arroyo Hondo, a creek halfway between Adaes and Natchitoches—and thus the old "neutral ground" established by St. Denis and Aguayo back in 1721 became a subject of dispute between the two nations.

But Spanish officials and settlers discovered rapidly that they no longer were dealing with polite French colonials. What they now faced was something more nearly resembling a race of human grizzly bears.

Even before the United States acquired Louisiana the first shadow of the inevitable fell across the Southwest when daring frontiersmen from east of the Mississippi went venturing out on the forbidden Texas plains to see what was there.

There was Philip Nolan, a strange, furtive character, though lacking nothing in courage, who began in 1792 a series of law-defying journeys into Texas. He went ostensibly on horse-hunting expeditions, but he also drew maps and explored uncharted areas, and his real objectives were shrouded in a mystery which has defied time.

It is known, however, that he took council with General James Wilkinson, a very slippery gentleman. During the War for Independence, Wilkinson served in the Revolutionary army, and was a close friend of Benedict Arnold and Aaron Burr. After the war, in 1798, he went west to Kentucky, where he took a secret oath of allegiance to Spain and began to intrigue with the discontented Kentuckians to detach their territory and Tennessee from the United States and join them to Louisiana—and the New Orleans markets. As a Spanish secret agent

Wilkinson was known officially as "Number Thirteen" and for his services he received a Spanish stipend which he continued to collect when, later, he returned to the military service of the United States. Yet even while taking Spanish money he connived against his Spanish friends. Philip Nolan's expeditions almost surely were part of his shadowy plans, which may have schemed as high as a conquest—for his own advantage—of the northern provinces of New Spain.

Thrice Nolan entered Texas, returning each time with horses—and maps and reports based on keen observation. Still he seemed dissatisfied and in 1800, with fourteen American frontiersmen, five Mexicans and a Negro slave, he once more rode out on those forbidden plains, defying the risk of capture and punishment.

This time he pushed his luck too far. Three of his men deserted and returned to American soil. Then, on March 21, 1801, a Spanish force of a hundred and fifty men with a piece of artillery surprised Nolan's party. Nolan and some of his men were killed and wounded, and after a brave fight, during which they defended themselves in an arroyo all day, the survivors surrendered. Nolan's ears were cut from his head "in order to send them to the governor of Texas," and the prisoners were sent to San Luis Potosí to await trial. Eventually they were tried at Chihuahua, convicted as *filibusteros,* and their final sentence referred to the Spanish Crown.

A long wait. The prisoners had been in custody five years before they learned their fate. The king's sentence was that every fifth man should be hanged. But by that time only nine of the party survived and after due consideration the authorities decided that one life was sufficient to satisfy the royal doom.

One morning a large drum was placed on the ground and the prisoners, blindfolded, were caused to throw dice on the drumhead. He who threw the lowest number would die. The Spanish adjutant inspector listed those who took part in this lottery as Ellis P. Bean, Lucian García, Jonah Walters, Solomon Cooley, William Danlin, Joseph Reed, Charles King, Ephraim Blackburn and David Fero.

There is a morbid fascination in the numbers these men rolled with the "devil's bones" in their dreadful gamble with death. In the order they cast—each taking precedence "according to his age"—here were their throws, as recorded: Blackburn, 3 and 1, making 4; García, 3 and 4, making 7; Reed, 6 and 5, making 11; Fero, 5 and 3, making 8; Cooley, 6 and 5, making 11; Walters, 6 and 1, making 7; King, 4 and 3, making 7; Bean, 4 and 1, making 5; and Danlin, 5 and 2, making 7.

Blackburn, the first and eldest, threw the lowest number. From the beginning he must have known his was a very low cast and one almost suffers with the poor fellow as the others spun the dice and the results were announced—his hopes rising and falling and finally dying when Danlin, the youngest and last, threw a 7.

On the day following, November 11, 1807, Blackburn was hanged "at the Plaza de los Uranges, in the Villa of Chihuahua." His comrades were forced to witness his execution.

Of the surviving eight, two escaped to the United States; Cooley was freed and settled at Santa Fe, New Mexico; and Ellis P. Bean, after serving in the Mexican army during the revolution, held several important offices, married a Mexican heiress named Ann Gorthas, and spent his final years in affluence on his wife's large estate near Jalapa. The fates of the other four are not known.

Nolan's full reasons for his expeditions were never publicly explained. But behind him was General Wilkinson. And behind Wilkinson was . . . a network of aims, plans and ambitions, so complicated, secret and often apparently conflicting that they have not been unraveled completely to this day.

Nolan was dead. But Wilkinson turned to Aaron Burr, then in disgrace for killing Alexander Hamilton in a duel, who had a fantastic plan known to history as the "Burr Conspiracy" to seize the Spanish territories west of the Mississippi and establish there an independent nation. Even while acting as governor of the northern Louisiana Territory, Wilkinson agreed to aid Burr, contrary to his orders and the treaties made by his government.

In 1806 he sent Lieutenant Zebulon M. Pike, who had explored the upper Mississippi, on what amounted to another armed invasion of Spanish territories. Its real object, like Nolan's, was perhaps to survey a favorable route for an armed campaign, but with his usual duplicity Wilkinson couched his orders in terms by which he could clear his own skirts if anyone ever charged him with disloyalty or exceeding his authority.

Pike did his best. Setting out from near St. Louis, July 15, 1806, he reached the Arkansas by October, and sending back part of his expedition, with sixteen men marched up the river and became, with his command, the first Americans to see the great Colorado peak which bears his name. Winter came down, with severe weather, and Pike became entangled among the high mountains, at last being politely captured by a Spanish detachment in New Mexican territory, equally politely deprived of his papers, and sent back to his own country, with all courtesy but with all firmness.

He brought back much information concerning the Spanish territories, but its value for the present had passed. In his absence Wilkinson had betrayed his fellow conspirator, Aaron Burr. Out of the long and important trial of Burr, in which the prisoner at the bar and those charged with him in the end were released "for lack of sufficient evidence," Wilkinson emerged with a reputation so badly tarnished that he never fully recovered from it.

The next *filibusteros* from the United States were brought in by the Mexicans themselves. Spain at that time had a three-continental empire, of which Texas and New Mexico-Arizona were no more than outposts of one viceroyalty. All through the Spanish provinces in North and South America—and even in European Spain itself—something of the ferment that caused the American and French revolutions was stirring. Administration was loose at the fringes of empire, and even in the capitals corruption had become so universal that a great explosion was building up.

It was brought to a head by the Spanish monarchs themselves. When a popular uprising against the court favorite, Godoy, occurred in Spain in 1807 and Charles IV abdicated, there was a brief period of enthusiasm for his successor, Ferdinand VII, who announced a policy opposing French aggression.

But the Spaniards were dealing now with Napoleon. Ferdinand's reign lasted only from March 19 to April 30, when he was forced to abdicate the throne he had scarcely warmed in favor of his predecessor, Charles IV (at the instance of Marshal Murat, who arrived with part of Napoleon's army), and Charles in turn abdicated May 10, in favor of Napoleon. For this complaisance the two Spanish princes were gives estates in France and handsome pensions, and Bonaparte promptly placed upon the Spanish throne his brother Joseph.

Crowning a Frenchman—and a plebeian—as king of Spain removed any lingering loyalties the majority of the Mexican people may have had for the mother country, and the inefficiency, venality and arrogance of royal officers appointed from overseas completed the discontent.

"The condition of Mexico at the beginning of the present [nineteenth] century," wrote the historian William Kennedy in the late 1830s, "was stamped with the repulsive features of an anarchical and semi-barbarous society, of which the elements were—an aboriginal population, satisfied with existing in unmolested indigence; a chaos of parti-colored castes, equally passive, ignorant, and superstitious; a numerous Creole class, wealthy, mortified, and discontented; and a compact phalanx of European [Spanish] officials—the pampered Mamlouks of the Crown—who contended for and profited by every act of administrative iniquity."

It was against those officials that the aroused people of Mexico turned their resentment. Napoleon's proclamations were publicly burned, the French emissaries were driven from the country, and Spanish officers who acceded to the new order were deposed and forced to seek refuge from the mobs. Juntas were formed and a plan of revolution adopted. It was betrayed to José Yturrigaray, the viceroy, who ordered the leaders arrested. That forced premature action and the revolution began—with a priest at its head.

Padre Miguel Hidalgo y Costilla, *cura* of the small town of Dolores, the population of which was chiefly Indian, had won the esteem of his people by his kindness and his efforts to improve their condition. Around him the rebellious forces rallied and in September 1810 he took the field "for the defence of religion and the redress of grievances."

Unfortunately for the good name of his cause, when he saw atrocities committed by royalist troops operating against him, he sought reprisals by turning loose his Indians to wreak all their resentments and natural cruelties on every Spaniard or European who fell into their hands. His "army" was disorderly and undisciplined and he was promptly defeated, captured and shot. His conqueror, General Calleja, a Spaniard of the most brutal type, eclipsed anything Hidalgo's Indians had done in the ferocity of his massacres in the rebellious towns and districts.

But the avalanche was started. Another priest, Padre José María Morelos y Pavón, stepped into Hidalgo's place as the revolutionary leader. He was defeated by General Agustín de Iturbide, a native-born Spanish-Mexican, in the royal service, who one day would declare himself emperor of Mexico. Betrayed by one of his followers, Ignacio Elizondo, Morelos was captured, degraded from his priestly office by the Inquisition, and, like Hidalgo, shot as a traitor.

Up to this time Texas had not been directly affected by the revolution, although Spanish officials and native peoples alike were deeply interested and excited by the events. But now something happened that was to forecast the future.

Before the defeat of Morelos, Bernardo Gutiérrez de Lara and José Alvarez de Toledo entered the United States to raise a force of Americans to invade Texas in behalf of the revolution. The frontier was filled with men eager to fight, and A. W. Magee, a graduate of West Point and a former lieutenant in the United States Army, had little difficulty in enlisting two hundred riflemen from Kentucky, Louisiana, Tennessee and Mississippi. He assumed the title of colonel, appointed Samuel Kemper lieutenant colonel, and marched into Texas with the avowed purpose of "freeing it from Spanish rule."

Gutiérrez was the nominal commander—it being policy to give the Mexicans the impression that one of themselves was the leader—but the actual commander was Magee and under him his American subordinates. By the time he neared Natchitoches his hard core of frontiersmen had been augmented by enlistments from the French, Italian and Spanish populations of Louisiana, and Mexicans from Texas, until he had under him five hundred men.

The "army" had little organization and no commissary, but it could fight. It now began a career of remarkable activity. At the Sabine River a royalist force appeared, was scattered by the first volley from the frontiersmen, and chased all the way to Nacogdoches, which the Americans occupied August 11, 1812.

From there the invaders marched with unexampled rapidity and audacity on Trinidad—which was evacuated as soon as the first coonskin caps were sighted—and then toward La Bahía, also called Goliad, which was the key to San Antonio de Béxar.

There they were besieged by Governor Manuel de Salcedo and General Simon de Herrera with fifteen hundred royalist troops. In their first assaults Salcedo's forces had a disheartening taste of the accuracy of the American frontiersmen's rifles, and fell back. Yet the numbers of the enemy and his artillery appeared so overwhelming that Colonel Magee agreed to surrender on condition his men be allowed to return safely to the United States.

These terms, when they were announced, his men promptly and unanimously repudiated, and shortly thereafter Magee was found dead in his tent, apparently by his own hand, since his "honor" had been besmirched.

Salcedo, perhaps justifiably angered at the failure of his negotiations, ordered a general assault. But the American long rifles began to speak their deadly message and the royalist columns fell back, stunned, with a loss of two hundred men. Salcedo raised the siege and retired.

It was now early March and with confidence vastly increased the filibusters marched toward Béxar—or, as the Americans preferred to call it, San Antonio.

Salcedo, who had been reinforced, attempted to ambush them in the dense chaparral of Salado Creek. What took place, the so-called Battle of Rosillo, is worth looking at, since it set a pattern of combat which would continue—the American rifle's mastery of many fields.

Salcedo's "trap" was easily discovered by the American scouts, who were accustomed to bush hunting. So the governor brought his army out and arranged it in the open, for better maneuverability, with his six pieces of artillery in the center.

When he observed this disposition, Colonel Kemper, who had succeeded Magee in command, assigned Captain Lockett, with a detachment of the finest marksmen in the American ranks, to pick off the artillerymen in the center. Then, placing Captain Ross in command of the left wing, and taking charge of the right himself, he issued a general order that his men should fire three volleys and then charge.

What followed was a devastatingly bloody demonstration of what accurate rifles could do. Under the withering blaze from Lockett's sharpshooters the royalist artillerymen melted to the ground before they could more than fire their first—and harmless—salvo. Up and down the entire line Salcedo's men were dropping under the relentless marksmanship of the frontiersmen. Suddenly the filibusters charged. The royalists broke and fled. Pursuing, the victors slaughtered them as they ran.

It was a foretaste of San Jacinto. Salcedo's army ceased to exist. Nearly one thousand of his men were killed or wounded, while of the victors only nine were killed and twenty-five wounded. Most of the defeated survivors scattered like rabbits, hid in the chaparral, and decamped from the country at night, never to be soldiers again if they could help it. Of the two thousand royalists who started the battle only about three hundred fugitives reached San Antonio.

The Americans advanced on San Antonio; and Salcedo and Herrera, with their men, surrendered, on the promise their lives would be spared. But here appeared a sinister attribute of this sort of Mexican fighting—bad faith. Though they were promised mercy, Gutiérrez had Salcedo, Herrera and some of their men marched out of the town to an arroyo of the river half a mile below. The Mexican escort of seventy men did not waste bullets on them. They simply stripped the prisoners, bound them, and cut their throats.

After that horrifying butchery Kemper, Lockett, Ross and many of the better class of Americans abandoned the campaign and returned to Louisiana. Those who remained, with reinforcements which came to them because of their success, defeated Colonel Elizondo, the renegade who had betrayed Morelos; but in turn, badly led by Colonel Toledo, who replaced Gutiérrez in command, were ambushed and almost wiped out by Colonel Arredondo with a royalist army of two thousand men and eleven pieces of artillery, near the Medina River. Only ninety-three of them escaped alive to Natchitoches.

The fight on the Medina ended the revolution in Texas—for a time. Arredondo took possession of San Antonio. Elizondo, the renegade, was given the task of providing a blood bath for the province, to him most congenial. He swept through the country, captured and shot seventy-four men, some on mere suspicion that they favored the insurgents, and imprisoned a hundred more. Then retribution overtook this treacherous brute. He was shot and fatally wounded by Miguel Serrano, one of his own lieutenants, who lost his reason, it was said, because of the inhumanity of Elizondo's executions.

Royalist troops were once more in control everywhere. Many liberal Mexicans fled to Louisiana, abandoning their lands and homes. Penalties were made stricter and more savage against foreigners who came into Texas without permission. But to hold back the Americans was impossible.

In the succeeding years numerous further efforts were made to gain footholds on Mexican-Texas soil, most singular among which was the piratical colony of Jean Lafitte on Galveston Island. With his brother Pierre, Lafitte long had engaged in smuggling goods up the mouth of the Mississippi to New Orleans, his headquarters being at Grand Terre, a beautiful island in Barataria Bay. From smuggling (winked at by the Creole merchants of New Orleans who profited by it) Lafitte turned to privateering when he found he could obtain letters of marque first from Colombia, then from Venezuela, countries then in revolution and hence at war with Spain.

A very thin line divided the privateer—especially one legalized by such shaky governments—from the outright pirate. Lafitte, however, liked at least a surface semblance of legality and always asserted that his ships captured and looted only Spanish craft.

But it appeared to be difficult for some of his captains—corsairs like Dominique You, Nez Coupé, René Baluche and Gambi—to distinguish between the flag of Spain and those of other nations. Because of their depredations, the Lafittes were declared outlaws; and Pierre, the elder brother, was imprisoned in the Cabildo in New Orleans. From this he "escaped" by virtue of some judicious bribes Jean Lafitte arranged.

At this point the War of 1812 intervened and for a time the Lafittes were submerged in greater events. They refused an offer—with an inducement of $30,000 cash—to aid the British when General Pakenham began his invasion and effort to take New Orleans. Although an American fleet occupied Barataria Bay and Grand Terre, to prevent the British fleet from using the harbor, the Lafittes tendered their services and those of their men to General Andrew Jackson, who commanded the United States forces. The latter, desperately trying to gather his defenses, accepted the Baratarians; and their piratical artillery played a conspicuous part in the defeat of Pakenham and his British army at the Battle of New Orleans.

Jean Lafitte and his men were given full pardons as a reward for their services. He attended the victory ball after the battle, and found himself a popular figure. Always dashing in appearance and making friends easily among influential people of the city, he might have become a respected citizen of New Orleans had he chosen.

But a career of peace was not in his nature. Enjoined from using American bases for his attacks on Spain, since the United States was at peace with that nation, he and his followers moved down the coast of Texas and occupied Galveston Island, from which they continued to scourge Spanish shipping, smuggling their captured goods and slaves into Louisiana. During this period Lafitte was visited by two Louisianans who bought slaves from him and illegally took them across the border into the United States to sell them—a violation of the laws so common that it was hardly condemned. They were brothers, Rezin and James Bowie. Of the latter Texas was to hear very much in the future.

Once again the shadow of General Wilkinson fell across Texas. Dr. James Long, who had married Wilkinson's niece and was firmly attached to that worthy's fortunes and schemes, organized in 1819 an "army of liberation" to invade the province. With three hundred men—among them young Jim Bowie—he occupied Nacogdoches and in a bombastic manifesto proclaimed a "republic," complete with a constitution, a system of laws, and himself as president and commander-in-chief. Shortly after, he visited Lafitte on Galveston Island and tried to enlist his aid; but the pirate, while royally entertaining him, thought the project too shaky and gave no help.

Spain lodged a sharp diplomatic protest with the United States and sent an army under Colonel Ignacio Pérez against the filibusters. The "republicans" at the time were scattered, and far too happily employed in enjoying themselves with the wine and women of the country to do much fighting. In separate contingents Pérez defeated them, killed Long's brother David, and drove them across the Sabine.

The defeat, however, did not discourage the "president and commander-in-chief." He gathered another "army" and invaded Texas again; and this was in 1821, after Mexico obtained independence from Spain, which removed the thin pretense of "liberating" the Mexican people and made it an outright territorial raid. The rash Dr. Long "captured" Goliad, but promptly was himself captured by his old adversary Pérez—now commanding for the Mexican government—and sent to the City of Mexico. There, though he was not confined, he made himself continuously troublesome and finally was shot by a sentry while trying, for some reason, to force his way against orders into the barracks of Los Gallos.

Long's death put a final period to Wilkinson's machinations. Discredited and disgraced, the scheming general died in the City of Mexico December 28, 1825.

The end came also for Lafitte. He had gathered on his island a populous settlement of choice rogues, who, including their women, with whom they lived without benefit of clergy, and the children of these extremely irregular unions, numbered more than a thousand.

On the island he had erected a fortified house called the Maison Rouge, and there was a good harbor for his piratical ships. Prosperity was enjoyed by the "colony," and its chief lived in barbaric splendor that impressed visitors to his fortress-palace.

But nature and the old inability of his captains to distinguish between national flags worked against him. A hurricane swept the island, destroying most of its piratical shacks and killing many of the people. Lafitte's mistress, a quadroon girl of considerable beauty named Catherine Villars, received injuries from which she never fully recovered.

To cap this, Lafitte's captains made the mistake of robbing American vessels. One day the brig-of-war *Enterprise*, Captain Kearny, anchored off the island and swung its guns on the settlement. Kearny, with some of his officers, went ashore and held a conference with the pirate chief. Lafitte was beginning to age, and was no longer the dashing figure of old. A young officer with Kearny left his word picture of him:

"My description of this renowned chieftain . . . will shock . . . many who have hitherto pictured him as the hero of a novel or melodrama. I am compelled by truth to introduce him as a stout, rather gentlemanly personage, some five feet ten inches in height, dressed very simply in a foraging cap and blue frock coat of a most villainous fit; his complexion, like most Creoles, olive; his countenance full, mild, and rather impressive, but for a small black eye, which now and then, as he grew animated in conversation, would flash in a way which impressed me with a notion that *Il Capitano* might be when roused, a very ugly customer."

Kearny notified him that he must get off the island and cease his piratical activities. Lafitte might have defied one ship, like the *Enterprise,* but he knew now that the full power of the United States Navy was arrayed against him. When the brig-of-war sailed away, he one day, early in 1821, destroyed all the buildings of the settlement by fire, disbanded his men, and sailed away with his ailing mistress and a special crew on his favorite vessel, the *Pride.* Five years later he died in Yucatán and was buried there.

CHAPTER TWO

New Spain Becomes Mexico

S P A I N had repelled every encroachment by peoples other
than her own, and Texas, after two centuries, was virtually empty. A few missions and *presidios* had been established but
it seemed impossible to colonize the great province.

Chief reason for this was the Indian problem. Of all the wild and
warlike tribes in New Spain, the most numerous and fiercest roamed
the immense expanses of Texas, where the cannibal Karankawas, the
swooping Comanches, the ever treacherous Caddos, Wacos and
Tawakonis, and the Apaches of endless bloody guile, created a peril
so continuous that Mexicans and Spaniards alike shunned the area.
Even the first Spanish *conquistadores,* who feared nothing, failed to
bring the country into submission. Save for such strongholds as
Nacogdoches, Goliad and San Antonio, most of the missions and
presidios by 1820 had been destroyed, their very locations sometimes
forgotten.

It now occurred to the Spanish administrators that there might be
merit in changing a policy of centuries. In 1819, therefore, after the
"Treaty of Amity," whereby, in exchange for the cession of Florida, the
United States confirmed Spain in her possession of Texas, the restrictions against Americans and other non-Spaniards entering the province
as colonists were removed.

It appeared safe enough to do so: the revolution seemed ended and
royalist power strongly established. Development of Texas lands by
the industry of American colonists would bring welcome revenue in
taxes to the Crown. Furthermore the officials of New Spain considered
that in the Americans, self-reliant and formidable, they might have a
solution for the Indian problem. Let Americans form a buffer for the
rest of New Spain!

The danger in which they were placed must have occurred to the
Americans, but that land hunger which always has characterized the
Anglo-Saxon race made them willing to undertake any risk and they
were not slow in taking advantage of the new dispensation.

First to apply for a tract of land, on which he agreed to introduce
three hundred families as colonists, was Moses Austin, a native of
Connecticut, who made a fortune producing lead from mines in

Missouri, then lost it when the Bank of St. Louis, in which he was a large stockholder, failed in 1818. With his remaining resources Austin sought opportunity in Texas and, traveling to San Antonio in 1820, offered his petition. His journey back to Louisiana was one of great hardship, and shortly after reaching Missouri he died, June 10, 1821, probably of pneumonia resulting from exposure.

Moses Austin did not live to learn that his petition had been granted, the news arriving a few days after his death. But anticipating success, he had charged his son, Stephen Austin, to carry out the venture. The latter did so in the troublous years that followed, to the best of his abilities and strength.

Between the time the father visited Texas and the son took over the colonizing enterprise, however, a startling change took place. Without warning the supposedly quiescent revolution broke out again in New Spain. Under Vicente Guerrero, who had been a lieutenant of Morelos, the insurgent Mexicans won victory after victory over royalist forces.

General Iturbide, who had put down the Morelos revolt, was sent with the principal royalist army against Guerrero. He found his antagonist superior to him and, after losing several skirmishes, resorted to treason. Making a secret compact with Guerrero, he transferred himself and his army to the revolutionary cause, and the two of them issued the so-called "Plan of Iguala," which declared Mexico independent of Spain, but accepted a Bourbon prince as a ruler, proclaimed the pre-eminence of the Roman Catholic Church, and "social and racial equality." The agreement was signed in February 1821, just a month after Moses Austin started his return journey from San Antonio, about the time Lafitte was destroying and abandoning his settlement on Galveston Island, and some time before Long's second expedition of "liberation."

With his army and general gone over to the other side, Viceroy O'Donojú, by the Treaty of Cordova, recognized the independence of the nation. In this treaty, incidentally, the country was given the official name *Mexico*, for the first time in history.

Spain's power was ended, but no Bourbon prince could be found who was willing to accept the "throne" of Mexico. In this impasse Iturbide, who may have been working toward this end the whole time, had himself proclaimed emperor in May 1822. The "empire" lasted less than a year. In March 1823, Iturbide was forced to abdicate by a new revolution launched by a figure destined to loom large in Mexican history—General Antonio López de Santa Anna. It was the beginning of a long succession of revolutions, counterrevolutions, massacres and bloodshed through which Mexico and Texas were to pass.

A look into the future: This Santa Anna, who would manage to lose for Mexico slightly more than half her territory—the states of Texas, New Mexico, Arizona, Nevada and California contain 765,540 square miles, while Mexico today contains 760,372 square miles—was to be the only one of the early Mexican leaders of note who escaped being shot. Iturbide was exiled to Europe, but when he returned to Mexico he was convicted as a traitor and shot. Hidalgo, Morelos, Leonardo and Nicolás Bravo, Matamoros, Mina, Guerrero, Victoria, Mexia, Pedraza, Santmanet, Herrera and Paredes—all, sooner or later, faced firing squads in the turmoil that overwhelmed the country until the rise of Benito Juárez, who himself executed Maximilian, the emperor installed by Napoleon III during the American Civil War. But Santa Anna, perfidious, vain, bloodthirsty and so selfish that he did not hesitate to sell out his country to save his own pusillanimous hide, lived out his life and died in bed.

So Mexico was free—at least from the bonds of Spain. It meant vast and sweeping changes in administration and politics. Stephen Austin, confronted by radical alterations in government, whereby his father's grant from Spanish authorities became ineffective, nevertheless undertook with the stubborn courage which was his great characteristic to carry on the task assigned to him.

The senior Austin's proposal was the foundation of what became known as the Empresario System—the word *empresario* meaning contractor. Under it, heads of colonizing families were to receive 640 acres of land, with 320 acres additional for their wives, 100 acres apiece for each child, and 80 acres for each slave. A premium thus was placed on procreation and slaveholding.

The Spanish government specified that all colonists must be Catholics, or become Catholics before entering Spanish territory; that they must show credentials of good character; and that they must take the oath of allegiance to the king of Spain.

Already, by December 1821, when Mexico was still trying to induce a Bourbon prince to come and rule her, some colonists had been gathered by Stephen Austin and were settling on land along the Brazos River, which though dangerous Indian country was fertile and productive. But it was necessary to induce the new government of Mexico to validate their claims, so Austin decided to go to the City of Mexico.

In a journey of extreme difficulty and danger—Mexico was chaotic and murder and robbery common episodes of every day—disguised in ragged clothes and a blanket, he finally reached the capital in April 1822. There he spent a year—twelve months of patient negotiation, frustrated again and again, until after the abdication of Iturbide he at last saw his grant confirmed by the Mexican Congress.

He even gained some extra concessions. The decree, dated February 18, 1823, increased land grants to the colonists. To the head of each family was granted one *sitio*, or square league, of grazing land, and one *labor* of tillage land, in all adding up to 4605 American acres. Unmarried men received one fourth of a *sitio*. The new arrangements encouraged matrimony, without putting any particular stress on big families.

At the same time *empresarios* were given various authorities, including the civil government of their colonies, the administration of justice and the command of militia, with the rank of lieutenant colonel. They could make war on Indian tribes which molested them, and import supplies free of duty through Galveston Harbor. Compulsory Catholicism, evidence of good character and an oath of allegiance were required as before.

From the first the Austin colony in Texas was a success. Other *empresarios* flocked in, among them Robert Leftwich, Hayden Edwards, Green De Witt, Ben Milam, James Powers and David G. Burnet, most of whom were prominent in later Texas annals. By 1835 the map of Texas was virtually covered by grants, some of which were never carried into effect, while others merged with stronger concessions. But the colony in the Brazos Valley remained chief, and its leader, Stephen Austin, was recognized as the head and spokesman of the American settlers, who came in such numbers that, whereas in 1821 the population of Texas, exclusive of Indians, did not exceed 3500, by 1830 it was almost 20,000.

The newcomers accepted unhesitatingly the role of facing the hostile Indians which was thrust upon them. In the spring of 1823 the Karankawas attacked the settlements in the lower Colorado Valley, killing two men and wounding two others. The colonists responded with a celerity and deadliness that must have astonished the aborigines. With a party of determined men Robert Kuykendall pursued the hostiles, surprised them on Skull Creek, killed nineteen of them, and destroyed their encampment.

It was an augury of unpleasant things to come for the Indians, yet the Karankawas continued their depredations until in a few bitter campaigns, some of which were led by Austin himself, they were almost exterminated and driven into Mexico, where they since seem to have disappeared entirely.

Other Indians, notably the Wacos and Tawakonis, were troublesome, for the lands surveyed and appropriated were their hunting grounds. To attempt to recite the small raids, ambuscades, skirmishes, pursuits and battles of this frontier war would be impossible, but one action deserves mention, because it forms one of the most mysterious and at the same time thrilling episodes in all frontier history.

Mention has been made of Miranda's discovery of silver in the San Saba country in 1756, and the *presidio* and mission established there. Following the destruction of the mission in 1758 by the Comanches, the *presidio* was abandoned also and for sixty years the silver workings reported on the San Saba lay idle, their very location forgotten.

About 1828 a remarkable adventurer arrived in Texas to become a permanent resident—big Jim Bowie, six feet two inches tall, weighing two hundred pounds, all hard muscle, bone and gristle, and active as a cat; a man with reactions so instantaneous that they made him the most celebrated duelist this country ever knew, and with the deadliest of all close-combat weapons—the knife.

Bowie was a rimrock American of his day, cut from the same piece of granite as Andy Jackson, Sam Houston and Davy Crockett. It was said of him that he respected nobody but the ladies, and feared nothing but running out of drinking liquor. Yet he was no drunkard, for though he drank like all men of his time, his exploits were those of a superbly trained athlete. He never lied. He loved to make money; but it was the making of it, and not the money itself, that was the prime attraction. And he loved danger better than money-making.

Legends persist of him in every part of the land where he ever passed. He was born on the frontier about 1799, roped and rode huge alligators in the bayous of Louisiana, and made dangerous cruises to deal with the pirate, Jean Lafitte, in his buccaneer's roost on Galveston Island. He was with Long's first filibustering expedition, but not with the second. He speculated largely in land deals and made a fortune.

During this time he gained the reputation of being the most terrible duelist in American history. His favorite weapon was the bowie knife, a fighting blade with a cross hilt and remarkably tempered steel, to which he gave his name. That he invented the knife has been disputed—no fewer than thirteen persons have claimed the honor. But it is notable that none of these claims was advanced until after Jim Bowie was dead and could not refute them. By the best evidence, he got the idea from an ordinary butcher knife his brother Rezin gave him, which was equipped with a brass cross guard. Working from that, he devised the fighting weapon which later was forged for him by James Black, an Arkansas blacksmith, and became the archetype for the most universal and deadly weapon of the frontier until it was supplanted by the nimble six-shooter.

Numerous duels were fought by Bowie, all under ferocious circumstances. Once he was locked with his antagonist in a pitch-dark room, he with a knife, the other with a sword, to feel for each other's lives in the blackness. He killed his enemy. On another occasion he fought a Spaniard with knives, the two of them seated on a log, their leather breeches nailed to it. Again he killed. Bloody Jack Sturdevant, chief of the Hole-in-Rock outlaws of the Ohio River, met him in a ten-foot chalked circle, their left wrists strapped together. Bowie crippled the outlaw's weapon arm for life. In the Vidalia sand bar duel, one of the most celebrated in history, he wounded two men and killed Major Norris Wright, after the latter had stabbed him with a sword cane when he was down with a pistol wound. Three assassins, sent to murder him by Sturdevant, waylaid him at night on a lonely wilderness road. He slew all three with his terrible knife. On another occasion he varied his fighting method by using pistols in a duel in which he killed a crooked steamboat gambler he had exposed. There were other episodes, some legendary, some attested, but contemporaries agreed that Bowie was never a bully and fought only when challenged. When he did fight, however, he was apt to stipulate conditions of combat so grim that the next man might hesitate to seek trouble with him.

John Myers Myers, writing in *The Alamo,* said, "Most dangerous men are apt to be either men of no control or men of limited emotions; men who are passionate lechers or drinkers, or men possessed of abnormal asceticism. Bowie astonishes investigation by his soundness. He was self-controlled but warm-hearted; he drank but he had other things to do; he got along with the women but he was no skirt chaser."

When he arrived in Texas Bowie already was a man of considerable property. Yet when he heard stories of the lost San Saba mine his old craving for adventure took possession of him. Making friends with the Lipan Apaches, he lived with them as a hunter and warrior for months, and eventually was shown, according to his own statement, the hidden workings, which he entered, appraised, and found very rich.

Returning to San Antonio, he made his plans, and on November 2, 1831, set out with ten other men, including his brother Rezin and Cephas Ham, an old Indian fighter. By November 19 they were within two days' travel of their destination, when Bowie was warned by friendly Indians that a large party of hostile warriors was on their trail. The night of the twentieth they camped in a grove of live oaks on a point of land made by the sharp bend of a creek. The neck of the little peninsula was heavily grown with thick chaparral brush and in this they took the precaution of cutting passages, with an open space in the center.

Next morning as they started the last day's ride, which would take them to the San Saba mine, the exact location of which only Jim

Bowie knew, the Indian war party which had been trailing them appeared—164 hostile savages, Caddos, Wacos, Tawakonis and probably Lipans, since Bowie's old friends had turned against him.

David Buchanan, who could speak the Caddo tongue, advanced with Rezin Bowie toward the Indians, to parley. But the savages fired, wounding him in the leg. Replying with his double-barreled rifle, Rezin Bowie took Buchanan on his back and bravely began carrying him back to camp.

Yelling, the hostiles pursued, intending to spear the two men; but Jim Bowie, with Cephas Ham and some others, ran out to meet them, and with accurate fire killed four, whereupon the others fell back.

A battle to the death was now certain. Protecting themselves as well as they could behind the trunks of the live oaks on their little peninsula, the Texans fought off the Indians until some of the savages crept behind and opened a raking fire on them from the rear. One man was killed and another wounded before Bowie could get what was left of his party into the chaparral thicket, where they could move about in concealment through the passages they had cut.

From this screened defense, under the keen leadership of Bowie, the handful of white men repelled charge after charge throughout that day. Twice the Indians tried to burn them out by setting fire to the prairie. The second time flames got into the brush which concealed the defenders, so that they had to beat it out with their coats and what little water was left in their canteens.

But by evening the Indians had enough of the deadly Texas rifles. They withdrew, taking their dead. In the day's furious fight, by their own account, they lost fifty killed and thirty-five wounded. Of the Texans, one was dead and three wounded.

Taken all around, this is possibly the most brilliant fight against heavy odds in the history of the West. In the battle the Texans were armed only with muzzle-loading rifles; whereas in some other notable fights against great odds, such as Forsyth's victory over the Cheyennes at the Arickaree, and the Wagon Box defeat of the Sioux, the white men used repeating, breech-loading Spencer carbines and six-shooters.

Because most of their horses were killed and their wounded men needed medical care, Bowie's party was unable to continue on to the mine after the battle. Instead they returned to San Antonio. No second attempt was ever made to reach the San Saba, and the secret of the location of the mine died with Jim Bowie when he was killed at the Alamo. J. Frank Dobie, in *Coronado's Children*, has recorded the many efforts since made to locate it. People still believe it is there, somewhere in the vicinity of the present town of Menard. But if there was a mine shaft, it was filled in—presumably by the Indians—

and so overgrown with brush that nobody has ever been able to find it again.

After the San Saba fight the Waco-Caddo-Tawakoni confederacy never again was a serious menace, and the Texas settlements were thereby relieved of one peril.

CHAPTER THREE

Mexican Autocrats and Texas Fire-eaters

THE character of the Texas settlers was by no means uniform. Among them were insolvent debtors, adventurers, soldiers of fortune, even fugitives from justice. It was during this period that "G.T.T."—"Gone to Texas"—became a byword in the United States when a defalcator with his bank's funds in his carpetbag disappeared overnight, or someone made a hasty exit from a community when the law began to smell too closely at his heels on a suspicion of horse larceny, highway robbery or murder

The overwhelming majority of settlers, of course, were honest, capable, hard-working and law-abiding (within limits). They were the builders of Texas, the solid community which, in spite of an infinity of different modes of thought, personalities and ways, managed to cleave together and in the end create out of the wilderness a land in which their descendants take a pride almost inordinate. Illustrative of the divergences among Texans at this time, two men, at opposite poles in policy and motive, furnish an interesting comparison.

Stephen Austin, head of the Brazos colony, was a composition of contrasts. A slender man of moderate height, he had a face suggesting thought rather than action and a temperament somewhat in keeping with that appearance. His forehead, slightly balding, was too high; his eyes were too wide, almost femininely so; his nose was too long, taking away from his small mouth and making his chin appear weak by comparison.

He had accepted the responsibility of the Texas colony when he was only twenty-seven years old, and he bore that responsibility like a burden. His habits were abstemious, he cared neither for the humor nor for the rough talk of the frontiersmen, and kept much to himself when it was possible to do so. He never married, living in the home of his sister and her husband, James F. Perry.

In the Indian wars of the early colony he proved his courage, as also in the journeys of hardship and danger he made to the City of Mexico in behalf of his colonists. But when called upon to command the forces of Texas later, his unhappy irresolution and overcaution showed he was not by temperament a soldier.

He was charged with being overfond of debates, oratory, rostrums, gavels and rules of order. Yet this was a manifestation of his desire to be in all things fair and just.

Of himself he once wrote, "My temper is naturally hasty and impetuous; the welfare of the settlement required that I should control it effectually, for one in my situation, falling suddenly into a fit of passion, might do hurt to the interests of hundreds. My disposition is by nature, also, open, unsuspecting, confiding, and accommodating almost to a fault. I have been, therefore, subject in a peculiar manner to imposition. Experience has enlightened me as to this latter deficiency, I fear, almost too late, for I am apprehensive of having fallen somewhat into the opposite extreme."

Austin took in all sincerity the oath of allegiance to the Mexican government, and strove honestly and earnestly to live as a loyal citizen of his adopted country. Constantly confronted, on a frontier between two clashing civilizations, with the necessity of restraining his over-zealous compatriots, he received much abuse. But his selflessness, which was heroic, enabled him to accept persecution with all patience and forgive his detractors. Though a conservative in the affairs of Texas, his sole interests were those of his people, and even when he was repudiated by them he accepted their rebuffs and faithfully tried to carry out the subordinate duties they assigned to him.

If Austin was at one extreme of the Texas body politic in his conservatism, the opposite extreme was William Barret Travis, a sandy-haired lawyer with a blazing blue-gray eye, who arrived in Texas sometime in 1831. He was a gentleman, obviously of the type produced by the Deep South, given to rhetoric, with a touchy sense of honor, and if need be a subscriber to the *code duello*. He also was possessed of more than his share of courage, and more than his share of willingness to promote and participate in any kind of excitement that would enliven the dull routine of life.

His early history was shrouded in some mystery. One version was that his real name was William Barr, not Barret, and that he was a foundling, the name (with defective spelling) being conferred on him when he was discovered, one morning in 1809, as an infant, tied to a bar of a gate on the farm of a man named Travis—who adopted him—near Saluda, South Carolina. This yarn has been denied by persons who said variously that he was born in Alabama and North Carolina.

Whatever the truth about his origin, he was a rebel by nature from his childhood. He attended school in a South Carolina academy, which he left—at the urgent request of the faculty—for fomenting a student riot against what he considered "tyrannical rules."

In the 1820s he appeared in Alabama, read law, was admitted to the bar, and practiced successfully in the somewhat rough and ready courts of the period. He married and was the father of a son and daughter; but in 1831, believing that "he had reasons to suspect her of unfaithfulness," he left his wife—who retained custody of their daughter and his entire bank account—and with his son went to Texas, penniless, to begin life over again. Mrs. Travis obtained a divorce and promptly remarried, but Travis never again attempted the rocky path of matrimony.

By 1831 the entry of Americans into Texas had been made illegal by Mexico. Travis refused to take the ban seriously, coolly took up headquarters in Anahuac, and began there to practice the very law he was violating. A born intransigeant with high-flown notions, an eloquent tongue and a flair for leadership, he was as if bound by destiny to become a focal figure in the troubles about to take place in Texas.

Already, when he arrived, there was much discontent evident in the colony, and that discontent was hastened and increased by events. Left without any support, military or otherwise, to shift for themselves on the frontier, the American colonists found it difficult to work up any great enthusiasm for the Mexican government. For one thing, changes occurred so frequently and unpredictably in the palace of Chapultepec that it was hard to keep track of them.

So the Texans kept their own modes, language and traditions, refused to absorb Mexican customs and habits, and remained in all essentials Americans. Their towns were laid out on the American plan; their systems of local government were American, although they used Mexican names—*alcalde* for mayor, *ayuntamiento* for town council, and so on. Their notions of justice and freedom were American. Farming and business methods were American, and more successful than those of the natives. The bustling, aggressive spirit was American . . . that universal Mexican habit, the *siesta*, was never adopted by the colonists; they had no time for it.

Mexico had, in 1824, adopted a constitution which has been called "the most complex form of government ever devised by man." Though it was better than nothing, and reflected only Mexico's lack of training in self-government after three centuries of subjugation to Spain, the constitution was a constant irritant to many Texans, who in particular resented the denial of trial by jury and absence of religious freedom.

Nevertheless, the time would come when Texas-Americans would pour out their blood in copious quantities for that poor, limping, imperfect constitution, when it became the symbol of freedom in the unhappy land.

As early as 1826 an abortive effort was made to set up an independent state by Hayden Edwards, an *empresario* whose license had been canceled. Some colonists were willing to help him and he gained the support of the Cherokee Indians who lived in the Red River Valley, through their chief, The Bowl, and John Dunn Hunter, a white man who had been taken by them as a child, grown up among them, and gained great influence over them.

The "Republic of Fredonia" was proclaimed in east Texas, but it was extremely short-lived. Ellis P. Bean—he of the Nolan expedition—was in Nacogdoches as Indian agent for the Mexican government. He persuaded the Cherokees that Edwards' cause was already lost before it started, and The Bowl and his warriors withdrew, murdering Hunter and his aide, a half-breed named Richard Fields, to show their good faith and repentance.

At this juncture a Mexican force of three hundred men under Colonel Matio Ahumada appeared, the "revolutionists" were demoralized by the sight of all those uniforms, Edwards skipped over the border, and the so-called Fredonian War collapsed after a single skirmish.

Brief as it was, the disturbance set some men to thinking. What would happen if *all* Texas should decide to break away from Mexico? It became a subject of considerable speculation and to some, particularly the political-minded, it presented some highly advantageous prospects.

Throughout the Fredonian trouble Stephen Austin and other American *empresarios* maintained strict loyalty to the Mexican government. Austin even arrested one of Edwards' emissaries who came to the Brazos colony seeking recruits. It was, of course, only good business policy to thus underline fealty toward a government under which the *empresarios* all held their contracts.

In spite of this, however, Mexican officials became increasingly suspicious of American settlers. And perhaps not without reason, for the United States at this time began to behave in a somewhat alarming manner.

General Andrew Jackson was elected President in 1828. The old war horse was a confirmed and avowed expansionist, whose illegal military activities in Florida had been condemned in Washington, but ended in the cession of that territory to the United States by Spain. Now, many Mexicans believed, his eye was on another former Spanish province, Texas—perhaps even the whole of Mexico! Their apprehension was strengthened when Old Hickory gave his forthright support to the theory that under the terms of the Louisiana Purchase the United States was entitled to all lands as far as the Rio Grande. And this apprehension colored their attitude when the President instituted negotiations for the purchase of Texas, authorizing Ambassador Poinsett to "go as high as five millions" for the province.

Mexico had no desire to sell and was offended by the offer. At just about this time, in 1829, owing to a revolution engineered by Santa Anna, General Anastasio Bustamente became *presidente*. One of his first acts was to issue a decree aimed directly at the American colonists in Texas. At a single stroke it prohibited further entry of Americans into Mexican territory, suspended *empresario* contracts, stopped further introduction of Negro slaves (without mentioning Mexico's parallel peon system), placed heavy duties on imported goods, and laid down other rigorous restrictions on the colony.

As if he anticipated that his decree would meet opposition, Bustamente simultaneously began to strengthen Mexican garrisons in Texas, placed new commanders at many posts, and gave them authority to supersede civil with martial law. At Nacogdoches, San Antonio, Goliad, Anahuac, Galveston, Velasco, Victoria and other posts, about thirteen hundred Mexican soldiers were distributed.

The new troops were of the worst description. Finding that it could not keep up an army on volunteer enlistments, the Mexican government had adopted the policy of filling its ranks with convicts from its prisons. And since not even by this method of putting uniforms on criminals enough men could be secured for the regiments, *ayuntamientos* (village councils) were instructed, "with the assistance of armed force, to proceed to make levies; vagabonds and disorderly persons shall be taken in preference for military service; recruits may be obtained by entrapment and decoy."

Such villainous soldiers, further brutalized by the harsh and often cruel methods of "discipline" to which it was deemed necessary by their officers to subject them, had hitherto been quartered in the subservient villages and cities of Mexico. There they had things very much their own way and learned such arrogance, viciousness and light-fingered activity that, when they were transferred to garrisons in a free-minded province like Texas, trouble was inevitable.

It came to a head in May 1832. And, oddly enough, it was not a native Mexican whose oppressions brought on the conflict, but an American—a Kentuckian by birth—Colonel Davis Bradburn, a soldier of fortune then serving as an officer in the Mexican army. A hard, self-important man, Bradburn believed he knew how to handle insubordination and he seemed to hold some sort of a grudge against the people of the land of his own birth. From the beginning, when he was placed in command at Anahuac, he was offensive, sneering and dictatorial toward the settlers.

Those who complained of his numerous injustices, which included dispossessing some persons of their land and property on various pretexts, found themselves nursing their wrongs behind the bars of Bradburn's specially built prison. He refused any redress for thefts, robberies and other crimes committed by his rascally troops. On the other hand, to stop smuggling—which since Bustamente's decree had vastly increased—he closed all the ports of Galveston Bay, except Anahuac, where no vessel of more than six feet draft could enter, and where he could personally inspect every cargo that came in or went out. This caused such protest that on the orders of his superior, General Mier y Teran, Bradburn reluctantly allowed the port of Brazoria also to remain open.

Late in May a woman, unnamed but presumably American, was seized one night, dragged to a vacant house on the outskirts of Anahuac, and brutally raped by five of the criminal soldiers of the *presidio*. A worthless and depraved Texan witnessed the outrage, and either participated in it or at least made no effort to prevent it.

When the victim's story became known, Texans, who held the virtue of their own women in high esteem, quickly gathered in an angry mob. The Mexican soldiers had escaped to their barracks, but the Texan who had been present was seized. Because there was some doubt as to his actual participation in the ravishment, lynching was decided against in favor of that ancient and accepted rite—tar and feathers. The prisoner was stripped naked. In a cauldron tar was heated to a fluid (and scalding) state, smeared over the naked body of the wretch, and feathers dumped over him which, adhering to the tar, caused him to assume the ludicrous appearance of some obscene and disgraceful fowl. Then he was told to get out of town.

At this point a detachment of Bradburn's soldiers appeared, fired several shots, and arrested some of the leading spirits of the crowd. As might be expected, one of those leading spirits was William Barret Travis, who in a few months had become a conspicuous resident of Anahuac. The prisoners were locked in Bradburn's jail, and when citizens demanded their release the colonel sneeringly refused.

Anahuac was thoroughly aroused and angry. Texans, transplanted from the bayous of Louisiana and the forests of Tennessee and Kentucky, always had a long rifle handy, over the door or mantel or leaning in a corner. Down came the guns from the racks, and Texans swarmed angrily toward the *presidio*, capturing a squad of Mexican cavalry on the way.

In the streets a few tentative shots were fired. Before anyone was hurt, however, Bradburn called a parley and agreed to surrender his prisoners in exchange for the Mexicans held by the Texans, on condition the Texans withdraw six miles out of town. The prisoners held by the Texans were released in good faith, but no sooner did Bradburn have his men than he opened fire and drove the settlers out of Anahuac, still keeping Travis and the other captives under lock and key in his jail.

It was now war between Anahuac and Bradburn. The colonists, however, were Americans, and to Americans of that day no tenet was more cherished than the belief that the proprieties should be maintained: which meant that before the shooting began a meeting must be held, proper officers elected, and a set of resolutions drawn up and passed.

The resolutions adopted in this instance were interesting in one respect. The name of Santa Anna bulked large in them. And to explain this a short discussion is necessary.

Bewildering changes in government had taken place in Mexico. Since 1822, when Juan O'Donojú, the last Spanish viceroy, left the country, the following successions had occurred: Agustín Iturbide, emperor, 1822; Guadalupe Victoria, president, 1824; Gómez Pedraza, president, 1828; Vicente Guerrero, president, 1828; Anastasio Bustamente, president, 1829. During this time an almost continual turmoil of revolts and counterrevolts went on in interior Mexico, so that one never knew, quite, from night to morning, who would be head of the government.

It might have been noticed that there was a certain bug under the chip in most of these revolutions, *coups d'état* and blood purges. The name of that insect was Antonio de Santa Anna. He fomented almost every revolt, made and unmade presidents, and gradually was working toward his own great ambition, which was to be dictator, with unquestioned and absolute authority over Mexico and perhaps—who could tell?—vast regions beyond Mexico, if fortune smiled on him.

The most recent series of manipulations by Santa Anna's dexterous political hand had included the following: Under the constitution of 1824, Pedraza was elected president in 1828. But Guerrero, who was defeated in the election, began a revolution—his chief general being Santa Anna, who previously had overturned Iturbide.

Santa Anna was defeated by Pedraza's troops, but the dogged half-Indian Guerrero fought on and captured the capital. Pedraza, the lawfully elected president, fled into exile and Santa Anna, who had been hiding in mountainous Oaxaca, came out from his refuge.

His reputation was tarnished, but shortly after this he regained his popularity by defeating at Tampico a weak Spanish force which made an abortive effort to resubjugate Mexico. Santa Anna returned to the capital a conquering hero and almost at once turned against Guerrero, forced him to evacuate his office late in 1829, and assisted Bustamente to become president January 1, 1830.

Bustamente was a usurper. He seized the presidency from Guerrero, whom he captured and shot. But Guerrero was a usurper also, having seized the government from Pedraza. After two troubled years, resentments against the Bustamente administration culminated in a tardy realization that Pedraza was, after all, the lawful president. In the summer of 1832 revolutionary forces sprang into being in Vera Cruz, Zacatecas, Jalisco, Durango and elsewhere, declaring for "legitimacy." And who suddenly appeared as leader of the revolt against Bustamente? The slippery Santa Anna, who had himself helped drive into exile this very Pedraza.

The Texans could hardly be expected to understand these kaleidoscopic changes. Mexican politics were too volatile. Yet, out of the turmoil, Santa Anna somehow managed to appear to the settlers as a champion of democracy. So, at Anahuac, the resolutions duly moved, seconded and passed by the Texans "adopted" Santa Anna's "cause."

Having adjourned, they went into action and the action flamed all around Galveston Bay. It even involved a "navy"—consisting of a single schooner, the *Brazoria,* commandeered at the town of that name by John Austin, who incidentally was no relation to the *empresario.*

Austin was a man of action. He mounted a single cannon on the deck of the little ship and provided it with defensive "bulwarks" of cotton bales. Then he sent it sailing down the Brazos River to Velasco, which lay above the mouth of the stream, while with 112 men, all experts with the rifle, he marched overland for the same destination.

Velasco was garrisoned by 125 Mexican soldiers commanded by Colonel Ugartechea. The latter, a good officer and loyal to his country, rejected Austin's demand that he surrender.

Thereupon a curious battle began. Placing on the schooner forty men, all good marksmen, who were protected by the cotton bales, Austin had the ship brought to anchor within two hundred yards of the fort, her single cannon bearing on it. The rest of his men he disposed on the landward side.

The schooner really won the fight. All day her cannon blasted away at the *presidio,* while her riflemen prevented the Mexicans from using their own solitary piece of artillery with any effect by dropping the men who served it until they flinched from the duty. At last only Ugartechea himself would point the gun. His courage was so admired by the Texans that they let him live.

But by nightfall fifty of Ugartechea's 125 men were on the casualty list—thirty-five killed and fifteen wounded. The large proportion of dead was due to the fact that the Mexicans were fighting behind walls and exposed only their heads. The head was sufficient target for the Texas riflemen, and a bullet striking that mark usually was fatal.

Meantime, the Texans had lost but seven killed and nineteen wounded, little more than half the Mexican casualties.

In the evening Ugartechea surrendered. He was permitted to evacuate Velasco with his surviving men, who were allowed to carry their arms and baggage, and even provisioned for their march to Matamoros.

While this was going on at Velasco, a rather surprising series of events took place at Anahuac. Colonel José de las Piedras, commandant at Nacogdoches, arrived there July 1 and, as Bradburn's superior officer, ordered the immediate release of Travis and the other prisoners. Offended by this, Bradburn threw up his command. Thereupon Piedras appointed Lieutenant Colonel Cortinas to succeed him.

No sooner had Piedras returned to Nacogdoches than the Mexican soldiers at Anahuac mutinied, declared for Santa Anna "the liberator," evacuated the city, and marched south. Bradburn, his life now in peril from both Mexicans and Texans, slunk out of Anahuac, boarded a ship for New Orleans, escaped arrest there by saying he was seeking aid for the Texans to drive the Mexicans out of the province, and eventually reached Vera Cruz by sea, where he was reinstated in the Mexican army. He entered Texas again in 1836, as an officer in Santa Anna's invading force.

These victories by no means appeased the Texans. By midsummer Santa Anna's revolution against Bustamente was in full career and it seemed as good a time as any to the Texans, who already had declared for "the liberator," to expel the garrison at Nacogdoches.

The action there was notable for the fact that one of its leaders was James Bowie, he of the famous knife, and afterward a spearhead of the Texas revolution.

Colonel Piedras was faithful to Bustamente. When, August 2, an "assemblage" of about three hundred men, including prominent Mexicans as well as Texans, entered Nacogdoches "peacefully" to invite the garrison to declare for the constitution of 1824 (which had become quite a sacred symbol), Piedras trotted out his cavalry and fired on the crowd. A distinguished old Mexican, Encarnación Chirino, the *alcalde* of the town, was killed, thus becoming an early Texas martyr.

The "peaceful" nature of the assemblage disappeared about as rapidly as that of a community of Texas red-tailed wasps when someone inconsiderately prods their nest with a stick; and the circumstance that most of those present had their shooting irons with them suggests something or other about their real original intentions.

Bullets began to sing up the streets and the cavalry retreated hastily, while the Texans—more a posse than an army—took possession of the houses around the central plaza, where stood the church into which Piedras had withdrawn most of his troops.

Adobe walls now hung out curtains of smoke and the keen crackle of rifles, with the duller reports of Mexican muskets, made the streets echo with ear-shocking clatter. Leaden slugs probed and searched the Mexican defenses, and here and there men began to crumple up in the church. By nightfall Piedras had forty casualties. He took advantage of the darkness to get out of there, retreating without bothering to remove his dead and wounded.

Here Bowie, who had just arrived in Nacogdoches, took charge. As soon as he learned from a wounded prisoner what direction Piedras was taking, he rode with twenty men "on good horses" by a lower road, circling Piedras and heading him off at the crossing of the Angelina River. His plan was to delay the Mexicans while the main force from Nacogdoches overtook them and hit them from the rear. But somehow the people in Nacogdoches got involved in passing more resolutions and never did arrive in time to help Bowie.

Of this Bowie was unaware. He hid his twenty men in the brush down by the ford and when Piedras' advance guard came to the river it was fired upon and retreated with some losses to the main body.

Piedras, thoroughly confused and convinced he was surrounded by an overwhelming force, camped a considerable distance back from the river. Next morning Bowie, tired of waiting for reinforcements that did not come, boldly sent two messengers to the Mexican camp demanding surrender. Piedras complied. His men stacked arms and it was not until then that Piedras discovered to his chagrin that he had given up three hundred soldiers to Bowie's twenty Texans.

The Mexicans were marched back to Nacogdoches, where the soldiers unanimously declared for Santa Anna and his "Plan of Vera Cruz," and were allowed to return to Mexico. Piedras was held for a time at Brazoria, but later was released also and returned to Mexico by way of Tampico. In the entire Nacogdoches action the Texans lost only three killed and five wounded.

By the end of August not a Mexican soldier remained in Texas, except a small force of about seventy men in the *presidio* at San Antonio.

Down in Mexico, Santa Anna defeated Bustamente's army and saw the "rightful" president, Pedraza, reinstated to serve out the remainder of his term—which had but four months to run. From Santa Anna's point of view, that was just about enough time to build up sentiment to which he could in due time turn a responsive ear, when the people of Mexico would "call" him to the presidency—from which he envisaged an even higher step for himself.

CHAPTER FOUR

The Leaders and the Revolt

T H E affairs at Anahuac and Nacogdoches made marked men of several persons, including Bowie, Travis and John Austin. But late in 1832 another arrived who was more important than any of them, more important than Stephen Austin—a strange giant named Sam Houston.

Born in Virginia in 1793, of Scotch-Irish ancestry, he went to Tennessee as a boy when his widowed mother took her brood of children across the Alleghenies to the new land. His educational opportunities were meager, but so all-encompassing was his mind and so retentive his memory that whatever he read he digested and kept. His taste in literature was in itself notable for an untrained youth of the frontier. The Bible, the *Iliad*, Shakespeare's works, *Pilgrim's Progress* and Caesar's *Commentaries* were the books over which he pored and from which, throughout his life, he was able to quote profusely, exactly and appositely.

He did not admire labor unless its rewards were exceptional and as a youth, tiring of clerking in a country store, he left civilization and went to the Cherokee country. There he lived and became a member of the tribe, being adopted as a son by Oo-loo-te-ka, a chief, who gave him the Indian name Co-lon-neh (the Raven)—a complimentary title, for the Cherokees considered the bird not an evil omen but the most sagacious of the feathered kind.

Among the Indians he took part in hunting, dancing and the game of lacrosse, in the rough sport of which he excelled with his size and athletic ability. But this did not stop him from reading, for when his brothers came from the settlements to try to persuade him to return home they found him beneath a tree, immersed in the lines of the *Iliad*, a translation of which he had taken to the woods with him.

He refused to return with his brothers and remained with the Indians for some time. In this period he acquired the curious habit of speaking of himself in the third person—a trait of the Indians, and, be it noted, also of Julius Caesar, whom he read continuously. He learned also the trick of forensic imagery which the red men used in their speeches, and which later gave a distinctive flavor to his public oratory as well as his private conversations.

In 1812, when he was nineteen years old, he returned to civilization and for a time taught school; but with the outbreak of the war with Britain he enlisted in the Tennessee infantry. His regiment never faced the redcoats. Instead it was led by General Andrew Jackson against the Creek Indians, who had been stirred into hostility by Tecumseh, the Shawnee chief, and who under their chief Weatherford captured Fort Mims with a great massacre and terrorized the whole frontier of Alabama.

At the Battle of the Horseshoe, Houston, already an ensign, led a charge of the Tennesseans against the Indians behind their barricade, and was the first man to leap down from the parapet among the savages. His bravery brought in his men after him, the ramparts were taken, and Houston, wounded by an arrow, caught Jackson's attention. It was the beginning of Houston's career.

Later in the day the young ensign was again wounded, leading an attack on a covered blockhouse. Such zeal solidified Jackson's regard for him. Houston was hospitalized at home while the general went to New Orleans and defeated Pakenham's British army, but when Jackson returned to Tennessee and to politics Sam Houston was one of Old Hickory's bright young men. Under the aegis of that leader he went to Congress, fought a duel with General William A. White—and put his opponent in bed for four months with a well-placed bullet—became a general of militia, and was elected governor of Tennessee.

His method of campaigning was remarkable. Each frontier community of that day had its "bully"—its acknowledged champion, who could whip every man in the country round and lorded it over all. Houston would go into a village and challenge the town bully to a wrestling match. When the match was over, he would address the crowd which had quickly assembled to see the contest. It is said that Sam Houston—who was, according to at least one account, in the neighborhood of six feet six inches tall and perhaps weighed 240 pounds of bone and muscle—never lost a wrestling match, or a precinct which he addressed.

Jackson was elected President and Houston, at the height of his career, was generally considered Old Hickory's political heir, who should go to the White House after him. Then disaster came, and through a woman.

Houston married a young lady of an aristocratic Tennessee family named Eliza Allen. She was very much younger than he and it is said that she preferred another suitor, marrying the governor at her father's command. Exactly what happened probably will never be known, but shortly after the wedding the bride, weeping, returned to her father's home; and Houston, evidently severely shaken, resigned his governorship and disappeared, eventually showing up among the Cherokees, who had in the interim moved to what is now Oklahoma.

It created a political sensation such as never before had been known in America. Everywhere were rumors but neither Eliza nor Houston offered any explanation of the separation. Before departing, however, Houston left a notice that "if any wretch ever dares to utter a word against the purity of Mrs. Houston, I will come back and write the libel in his heart's blood."

All this happened in 1829. For three years he lived with the Cherokees near Fort Gibson, drinking far too much for his own good. Once he traveled to Washington as "ambassador of the Cherokee Nation," presenting himself at the White House in a buckskin coat, blanket, moccasins and other habiliments of the Cherokees. President Jackson received him with joy and embraced him publicly. Before Houston returned to the Cherokees there may have been a strong understanding between them on certain matters concerning the Southwest. A year later Houston was in Texas.

The episodes above form only the briefest outline of his extraordinary career, but now in Mexican territory, ostensibly as a private lawyer, his presence could not fail to produce enormous speculation. Sam Houston was such a man of tumbling passions and mighty achievements as comes not once in a generation, but perhaps once in a people's history.

At San Felipe de Austin he encountered Bowie, now married to Ursula, a daughter of Juan de Veramendi, vice-governor of Texas, and living in San Antonio. From the beginning they were friends and understood each other. With Bowie, Houston visited San Antonio, and when he returned to Natchitoches, Louisiana, he wrote on February 13, 1833, a letter to Andrew Jackson which is at least significant. It began:

"Having been so far as Béxar, in the province of Texas . . . I am in possession of some information that . . . may be calculated to forward your views, if you should entertain any, touching the acquisition of Texas by the United States."

The letter continued; its writer believed Texas would be transferred to some other power than Mexico—perhaps England—within the near future, unless the United States intervened; and added that nineteen twentieths of the people of the province desired union with the United States. Perhaps all this was only a suggestion: but it may also have been a report.

Disturbing news sifted up from south of the Rio Grande as Santa Anna began the final devious series of shifts whereby he became dictator. In May 1833 he became president, elected as a proponent of religious freedom, liberal political rights and equality between races. Almost at once a *coup d'état,* promoted by him to give him dictatorial powers, was attempted but failed. By December it was clear that he had changed his political beliefs and was on the reactionary side of the *ricos* and the Church.

The Texas settlers wanted their province separated from Coahuila, to which it had been joined since the days of that French genius of disruption, St. Denis, and from which it was badly administered. Other reforms were desired also and a state constitution was drafted which embodied them. With this document Stephen Austin, the patient and long-suffering leader of the colony, traveled to the City of Mexico, to present it to the government for ratification.

Texas did not see him again for two years. When he reached the capital his petition was heard and he was allowed to begin his return journey. But on the way he was arrested at Saltillo and sent back to the City of Mexico, where he was lodged in the dungeon of the old Spanish Inquisition. Though later he was transferred to a better prison, he was not released to return to Texas until September 1835, never having been tried on any charges.

Meantime Santa Anna at last came out in his true colors. By the "Plan of Cuernavaca," proclaimed in May 1834, he made a public apostasy of his declared beliefs; joined the clergy in pronouncing against religious reform; supported the wealthy property owners; discarded the slogan of equality between races on which he had been elected; repealed the constitution of 1824 and substituted a new constitution written by himself; and in October seized absolute power as president-dictator.

In all Mexico only Zacatecas, Coahuila and Texas opposed this usurpation. The rebellions in the first two named states were put down bloodily, but Texas proved a nut somewhat harder to crack.

Though most of the colonists as yet wished only to have the constitution of 1824 restored and a true liberal in Chapultepec palace, firebrands like Travis began urging complete independence. Santa Anna recognized the danger he faced and, acting before Texas resistance was fully formed, sent a strong force to occupy it at once.

It was Bowie who gave the first warning. He had lost his wife and two children in a cholera epidemic which swept Texas and Coahuila in 1833; and had since wandered, restless as a lost soul, drinking heavily, indulging in land speculations and political maneuverings in the unstable legislatures of Coahuila, for which later he was severely criticized —a man deprived of purpose and aim in life by the grief that overwhelmed him.

Early in June 1835 he was in Matamoros, across the Rio Grande near the gulf, when the Mexican provost marshal posted notices forbidding all foreigners to leave the city. Bowie, however, took his horse from the stable of the inn where he was staying and escaped by night back across the river into Texas. At Hatch's plantation on the Lavaca River, a hundred and sixty miles away, he wrote a letter to Dr. J. B. Miller, the *jefe politico* of Brazoria:

I have just arrived here from Matamoros, and as all communication is cut off between Texas and all other parts of the republic, I take this opportunity of giving you some information that may be useful to Texas. I left Matamoros on the 12th of the present month. All the vessels in the port were embargoed for the purpose of transporting troops to the coast of Texas. The commandant, General Cos, forbid all foreigners from leaving the city under any circumstances. I run away and succeeded in getting this far safe. Three thousand troops had reached Saltillo on their way to Texas. All this may or may not be news to you.

It *was* news to Dr. Miller—and to all of Texas. The substance of Bowie's letter crossed Texas with a celerity which only fear could impart. Committees of Safety were formed and men began gathering at night to drill as informal companies of volunteer soldiers.

Houston had recently returned from Washington, Philadelphia, New York and elsewhere, where he had been engaged in some mysterious business which, it was whispered, had to do with financial and manpower help for Texas. He received a letter from Samuel Swartwout—Aaron Burr's go-between in the conspiracy with General Wilkinson—in which that worthy said, "If I mistake not Texas will be U States in 5 years, or an independent Empire, when you'll be King."

But Houston had no ambitions to be a king. He had a different aim, and it was linked closely to the policies of Andrew Jackson. He began organizing the Department of Nacogdoches, set up a Committee of Vigilance and Safety, and was in turn commissioned by it "Commander-in-Chief of the forces of the Department to sustain the principles of the Constitution of 1824."

Trouble started quickly. An armed mob, led by the ever turbulent Buck Travis, in June expelled Captain Tenorio and his twenty Mexican soldiers from Anahuac. Disarmed, the Mexicans were marched to San Felipe de Austin, the colony's capital. Some of the council there denounced the proceedings as highhanded. Tenorio and his men, their arms restored, were treated well and sent on to join the garrison under Colonel Ugartechea in San Antonio, where the Mexican forces, including the first detachment from Cos's army across the border, now numbered five hundred men.

There were some clashes at sea between Texas ships and Mexican ships, and a Mexican armed schooner, the *Correo,* was captured by the *San Felipe,* a hastily converted ship manned by Texans and commanded by Captain Hurd, and brought into Anahuac as a prize of war in July.

Then, early in September, Stephen Austin arrived back in Texas. He had been released by Santa Anna, who believed he could keep Texas in line as previously. But Austin had had his fill of the dictator and his methods. At a banquet honoring him in Brazoria he gave an address urging unity, then offered a toast, "To the constitutional rights and the security and peace of Texas—they ought to be maintained."

When word came that General Cos was sending substantial reinforcements to Ugartechea, the Committee of Safety of the Austin colony, at Austin's direction, drew up a circular for the direction of the colonists, in which these fateful words occurred:

This committee deem it to be their duty to say that, in its opinion, all kind of conciliatory measures with General Cos and the military at Béxar are hopeless, and that nothing but the ruin of Texas can be expected from any such measures. They have already, and very properly, been resorted to without effect. War is our only recourse. There is no other remedy. We must defend our rights, ourselves, and our country, by force of arms.

The great *empresario* had declared for war and called on the people for unity. Texas rallied around him.

But though Texas was at last united, Texas was hardly prepared. Without opposition General Cos occupied San Antonio in force.

Shortly after, hostilities began. The town of Gonzales, on the direct road between San Antonio and San Felipe, had for four years been the proud possessor of a six-pound cannon. Ugartechea demanded that it be surrendered and sent Lieutenant Colonel Francisco Castañeda with two hundred cavalry to seize the piece. Texans gathered to repel this "invasion." When, September 20, Castañeda tried to cross the Guadalupe River, he met a hot fire from eighteen riflemen under Captain Albert Martin and fell back from the ford and camped on a hill.

That night 168 Texans, of whom fifty were mounted, led by Colonel John H. Moore, crossed the river to attack the Mexican position. At four o'clock on the morning of September 21, under a heavy fog, the assault began. With the disputed cannon booming in the center and the rifles of the Texans crackling, the Mexicans were routed and fled all the way back to San Antonio. A few of them remained behind, dead. The Texans lost not a man.

Militarily the affair at Gonzales was insignificant, but to the Texas revolution it was what the Battle of Lexington was to the American

War for Independence. Every Texan knew that from this time forth he would be treated as a rebel. There was no alternative but to fight.

Men came flocking to Gonzales, each bringing his own arms and ammunition—long rifles, chiefly, though some carried shotguns loaded with buckshot, a few bore muskets, and almost all had, sheathed at their hips, the sinister bowie knives which had become almost a symbol of the frontier fighting man. So many camped about the small town that Ugartechea, who was about to march with five hundred men to wipe out Castañeda's disgrace, decided not to attempt it.

From Goliad, on October 9, came word that Captain Collingsworth, with about fifty men, had by a surprise night attack captured that important point, which commanded lower Texas—and with it $10,000 in money for the payment of the Mexican troops, two pieces of artillery, three hundred stands of arms, and the entire garrison, including its commander, Lieutenant Colonel Sandoval.

Perhaps as important as any of the foregoing was the finding by Collingsworth's men of Colonel Ben Milam, hiding in a thicket. He was an *empresario*, and a veteran of the War of 1812, of the Mexican revolt against Iturbide, and of various Indian battles—a proved fighter and a man with capacity for leadership. Milam had been captured by Santa Anna's troops in Monclova, escaped from his prison in Monterrey, and had ridden six hundred miles through enemy country to join his fellow Texans.

Soon after, Austin arrived at Gonzales and was elected commanding general of the Texas army. It was an "army" by courtesy title only, for Austin had less than 350 men, ill armed and undisciplined, without organization, commissary or proper officers. He did what he could to form them into companies with commanders, to organize a commissary, and otherwise to bring order out of confusion; and on October 13 he moved south to the San Antonio River, where he took up a position eight miles below the capital and sent couriers to San Felipe begging for reinforcements.

Sam Houston and others had been appealing for aid in the United States—and not in vain. In New Orleans two companies of cavalry, calling themselves the New Orleans Grays, were sent to Texas at their own expense, while volunteers hurried in from elsewhere, notably Arkansas, Tennessee and Louisiana. Austin's army grew.

An interesting development of this period was the first organization of that famous body of fighting men known as the Texas Rangers. It was authorized by the Texas General Consultation at San Felipe, October 17, 1835, and was at first limited to three companies: one of twenty-five men under Silas M. Parker on the Indian frontier between the Brazos and the Trinity; a second under Harrison Greenwood, of ten men, patrolling east of the Trinity; and the third, of twenty-five men, under D. B. Frayer, to guard the territory between the Brazos and the Colorado. The organization would eventually take on far broader duties and grow in strength, and would win fame not shared by any other similar organization on the continent, save the Royal Canadian Northwest Mounted Police.

The Consultation also adopted a bill of rights, appointed Henry Smith governor, and outlined the powers of a provisional government in a declaration of twenty-one articles. It is to be noted that this was not a declaration of independence. Many of the delegates were in favor of that step, but the majority were not yet ready.

CHAPTER FIVE

"We Will Rather Die in These Ditches"

HAVING reached Salado Creek, which enters the San Antonio River just below San Antonio, Austin ran into excitement. One of his officers was Jim Bowie, now bearing the rank of colonel. A turbulent and restless adventurer, but a notable fighting man, Bowie did not enjoy the entire confidence of Austin, who regarded him as a disturbing influence.

Nevertheless, when it was necessary to send forward a scouting expedition of some peril, Austin selected Bowie for the task. So on October 27, with Captain James W. Fannin as second in command, and ninety-two men, Bowie rode out to reconnoiter the old missions which formed a sort of ring around San Antonio, and to find a suitable advanced camping place for the main army. His instructions were to choose the site, send back a messenger announcing its position, and await there the coming of Austin.

As ordered, the detachment advanced, encountered no enemies at the San Juan Capistrano and San José missions, and went on to Concepción mission, a two-towered century-old Franciscan church situated only about two miles south of San Antonio's main plaza. There Bowie chose a camp site in a bend of the San Antonio River, and sent back his courier to Austin, expecting immediate support.

But Austin failed to move as he had promised. That night Bowie lay with his small force in his terribly exposed position, wondering how soon the Mexicans would discover him. Morning came, with a heavy fog that obscured all vision. Suddenly a rifle cracked out—a warning signal from a sentry, placed in a tower of the mission. A Mexican force had arrived and was already deployed before them, pinning them against the river.

Bowie made his dispositions coolly. The shelving bank of the river behind his camp offered protection and there he posted some of his men. The rest, in two companies, he sent into the woods which stretched out on either side of a level plain in front like extending arms.

All at once the fog lifted. Before them, occupying the triangular plain between the wooded areas, Bowie's men saw the long rank of blue uniforms with white crossbelts in an X pattern—Mexican infantry. The Texans were in a trap from which they must fight their way out.

Frontier habits paid dividends. Many of the men that night had slept cold so that they might wrap their blankets about their guns against the foggy damp. The keen crackling of Texas long rifles sounded, and empty places began to appear in the blue line.

From the Mexican array crashed a heavy volley. Then a small brass cannon was wheeled forward and grapeshot began tearing through the woods.

Making his way through the timber in which Fannin's men lay firing, Bowie directed several sharpshooters to devote themselves to the cannoneers. Rifles began looking at the brass gun. Gunner after gunner spun to the ground, and the rest fell back, leaving the loaded cannon standing alone, far out ahead of the infantry line.

"Boys, let's get that gun!" shouted Bowie. Waving his great knife over his head, he bounded from the woods.

After him leaped his men. They did not march forward in an orderly line, according to the rules of the military textbooks then current. They ran, stopping now and then to fire with deadly effect, then dashing on again. Blue-clad Mexican soldiers in increasing numbers began to flop and kick on the ground.

First to reach the cannon, Bowie ordered it swung around, himself seized the burning fuse stick from the dead hand of the gunner who last had held it, and applied it to the vent.

At the roar of the gun a great hole was torn in the Mexican front. Onward whooped the Texans.

The Mexican soldiers, though well drilled in close-formation maneuvers, had little stomach for the fight. They were mostly impressed into the service, being convicts, or peons who had been waylaid and kidnaped, or vagrants forced to don uniforms. With sudden, overwhelming panic, they broke and stampeded before the Texas charge.

Jim Bowie had won the first pitched battle of the war. The Mexicans suffered a loss of sixty-seven killed and almost as many wounded, while the Texans had one dead and no wounded. The deadly shooting of the frontiersmen, the furious charge and the ferocious pursuit which followed foreshadowed once again the decisive Battle of San Jacinto.

After the battle Austin moved up the main army, but instead of occupying the ground defended by Bowie, he passed on north and took a position on the river above the city. Though he now had more than a thousand men, including the New Orleans Grays, he hesitated, too cautious to follow the urgings of his officers and attack the town itself. The indecision enabled General Martín Perfecto de Cos, Santa Anna's brother-in-law, who was now in command in San Antonio, to strengthen his position by barricading the streets, erecting batteries, and sending to Laredo for a reinforcement of five hundred more soldiers.

With all his great qualities, Austin was not by character a soldier. He spent his time quarreling with some of his commanders, once receiving—and refusing to accept—the resignation of Bowie, perhaps the best of them, while he lay idle, fearing that he could not long keep his army together.

Meanwhile the Consultation at San Felipe took some decisive actions. General Sam Houston was named commander-in-chief of all the Texas forces—over Austin's head—and Austin himself was appointed on a commission to visit the United States to gain help. It must have been a bitter disappointment to Austin. Smith was governor in his stead, and Houston commander-in-chief, replacing him. Nevertheless, with the patience and self-sacrifice which were his nature, he surrendered the command of the army before San Antonio to Colonel Edward Burleson, and on November 25 departed for his new duties.

The day following, November 26, there was another skirmish and again Bowie was the leader. Erastus Smith, better known as Deaf Smith, a giant who, in spite of defective hearing, was the army's best scout, brought word that a Mexican convoy of loaded pack mules was approaching San Antonio from the south. It was believed to be Ugartechea, returning from Laredo with the five hundred soldiers, and with pay for the troops.

Bowie galloped with his company to intercept them. Some shooting took place, the convoy was driven back, and when Cos sent out a detachment from the city to relieve it Colonel Burleson arrived with the main force of Texans and turned the affair into a rout. But when the loads of the pack mules were examined they did not contain silver, as expected, but only grass—fodder for the animals in the San Antonio garrison. This occasioned mirth among the Texans, and the sharp little battle has always been called "the Grass Fight."

Still the Texas army lay idle, and discontent grew. Tired of doing nothing, many of the free and easy "soldiers" walked out of camp and went home, until not more than eight hundred remained before San

Antonio. At last, December 3, Burleson announced that he intended to attack. This was received with enthusiasm by the army. Almost at once, however, Burleson rescinded his plan on the ground that the enemy had learned of it, and proposed instead to withdraw.

Before the men, drawn up in ranks, stepped Colonel Ben Milam, carrying his rifle on his shoulder. He waved his rakish hat and cried out in a humorous, drawling voice, "Who'll go with old Ben Milam into San Antonio?"

A roar greeted the words. Followed one of the strangest assaults in history. Virtually ignoring Burleson, the Texans moved forward the night of December 4 in two columns, led by Milam and Colonel Francis Johnson. Before dawn, December 5, the attack began. Military precedent was ignored, and each Texan was, in a manner of speaking, his own commander.

While Colonel J. C. Neill made a noisy diversion before the Alamo—the old mission church which had been converted into a fort—the attacking columns, carrying in addition to their firearms crowbars to break through the walls of adobe houses, surprised the garrison of San Antonio and gained entrance into the city.

A tremendous cannonade began, Cos directing his artillery to sweep the streets. But the Texans did not use the streets. Instead, they worked their way from one house to another, by opening holes through the soft adobe walls, and from the windows the deadly rifles did their work so effectively that several times that day enemy guns within range had to be abandoned.

Night came. The attackers strengthened their positions by opening trenches for communication and defense. With dawn the battle was resumed. Working their way steadily forward, the Texans penetrated almost to the *presidio,* the center of the Mexican defense.

During this assault Ben Milam, the moving spirit of the attack, while crossing the courtyard of the Veramendi house, was killed by a bullet which struck him in the head. But the Texans fought on. By night they were near the central square, making their progress from house to house, almost fighting their way from room to room.

The night of December 7 once more interrupted the fighting. In the darkness Ugartechea arrived with his reinforcements. The lack of quality in these is seen by the fact that four hundred of the soldiers were uniformed convicts, who had to be guarded on the march by the other hundred regular and trustworthy soldiers. Their arrival did not daunt the Texans, who with the first light of day began again their attack.

That morning of December 8 was signalized by a charge of the New Orleans Grays and a company from Brazoria, which captured buildings that commanded the plaza and the *presidio*. During this day intense cannonading continued. It did little harm to the attackers, but under its cover Cos withdrew from the city into the Alamo. His troops by this time were demoralized, many deserting and fleeing from the city. Disorganization grew so complete that on the morning of December 11 Cos sent a flag of truce to Burleson, and gave up the fort and city to the Texans.

In the four-day assault the Texans lost two killed and twenty-six wounded, while the defending Mexicans suffered casualties never fully enumerated, but estimated at between three hundred and four hundred, counting dead, wounded and desertions.

Cos marched south across the border into Mexico, having given his parole of honor that he would not again fight the Texans. He took with him 1105 men, provisioned but carrying no arms—except for the hundred regular soldiers who were to guard the convict troops. He had surrendered the city, the Alamo fortress, twenty-one pieces of artillery, five hundred muskets, much ammunition and other booty of military value.

As far as it went, the victory was complete. Not a Mexican soldier was now left north of the Rio Grande and many Texans were so sanguine as to believe the war was over. But their leaders, especially those who knew anything of the nature of Santa Anna, were under no such delusion. In addition to the rebellious nature of the capture of San Antonio, a personal affront had been given the Mexican dictator, for his brother-in-law, General Cos, had suffered a deep humiliation. Already Santa Anna had displayed bloodthirstiness in crushing a revolt in Zacatecas. He could be expected to be even more ferocious against the *Americano* Texans, whom he detested anyway.

One who realized the danger most keenly was Houston, who had the responsibility of rallying an army to meet the expected invasion. He had managed to get the Consultation to pass ordinances under which an army might be organized, including land bounties for soldiers who served in it. But the capture of San Antonio, rather than strengthening, seemed to weaken his position. He had not been present at the fighting. Not Houston, but Colonel Johnson and Dr. James Grant, an adventurer who had been wounded, were the idols of the army.

This pair, and many other officers and men, overconfident after the victory, began to propose an invasion of Mexico itself; to capture Matamoros and from it campaign into the country which, it was represented by schemers like Grant, contained thousands of "liberal Mexicans" who would rise to join them and sweep forward irresistibly with them, perhaps to the halls of the Montezumas themselves. Grant had a heavy personal interest in promoting such a campaign—he had mines below the Rio Grande which had been seized by Santa Anna, and he wanted the army to get them back for him.

Houston knew that the Mexicans would resent rather than rejoice at the projected invasion, and opposed the Matamoros expedition. So also did Bowie and many other thinking Texans, who knew the Mexican temperament. But the majority in the army—now increased by many new recruits—believed in an easy victory and a march supported by the spoils of rich cities: a looting expedition in every sense.

To check this move, Houston sent an order to Bowie to organize a force and proceed ahead of the army to Matamoros. At least a seizure of that city under Bowie's direction would be at the command of the recognized authorities. In some manner the order was not delivered to Bowie, so he did not move. Then a message came from Colonel Neill, who had been left in command of the Alamo with eighty men, mostly sick and wounded, that Johnson, Fannin and Grant already had marched with the army on their expedition.

A sorry and humiliating condition of affairs confronted the commander-in-chief at this news that he had lost his army. Houston rode hard to Goliad, where he found Bowie. He also found Grant, styling himself "Acting Commander-in-Chief," and the runaway army in high fettle, so cocksure and determined on its course that he did not even attempt to assert his authority as it marched away.

At this grave moment another messenger came spurring from Neill at the Alamo, saying that the Mexican army again was invading Texas, and Santa Anna in person, with a large force, was about to attack San Antonio.

The despairing Houston had only one man on the spot on whom he could depend—Bowie. Raking together a handful of men, about twenty in all, the commander-in-chief sent Bowie with them to San Antonio, with orders to demolish all fortifications, blow up the Alamo, abandon the place, and bring all cannon north for the use of the Texas defense.

While Bowie marched to take command of the Alamo under these orders, Houston rode on, overtaking the army at Refugio, where Colonel Johnson informed him that the General Consultation had deposed both Governor Smith and himself, and that Fannin was the new commander-in-chief.

There was little Sam Houston could do. He did what he could, addressing the soldiers with such a gloomy yet realistic picture of what they would face in Mexico that he greatly reduced the enthusiasm for the venture. Then he rode back to San Felipe. Deprived of his command, he announced himself as a candidate for the new convention which was to meet March 1 to reorganize the government. When beaten at one point, Houston was always ready to fight at another, and he had equal facility in politics and war.

Meantime Bowie, of whom Houston had written Governor Smith, "There is no man on whose forecast, prudence, and valor I place a higher estimate than Colonel Bowie," reached San Antonio. He conferred with Colonel Neill and saw that it would be impossible to transport the cannon. Furthermore, he became convinced that the Alamo was a key defense point, where Santa Anna might be checked. He perhaps felt also that he had some latitude to act, owing to Houston's removal from command.

He therefore took the responsibility of disobeying the orders given him and began to prepare the place for defense. On February 2, 1836, he sent to Governor Smith, who still held his office in the absence of a successor, the following message:

Relief at this post in men, money, and provisions, is of vital importance. The salvation of Texas depends on keeping Béxar out of the hands of the enemy. Colonel Neill and myself have come to the conclusion that we will rather die in these ditches than give up to the enemy. The citizens deserve our patriotism, and the public safety demands our lives rather than evacuate this post to the enemy. Again we call aloud for relief. Our force is small. The returns of the day show only 120 men and officers. It would be a waste of men to put our brave little band against thousands. I have information just now from a friend that the forces at Presidio is 2,000 complete. He states further that 5,000 more are a little back and marching on. The informant says that they intend to make a descent on this place in particular, and there is no doubt of it.

Thus was made the decision to fight it out at the Alamo, and Bowie made it. He generously gave equal credit to Colonel Neill, but that gentleman rather eliminated himself from the consideration shortly thereafter by taking leave and departing from the doomed place on a plea of illness in his family. On Bowie alone was the responsibility.

The harried Governor Smith did what he could to help the Alamo garrison. He could not give orders to officers with any assurance that they would be obeyed, but he wrote to William Barret Travis, now a lieutenant colonel and on recruiting duty, telling him to go to the Alamo with as many men as he could gather. Buck Travis disliked the assignment. Twice he wrote Smith, begging to be relieved of the order, once complaining that he was being "sacrificed," and once threatening to resign his commission. But in the end he unwillingly went, reaching San Antonio a few days after Bowie had written his decisive letter and bringing with him thirty men.

From the outset there was friction between Bowie and Travis. When he left the Alamo, Colonel Neill had taken it upon himself to "appoint" Travis to the command of the post—which he had no authority to do, since Bowie had written orders giving him that authority. The act created endless trouble. Travis was ambitious, a politico-soldier who possibly had his eye on future prestige, and he used Neill's unauthorized appointment to divide the loyalty of the men. In the end he was to prove himself flawless in bravery and self-sacrifice, but at this time his personal rivalry with Bowie took the form of letters of complaint to the governor, in which he accused Bowie of drinking too much, and of leaving him to shoulder the whole burden.

At this juncture an unexpected and welcome reinforcement of eighty men from Tennessee arrived, bear and deer hunters all, and led by one of the legendary characters of the frontier—Davy Crockett. The Tennessean and Bowie had heard of each other before, and from the beginning they were friends.

Crockett later told of how he asked to see the original hand-forged knife, and when Bowie handed it to him, he said, "Tarnation, if the very sight of it ain't enough to give a man a squeamish stomach, specially before breakfast."

To which Bowie replied, grinning, "You might tickle a fellow's ribs a long time with that before you'd make him laugh."

An election was held to settle the disputed question of command. The Tennesseans swung it in favor of Bowie. He was declared commander of all the volunteers and Travis commander of the "regulars and cavalry"—his own thirty men whom he had brought. Thenceforth they signed all orders and communications together.

But a stroke of fate intervened to put all authority in one man's hands and avert a divided command. While supervising the mounting of a cannon on the wall of the Alamo, Bowie made a misstep and fell fifteen feet to the ground. One hip was smashed and some ribs broken, evidently with a penetration of the lungs. Confined to a cot in the infirmary, with pneumonia setting in because of his lacerated lungs, Bowie could no longer be a leader. Travis took over.

Shortly thereafter, on February 23, the vanguard of Santa Anna's army, four thousand strong, appeared before the Alamo.

The Texas convention had begun to gather at Washington-on-the-Brazos—up the river from San Felipe—and the vanguard of refugees from the Mexican invasion was beginning to appear, when on February 28 a courier rode in with what has been called the most heroic message in American history. It was dated February 24, and read as follows:

Fellow Citizens and Compatriots: I am besieged by a thousand or more of Mexicans under Santa Anna. I have sustained a continual bombardment for twenty-four hours and have not lost a man. The enemy have demanded surrender at discretion; otherwise the garrison is to be put to the sword if the place is taken. I have answered the summons with a cannon shot and our flag still waves proudly from the walls. I shall never surrender or retreat. Then I call upon you, in the name of liberty, of patriotism, and of everything dear to the American character, to come to our aid with all dispatch. The enemy are receiving reinforcements daily and will no doubt increase to three or four thousand in four or five days. Though this call may be neglected, I am determined to sustain myself as long as possible and die like a soldier who never forgets what is due to his honor or that of his country. Victory or death!

W. Barret Travis, Lt. Col. Commanding

Thus the gallant Travis endorsed Jim Bowie's equally gallant decision to "die in these ditches," in order to halt, or at least delay, Santa Anna's overwhelming invasion.

After that, silence closed about the Alamo as far as the rest of Texas was concerned. March 1 came, and the convention went into session. Houston, attending as a delegate, was the dominating figure, his personality such that in that hour of great crisis all, even his enemies, turned despairingly to him.

A harebrained resolution to adjourn the convention and march in a body to the relief of the Alamo was defeated by Houston, who was grimly determined to have here created a government, without which to fight a war would be impossible. Through the first night, with a "blue norther" howling down so that they shivered in the unheated cabin where they worked, the delegates labored. Next morning, March 2, they completed a declaration of independence, by which all political connection with Mexico was ended, and Texas proclaimed a free, sovereign and independent nation.

In its statement of grievances, the document included charges of despotism of the sword and priesthood; unlawful overturn of the constitution of 1824; depriving the colonists of the right of trial by jury and representation in the legislatures; inciting the savages to massacre inhabitants on the frontier; and armed invasion of Texas for the purpose of driving the colonists from their homes.

The declaration was adopted and signed without a dissenting vote, and on it Houston's signature was the most prominent. Among the signatories were three Mexicans of prominent family and political influence, Antonio Navarro, Lorenzo de Zavala and Francisco Ruiz.

Two days later General Sam Houston was once more appointed—this time unanimously—commander-in-chief of the Texas military forces.

CHAPTER SIX

Santa Anna's Blood Bath

A DREAD though heroic tragedy was being enacted at the Alamo. The mission, which stood across the river and just east of San Antonio, was poorly designed for a fort. Its main plaza was a long parallelogram, about 50 by 150 yards in extent, with the major axis north and south, enclosed by a wall of adobe bricks eight feet high and three feet thick. Within the west wall stood a row of one-story buildings, and at the middle of the east wall a two-story convent. East of the convent was a yard, enclosed by an embankment built by the Mexicans under General Cos during the Texan siege of San Antonio, and southeast of this second enclosure stood the church, built of stone, cruciform and properly oriented, its walls five feet thick and two stories high. The church had long been dismantled and part of its roof had fallen in. A log stockade connected the corner of the church with the corner of the main plaza wall. Along these defenses at various places were distributed fourteen pieces of the artillery captured from Cos.

Military experts have agreed that it would have required at least a thousand soldiers to man properly the extensive walls of the Alamo. Yet the garrison consisted of less than 190, including Crockett's Tennesseans and thirty-two brave volunteers from Gonzales, who cut their way through the Mexican lines to join the defenders. The exact number is not known: according to various counts, it ranges from 181 to 187. Seven of these were Mexicans, fighting valorously with the Texas-Americans against the oppressor. Man for man, the Alamo's defenders were as courageous and deadly a group of fighters as then existed, but they were far too few.

From the first day of the investment, the defenders knew what their fate would be, for on that day, February 23, Santa Anna displayed on the tower of San Fernando church, in full view of the Alamo, the blood-red flag that signified "no quarter."

There was some bombardment and skirmishing but no direct assault in the days that Santa Anna waited for the bulk of his army and his artillery to come up. Though the walls were thin and of adobe, the cannon did not greatly damage them because they were light field-pieces rather than siege guns. By March 3—the day after the Texas declaration of independence—the Mexican dictator had completed his dispositions. On that day the last courier went out from the Alamo. He was Captain John W. Smith. The following day he reached Washington-on-the-Brazos, and the convention gathered to hear the message. A few lines reveal the feelings of Travis, who wrote it:

"The spirits of my men are still high, although they have had much to depress them. . . . Col. Fannin is said to be on the march to this place . . . but I fear it is not true, as I have repeatedly sent to him for aid without receiving any. . . . I hope your honorable body will hasten on reinforcements. . . . Our supply of ammunition is limited."

The reference to Fannin needs elaboration. He did not, after all, accompany Johnson and Grant toward Matamoros but, considerably chastened in spirits, begged Houston to permit him to redeem himself as an obedient "company officer." Repeated messages came to him at Goliad from Travis, imploring assistance; and as he had under him at the time 402 men, he might have changed the course of events at the Alamo. But he seemed rooted by indecision to Goliad. Once he began a march with part of his forces, but returned to Goliad quickly, explaining that he did not have sufficient provisions.

It was Colonel James Butler Bonham, a South Carolinian and a personal friend of Travis, who on this last occasion brought the appeal for help. Fannin tried to persuade Bonham to stay with him, but the courier, a magnificent horseman, said, "I will report to Travis or die in the attempt." After a long and very dangerous ride he actually succeeded, at one o'clock on the morning of March 3, in reaching the Alamo, where he must have known he faced certain death.

The news Bonham brought of Fannin's return to Goliad convinced Travis that hope was ended. That was the day called by Sidney Lanier "one of the most pathetic days of time," when the legendary drama occurred within the walls of the Alamo. Travis, according to tradition, assembled his men in ranks, explained to them the doom that awaited them and that he no longer hoped for aid. He added that he left each man to his own choice, but would himself remain and die in the fort. Then, with his sword, he drew a line on the ground, and invited those who would die with him to step across it.

They stepped across—every man but one. Even Bowie, who had been carried out on his cot, dying from pneumonia and helpless with his smashed hip, asked that his cot be lifted across the line. The one who did not cross was Moses Rose, who climbed the wall and succeeded in making his escape, to bring the story to the world. It has been discredited by some historians and upheld by others. But even those who say it is not proved fact, being based on a story published many years after, agree that it is at least plausible. Certainly it is a part of the heroic legend of the Alamo.

His main army having arrived, and rested for three days, Santa Anna ordered the stubborn Alamo to be taken by direct assault, a decision later condemned even by Mexican writers, such as General Vicente Filisola, who wrote:

"In our opinion the blood of our soldiers as well as that of the enemy was shed in vain, for the mere gratification of the inconsiderate, puerile, and guilty vanity of reconquering Béxar by force of arms, and through a bloody contest."

The night of March 5 the Mexican dictator formed his infantry into four columns for the attack. One was commanded by General Cos—who had broken his parole of honor. Another was led by Colonel Francisco Duque, a third by Colonel José Romero, and the fourth by Colonel José Morales. The cavalry, under General Ramirez y Sesma, was arranged at places in the rear of these columns, to prevent escape of any fugitives from the Alamo—and, incidentally, to prevent their own troops from fleeing, if a rout occurred.

At three o'clock the morning of March 6, without any preparation by artillery, the four-pronged assault began. Francisco Ruiz, the *alcalde* of San Antonio, who witnessed the entire battle, stated in writing that four thousand men took part in the attack. They were provided with scaling ladders, axes and crowbars, in addition to their weapons.

Shouts of the Mexican soldiers crying *"Viva Santa Anna!"* must have been the first warnings to the defenders. Immediately every able-bodied man in the Alamo was at his post. The sinister assassin notes of the *degüello*—a bugle call meaning "no quarter"—announced the charge. Then through the gloom the Mexican columns were seen approaching.

The principal assault was against the north wall—the weakest part of the Alamo's too extended defenses. It was led by Colonel Duque. Simultaneous attacks were directed against the east and west walls, and from the south on the church and convent yard.

From the Alamo every piece of artillery slammed grapeshot and the snarling rifles of the Texans and Tennesseans began spraying death. Forward rolled the dark lines of Santa Anna; then hesitated; and finally recoiled in retreat.

The first attack had been repulsed; the ground was covered with Mexican wounded and dead. The east and west columns of assault fell back toward the north, and Colonel Duque, a gallant officer, formed them on his own brigade.

Again the Mexicans charged, and once more the Texas rifles began their crackling. So rapid was the fire that, according to Santa Anna's own report, it "illuminated the interior of the fortress and its walls and ditches." Colonel Duque, leading his men, was mortally wounded. The second Mexican attack swirled up to the walls, halted before the deadly blast of Texas lead, and fell back.

Now the fatal weakness of the Alamo became apparent. The thinning numbers of Travis' men were not sufficient to defend the walls. Santa Anna rushed forward his reserves and the increased attacking forces once more returned to the assault, coming at several points at once.

Crockett and his Tennesseans fought behind the log stockade that connected the church with the plaza. Travis himself directed the artillery. This time the attack, overwhelming in its weight and numbers, was pressed remorselessly home. As the Mexican troops reached the walls the cannon were rendered useless because their muzzles could not be sufficiently depressed to bear on the assailants. The few Texans, scattered along the walls, suffered heavily for, as Filisola said in his later account of the battle, "because the wall having no inner banquette, [the defenders] had, in order to deliver their fire, to stand on top where they could not live one second."

Over the west barricades of the plaza lapped the Mexican horde; and turned the cannon on that side against the houses along the eastern wall where some of the defenders had taken refuge. Travis died, shot through the brain and falling across the trail of a cannon he was trying to fire. Bonham, also serving a gun, was likewise slain. Crockett, hemmed in, his men all dead about him, fought like a cornered wolf, using his clubbed rifle to smash heads until he was bayoneted.

The Mexicans burst into the church, which was the last redoubt, and the wounded and those fighting within it were ruthlessly slaughtered. It is probable that the last fighting man in the Alamo was Jim Bowie. His cot was in the baptistery of the church, where he lay coughing and spitting blood, very weak, but indomitable, with four pistols and his famous knife beside him. The Mexicans broke in the door. How many of them died before they reached him is a matter of dispute; it ranges from two to nine, according to different accounts. In the end they got Bowie. Five bayonets impaled him; one, through the neck, breaking off short and pinning him to his bed. Then they lifted the magnificent dead body on their bayonets and carried it out, dumping it on the ground.

Lieutenant Governor James W. Robinson of Texas, who made an investigation based on the testimony of all available witnesses—a few women and children, and a slave, who were spared—was convinced that Bowie was the last fighting man in the Alamo. Others died after him, but these were fugitives, no longer fighting, hunted out where they sought refuge, dragged forward, and slaughtered.

When it was over Santa Anna viewed the carnage with mixed feelings. There were, according to Ruiz, the *alcalde*, 182 dead Texans. *El Presidente* ordered them burned, and Ruiz was told to oversee the task of gathering them up and consuming them on two huge funeral pyres, so he had the best chance to make a complete count.

Santa Anna asked to be shown the bodies of Travis, Crockett and Bowie. He had been godfather to Bowie's wife, Ursula de Veramendi, and when he saw the dead man, he said, *"Era hombre muy valiente, no déjale como un perro* [This was a very valiant man, he ought not to be treated like a dog]." Then he changed his mind, shrugged his shoulders, and added, *"Pero no importe; échale dentro* [But it's of no importance; throw him in]." So Bowie's body was consumed on the pyre with his comrades, as no doubt he would have preferred.

Santa Anna had wiped out the Texans; but when he looked over his own army, the results must have shocked him. He admitted later that he lost 600 killed and wounded, but his total loss must have been much greater. Ruiz, who had charge of disposing of the Mexican bodies as well as burning the Texans, said the Mexican loss was 1600 killed and wounded. After the Battle of San Jacinto, Ramón Caro, Santa Anna's private secretary, who was captured, made the following statement which has the flavor of authenticity, since Caro certainly knew his chief's personal records and correspondence:

"We brought to San Antonio more than 5,000 men and we lost during the siege 1,544 of the best of them. The Texans fought more like devils than like men."

Part of the Mexican loss was due to their own gunfire, for the arrangement of the assault was such that sometimes Mexican columns were cross-firing into each other. Ruiz, finding himself unable to bury all the Mexican bodies, had many of them thrown into the San Antonio River. For weeks afterward great flocks of buzzards hung over the city and river, feeding on the corpses that lodged against the banks, and many people left the city, fearing a pestilence.

Some military writers have said that the Alamo was a useless sacrifice. But others have pointed out that Santa Anna's forces suffered a serious loss in morale from the battle; that he was forced to reorganize his units; and that the loss of so many of his best troops weakened some of his enterprises afterward. At a minimum, the heroes of the Alamo bought the time which gave the convention its chance to make the all-important declaration of independence and the constitution of legal authority to which Houston relentlessly led it. And the cry, "Remember the Alamo!" was of priceless value in giving fury to Texas arms in future conflict.

Houston received first news of the fall of the Alamo at Gonzales, where he went after his appointment as commander-in-chief. He hurried orders to Fannin, at Goliad, to blow up his defenses and retreat; and in a letter to a friend he severely censured Fannin for failing to relieve the Alamo. Fannin failed to move as ordered. At Gonzales Houston gathered up a small force of 374 men, camped under the command of Colonel Moseley Baker, which was rapidly increased by volunteers who came hurrying in.

Word came that Fannin, after all his vacillations, had decided to remain and defend Goliad. When he heard it, Houston, with a groan, gestured at his handful of men and remarked, "*There* is the last hope of Texas. We shall never see Fannin, or his men."

The prediction was correct. Poor Fannin could not make up his mind and he and his men died for it.

Farther south, Grant and Johnson, with what remained of their "invading force," were experiencing fatal vicissitudes. These two had intended to capture Matamoros but the effect of Houston's oratory at Refugio had so dampened the ardor of their followers that most of the latter abandoned the invasion project. On March 2, General José Urrea, with one of Santa Anna's columns, surprised Grant on the Nueces River. The flamboyant physician and forty-one of his men were lanced to death. Only one of the company survived, Rueben R. Brown, who was saved by the intercession of a priest and a Mexican woman, and eventually escaped to bring the story to the Texas lines.

Johnson, at San Patricio, was attacked the morning of February 27 in a driving rain. Though his men fought stubbornly the place was carried. Forty Texans died in the defense, but Johnson and three companions managed to escape. Johnson afterward wrote a memoir of this ill-fated and ill-advised expedition and a history of the early Texas republic.

In his cleaning-up operation, Urrea continued northward toward Fannin's post at Goliad. He had between nine hundred and a thousand men, against whom Fannin, who now had about five hundred men, might successfully have defended himself. Unfortunately Fannin took this time to divide his forces.

He sent Captain King with 28 men to bring away several terrified families of Texans at Refugio; then sent Colonel Ward with 120 men to rescue King.

Unhappily for this movement, Urrea was a skillful and decisive officer. He attacked Ward and King, killed the latter and many of the Texans; and, though he suffered severe losses himself, forced Ward, who had retreated into a swamp, to surrender, when his men exhausted their ammunition. The prisoners were taken to Goliad by the victorious Mexicans.

When Fannin learned the fate of Ward and King, March 17, he changed his mind once more. He now began to retreat from Goliad as Houston had directed him to do in a dispatch three days before. But he had waited too long. The enemy appeared in force March 19 and when Fannin began to fall back it was in the face of the opposing army. He had now only about three hundred men and nine pieces of artillery, having frittered away the rest of his force. Though he made his withdrawal safely under cover of a fog, he failed to use the ordinary military precautions of scouts and outriders. Suddenly, near the Coleto River, he found himself surrounded by overwhelmingly larger forces.

Nevertheless he prepared to fight. His soldiers, consisting chiefly of several companies from the United States with high-sounding names—the Red Rovers, the New Orleans Grays, the Kentucky Mustangs, the Mobile Grays and so on—were formed in a hollow square. Urrea attacked. Three times his troops were beaten back. Night came, but when the main battle ceased, Campeachy Indian auxiliaries crept forward in the long grass and harassed the Texans with destructive fire, wounding Fannin himself.

Morning dawned at length—Sunday, March 20. With its early light a strong reinforcement was seen coming up to join the Mexicans. After some fighting Fannin surrendered, on the promise the lives of his men and himself would be spared. The Texans were marched to Goliad, where they joined as prisoners the survivors of Ward's detachment.

Santa Anna, who was still at San Antonio, was apprised by Urrea of his success. Some time prior to his invasion of Texas the dictator had caused a law to be passed by the Mexican Congress, by which all foreigners found in Mexico with arms in their possession were considered pirates, to be punished as such. Many of Fannin's men, from Tennessee, Kentucky, Mississippi or Louisiana, fell under this heading. Santa Anna sent an order to Lieutenant Colonel Nicolás de la Portilla, whom Urrea had left in command at Goliad, to execute the prisoners.

His officers were horrified. Urrea, who had outmaneuvered and captured the Texans, personally asked mercy for them—and received for doing so a sharp reprimand. Portilla, directly commanded to perform the executions, hesitated and spent a whole night wrestling with his conscience and his duty, before he decided to follow what were, indeed, peremptory orders. Colonel Garay withdrew four Texan doctors from the hospital and, with one company of Texans which did not come within the massacre orders, held them apart; and even concealed two doomed soldiers in his own tent to save their lives. Señora Alvarez, a Mexican woman, hid several men in her home, so that they escaped.

But as to Santa Anna, Hubert Howe Bancroft, the historian, wrote,

"No ray of mercy or of pity illumined the dark and cruel soul of the general-in-chief. He was the incarnation of an inhumanity at once revengeful and cowardly. The slaughter of his troops at the Alamo still rankled in his mind, and he would not have spared a single life."

What followed was the worst of the crimes charged against Santa Anna. On the morning of March 27, Palm Sunday, the Texas-American prisoners were marched out of their barracks. Knowing nothing of their doom, they were in good spirits, expecting soon to be allowed to return to their homes.

Instead, guarded by files of soldiers, they were led into a field and there halted. At a sudden order, the soldiers raised their muskets and began shooting down the unarmed victims. Most fell at the first treacherous fire. A few tried to escape but were mercilessly hunted down. Those who were wounded were put to death. Fannin and Ward were both shot, their bodies left to the wolves and vultures. In this massacre more than three hundred men were murdered without warning; and without sentence being pronounced upon them.

Santa Anna, with the Alamo reduced, Johnson's and Grant's men slain, and Fannin's force massacred, possibly believed that the war was over and Texas under his foot. But there was another with different thoughts.

Sam Houston was yet in the field. Though he had only a handful of men and no supplies, he still had to be defeated.

CHAPTER SEVEN

"Remember the Alamo!"

WITH the fall of the Alamo and Fannin's failure to join him at Gonzales, Houston had but one alternative. Mexican forces to the south and west were too great for him to face with the little force he had called "the last hope of Texas." He must keep this small handful from being engulfed with the others, and use it as a nucleus with which to build an army that might have some chance against Santa Anna's thousands.

Retreat was his only possible strategy. He did not yet know what had happened to Fannin, but by withdrawing he could hope for two advantages: as he passed through east Texas he might pick up additional men and arms; and by drawing on Santa Anna into lengthening his lines of communication, he might weaken the Mexican forces through the necessity of leaving garrisons and the difficulty of transporting supplies, artillery and ammunition.

Yet retreat would not be popular. He would have to abandon Texas towns and plantations to an enemy who looted and destroyed invariably. Furthermore, the Texas instinct was to stand and fight, whatever the odds—a headlong trait exemplified by Travis, Bowie and Fannin, with results so disastrous that of all the available men under arms and regularly organized in Texas, totaling perhaps eleven hundred, more than seven hundred had been lost at the Alamo, Goliad and San Patricio.

Houston was almost the only man in Texas with any conception of strategy as against tactics. He was so much alone in having military training that in his little army only he knew how to play the usual signals on a drum, and it was the general who acted as drummer boy in the Texas camp and on the march.

He gave the order to retreat. Almost instantly it set in motion what Texans still call "the Runaway Scrape." The families at Gonzales—thirty of which had lost fathers and husbands at the Alamo—accompanied Houston's army with what they could carry in baggage wagons. The "government," headed by the new president, David G. Burnet, a Bible-reading adventurer who had been an *empresario*, decamped in some trepidation to Harrisburg, on Buffalo Bayou, which ran into Galveston Bay. Everyone else in Texas seemed to be running also. Wagons, carts and animals, bearing women and children and household effects, choked the muddy roads in terrified flight from the Mexicans. Behind the refugees columns of smoke showed where homes and property were being destroyed by the invaders.

As the army left Gonzales a series of explosions was heard. A momentary panic—Santa Anna's artillery must be coming up! But Houston smiled and shook his head. Some overzealous persons had poisoned a quantity of liquor and left it, hoping the Mexicans would drink it. Houston had his own ideas of the conduct of civilized war. He had detailed Deaf Smith and a rear guard to gather that liquor and blow it up.

Hampered by the fleeing settlers, his army angry and humiliated by the retreat and almost insubordinate, the general doggedly continued his withdrawal, explaining his plans to nobody. He did, however, seek to encourage his men, who by now numbered some four hundred. Riding beside his column, as if counting them, he said to them, "We are on the rise of eight hundred strong and with a good position can whip ten to one of the enemy."

Probably nobody believed him, but his cheerfulness and courage won the loyalty of most of his men. Some deserted in discouragement, but more came in. By the time he reached the Colorado River, where he remained several days to see that every refugee family was safely across, he had about seven hundred in his "army," and had sent his aide-de-camp, William T. Austin, far ahead to the mouth of the Brazos, to fetch from there cannon and ammunition. He meant to fight—when conditions made it possible. And not before, no matter what anyone might say or think.

He was still at Beason's Crossing of the Colorado on March 23, when the advance guard of the pursuing Mexicans, under Generals Sesma and Woll, reached the river and camped across it, about two miles above him. Detachments under Captain Karnes and Colonel Sherman were sent to prevent their crossing, and for six days the Texas and Mexican forces lay in striking distance of each other, with only one skirmish, in which Karnes's men killed one Mexican and captured another.

Houston's forces were increasing daily. By March 25 he had more than a thousand men. Sesma and Woll, with only about eight hundred, preferred to wait for their main body before attacking him.

In his army orders of March 21, Houston had said, "In a few days I hope to have force sufficient to capture the enemy before he can reach the Guadalupe." And he told Captain Shape to "tell the people not to run any farther . . . there would be no more retreating; and that the next news they will hear from the army would be of a battle, the result of which no one could doubt."

This sounded like immediate action along the Colorado. But on March 25 dread news came. A man named Peter Kerr rode in to tell of the capture and massacre of Fannin's command at Goliad. It ended the last hope of junction with that force; and furthermore it indicated that Urrea, the victor over Johnson, Grant and Fannin, must be pressing close on the Texans' rear. While Houston might have beaten Sesma and Woll, such a victory would not have been decisive, for he dared not pursue them under present conditions.

He therefore ordered another retirement March 26. The command was received with bitter dissatisfaction by his men, who wanted to fight, and had no conception of the problems being faced by their general. Many asked furloughs to move their families to places of safety. Houston invariably granted these requests. As his retreat continued, more and more asked, until his force was reduced by half. And when he reached San Felipe and decided to leave it and move up the Brazos River, there was outright insubordination.

Many of the angry Texans said that the chief settlements which should be protected were *down* this river, instead of up; and two companies, under Colonel Moseley Baker and Captain Wylie Martin, refused to come into line.

Houston knew all too well the weakness of his position. The "authority" by which he acted as "commander-in-chief" was, at the moment, almost as shadowy as the future of Texas appeared to be. Thus far he had kept his army together solely by force of personality, and he could not risk a clash which might divide the loyalties of his men, for he was in no position to deal with mutiny.

He therefore made as much of a virtue of necessity as he could, gave "orders" to Baker to guard the crossing at San Felipe, and to Martin to go downstream—in other words to do exactly what they wanted to do—and with only 520 men remaining to him, pursued his own plan. On March 31 he camped on the right bank of the Brazos, opposite Groce's plantation, where he planned to cross. But exceptionally heavy rains raised the river to a height never known before, so high that the Texan camp ground was at one time converted into an island by the flood and there was no possibility of crossing it until the waters receded, which was not until April 13.

Meantime Sesma and Woll were reinforced at the Colorado by a force under General Tolsa, raising their division to fourteen hundred men. Sesma, the chief commander, decided he was strong enough to pursue the Texans and crossed his force over the river in rafts.

This was a time of peril for Houston, caught with reduced forces on the wrong side of the Brazos. Fortunately, however, Sesma received orders to wait for Santa Anna, who had decided to take personal charge of pursuing and annihilating the last Texas military force.

El Presidente, flushed with the success of his early operations, had been a little surprised to learn that there still remained a stubborn concentration of insurgents in the Colorado and Brazos area. With his peculiar vanity, he wanted to be present and take all the credit for finally crushing the rebels. He had also a feeling, perhaps, that his own role thus far had been none too brilliant or admirable. His useless battering against the Alamo, with the loss of a large part of his best army, when he might easily have reduced it by starvation, smacked of bad strategy; and revealed a kind of arrogant impatience as well as a disregard for human life. He must have known that his own officers, such as Generals Filisola and Urrea, were criticizing his wasteful and bloody tactics. Furthermore, his massacres of prisoners who fell into his hands found dissent among his best officers and many influential Mexicans in private life. To a nature like his, such censure, even though not openly spoken but only felt by him, would further stimulate his fury against the Texans who, in one way or another, had placed

him in a bad light. All in all, *El Presidente* felt he needed to recoup his
lost prestige by obliterating personally the last of the rebels.

This vanity saved Houston, who had sufficient time to get over the
Brazos before he was caught by overwhelming forces, and further to
build up his army beyond that flooded river.

Santa Anna started from San Antonio, where he had been reorganiz-
ing his forces, with his army proceeding in three divisions to sweep up
all possible lingering insurgent bands and concentrate with the advance division under General Sesma. General Ganoa took the northern
route, crossing the Colorado at Bastrop. Urrea marched by the southern coastal route, to take possession of Matagorda. Santa Anna, with
his staff, including General Filisola, and a considerable part of the
army, took the most direct, central route, by way of Gonzales and San
Felipe, to join Sesma and proceed—as he believed—triumphantly on.

Now Houston's strategy—to drain the Mexican strength in the Texas
distances—at last began to tell. The rains which had held him at the
Brazos continued and proved now as much of a help as they had been
a hindrance. Finding the Guadalupe too swollen to move his main
command across it, Santa Anna left it with Filisola, who was to bring
it along as soon as possible, and with only his staff and an escort proceeded rapidly to join Sesma.

Meantime his left wing, under Ganoa, after crossing the Colorado,
became entangled in the canyons, mesquite and mud of the intervening
country, lost its way, and failed to arrive at the concentration point
until too late. Urrea, with the right wing, found Matagorda vacated
and marched on down the coast, capturing Brazoria April 22, with a
large quantity of supplies and goods. Urrea was the best of Santa
Anna's commanders, and the celerity of his march was in itself excellent; but its very boldness placed him out of the immediate field of
action.

Filisola took days getting the central army across the Guadalupe to
follow his commander. And Santa Anna, having found Sesma's advance
division, impatiently began pressing forward with it, his impatience
increased by the report that the Texas seat of government had been
moved to Harrisburg, on Galveston Bay. If he could capture the president and congress of the rebellious state and neatly execute them, he
might end the revolution at a single stroke.

Baker's detachment opposed his crossing at San Felipe. Leaving
Sesma with 489 men to occupy the colony's capital and with orders to
follow as soon as Filisola came up with the main command, Santa
Anna proceeded down the river and put his force of 700 men and a
six-pounder gun across at a point where Wylie Martin's force was too

weak to prevent him. From there, by forced marches, Santa Anna proceeded to Harrisburg.

Only another very prompt decampment by the Texas government prevented his capturing it. President Burnet, indeed, almost was overtaken by a flying squadron of Mexican lancers early on the morning of April 17; but he displayed considerable nimble-footedness on this occasion, and with his cabinet and congress managed to get across the bay to Galveston Island, where, at the extremest limit of Texas, the forlorn government again set itself up and waited anxiously for news from Houston.

Santa Anna burned Harrisburg to the ground. His only captives were three printers. From them he learned that Houston and the Texas army were near; and also—this was mere rumor—that Houston intended to fall back to the Sabine River, at the border of Texas, where he expected to be reinforced by volunteers from the United States and make his final stand. Houston actually never had this design, but he did not deny it, and report of it, reaching Santa Anna, affected the latter's movements, since he expected to have to extend his pursuit farther.

While *El Presidente* was thus marching his forces across Texas, Houston experienced troubles sufficiently serious. He himself beat the reveille and mess calls, as well as all other signals, on an old drum—the only one in camp. He also turned his hand to many other tasks usually assigned to subordinates, including helping the farriers in repairing rolling stock and in cutting up old horseshoes for artillery ammunition.

A young recruit complained to a blacksmith he saw working at an improvised forge that the lock on his gun would not work.

"Leave it and come back in an hour," said the smith.

Later the youth returned with a stammered apology. "I was told you were the blacksmith, sir. I didn't know you were the commanding general."

"You were told quite right," said Sam Houston. "I'm a damned good blacksmith. Here's your gun. The lock works all right now."

But there were greater problems. Part of the army was almost mutinous. President Burnet was Houston's enemy, continuously wrote critical letters, and even kept a spy in camp to report on the general.

When things reached a crisis, Houston caused two graves to be dug and nailed notices to the trees at the foot of which they lay, to the effect that they would be occupied by the first men who mutinied. It quieted the threatened insubordination and, when he ordered, the men marched. Another triumph of personality could be chalked up for Houston, for he was not even backed by a shadow government now, since it was no secret that the president of the republic wished to have him replaced by a commander who "would fight."

At last Houston received two field pieces—six-pounders which his men christened the Twin Sisters—and volunteers came drifting in, making up for the defections in his ranks and more, so that he had perhaps eight hundred men. Some of these, among themselves, accused him of incompetence, timidity or worse. Burnet's spy, in a letter to the president—which was intercepted—quoted a report that Houston had "given up drunkenness in favor of the opium habit." Yet in spite of all the discontent and criticism, Sam Houston somehow compelled his men to march through the incessant rain and mud, explaining himself to nobody, telling them nothing.

He arrived at Buffalo Bayou, opposite Harrisburg, April 18. The town was in ruins, still smoldering. Santa Anna had been there only the day before.

That evening the indefatigable Deaf Smith and a few scouts swam the bayou and captured two prisoners, one of them a courier. The saddlebags of the courier bore the name of W. B. Travis—a memento of the Alamo. But the saddlebags contained something more important at the moment—letters to Santa Anna from Filisola, who was marching to join his chief. For the first time Houston learned that the Mexican force immediately confronting him was commanded in person by the dictator.

It crystallized his determination. Other armies were converging on him and there was risk in fighting just at this point. But the archenemy was there—just on the other side of the river. Houston would seek personal conclusions with Santa Anna.

The morning of April 19 he assembled his soldiers and made a short speech, telling them that Santa Anna, the murderer of their comrades, was across the bayou and that they were to cross and meet him. He concluded his speech with these words:

"The army will cross, and we will meet the enemy. Some of us may be killed, must be killed; but, soldiers, remember the Alamo! The Alamo! The Alamo!"

The army took up the words with a roar. *"Remember the Alamo!"*

Texas at last had a battle cry.

Leaving his sick and the baggage with a small guard, Houston moved down the bayou two miles and got his army across, using an old boat and the floor torn from a cabin which served as a raft, the horses swimming. By nightfall the crossing was complete and in the darkness the Texans pushed forward to Lynch's Ferry—toward which Santa Anna also was marching, from the south. Houston reached the ferry first; and captured a boatload of flour which, with some cattle that were grazing in the vicinity, provided his men with a welcome barbecue to strengthen them for the battle to come.

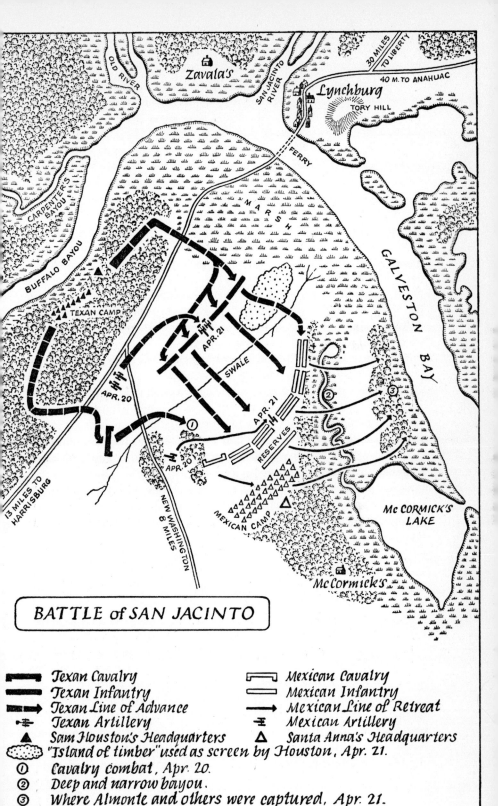

BATTLE of SAN JACINTO

Zavala's

OLD RIVER

SAN JACINTO RIVER

30 MILES TO LIBERTY

40 M. TO ANAHUAC

Lynchburg

TORY HILL

FERRY

MARSH

CARPENTERS BAYOU

BUFFALO BAYOU

TEXAN CAMP

APR. 21

APR. 20

SWALE

GALVESTON BAY

APR. 21

APR. 20

①

APR. 20

②

③

RESERVES

13 MILES TO HARRISBURG

NEW WASHINGTON 8 MILES

MEXICAN CAMP

McCORMICK'S LAKE

McCORMICK'S

▬▬ Texan Cavalry	⊏▭⊐ Mexican Cavalry
◤ Texan Infantry	▭ Mexican Infantry
➤ Texan Line of Advance	→ Mexican Line of Retreat
⅏ Texan Artillery	⚑ Mexican Artillery
▲ Sam Houston's Headquarters	△ Santa Anna's Headquarters
☁ "Island of timber" used as screen by Houston, Apr. 21.	
① Cavalry combat, Apr. 20.	
② Deep and narrow bayou.	
③ Where Almonte and others were captured, Apr. 21.	

With a choice of positions, Houston arranged his men in a fine belt of timber which ran along Buffalo Bayou just above the place where the San Jacinto River ran into it and very close to Galveston Bay. In front of the position was an open prairie broken by a few clumps of trees; to its left a marsh prevented its being flanked; and behind it ran Buffalo Bayou itself. It was a position from which there could be no retreat and Houston's selection of it proved his deadly determination to conquer at this point or perish with his army.

About two o'clock in the afternoon of that day, April 20, Santa Anna's vanguard appeared. *El Presidente,* who had been at the hamlet of New Washington the previous night, had a bad scare when a false report came that Houston was upon him. He is said to have ridden like a madman out of the town, crying out at the top of his voice that the enemy was coming and knocking down and riding over people in the street as he galloped out of the place. He was tactfully informed that the report was unfounded and, somewhat shamefaced, formed a column and marched toward Lynch's Ferry.

Near there he at last found Houston. There was a brief skirmish, in which the Texas guns called the Twin Sisters disabled the one Mexican piece of artillery and a few men fell on each side. Colonel Sidney Sherman—who was Burnet's candidate to succeed Houston as commander-in-chief—made a charge to capture the Mexican gun and failed. It was just the chance Houston had been awaiting. He gave Sherman a tongue-lashing which was heard by the whole army and took away from him the command of the cavalry—consisting of fifty-three mounted men. In his place he promoted to colonel a private with the flamboyant name of Mirabeau Buonaparte Lamar, and put him in command of the mounted force. It was the beginning of a career for Lamar, who would one day become president of the Texas republic on the strength of this day.

Night fell. The Mexicans camped to the southeast, across the plain, with the marsh to their right and a wooded ravine to their left. Morning dawned with no movement from either army. For some reason Houston was waiting—nobody knew why—and again there was bitter complaint from the men, who were anxious to get at their enemies.

In the middle of the morning Deaf Smith rode into camp, saying that reinforcements were arriving for Santa Anna. Houston spoke to him aside and the scout went out again. As Houston watched him go, he remarked aloud, so that a group of soldiers heard him, that it wasn't often that Deaf Smith got fooled like that—Santa Anna had been marching his men around a grove of trees to make it look like a reinforcement. Smith came back at a gallop and said that the general was right—the whole thing was a fraud and no reinforcements had come.

But, having thus carried out Houston's instructions, he privately told him that it *was* a reinforcement—General Cos, with 500 soldiers, raising Santa Anna's force to 1300 men, against whom the Texans could oppose exactly 783 men.

Later, Houston told Santa Anna that the reason he did not attack before the arrival of Cos was that he did not want to make "two bites of one cherry."

As a precaution—to prevent Filisola, who was approaching with another large force, from joining Santa Anna during the battle—Houston sent Deaf Smith to destroy Vince's Bridge, over which Cos had marched. By this he also cut off the last slender chance of his own men to escape if they were beaten.

About noon Houston held a council of war; his first and last during the campaign. The question was, "Whether they should attack the enemy in his position, or await his attack on theirs." Opinion was divided and Houston said nothing. Instead he sounded out the captains of his companies as to whether they should attack at once or wait until just before daybreak of the morrow. The captains voted overwhelmingly in favor of immediate attack.

Thereupon Houston mounted a great white stallion and deployed his men in battle formation. On this day of days he wore "an old black coat, a black velvet vest, a pair of snuff-colored pantaloons, and dilapidated boots," with his trousers tucked in them. "His only badge of authority during the campaign was a sword with a plated scabbard which he tied to his belt with buckskin thongs."

Thus the leader of one of the most forlorn hopes in history prepared to fight a battle which, for all the small numbers of combatants involved, deserves to rank among the decisive battles of the world, for it would decide the mastery of half a continent between two rivals not only in race but in basic ideals. As Marquis James wrote in his magnificent biography of Houston, *The Raven*, "On an obscure meadow . . . wet steel would decide which civilization would prevail . . . in the clash of men and symbols—the *conquistador* and the frontiersman, the Inquisition and the Magna Charta, the rosary and the rifle."

In the shelter of the small groves of trees before his position, Houston placed Burleson's regiment in the center, Sherman's on the left, and the Twin Sisters on the right, supported by Millard and Lamar with his cavalry. Then he rode out in the van on his white stallion, raised his hat, and gave the order to advance. A single fife struck up a then popular air, "Will You Come to the Bower?" and the Texans went forward to come at last to grips with the foe from whom they had so long retreated.

As they broke into view of the Mexican camp, Deaf Smith careered down the line on a foaming horse, shouting in his high-pitched voice so that all could hear, "Fight for your lives, boys! Vince's Bridge has been cut down!"

Not a man missed the significance. It was grim victory or death for those ragged Texas fighting men. Not one of them broke stride or paled. Instead they began running forward, and across the plain into the Mexican camp thundered the cry, "Remember the Alamo! Remember Goliad!" It was the voice of a new people, a cry of fury and deadly retribution.

So suddenly came the attack that the Mexican camp was caught completely by surprise. Cos and his men were sleeping off the weariness of their forced march. Santa Anna, who campaigned in style, was taking his *siesta* in his tent, which was carpeted and furnished in something like splendor. A few sleepy sentinels drowsed, for nobody dreamed that the Texans would advance at this hour.

A bugle sang sudden alarm and Mexican soldiers, hastily buckling on ammunition belts and seizing muskets, ran to a low barricade of pack saddles and carts, and began to fire. Some Texas rifles replied.

"Hold your fire! God damn you, hold your fire!" roared Houston, spurring forward.

The white stallion reared and fell under him, killed by a bullet. He took the horse of a cavalryman, threw himself on it, and resumed his riding up and down the line.

The Twin Sisters bellowed and part of the barricade was blown flat. Now Houston loosed his Texans. Their rifles began to speak; and, howling, they swept over the torn barricade.

Everywhere Mexicans were fleeing. After them roared the avenging Texans, mad with rage and lust for revenge. Without mercy they slew all upon whom they came.

Some of the Mexican officers died bravely, notably General Castrillon, who vainly tried to rally his men, then stood on an ammunition box, his arms folded, sternly awaiting death, which came to him there. General Almonte managed to hold together a body of four or five hundred soldiers by sheer coolness and intrepidity; though later in the day, hemmed in the morass at the rear, he had to surrender them.

But among those who did not await the onslaught of the Texans were Santa Anna and his shifty brother-in-law, General Cos. Both fled at the first attack.

Hardly ever in history was an army so completely obliterated as was Santa Anna's that day at San Jacinto. The figures reported by Houston showed 630 of the enemy killed, 208 wounded and 730 prisoners. The wounded probably were included among the prisoners, but even that adds up to a loss of 1360—the entire force Santa Anna had after he was reinforced by Cos.

Six Texans were killed and twenty-five wounded, of whom two later died. Among the wounded was General Houston. He had a musket ball in the ankle, but continued to ride with his boot full of blood until the Mexicans were in full rout.

Captured were all the Mexican arms and ammunition, several hundred horses and mules, all the baggage and camp equipment (including Santa Anna's carpeted tent) and the military chest, containing $12,000.

Next day there was an even more important capture. Santa Anna had mounted a fine horse to save his precious hide, taking the road to Vince's Bridge, hoping to join Filisola's oncoming force. He found to his consternation that the bridge was destroyed. Nevertheless he tried to cross the creek, only to mire down his horse. Abandoning the animal, he hid until night, then got across the little stream, stripped off his gaudy general's uniform, and donned instead the garb of a common soldier—the blue cotton jacket and linen trousers, with a leather cap—which he found, as he said, in a house, but more likely took from the body of one of his own men who had been killed. Thus disguised, he tried to escape on foot.

But a detachment of Texas riders, headed by Joel Robinson, soon scooped in the undersized, mud-spattered and abject little figure and took him back to Houston. Santa Anna tried to hide his identity, but a group of Mexican prisoners, seeing him, took off their hats and murmured among themselves, *"El Presidente! El Presidente!"*

Thus unmasked, he was conducted to where Houston lay under a tree in the captured Mexican camp, his shattered leg stretched out before him. The Texans had spent the night roistering and captured liquor had left many an aching head, while discipline was almost lost. Well did Santa Anna know that these people held him responsible for the butcheries that had taken place, and he must have felt a choking dread as he stood before the victorious commander who, though too crippled to move about, was writing dispatches, questioning prisoners, and trying to restore some sort of order in his army.

Calmly Houston looked over his unwilling guest and told him to be seated on a box. Even while he trembled for his life, Santa Anna could not help being grandiloquent.

"That man may consider himself born to no common destiny who has conquered the Napoleon of the West," he said. "It now remains for him to be generous to the vanquished."

Houston gave him a grimly piercing look. "You should have remembered that at the Alamo."

It shook the Napoleon of the West. He asked for some opium and swallowed a piece of it when it was furnished him from one of the Mexican medicine chests. With his composure somewhat restored, he began to try to excuse his crimes, saying he had only followed the dictates of the Mexican Congress, which had made the laws under which he acted. He did not mention that the Mexican Congress, in enacting those laws, had obeyed his own commands. So much was he in terror of his life that he was willing to do anything—sell his own country if necessary—to save himself. Around him crowded the Texans with hate in their eyes and his fear rose.

But he need not have felt such trepidation. One man present saw past this moment of triumph and revenge and already was planning the future. To Sam Houston, Santa Anna was worth much more alive than dead.

Keeping the dejected little Mexican dictator seated before him, Houston called for pen and ink and paper, and dictated to Santa Anna orders, which the latter eagerly wrote and signed, commanding all his armies to evacuate Texas immediately. Filisola was at the Brazos, where at last he had been joined by Ganoa. Urrea was at Brazoria. There were other Mexican contingents.

When Urrea joined Filisola, April 25, after news of the disaster at San Jacinto, their combined forces totaled 2573 men of all arms. There were besides 1505 more, stationed at San Antonio, Goliad and Matagorda. The numbers were more than sufficient, if promptly brought to bear and well led, to defeat the jubilantly victorious army of Houston, which still numbered less than 800 men.

But these officers were loyal to Santa Anna; and, though he was a prisoner, still regarded him as their commander. When Deaf Smith arrived at their camp the afternoon of April 27, bearing dispatches with Santa Anna's authentic signature, they obeyed. The retreat began as ordered.

Now President Burnet and his cabinet—after sufficient reassurances —felt it safe to return to the mainland from Galveston Island. They did so, and caused trouble of every annoying kind, from the moment they arrived at Houston's camp. Some of them, and a good many of the soldiers, were for lynching Santa Anna at once—and also General Cos, the parole violator, who had been captured. Both richly deserved the fate. But Houston calmly resisted all suggestions along this delectable line. His judgment in saving the two prisoners was presently vindicated.

Nobody understood Santa Anna's perilous situation better than *El Presidente* himself. He agreed rather precipitately to a treaty when Houston proposed it—he would have agreed to almost anything at the moment. The sense of the treaty which Houston dictated was that Texas was independent, and Mexico renounced all claims to it, territorially or otherwise. With a copy of this treaty Colonel Benjamin F. Smith and Captain Henry Teal, as commissioners, set out on horseback after Filisola's retreating army, overtook it between Goliad and San Patricio, and had the Mexican generals ratify its provisions.

It was a very informal treaty. Some time was going to pass before a formal treaty would be made. But for the present it would do and never again would Mexico seriously threaten to repossess its lost province.

Houston, his wounded leg badly infected, was taken by ship to New Orleans for treatment. When he returned to Texas, still on crutches and far from recovered, he found the republic in turmoil and Burnet, his enemy, unable to control either the government or the people.

Santa Anna was still a prisoner. An attempt had been made to assassinate him by shooting at him through the window of a house in which he was confined, but the bullet missed. A plot also had been made to rescue him via the connivance of a Spaniard named Bartolomé Pages, but it was discovered and failed.

Burnet threw up his hands, announced his resignation from an office he could not cope with, and called an election to ratify the constitution and elect a new president. Some difficulty was experienced in finding a copy of the constitution for ratification, but candidates for the presidency were not so hard to discover. Stephen Austin and Henry Smith, the former governor, offered their names. At the last minute friends of Sam Houston persuaded him to become a candidate. In the election, September 5, Houston received 5119 votes, Smith 743 and Austin only 587.

To Austin it was a crushing humiliation. Though he accepted the post of secretary of state—as Smith accepted that of secretary of the treasury—and labored conscientiously on the problems of the infant nation, he died December 7. Houston's announcement gave him the fitting recognition he deserved: "The Father of Texas is no more."

With Houston as president, affairs moved in Texas. Santa Anna was saved again from lynching—this time by New Orleans volunteers under General Thomas J. Green. Thoroughly cowed, the Napoleon of the West, at the suggestion of Stephen Austin, then in the last days of his life, wrote a letter to President Andrew Jackson, filled with flowery compliments and humbly appealing to Old Hickory to exert his good offices. Jackson, who had received with every evidence of joy a report of his favorite subaltern's victory at San Jacinto—written on the field of battle and in his own hand by Houston while he lay wounded—replied with a carefully worded message, disclaiming any intent to interfere, but expressing willingness to assist in working out matters if the government of Mexico so desired.

The "government of Mexico"—Santa Anna—did so desire, and said so, promptly. He was most eager to leave the uncomfortably perilous soil of Texas where people organized impromptu lynching parties in his honor. So he was conveyed overland to the Mississippi, passed by steamboat up that stream and the Ohio to Louisville, Kentucky, and thence by coach to Washington.

Crowds everywhere gathered to see "the illustrious prisoner." One who saw him described him thus: "A graceful figure, with a small oval face, stamped by thought and energy, a bilious complexion, with closely set eyes, brilliantly reflecting an impulsive nature and talented mind. A sprinkling of gray hair added dignity . . . when enraged his face changed into repelling fierceness. His character for licentious indulgence was well known, and he abandoned himself to every form of dissipation. He was an inveterate gambler and his favorite form of diversion was the cockpit."

He conferred with Jackson, agreeing to the treaty terms setting Texas free. From Washington he was liberated to return home by sea. He landed at Vera Cruz July 26, 1837, discredited in his own country and very soon displaced as Mexico's ruler.

In the last days of the Jackson administration the United States recognized the new Republic of Texas, a mighty milestone in its history. Sam Houston turned grimly to the inevitable reorganization work and the administration of his new nation.

BOOK 5

The
Giant
of the
North

The Strange Story of Cynthia Ann Parker

WHILE Houston enacted the drama of the Mexican campaign in the south, northern Texas suffered its own tragedy. Indian hostility in the Red River region was somewhat chronic, but in the Texas revolution agents of the Mexican government were among them, and the plans of the warlike tribes were directed by representations and gifts made by those agents, so that the danger was something bigger and more terrifying than mere horse-stealing raids with incidental scalping.

Particularly active and ferocious were the Comanches. On April 14, 1836, seven days before San Jacinto, a band of those vicious raiders massacred the Horn party of refugees—fleeing before the Mexican invaders—killing nine men and three children and carrying away two young wives who saw their husbands and babies murdered before their eyes. The two unfortunate women, Mrs. Horn and Mrs. Harris, after the usual treatment accorded to captive women by the Indians, were ransomed months later and one of them wrote a pamphlet recounting her experiences, which were not pretty.

Other depredations of like nature occurred. Most important of these was the massacre at Parker's Fort, on the Navasota River, about forty miles east of the present city of Waco.

That rainy April nobody dreamed of trouble at Parker's Fort. For the time and place it was strong, consisting of a group of log cabins, the outer walls of which formed a stockade with blockhouses at the corners and loopholes for rifle fire. Elder John Parker and his wife "Granny" Parker were the patriarchs of the settlement. Parker was seventy-nine years old, a Virginian who had moved his family to Georgia, Tennessee, Illinois and finally to Texas. One of his sons, Silas M. Parker, was captain of one of the first Texas Ranger companies organized and was at this time away on frontier duty.

So long had this part of Texas been free from hostile incursions that the people of the settlement became careless, preferring to sleep in their cabins on their farms, which were scattered about, rather than go to the fort each night as was the original plan. Most of the men and many of the women were thus scattered when, on the morning of May 19, a large party of seven hundred Comanches and Kiowas, led by Peta Nokoni, a celebrated Comanche chief, suddenly appeared about the fort.

As soon as the Indians made sure that the place was open and undefended, they rushed the fort. Screams, shots, yells, the trampling of feet and the sound of blows made the morning hideous. When the Comanches drew off they had killed and scalped Elder John Parker and several other persons; and carried with them as prisoners two women, Mrs. Elizabeth Kellogg and Mrs. Rachel Plummer, and three children, James Pratt Plummer, Mrs. Plummer's little son, and the two children of Silas M. Parker, the Ranger captain, Cynthia Ann Parker, nine years old, and her brother John, some years younger.

The adventures of these prisoners hold interest as revealing what commonly happened to captives of this kind among the Plains Indians.

With their loot and scalps the Comanches and Kiowas rode back toward the Staked Plains. The first night they held a scalp dance and the two white women came in for the usual abuse. A little later the party was divided, Mrs. Plummer and her child were separated, and Mrs. Kellogg and the Parker children distributed among the Indians according to the custom when children were intended for adoption. As for adult women under such circumstances, General Richard I. Dodge, writing in *Our Wild Indians,* published in 1882 and relating his thirty years' frontier service against primitive tribes, said:

Cooper, and some other novelists, knew nothing of Indian character and customs when they placed their heroines as prisoners in their hands. I believe I am perfectly safe in the assertion that there is not a single wild tribe of Indians in all the wide territory of the United States which does not regard the person of the female captives as the inherent right of the captor; and I venture to assert further that, with the single exception of the lady captured by the Nez Percés, under Joseph, in Yellowstone park, no woman has, in the last thirty years, been taken prisoner by any wild Indians who did not, as soon after as practicable, become a victim to all the brutality of . . . her captors.

When a woman is captured by a party, she belongs equally to each and all, so long as the party is out. When it returns to the home encampment . . . she becomes the exclusive property of the individual who captured her. In some instances he takes her to wife, and she has protection, as such; but in the very large majority of cases she is held by him as a slave, for the vilest purposes, being sold by her owner to anyone who wants her. In nearly all the tribes there are more or less of these slaves.

The life of such a woman is miserable beyond expression, for the squaws force her to constant labor, beating her on any, or without, provocation. . . . She brings her owner more or less revenue, dependent on her beauty; and, as property, is worth quite as much as an equally good-looking girl of virtue. She is a favorite stake at the gambling-board, and may change masters half a dozen times a day, as varies the fortune of the game; passing from hand to hand; one day the property of a chief, the next, of a common warrior. . . .

Indians always prefer to capture rather than kill women, they being merchantable property. White women are unusually valuable, one moderately good-looking being worth as many ponies as would buy from their fathers three or four Indian girls.

From which it is evident that, if the Indians had no general understanding of slavery when Coronado entered the Southwest, the enlightening influence of the white man had so illumined these ignorant savages by now that they fully comprehended the institution in its worst forms.

Mrs. Plummer and Mrs. Kellogg both eventually were ransomed. The former died shortly after she was freed from captivity, February 19, 1839. The unhappy woman did not live to learn that her little son, James Pratt Plummer, was ransomed also, late in 1842.

But what of the two Parker children, Cynthia Ann and John? Continuous efforts were made to trace them, but their particular band, the Quahada Comanches, went so far out into the plains that these efforts failed.

There is a fairly authenticated story that a party of traders, including Colonel Len Williams, a man named Stoal and a Delaware Indian guide, Jack Henry, saw her in a Comanche village on the Canadian River in 1840. She was then thirteen years old. Williams asked to talk with her. This was granted. The girl came to him and sat down at the foot of a tree. She did not reply to any question he asked, but remained perfectly silent as if she did not hear, or understand, anything he said. Probably she had been told to refrain from speaking and was being watched. By this time also she was becoming pretty thoroughly Comanche in her thoughts and ways and perhaps did not wish to return to the settlements. Williams' offer to ransom her was refused by the Indians.

Once more she was seen, fifteen years after her capture, by a party of white hunters, in a Quahada village on the upper waters of the Canadian. At that time she was twenty-four years old and had been married for several years—by Indian custom—to Peta Nokoni, the chief who led the sack of Parker's Fort. By him she had several children, but only one survived to maturity. This was a son, who came down in history as Quanah Parker, the greatest of the Comanche chiefs.

On this second occasion Cynthia Ann was asked if she would like to return to her people. She shook her head and was quoted as saying, "I am happily wedded. I love my husband, who is good and kind, and my little ones, too, are his, and I cannot forsake them."

If she did make such a speech it must be a very free (and stilted) translation of something she uttered in the Comanche tongue, for five years later, when she again appeared, she knew not one word of English.

In 1856—twenty years after the massacre at Parker's Fort—Captain Lawrence Sullivan Ross, later a Confederate general, governor of Texas and president of Texas A. & M. College—with a force of U.S. dragoons, Rangers and armed civilians, surprised a Comanche hunting camp on the Pease River in the Texas Panhandle. A few Indians were killed and the Rangers captured a "squaw" whose face was bronzed by the elements, but whose hair was blonde and whose eyes were blue. In her arms she carried a baby girl.

The "squaw" was taken to the settlements by Ross, who sent for Isaac Parker, one of the survivors of the massacre at the fort, and brother of Silas M. Parker, deceased, thinking the woman might be the lost Cynthia Ann. The old account of the meeting in the Ranger camp says:

"Her age and general appearance suited the object of his [Parker's] search, but she had lost every word of her native tongue. Colonel Parker was about to give up in despair, when he turned to the interpreters and said very distinctly that the woman he was seeking was named Cynthia Ann. The sound of the name by which her mother had called her, awakened in the bosom of the poor captive emotions that had long lain dormant. In a letter . . . Captain Parker says, 'The moment I mentioned the name she straightened herself in her seat and patting herself on the breast, said, "Cynthia Ann, Cynthia Ann!" . . . Her countenance changed and a pleasant smile took the place of sullen gloom.'"

In spite of this recognition she was unhappy and considered herself a captive. When she was exhibited to the state convention at Austin she showed distress, thinking the assemblage was a meeting of "war chiefs," sitting to decide how to put her to death. The legislature appointed her uncle, Isaac Parker, her guardian and voted a pension of $100 a year for her support. Yet every effort to reconcile her to civilized life failed. She had become so thoroughly a Comanche that she desired only to return to her savage people. Three times she tried to escape with her child, and each time she was pursued, recaptured, and brought back. At length her little girl, who bore the name Topsannah—Prairie Flower—died. Soon after Cynthia Ann also died. I have been told by her descendants, the children of Quanah Parker, that she starved herself to death in despair at being prevented from rejoining the people whom she considered her own.

John Parker, her brother, also grew up among the Comanches and became a warrior. During a Comanche raid into Mexico, his party captured a Mexican girl. On the trail back to the Staked Plains, John was stricken with smallpox. In consternation the other warriors fled from him, for smallpox was worse feared by the Indians than bullets. He would probably have died alone and neglected, had not the Mexican girl remained with him and nursed him back to health. When he recovered he took the girl back to her people south of the Rio Grande, married her, and remained there. During the Civil War he served in a Mexican company in the Confederate Army, and after the war died on a ranch in Mexico.

The experiences of this group of prisoners, and particularly Cynthia Ann's adoption and love of the savage life of the Indians, are by no means exceptional. Many white men, of course, took up Indian life, married Indian women, and gave up any thought of returning to civilization. This can easily be understood when one considers the adventurous and rather lawless nature of some frontiersmen. But there are also numerous instances where white women, though at first unwilling participants in the barbaric existence, at last so fell under its strange spell that they were unwilling to leave it, even when given the opportunity.

As far as Texas in general was concerned, the immediate effect of the massacre at Parker's Fort in 1836 produced a minor international incident. Shortly after that Comanche raid, an alarming report was circulating that a Mexican army, seven thousand strong, had been mobilized to march into Texas, Bustamente, who had succeeded Santa Anna as president, having repudiated the latter's treaty.

General Edward Gaines, commanding the United States troops on the Louisiana border, was under orders to observe strict neutrality, but to give aid if needed against hostile aggression by Indians "against either Anglo-American or Mexican states."

The Parker's Fort incident, Gaines felt, gave him freedom to act under his orders and early in July 1836 he moved a detachment of regulars under Colonel Whistler across the Sabine, to occupy and fortify Nacogdoches. At this the Mexican ambassador in Washington made strong representations, refused to admit that Texas was independent, asked for his passports, and returned to Mexico. Shortly after, diplomatic relations between the two nations were broken off.

General Arbuckle relieved Gaines in October, but Arbuckle's orders were the same, giving him discretion to maintain troops in Nacogdoches; which he did, and there they remained for some time.

However one may look at it, this was an act of aggression by the United States, covered by a subterfuge and given technical legality by a provision of the treaty with Mexico, whereby both contracting nations agreed to prevent hostilities of Indian tribes against the citizens of either. Nacogdoches, however, was not threatened by any Indian tribe. Gaines's occupation of the town, therefore, was nothing less than an extension of military support to the Texans, who feared another Mexican invasion—under a bland pretext of a "neutral" protective move.

It caused Bustamente to reconsider his invasion plans, if he had made them, and the march of the Mexican army did not materialize, perhaps owing to the indication of the attitude of the United States. Mexico felt affronted, and the occupation, with other incidents, developed a national spirit of hatred against the United States. The Parker's Fort massacre and the Nacogdoches occupation to which it gave excuse were among the steps which led to war later between Mexico and the United States.

CHAPTER TWO

The Scalp Hunters

I T I S time to return to New Mexico-Arizona, leaving Texas for the time being struggling in the usual throes of disorganization and jealousy which seem always to afflict a new nation.

Indian troubles had become acute along the northern frontiers of Mexico, particularly in the settlements in the Rio Grande and Gila valleys, where the Apaches never ceased raiding. Mexican weakness was responsible for Apache aggression. There never had been much control of the wild tribes, even during Spanish rule, although some of the Spanish military governors did campaign against and sometimes punish foraying bands. Under Mexican administration—which lacked organization and firmness, since there was a constant changing of presidents and consequent confusion in the lower echelons of government—the Apaches had almost a free hand and became more and more insolent and bloody-minded in their operations against the villages and ranches.

In spite of this agony the Mexicans clung to their fringe of settlements in the Rio Grande Valley and along the southern border of New Mexico-Arizona, where missions like San Xavier del Bac and La Purísima Concepción, and towns like Tucson and Santa Rita del Cobre were buttresses.

The copper mines of Santa Rita were discovered about 1800 by Lieutenant Colonel Carrisco, who, however, had little benefit from them, since the Mimbreño Apaches considered them the heart of their country and made impossible not only the working of the mines but the conveying out of the ore. In 1804 Carrisco sold the mines to Francisco Manuel Elguea, a *rico* of Chihuahua, who began negotiations with the Apaches. By dint of gifts and promises he succeeded in gaining the consent of the Mimbreño chief, Juan José, for the working of the mines under certain conditions: the Mexicans were not to leave the mining town of Santa Rita del Cobre without permission; and even then they must follow only two specified trails back to Mexico, one toward Chihuahua and the other toward Sonora. Under these restrictions mining began and before long the *conductas* carrying copper were making regular journeys, while the population of Mexicans at Santa Rita del Cobre continuously increased.

An unusual Indian was Juan José, the Mimbreño chief, in that he had enough education to read, having been taught in his youth by a Mexican priest who hoped to win him to Christianity. The Apache, however, returned to his people and used his learning by causing messengers and carriers of mail to be intercepted, reading the letters and dispatches, and thus forestalling by lightning escape or well-planned ambush the military movements against him. For this reason he was so respected by his people that when he forbade hostilities against Santa Rita del Cobre the injunction was scrupulously obeyed.

In no way, however, did the Apaches consider themselves hampered by this in their activities elsewhere. They carried on their great raids deep into Sonora and Chihuahua, bringing back horses, plunder, scalps and captives.

Although Mexican authorities for a time continued the Spanish policy of forbidding aliens—particularly Americans—to enter their territories, the inevitable mountain men, or free trappers, could not be kept out. Records of their furtive visits are scanty because the men who made them often were totally illiterate. It is certain, however, that Ceran St. Vrain of the famous fur company of Bent & St. Vrain trapped on the Gila River in 1826, with a company including the famous mountain man, Bill Williams. The appearance of this party near Tucson caused a diplomatic protest by Mexico to the United States; but since St. Vrain had taken the precaution of getting passports at Santa Fe, he was not arrested. One of his trapping parties, headed by Michel Robidoux, was, however, almost exterminated by Indians on the Gila.

George C. Yount trapped in the same district in 1828; and Ewing Young with a party in 1832. One of the best-documented expeditions was that of Sylvester Pattie, in 1827, when with six men, including his son, James Ohio Pattie, he worked clear down to the Santa Rita copper mines. The party was arrested by the Mexicans and the elder Pattie died in prison. James Ohio Pattie left a colorful account of the expedition, its hardships and its failure.

These were only a few of many. One such party, headed by James Johnson, precipitated bloody history.

The activities of Juan José and other Apache chiefs became so maddening that in 1837 the *junta* of Chihuahua promulgated the *proyecto de guerra* (project for war) against the Apaches. It was a barbarous law, a law conceived by men who despaired of ever meeting the Apache menace by civilized means. It was a last-ditch law, dictated by fear. The state promised to pay a bounty for *human scalps*: a sum equivalent to $100 for the scalp of every Apache man; $50 for the scalp of each woman; and $25 for the scalp of each child. Sonora also adopted such a law.

It must not be supposed that the Mexicans invented this kind of a law. They had excellent precedent. The British and French colonial governments both had offered rewards for enemy scalps. The Massachusetts colony once offered as high as £100 for the scalp of a grown warrior, and the Pennsylvania colony in 1784 offered 134 pieces of eight for the scalp of a male enemy and 50 pieces of eight for each female. As for the United States, the former Grant County, Arizona, as late as 1866 offered a bounty of $250 each for Apache scalps.

At once, with the *proyecto de guerra* in force, the scalp hunters grew busy, Johnson, the mountain man referred to above, hit upon a plan of wholesale collection of scalps, which eliminated the labor of bushwhacking individual Indians. He took his party of trappers to Santa Rita del Cobre and arranged to have the Mimbreño Apaches invited to a feast, which took place probably in the village plaza, though one account says it was on the Gila River, perhaps in present Arizona.

J. P. Dunn, whose facts usually were pretty straight, placed it at Santa Rita del Cobre; and added that in addition to the scalp bounty Johnson was to be paid a bonus for dead Indians by the owners of the copper mines, making the transaction doubly attractive to him.

To quote Dunn, in *Massacres in the Mountains:* "He [Johnson] made a feast and invited to it a number of Mimbreño warriors, who accepted his hospitable bidding. [Squaws and children were invited to the feast also, and shared its tragic and brutal aftermath.] To one side of the ground where his feast was spread, he placed a howitzer, loaded to the muzzle with slugs, nails, and bullets, and concealed under sacks of flour and other goods. In good range he placed a sack [or sacks] of flour which he told the Indians to divide among themselves. Unsuspicious of wrong, they gathered about it. Johnson touched his lighted *cigarillo* to the vent of the howitzer, and the charge was poured into the crowd, killing and wounding many. The party of trappers at once followed up the attack with their rifles and knives. A goodly number of scalps were secured, that of Juan José among others, but the treachery was terribly repaid."

The surviving Apaches stampeded to the hills. But there they soon rallied, and sought revenge. A new leader stepped forward to take Juan José's place. He was Mangus Colorado, which means (in defective Spanish) "Red Sleeves"—a name he is said to have won when he robbed a cache of furs left by a trapping party, and appropriated for himself a red flannel undershirt with the rest of the loot.

Mangus Colorado was that anomaly among the short-statured Apaches: a giant. According to Charles F. Lummis, he was six feet six inches tall, with the strength of two or three men. He had won renown in a number of exploits, one of which was the following, vouched for by Captain John C. Cremony, in his *Life Among the Apaches:*

Although he already had two Apache squaws in his *jacal*, Mangus captured a beautiful Mexican girl and added her to his household. This was contrary to custom, under which he should either have killed her or turned her over to his wives as a slave. But Mangus Colorado made his own customs. He was challenged by a brother of each of his wives to a duel with knives, accepted both, and before the assembled tribe slew both his challengers. After that nobody dared question his right to bring anyone he desired into his lodge.

Under Mangus Colorado the Mimbreños set out to exterminate every Mexican and white man in the country. Two trapping parties were on the Gila River, one of twenty-two men under Charles Kemp, another of three under Benjamin Wilson. They were surprised and wiped out, only Wilson living to tell the story.

But Santa Rita del Cobre was the chief objective. Mangus placed about it his warriors in a kind of siege made the more fearful in that the besiegers never were seen by those they surrounded. War parties waylaid and destroyed *conductas* bringing supplies to the village. Provisions were almost exhausted and the supply of ammunition nearly gone. Weeks passed, and it dawned on the people at the copper mines that they were cut off from the world—doomed to starve or die at the hands of their deadly enemies, the Apaches.

At length a retreat had to be attempted. The whole population of the village began the march southward, most of them on foot, the soldiers of the *presidio* trying to guard the noncombatants. But the Apaches hung about them, cut off stragglers, and waylaid them in every gorge through which they had to pass. There is no detailed account of this tragic *via dolorosa,* but this much is known: of the three or four hundred who left Santa Rita only half a dozen or so ever reached Janos, the first military post in Chihuahua to the south. A very full payment indeed had been made for the massacre of Apaches by Johnson.

Yet Mexican bounties continued in force for some time and caused many unscrupulous and villainous men to operate in the Indian country, sometimes with results hardly expected by the authors of the laws.

John Glanton (also called Gallantin and Gallatin) made the gold rush to California in 1849. As conscienceless and bloody-minded a scoundrel as ever lived, he departed from California just ahead of a vigilance committee which earnestly desired to confer upon him a hempen necktie for his crimes. Taking refuge in Chihuahua, he gathered about him a set of rogues and outlaws as bad as himself.

In an effort to make this dangerous element useful, General Carrasco, governor of Chihuahua, employed them to hunt Apaches. Glanton and his merry men went to work with a will and no scalp hunters brought in more scalps than they. Judging from the harvest of grisly trophies for which they were paid bounties, the Apache tribes should have been decimated. Yet reports of Apache raids continued and even grew in numbers and bloodiness. Friendly Indians and Mexicans were slaughtered and scalped sometimes in the very midst of settlements.

The suspicions of the Mexicans were aroused, and presently Glanton and his men were discovered in the act of taking the scalps of some Mexican citizens they had just murdered. Now the growing number of "Apache raids" was explained. Glanton and his scalp hunters had been murdering and scalping the very people they were supposed to be defending—and collecting money from the Mexican government for those scalps.

With his men, Glanton barely escaped north into what—by that time —had become part of the United States. That his hegira might not be unprofitable, his men took along a herd of two thousand sheep they had appropriated, eventually arriving at the confluence of the Gila and the Colorado, where the present city of Yuma stands.

At that place was a ferry, operated by a Dr. Langdon. The Yuma Indians previously had derived some profit by ferrying immigrants across the Colorado with crude rafts and a scow. But Langdon ran the better ferry. He built a stockade on the California side, which he named Fort Defiance, and got most of the business. Still, the Indians continued to operate their scow, getting a little custom here and there, which prevented Langdon from charging as high a fare as he would have liked.

When Glanton and his outlaws arrived at the ferry, they first contented themselves with robbing immigrants and committing other outrages, which they blamed on the Yumas, a peaceful and rather law-abiding people. The Yumas did not relish being scapegoats, but they endured it silently.

Then Glanton became associated with Dr. Langdon—probably through the method later known, by modern racketeers, as "muscling in." As soon as he had interest in the ferry, which was the chief means of crossing for the great tide of immigrants to California, Glanton decided to eliminate competition. Result: the Yuma who operated the rival scow was murdered. The Langdon-Glanton ferry had the field to itself and prices for crossing immediately became extortionate.

But the Yumas were now very weary of Glanton and his doings. Their chief, Caballo en Pelo (Naked Horse), arranged to dispose of the unwelcome intruders. Sometime in 1851 he and his warriors, with great professions of friendship, wandered as if aimlessly and casually from different directions into the desperado camp at Fort Defiance. There was a signal, Yuma weapons came out, Yuma yells resounded, and it is a pleasure to record that only three of the Glanton gang escaped their just deserts; all the rest, including the archcriminal Glanton, were slaughtered on the spot.

After this wholesome elimination the Yumas appropriated the money which the outlaws had accumulated, reported as from $15,000 to $30,000 in gold, and used it in purchasing trinkets, luxuries and supplies from the immigrants. Not knowing money values, they frequently gave four or five doubloons for a worn-out blanket, or a gold eagle for a tattered shirt. They also resumed the ferry traffic, but did not enjoy it long, because it was too profitable. L. J. Ieger, with a party of men from San Diego, California, built a new ferryboat and pre-empted the business.

The Glanton episode is ahead of our story, but it belongs in a chapter about scalp hunters, since it illustrates the atrocities committed, which had deadly repercussions for half a century in the desert.

Prior to the bloody work of Johnson, Glanton and their ilk, the Apaches had shown surprisingly little hostility toward Americans, considering the Mexicans their real enemies. But after the scalp hunters began to operate, from 1837 on, Mangus Colorado, the greatest chief in the history of the Apache people, made the Southwest all but untenable for Americans and Mexicans alike. No Mexican dared enter Apacheria. Gold and silver mines which had been operated were abandoned and lost, many of them forever, and the great copper workings at Santa Rita crumbled in idleness.

CHAPTER THREE

Texans Can Also Be Treacherous

IN THE sorry story of the treatment of Indians, Texas was about as bad as New Mexico. Sam Houston's first term as president ended in 1838, and he was succeeded by Mirabeau Buonaparte Lamar, the buck private he had promoted to colonel on the field of San Jacinto—who belonged to the Burnet party and devoted himself to the destruction of Houston's policies.

Houston, an adopted member of the Cherokee nation, understood the Indian's side of the argument with the white man. He also desired annexation by the United States as the only safe future for Texas. In the latter policy he was, without much question, also carrying out the wishes of his old friend Andrew Jackson, now, after his second term as President, in retirement on his plantation, the Hermitage, near Nashville, Tennessee.

In his inaugural speech Lamar expressed opposition to annexation. He also proclaimed a war of extermination against the Indians which would "admit of no compromise, and have no termination except in their total extinction or total expulsion."

It was a politician's agreement with the demands of the land grabbers. Following San Jacinto a flood of immigration poured into Texas. New towns were established, new lands opened up, and promoters and land speculators, greedy for anything on which they could get their hands, appeared like the proverbial clouds of voracious grasshoppers. Indians and Mexican dwellers were victims of ceaseless fraud, pressure and outright violence, as their lands were taken from them. To cloak their own knavery, the land grabbers continually raised an outcry that the Mexicans were fomenting rebellion and the Indians were their allies. Very naturally there was resentment among the

Mexicans at their treatment, but except for one futile, bloodless uprising, known as the Nacogdoches Rebellion, they actually made no great trouble.

The Indians were another matter. In the upper valleys of the Angelina, Neches and Trinity rivers dwelt a division of the Cherokees, a civilized, farming people, on land assigned them by the Mexican government in 1824, long before the independence of Texas. Had Houston been president the Cherokees, who had stood good friends to the Texans, even fighting their Indian enemies for them, would never have suffered the treatment they received in 1839. Houston, in his administration, had gone to the length of making a treaty with these Cherokees, confirming their rights to their lands. But the treaty was repudiated by the Texas Congress in the Lamar administration.

No sooner was Lamar president than he notified the Cherokees that they were to be removed, adding, "Whether it be done by friendly negotiations or by the violence of war, must depend on the Cherokees themselves." In his message he made all the usual charges that the Cherokees had committed murders and robberies and had conspired with Mexican irreconcilables—charges in many cases without foundation.

Following this he sent Colonel Edward Burleson and General Thomas J. Rusk with a thousand men—as a threat—and a commission, consisting of David G. Burnet (now vice-president), Rusk, J. W. Burton, James S. Mayfield and General Albert Sidney Johnston, to confer with the Cherokee chiefs. It is interesting to note that Johnston, later one of the great Confederate leaders and a notably fair-minded man, was appointed at the request of Diwa-li (The Bowl), chief of this division of the Cherokees.

The Bowl, a venerable patriarch eighty-four years old, was the son of a Scottish trader and a Cherokee mother, and had been in his younger days a notable warrior. But now, seeing the hopelessness of their situation, he advised his people to accept the best terms they could get and retire from their lands as demanded. The Cherokees, however, indignantly refused. Thereupon The Bowl told them that he would live or die with them and exhorted them to fight bravely.

With the failure, July 14, 1839, by the commissioners to achieve a peaceful abandonment of the Cherokee lands, the most shameful act in the history of Texas began—the murder and robbery of a people whose rights were equal to theirs, and who had been their steadfast friends in the past.

On July 15, Burleson and Rusk, with their thousand men, attacked the Cherokees, who numbered about eight hundred warriors—including young boys and old men—and who had retreated from their own settlement to a Delaware village on the Neches River, where they had a somewhat stronger position for defense.

Texans invariably fought well, even in a bad cause, and in two days' fighting the Cherokees, resisting bravely but outnumbered and outflanked, were driven from their defenses, with a loss of a hundred in dead and wounded, to a small Texas loss of eight dead and thirty-five wounded.

In the second day's battle The Bowl, the aged chief, when he saw the fight was lost, gave the signal to retreat. But he himself remained. "I am an old man," he said. "I die here." When he was found his hand grasped a sword which had been given him by his one friend among the white men, Sam Houston.

The Cherokees retreated toward the Red River, and the Texans, pursuing them, "destroyed their houses and cut down their corn. This devastating march was continued up to the twenty-fifth, until the entire Cherokee country had been traversed. . . . Houses were burnt and crops and improvements destroyed every day until none remained. All cattle and other stock were appropriated."

No Texan can be very proud of this chapter in his state's history. The Cherokees, destitute and miserable, made their way north and took refuge among their kinsmen in the Indian Territory, while Texas landhogs took over their fields and the charred sites of their villages.

When Sam Houston, who was in Tennessee visiting Andrew Jackson, heard of the expulsion of the Cherokees, he returned to Texas, raging. At Nacogdoches he made a savage speech. The Bowl, he said, was a better man than his "murderers." For that outspoken declaration threats were made against his life; yet shortly after, when he ran for Congress from the Nacogdoches District, he was elected overwhelmingly. In Lamar's turbulent administration, Sam Houston became the constant and scornful opponent of the ex-private of San Jacinto.

Among other tribes included in Lamar's anti-Indian policy, the Comanches, always hostile and troublesome, were the most powerful. Presently they were further inflamed by one of the ugliest pieces of treachery in the history of the frontier, part of Lamar's "policy of destruction"—the so-called Council House Fight in San Antonio, March 19, 1840.

On that day a party of Comanches, thirty-two warriors and thirty-three women and children, arrived in San Antonio for the advertised purpose of making a treaty of peace. In inviting them, the Texas authorities had promised them safety but told them to bring all prisoners in their hands. When this band arrived they had with them only one captive, a young girl named Matilda Lockhart, who had been carried away during a raid along the Guadalupe River in October 1838. Probably this prisoner was the only one in the hands of this particular band, and they came in good faith to deliver her. The Texans, however, had the habit of regarding the entire Comanche people, not as a loose confederation of wandering bands, each autonomous, but as a nation, with a government which had some sort of authority and could compel obedience.

All told, thirteen captives were believed to be held by the Comanches, and there was anger when the other twelve were not brought in. Furthermore, the condition and story of Matilda Lockhart excited indignation. The girl's body was covered with bruises and sores, her hair had been singed to the scalp and her nose burned to the bone, evidently some time before, as the wound had healed. She told of brutal treatment and the usual indignities to which female captives were subjected.

Conferring in the courthouse with Texas officials, the Indians said she was their only captive, but the girl said she had seen other prisoners a few days previously. The Texans charged that it was Comanche policy to bring in captives one at a time, thus extorting larger ransoms. Perhaps this was true. It does not, however, excuse what took place.

In the midst of the conference Colonel William S. Fisher marched two companies of soldiers into the room and notified the twelve chiefs there that they were under arrest, to be held as hostages for the return of other prisoners in the Comanche camp. It violated every promise, and a Comanche was like a catamount when his freedom was threatened.

A war whoop sounded, followed by rapid gunshots. Every one of the twelve chiefs was slaughtered, while one Texan was wounded—Captain Howard, who was stabbed by one of the Indians in a desperate lunge for the door. Quick as it was, the bloody work within the building was not completed when a company of soldiers came around the corner of the courthouse and opened fire on the Indians who were within the enclosure outside. The Comanches, fighting with bows and arrows against Texas rifles, retreated toward the river, but were pursued relentlessly and killed. Twenty-eight Indian women and children were lodged in jail as prisoners. Thirty-one chiefs and warriors and three women and two children were slain. One escaped—a renegade Mexican —who carried the report of the treachery back to the Comanches. The imprisoned women and children later were exchanged for white captives and this much good, at least, came out of the episode.

The Council House treachery had its natural outcome. Next August the Comanches made the greatest raid in Texas history. A huge war party, estimated at a thousand warriors by some Texas writers of the period, swept across Texas from San Marcos to Lavaca Bay and the coast, burning and looting Victoria and Linville, then turned back by way of the Colorado River Valley toward Austin.

But the alarm had spread and armed men began to swarm on the trail of the marauders. General Felix Huston—no relative and no friend of Sam Houston—who was commander of the Texas army, intercepted the raiders on Plum Creek, near present-day Lockhart. There the Comanches were defeated by the Texans, who were led by such renowned fighters as Ben McCulloch, "Paint" Caldwell, "Old Gotch" Hardeman, John H. Moore, Edward Burleson and others, under the command of General Huston.

The Texans recaptured more than two hundred head of stolen horses and mules, but of the prisoners—several kidnaped women and children —only one was recovered alive. This was Mrs. Watts, bride of Captain H. O. Watts, collector of customs at Lavaca, one of the men killed in the raid. The young woman was shot by an arrow in her body and left for dead, but was found and eventually recovered. Among the prisoners killed was Mrs. Crosby, a granddaughter of Daniel Boone, who with her child and its nurse was speared to death.

Huston reported that "upwards of forty Indians were killed," and a squaw and a child captured. His loss was two dead and six wounded. Instead of a thousand, as some writers said, Huston estimated the Comanche strength as "upwards of 400," which is nearer the probabilities, allowing still for a little Texas exaggeration.

The Comanches retreated into their wilderness. They had been defeated but they also had inflicted great damage, killed twenty-two settlers, and carried off some captives. Texans charged that this raid was planned by Mexicans, including General Canalizo, commandant at Matamoros. The Comanches expected Mexican troops to join them at the seacoast, which is why they raided that far. At the failure of the Mexicans to appear the Indians were bitterly resentful, and the following October, in retaliation, made a very bloody raid into Mexico itself. More than four hundred Indians penetrated four hundred miles into Nueva León and Coahuila. "Their track could be traced for miles by burning ranches and villages. They carried off a great many female captives, and thousands of horses and mules, escaping safely to their strongholds in their mountains with their booty."

The Texans were not content with merely repelling the Comanches. That October—probably while most of the warriors were absent on the great raid into Mexico—Colonel John H. Moore, with ninety Texans and seventeen Lipan scouts, surprised a Comanche village on the Red Fork of the Colorado, at daybreak of the twenty-fourth. Unprepared to fight, the Indians fled in every direction. Many were killed in the village and others were shot or drowned as they tried to ford the stream toward which they stampeded.

Moore did very well in carrying out Lamar's "policy of destruction." All told, he killed 128 Comanches, including many women and children. Thirty-four prisoners were taken, but of these seven escaped when Moore's horses were stampeded in the night, and three others were abandoned, probably because they were too badly wounded to travel. The village was burned. Two Mexican boys, captives of the Indians, were rescued.

These defeats, however, rather than diminishing Comanche hostilities, seemed to increase them. In the years following, the hair sat light on a man's head on the Texas frontier, and there was an oversufficiency of death and excitement, especially when the moon was full in September—the time when the Comanches usually made their greatest forays —called by Texans *Comanche moon*.

CHAPTER FOUR

Treasons, Stratagems and Spoils

I T W A S Lamar who made Austin the capital of Texas. Founded as a frontier village in 1838, it was named for the Father of Texas and became the seat of government in 1839, when it was a mere collection of log huts, with a stockaded building used for sittings of Congress when that body was in session, and as a defense from Indians at other times.

Admittedly, Lamar's purpose was to push the Indians westward as far as possible by shoving the tide of settlement forward. Austin was much exposed and as an administrative site was strenuously criticized by those opposed to Lamar's government. As one early writer said, "The nearest settlement on the west was San Antonio, about eighty miles away. To Lavaca bay, 150 miles distant, the only settlements were Gonzales and Victoria. To Houston, a distance of nearly 200 miles, the only settlements were about Washington. To the settlements on the Red River, nearly 400 miles distant, was a region unoccupied save by roving and murderous bands of Indians."

Yet to this outpost President Lamar and his cabinet moved by October 1, 1839. "The Court of King Witumpka," which was the derisive title given by Sam Houston to the Lamar entourage, was finding the going more and more difficult. An invasion by the Mexicans, during the Lamar administration, was averted only by a curious side uprising, in which Federalists of Mexico attempted to establish a "Republic of the Rio Grande" in the northeastern states of that nation by driving the Centrists out. This abortive revolution was joined by some adventurous Texans, including Colonels Reuben Moss, S. W. Jordan and William S. Fisher.

One of the strangest, treachery-ridden campaigns in history followed. After one battle, in which the valor of the Texans gave victory to the Federalists at Alcantro, Mexican officers of the Federalist army conspired to deliver their Texas allies to their own enemies, the Centrists. A pair of colonels named Lopez and Molano were chief figures in the projected treachery, and General Antonio Canales, if he did not help form the plot, at least lent himself to it.

Colonel Jordan, commanding the Texas forces, successively captured Laredo, Guerrero, Mier and Camargo. From the last-named place, June 26, 1840, he marched for Saltillo, guided by Lopez and Molano. Since the Texans did not know the route, this pair actually conducted them toward San Luis Potisí, where large Centrist forces were waiting to overwhelm them.

Through an honorable Mexican, Captain Pena, who revealed the direction in which they were going, Jordan discovered the plot and changed the route of march. But much time was wasted in the countermarching and when, October 22, the Texans reached a hacienda one day's journey from Saltillo, Jordan received a message from a friend in Victoria, confirming Captain Pena's revelations and stating that for "a sum of money" the Mexican leaders had agreed to place the Texans in a position where they could be destroyed.

Profoundly worried, Jordan nevertheless continued his march for Saltillo. Next day the Mexican Centrist army, under General Arista, was discovered entrenched on a hill three miles south of the city. Against this force, 1000 strong, with two nine-pounder guns, Jordan had only 110 Texans, 150 mounted Mexican *rancheros* and 75 Mexican infantry, a total of 335 men, the loyalty of the Mexican allies dangerously questionable.

Fairly certain that his Mexican soldiers were only awaiting the chance to desert him, Jordan placed his Texans in an old hacienda building about a hundred and fifty yards from the enemy position. True to his misgivings, when he ordered his Mexican infantry to occupy a stone house near the hacienda, they turned and marched without hesitation over to the enemy lines, where they were received with cheers. A moment later the Centrists opened fire with their two cannon and at the first shot Lopez, Molano and 150 *rancheros* rode over to the Centrists, taking with them most of the ammunition.

In a desperate position, confronting now an enemy force of 1225 men against their 110—more than ten to one—and with artillery where they had none, the Texans, far from being cowed by the desertion of their allies, were only sternly angered by it.

Since they had so little gunpowder that they could afford to risk only sure shots, they lay grimly silent behind the old walls into which crashed the enemy cannon balls. At four o'clock in the afternoon, thinking that after the long bombardment the few Texans had little resistance left in them, Arista ordered his men to charge.

Not a shot came from the old hacienda until the advancing Mexicans were within thirty feet of the walls. Then, with their peculiar high-pitched yell, the Texans rose and blasted out a volley so devastating that hardly a bullet missed its mark. The Mexican ranks broke and fled.

But the fight was by no means ended. Many of the inhabitants of Saltillo, having been told that victory was certain for Arista's force and wishing to see the destruction of the *Americanos,* had gathered on the heights to see the battle. Encouraged by the shouts of these spectators, column after column charged the old hacienda, only to be met by the same withering fire and retreat. The final repulse so disorganized the Centrists that there was general panic. In full rout, Arista's army stampeded to Saltillo—accompanied by the spectators, who now frantically feared they would be the next targets of the Texas rifles. The retreat came hardly a moment too soon. The ammunition of the defenders of the hacienda was almost all gone and they might not have been able to stop another determined assault.

In this singular engagement the Mexicans lost 408 killed and wounded, their two guns, and a great quantity of small arms and ammunition. The Texas loss was five killed and seven wounded.

With both Centrists and Federalists now against him, Jordan began a retirement to the Rio Grande. Once he was attacked by four hundred Mexican cavalry, but again the Texas rifles dispersed their foes. The heroic little band completed its successful anabasis of a hundred and fifty miles through hostile territory and without further loss crossed the Rio Grande to safety.

Jordan's fight was brilliant and his retreat masterly. The "revolution" ceased as soon as the Texans withdrew from it; the "Republic of the Rio Grande" disappeared as if in vapor; and nothing was accomplished save such another convincing demonstration of the deadliness of Texas riflery that Mexican leaders who may have been planning any invasion of Texas abandoned the idea, at least for the time being.

Except for this *émeute,* in which he had no part but which saved him from embarrassment, Lamar failed as an executive. His policy intensified Indian wars on the frontier; his financial practices made four times greater the national debt, while reducing the national credit to zero; and exports were ruinously on the debit side—in his administration the balance of trade showed $4,625,843.98 imports, against $687,-242.24 exports, or a trade balance against Texas of $3,947,600 in round figures.

In this critical situation Lamar decided on one last gamble. The bold traders of the Missouri frontier in the United States had broken down Mexican official opposition to their commerce with New Mexico. Santa Fe, the capital, was rich in silver, wool and mules, but lacked the simplest manufactured articles; and the Santa Fe trail had been pioneered in 1821 by William Becknell, of Arrow Rock, Missouri, who, hearing that Mexico had gained independence from Spain, reached Santa Fe with a mule pack train November 6 of that year and sold his goods at ten to twenty times their prices in St. Louis.

Becknell's route started from the steamboat landing of Franklin, Missouri (near the present site of Kansas City), followed the prairie divide between the tributaries of the Kansas and Arkansas rivers to the great bend of the Arkansas, then pursued the latter river upstream almost to the mountains before turning south to New Mexico. There were later mutations of this route, but in general it was the Santa Fe trail.

On his second journey, in 1822, Becknell carried part of his merchandise in wagons. The feasibility of rolling stock having thus been proved, wagons thereafter were generally employed in the Santa Fe trade. In spite of Indian attacks and other dangers, trade grew continually, until in 1843 Josiah Gregg reported in his *Commerce of the Prairies* that $450,000 worth of goods at St. Louis prices—much higher in Santa Fe—had been transported over the trail that year, this lucrative business being monopolized by American traders.

Lamar believed that if he could capture the Santa Fe trade for Texas he could do much to mend the republic's financial fortunes. But he also had a larger scheme in mind.

When Texas won its independence it set forth claims not only to its territories lying within the present state but to all of New Mexico to the Rio Grande, the parts of Oklahoma and Texas lying south of the Arkansas River and west of the present north-south border of the Texas Panhandle, and a liberal segment of Colorado, extending to the headwaters of the North Platte in southern Wyoming. It was a very large claim, including the cities of Santa Fe and Taos and other New Mexican towns along the Rio Grande; and it could not be maintained legally, but Lamar was willing to use extralegal methods, if necessary.

Followed the fantastic Texas–Santa Fe expedition of 1841. The president first tried to gain for it government financing, but the Texas Congress, faced with an already disastrous national debt, rejected this in

WYOMING

NORTH PLATTE R.

Ft. Laramie

PLATTE R.

SOUTH PLATTE R.

Ft. St. Vrain

COLORADO

MISSOURI R.

Independence

Bent's Fort

KANSAS

MO.

ARKANSAS R.

Ft. Gibson

Santa Fe

Ft. Smith

ARK.

Albuquerque

OKLAHOMA

Ft. Towson

NEW MEXICO

RED R.

SABINE R.

BRAZOS R.

Nacogdoches

LA.

COLORADO R.

Harrisburg

Anahuac

PECOS R.

T E X A S

San Felipe de Austin

RIO GRANDE

San Antonio

Velasco

Goliad

NUECES R.

MEXICO

San Patricio

Laredo

GULF OF MEXICO

Present state of Texas

Claimed by Texas

Present state borders

Scale of Miles

0   100   200   300

both houses. Lamar, thereupon, organized it on a non-official basis, its recruits to furnish their own weapons, horses and outfits, although the government "sequestered" to them some supplies, including wagons and beef cattle. In spite of this self-financing aspect, Lamar's call for "volunteers to meet at Brushy Creek for an expedition to New Mexico" brought adventurers not only from Texas but from all over the United States, England, France and other foreign countries.

Among these was George Wilkins Kendall, an editor of the New Orleans *Picayune,* who left a spirited and minute account of the mis-adventures of the expedition in his *Narrative of the Texan Santa Fé Expedition.* The commander was General Hugh McLeod; and with it went three "commissioners," William G. Cooke, Dr. R. F. Brenham and J. A. Navarro, whom Lamar instructed to offer to the people of New Mexico the priceless privilege of having "the laws [of Texas] extended over that territory; but in case the people were averse to changing their allegiance, then . . . to establish friendly commercial relations with New Mexico."

The expedition was military in character, with five companies of "mounted infantry" and one artillery company with a brass six-pounder—in all 270 men. Yet it was repeatedly proclaimed that the objective was entirely pacific and the troops were only for protection against the Indians who might be encountered on the way. Some fifty other persons—traders, teamsters and adventurers—made up the full total of about 320 men in all who set out from the Brushy Creek camp ground, about twenty miles from Austin, June 20, 1841.

A skylarking spirit was abroad, with hunting and merriment; ex-pectations were high and the adventurers looked for excitement and perhaps danger and welcomed them; the traders believed they would reap rich profits on the goods they were conveying; and the emissaries of Lamar had every anticipation of winning enthusiastic approval for their proposal to have Texas annex New Mexico's eastern areas. Ex-cept for the danger and adventure, not one of these hopes was to be fulfilled.

From the outset the expedition suffered the consequences of its amateur organization and leadership. Wagons were overloaded, guides ill acquainted with the route, distances far underestimated, and the actual hardships and difficulties of the journey little understood. Evi-dence of their lack of knowledge was the lateness of the start. Although it gave President Lamar opportunity to make a fine oratorical address when he reviewed the men on Brushy Creek, it was so far along in the season that rainfall was sure to be lacking, water hard to find, and grass scarce for the animals.

The expedition blundered along, got lost, mistook the Quitaque River for the upper waters of the Red, and was baffled by the escarpment of the Staked Plains, which seemed to defy being surmounted by wagons. Kiowa Indians, the fierce allies of the Comanches, cut off a party of five scouts, including young Lieutenant Hull, the only son of Major General Trevor Hull of the British army, killing and scalping all five.

The disaster convinced the leaders of the grave necessity of getting on with their journey and somehow climbing the escarpment, with its caprock, to the plains above. A horse party of ninety-nine men under Captain Lewis, the artillery officer, was sent ahead to find the settlements; while General McLeod followed with the wagons.

Kendall, historian of the expedition, wrote, "However impolitic it may be considered to divide a command, in this instance such a course could not be avoided. We were completely lost, and without power of moving forward; our provisions, which for weeks had been scanty, were now almost entirely exhausted."

Across the Staked Plains, Lewis led his men, preceded by three "envoys," Howland, Baker and Rosenberry, who were to sound out the disposition of the New Mexicans and obtain, if possible, provisions for the starving expedition. When the three reached San Miguel, however, they were immediately arrested and transported to Santa Fe as invaders. Escaping, they were overtaken, Rosenberry killed when they resisted, and Howland and Baker executed later.

Governor of New Mexico at this time was General Manuel Armijo, one of the typical tyrants that have risen periodically to rule despotically in Spanish-Indian countries. Cruel, corrupt and pompous, he was assuredly the last man to consent to have his power taken from him.

Proclaiming that the Texans were coming to "loot and destroy," he marched against them with a strong force of soldiers. As the two Texas columns appeared, one after another, starved, ragged, continually harassed by the Indians, and forced to abandon almost all their baggage, including their wagons, they were, to quote Kendall again, "so reduced in both body and spirit that surrender was inevitable." Captain Lewis, now a prisoner of the Mexicans, induced his comrades to lay down their arms on a promise that they would receive good treatment.

The promise was not kept. At Armijo's orders the prisoners were plundered, tied together in groups of four, six or eight—depending on the different lengths of the lariats which bound them—and prodded on a cruel, two-thousand-mile march all the way to the City of Mexico. No complete record ever was made of the fate of these men. Some few escaped; some were executed; and some died on the journey, or in the prisons where they lay for months and even years, in Puebla, Perote and the City of Mexico. Those who were citizens of the United States or of European countries were the most fortunate, for the diplomatic forces of their various nations labored for their release.

And here the ineffable Santa Anna played a part once more. When he returned to Mexico from the United States after the Texas revolution, he was ignominiously defeated in a presidential election by his old rival Bustamente, and retired to his estate at Manga de Clavo in eclipse. That would have ended most careers. But Santa Anna had the regenerative powers of a phoenix. Within less than a year opportunity came in a strange guise, enabling the extraordinary opportunist to become once again the idol of his people.

Late in 1838 a French squadron anchored off Vera Cruz to demand reparation for damages sustained by French subjects in one of the sacks of the City of Mexico. One item included the loss suffered by a French baker, whose shop was destroyed during Guerrero's occupation in 1828, whence the affair has been called the Pastry War.

The French squadron bombarded and occupied Vera Cruz. Now Santa Anna came from retirement and accepted command of the Mexican army which was to oppose the French. The commander of the fleet, having accomplished his purpose, withdrew from the city, but the Napoleon of the West, wanting it to appear that he was driving this foe from the sacred soil of Mexico, advanced with a small army to the outskirts of Vera Cruz.

Some shooting occurred. Santa Anna, approaching closer to the firing line than he intended, was struck in the knee by a French bullet. It was necessary to amputate the leg below the knee. Loss of such a member would have been deemed a calamity by most men, but to Santa Anna it was like a benison from heaven.

First, he pretended to be at death's door, issuing a pathetic "farewell" to the Mexican people, containing among other things this sentence: "My dying request is that my country permit my body to be buried in these sand dunes that my companions in arms may know that this is the line of battle I have marked for them."

He thereupon rapidly recovered.

But the amputated leg had not recovered. Santa Anna considered that it was a part of his sacred person, and it had died for his country. It must receive proper honors.

When he was once more back in power—which was quite soon—the martyred extremity was tenderly exhumed from the ground where it had been inconsiderately buried by the surgeons who removed it, carried to the City of Mexico, and there interred with impressive ceremonies of both church and state, with Santa Anna, as chief mourner, dropping a pensive tear over it. The Mexicans were touched by this evidence of tender sentiment on the part of *El Presidente*.

Santa Anna became stronger with only one leg than he had ever been with two.

It was he who was head of the state when the Texas prisoners were brought in, and on June 13, 1842—his birthday—he released 113 of them, who could prove citizenship other than Texan, to return to their countries. Of the remainder of the 320 who started the journey from Brushy Creek, few ever reached Texas again.

Meantime, in Texas, no word had been heard from the Santa Fe expedition and an election was due. Santa Anna, once more dictator, was adopting a threatening attitude and in this crisis, complicated by the fall of Texas currency to as low as three cents on the dollar, Sam Houston was overwhelmingly elected to his second term as president.

Four weeks after he took office, Houston announced sadly that the Santa Fe expedition had been captured and was being marched, with excessive brutality, to the City of Mexico. Texas was infuriated. A resolution was adopted by the Congress "annexing" New Mexico, upper and lower California, and four other Mexican provinces. Houston vetoed the measure, remarking that it was a poor time for a "legislative jest." Congress repassed it over the veto. It was never implemented. Texas soon had so many troubles that such ambitions were forgotten.

In March 1842 a Mexican force under General Rafael Vasques invaded Texas, occupied San Antonio, Goliad and Refugio for a few days, then retired. It was intended as an iteration of Mexican claims that independence had never legally been granted Texas and it set all the young republic aflame.

An unauthorized communication sent to Santa Anna by James E. Hamilton, who with Bernard E. Bee was in Mexico seeking to obtain good treatment for the Texas-Santa Fe expedition prisoners, further complicated matters. Hamilton suggested that Mexico recognize the independence of Texas—already recognized by the United States, Britain and France—and receive as compensation $5,000,000 together with "$200,000 to the secret agents of the Mexican government." This last not very adroit attempt to bribe *El Presidente* became public knowledge, thus losing any effectiveness it may have had.

Santa Anna, of course, chose to be affronted. He called the offer "an insult and infamy unworthy of a gentleman," and sent to Houston a message proclaiming that Mexico would not vary her hostile attitude until she had "planted her eagle standard on the banks of the Sabine."

Houston could write a magniloquent letter himself. He now penned it, ending as follows, "Ere the banner of Mexico shall triumphantly float on the banks of the Sabine, the Texan standard of the single star, borne by the Anglo-Saxon race, shall display its bright folds in liberty's triumph on the Isthmus of Darien."

With this exchange of presidential courtesies both sides might have rested on their laurels, such as they were, but in September General Woll, with a thousand Mexican troops, again occupied San Antonio. He fought three engagements with hurriedly assembled bodies of Texans, each far fewer in numbers than his force, was defeated in the most important of the three, and fell back across the Rio Grande, pursued by the Texans under Colonel Matthew (Old Paint) Caldwell, who had been a Texas-Santa Fe expedition prisoner but had escaped.

Texas demanded retaliation. Brigadier General A. Somerville, with 750 men, marched from San Antonio, November 18. The personnel was inferior, "a rabble of adventurers and self-willed individuals assembled in the hope of participating in any excitement but with little expectation of subordinating their impetuous desires to the general good."

They plundered Laredo and, when Somerville returned the plunder to the *alcalde* of the town, 200 of them marched back home. Somerville occupied Guerrero, across the Rio Grande, but soon returned to the Texas side. His men were so critical of this movement that he resigned his command and returned to Gonzales. With him went about 250 more of the best officers and men, including Major Jack Hays and Ben McCulloch, both famous later with the Texas Rangers.

That left 300 men on the Rio Grande. They elected Colonel William S. Fisher commander, and marched to Mier, a desolate adobe town a few miles south of the Rio Grande. The town was occupied by a Mexican force under Generals Ampudia and Canales when the Texans approached, December 23.

Desperate fighting followed, the Texans seeking to force their way into Mier, from building to building. Colonel Fisher was wounded and Captain Berry killed. The Texans, led by Captain Ewen Cameron, a powerful Scot, were gaining headway when reinforcements arrived for the Mexicans.

Confronted and practically surrounded by 1700 enemies, against whom he had only 261 men, and with his ammunition running low, Fisher, sick from his wound, surrendered. The Texans lost sixteen killed or mortally wounded, seventeen severely wounded and many more slightly wounded. The Mexican loss was never announced, but Bancroft, a rather reliable investigator, suggests that it may have been at least 600 in killed and wounded.

A desperate effort was made by 193 of the Texans to escape from their guards at Rinconada, January 11, 1843. Led by Cameron, they broke out of their prison and tried to reach Texas. All were recaptured, except ten who died in the desert mountains and four who got back to the Rio Grande.

They were imprisoned once more at the Hacienda del Salado and

Santa Anna sent orders to decimate them. What followed was the celebrated "black bean" episode. On March 22 the prisoners were lined up before an earthen jar in which were 159 white beans and 17 black ones, representing 176 prisoners, the sick not being included. Each was to draw out a bean, those receiving the black ones to be executed.

Cameron, the leader in the escape, was made to draw first. He "dipped deep" and came up with a white bean. Three fourths of the beans in the fatal urn were drawn before the last black one came up.

The seventeen men condemned by this deathly lottery were blind-folded, seated on a log, and shot.

Thereafter the survivors were marched on foot to the City of Mexico, several dying on the way. At Huehuetoca, about six leagues from the capital, Captain Cameron, although he had drawn a white bean, was executed on special orders from Santa Anna.

Of 245 prisoners taken at Mier, 68 were executed or died, 25 escaped, and 121 subsequently were released. The 31 not accounted for in those figures probably perished.

So ended another piece of foolishness.

Yet the Santa Fe and Mier expeditions, disastrous as they were, had a far-reaching effect. Together, they hastened the annexation of Texas by the United States, both by arousing sympathy in the United States and by quelling opposition in Texas. Hence they also helped bring on the Mexican War, by which the entire Southwest and California came into the domain of the Union.

CHAPTER FIVE

"Manifest Destiny"

ANDREW JACKSON finished his second term as President in 1837 and retired to the Hermitage. He was not, however, out of reckoning in the government.

Martin Van Buren, who succeeded him, proved less than satisfactory as an Executive and inherited also a panic, wherefore the Whigs swept into power in 1840, electing as President General William Henry Harrison, the hero of Tippecanoe; and John Tyler of Virginia as Vice-President.

Jackson, as the moving spirit in the Democratic party, seemed in eclipse, but fortune again favored the old tiger of Tennessee. One month after his inauguration, Harrison died; and Tyler, who succeeded him, became so involved in disputes with the Whigs, of whom Daniel Webster was the leader, that his entire cabinet resigned and he was a man without a party. He therefore threw the weight of his influence into the scales for the annexation of Texas, which though opposed by the Whigs was desired by most Virginians.

The Texas Congress, in 1836, had voted almost unanimously in favor of annexation to the United States, but Van Buren refused to consider it. The matter came up again in 1842, prompted by fears of British designs on Texas—fostered, incidentally, by crafty Sam Houston in his correspondence.

The underlying reason for the laggard tactics in the Texas annexation was not fear of war with Mexico (although Mexico was making belligerent gestures and threatening hostilities if the annexation took place) but the struggle for power between the free states of the North and the slave states of the South. If Texas entered the Union, it would be as a slave state, and Northern senators bitterly opposed it.

When Tyler, turning against the Whigs and joining his old foe, John C. Calhoun, submitted to the Senate, in April 1844, a treaty of annexation for Texas, it was rejected; but by now the movement had gained resistless power.

That fall, the gray and ailing master of the Hermitage reached out his hand and placed before the Democratic presidential convention James Polk. "Who is Polk?" many in the nation asked. It developed that he was a veteran of nine terms in Congress, one of Andrew Jackson's right-hand men, and a Tennessean, part of that remarkable political force built up about the personality of Old Hickory, which included another Tennessean, Sam Houston of Texas.

Polk ran as a dark horse, was nominated over Van Buren and Tyler by the convention, and in the election defeated Henry Clay, the Whig candidate, on a platform which boldly pledged annexation of Texas. His election was a mandate from the people who were in sympathy with Texas and in no mood for political juggling by the Senate—so much so that the opposition of the North weakened, especially in view of sudden diplomatic activity in Mexico and Texas by Britain.

Santa Anna sent a trumpeting warning to the United States that annexation of Texas would be a signal for immediate hostilities.

Houston, playing a game so obscure that he was accused of everything, including being in the pay of both Britain and Mexico, feigned indifference and blandly suggested to General Murphy, *chargé d'affaires* of the United States, that there were numerous "advantages" which might accrue to Texas if annexation did not occur. Should negotiations fail, he said, "the glory of the United States has already culminated. A rival power [Texas] will be built up."

He went on to outline a possible future division of the continent. The slave states of the South, including the "border states" of Virginia, Tennessee, Arkansas and what is now Oklahoma, would join with Texas and extend their domain to the Pacific, as far north as the border of the Louisiana Purchase—including Oregon, upper and lower California, Chihuahua, Sonora and the present states of Nevada, Utah, Arizona, New Mexico, half of Colorado, most of Idaho and part of Wyoming.

History was to show that this conjecture was not chimerical. Houston foresaw almost exactly the division of the nation which took place in the Civil War; and he envisaged the certain westward thrust which would carry the borders of the United States to the Pacific, over-estimating the latter only in the matter of the northern Mexican states, which did not become part of the Union.

It caused some worried speculation in Washington and it alarmed Andrew Jackson, now not long for this world, who wrote pleadingly to Houston, beseeching him to "act & that with promptness & secrecy" in the annexation of which Jackson had always dreamed.

Houston replied with assurances of his affection and prayers for his old chief's health and happiness, and then laid before Jackson in his letter the cold situation: "Now, my venerated friend, you will perceive that Texas is presented to the United States, as a bride adorned for her espousal. But if, so confident of the union, she should be rejected, her mortification would be indescribable. She has been sought by the United States, and this is the third time she has consented."

Were she now spurned, he added, it would forever terminate the possibility of annexation.

Having read the letter, Jackson roused himself from his sickbed to dispatch what amounted to orders to Washington. The resolution of annexation was passed by the two-thirds majority required, Tyler signed it March 1, 1845, just three days before his term expired, and Polk was left to carry through its momentous provisions.

Houston concluded his second term as president of Texas and Anson Jones succeeded to what was to be a forty-day term of office. After a little maneuvering the Texas Congress accepted the annexation resolution.

Already Houston, with his wife and son, was hurrying with all the speed the conveyances of the time could muster to pay his final respects and lay Texas in the hand of his old leader, to whom, for all his devious strategy, he had never once wavered in loyalty. A letter sent by special courier outspeeded his coach. Jackson received it June 6, 1845, as he lay on his deathbed.

It announced that the long fight was won. The old general rallied and spoke with joy and a sense of great fulfillment of this achievement of his hopes for his country.

"All is safe at last," he said. "I knew British gold could not buy Sam Houston."

But he could no longer wait. "My lamp is nearly burned out, and the last glimmer has come," he said. For two days he fought, to see "his old friend and comrade in arms," but when Houston at last reached the Hermitage, his coach driving through the gate at a gallop, Jackson had been dead three hours.

War between the United States and Mexico was now a certainty. Santa Anna, twice dictator of that country, had again been overthrown, in spite of his martyred leg, and exiled in May 1845 to Cuba, where he devoted himself to continual intrigue and graft. As a curious side note of the coming conflict, President Polk attempted—and almost succeeded—to conspire with this untrustworthy man to gain a bloodless victory over Mexico. Colonel Atocha, as "unofficial envoy" from the exiled man, visited Polk and suggested certain sums of money— $30,000,000 to the nation and, say, $500,000—"to meet present purposes" for a certain personage for whom he could speak, who would, if he returned to power, conclude a peace at a show of force by the United States, ceding Texas and certain lands to the west of Texas.

Unfortunately the agent selected to arrange the negotiations, Captain A. Slidell Mackenzie of the United States Navy, lacked discretion. He arrived at Havana with pomp and in full uniform, giving such publicity to the matter that, though Santa Anna was allowed to pass unmolested through the American naval cordon to Mexico—under the impression, apparently, that he would co-operate in the scheme he had himself instigated—he repudiated the matter in tones of such virtuous indignation that it served to reinstate him in the favor of the Mexican people. In December 1846, Santa Anna once more was elected *El Presidente*, announcing that he would "punish the foreigners."

In the United States, meantime, a new slogan had been coined. Writing in the *United States Magazine and Democratic Review* for July–August 1845, John L. O'Sullivan spoke of "our manifest destiny to overspread the continent allotted by Providence for the free development of our yearly multiplying millions."

Manifest destiny! It became a watchword, the expression of the devotees of expansion. What a fine, large sound it had! And who would cavil at *destiny*, especially when *manifest*—and so enticing?

After some preliminary maneuvers, including an unsuccessful effort made through John Slidell to purchase New Mexico, Arizona and California for $30,000,000, General Zachary Taylor, who had landed with a force of United States troops at Corpus Christi, Texas, was ordered by President Polk to proceed to the Rio Grande.

Mexico recalled her minister from Washington and handed the American minister his passports. General Ampudia advanced toward the Rio Grande from the south, and sent a note to Taylor, politely inviting him to evacuate to Texas. General Taylor, equally polite, declined the invitation, saying he was in United States territory. When Ampudia displayed some hesitation as to what to do next, he was replaced by General Arista, with orders to fight.

Learning that two vessels with supplies for the Mexican army were about to enter the Rio Grande, Taylor ordered the river blockaded. Arista pronounced this an act of war and prepared to attack a newly built American fort, across the river from Matamoros, called Fort Taylor but later renamed Fort Brown (this was the beginning of Brownsville, Texas).

Mexican troops were thrown across the Rio Grande by Arista to cut communications between Taylor and his base of supplies at Point Isabel. On April 24, 1846, Captain Thornton and a company of dragoons who were reconnoitering this movement fell into an ambush by a superior force. After a loss of sixteen men killed and wounded, the whole company was captured save for Thornton himself, who escaped by a tremendous leap of his horse over a high hedge, in a storm of bullets.

First blood had been shed—and on Texas soil.

"Old Rough and Ready" Taylor knew he was heavily outnumbered and in a perilous position but he was never unwilling to fight. Leaving Major Jacob Brown to defend the new fort with a hundred men, he marched first to Point Isabel to secure his supplies. Interpreting this as a retreat, the exultant Mexicans attacked the fort, in the defense of which Major Brown was killed.

But Taylor, picking up reinforcements of Texas volunteers and United States marines from the fleet, hurried back to relieve the fort at the head of two thousand men. Arista still had the heavier battalions. With six thousand men he posted himself in a strong position at Palo Alto, about nine miles north of the beleaguered fort, where Taylor found him. Old Rough and Ready did not hesitate.

Wrote historian Bernard de Voto, "What did he [Taylor] have? A sound principle: attack. A less valuable one which was to serve him just as well in this war: never retreat. Total ignorance of the art of war. And an instinct, if not for command, at least for leadership."

The Battle of Palo Alto was significant as the first major engagement of the Mexican War, and also the first demonstration of artillery fire power. American artillery outranged the Mexican guns and American small arms outshot Mexican muskets.

As always the Mexican soldiers were handsomely uniformed, with buckles, plumes, epaulettes, sashes and all the glittering panoply which their Latin hearts loved. But they had a deplorable tendency to shut both eyes at the moment they pulled the trigger, which made for very bad marksmanship. After a time they perceived that pretty costumes were a poor substitute for execution in the enemy's ranks and went away from there in a body—and at a speed that made pursuit hardly practicable. In the battle the Mexicans lost close to 600 killed and wounded; the Americans 53 killed and wounded.

Among the young West Point officers who took part in this day were Lieutenants Ulysses Simpson Grant and James Longstreet, who would win lasting fame in a greater war, when they would fight on opposite sides.

Next day Taylor moved forward and discovered that Arista had rallied his army and formed it in a heavily wooded ravine. The Americans went forward to engage the Mexicans, who were well concealed in the dense chaparral. It was hide and seek, almost a series of single combats in the thorny brush, with commanders unable to see the enemy or even their own men, the fighting so close that the smoke of gunfire of both sides seemed to rise from the same places in the choked jungle.

Once the Mexicans charged the American artillery and almost captured it. That annoyed Old Rough and Ready. He called to him Captain Charles A. May, son of a member of the Boston Tea Party and commander of a company—the word "troop" was not used in cavalry until after the Civil War—of eighty dragoons. In an army filled with spectacular personalities, May was the most spectacular. Six feet four inches he stood without boots, and he wore his beard full and his unshorn hair falling in dark brown locks down his back. A superb horseman and impatient of restraint, he had been in difficulty with the law once or twice in the East, for riding his horse up and down the steps of local hotels and public buildings.

Taylor indicated that he desired the capture of the Mexican artillery. May undertook to comply. Away he went, beard and long hair streaming, his eighty dragoons hell-bent after him, their horses clearing bushes and rocks at the dead run. They leaped the parapet and began sabering the gunners. The guns were captured and with them General La Vega. A surge from the Americans bore back a Mexican flank and the battle was over, the better-costumed army again in full and frantic flight.

This battle—called Resaca de la Palma because it was there that

Taylor later wrote his report of it—cost the Mexicans (an estimated) 1000 men, against an American loss of 100. It cleared the Mexicans out of Texas, and the reports of the newspaper correspondents not only filled the United States with excitement and enthusiasm but set off the boom which carried Old Rough and Ready Taylor to the White House.

Taylor relieved the fort and renamed it Fort Brown after its slain commander. Then he moved across the river and occupied Matamoros. There he kept his army idle while he awaited reinforcements, conferred with political friends, and gave his "consent" to their opening his campaign for the presidency. Having so done, he moved lumberingly—American transport and logistics were incredibly bad—to Monterrey.

Ahead of his army rode a body of Texas Rangers under Ben Mc-Culloch and Jack Hays. "In outlandish dress with huge beards, looking almost like savages," they threw a chill into the Mexicans wherever they appeared, and with some reason. When Mexican lancers—Santa Anna's favorite cavalry—tried conclusions with them, the Texans simply sat their saddles and, after one blast from their rifles, drew their Colt's five-shooters—the first really practical repeating weapons—and continued cutting down their enemies who carried those foolish spears. The lancers—what was left of them—quickly lost enthusiasm for the combat and went elsewhere.

Encircling Monterrey, Taylor captured it in some sharp street-to-street fighting, from September 21 to 24. The Rangers, spearheading this combat, signalized it with the yell already well known to Texans, and later to be famous as the Rebel Yell, when the Texas troops introduced it to the Confederate Army. A combination Indian war whoop and cattle call, "it started with a low bass rumble and rose in a crescendo to a frenzied treble shriek which suggested a sort of berserk mania of blood lust," as one writer described it. Blood-chilling it was, and quite effective, as Union troops in the Civil War later agreed.

By the time American detachments occupied most of the cities of northeastern New Mexico, Taylor received orders depriving him of some of his best men, particularly cavalry, which were sent by ship to reinforce General Winfield Scott, who was advancing on the Mexican capital by way of Vera Cruz. He was left with about forty-five hundred men, but when his scouts reported that Santa Anna, who had learned of his weakened army, was advancing against him in person with twenty thousand troops, Old Rough and Ready did not quail.

At Buena Vista, February 22, 1847, he met the full power of Santa Anna's attack. The enemy was overwhelmingly superior in numbers, but Taylor, inept as a general but courageous and cool as a man, sat his horse in the midst of all the fury of battle, letting his subordinate officers run the battle. It raged for two days. Once an Indiana regiment, through a mistaken order, gave way and it appeared that the American array was in peril. But Mississippians and Kentuckians, led by Colonel Jefferson Davis, threw themselves into the breach and the line was maintained. The young colonel who thus distinguished himself later became United States secretary of war and president of the Confederate States of America.

On the second day Taylor thought he saw signs of wavering in the Mexican front. Near him was a battery of artillery commanded by youthful Captain Braxton Bragg—who would one day be famed as a Confederate general.

"Give 'em a little more grape, Captain," said Old Rough and Ready. It was his only direct contribution to the orders of battle.

Captain Bragg did as ordered. The signs of wavering became more apparent and presently the Mexicans broke and fled. Taylor had won the bloodiest battle of the war and insured himself residence in the White House.

Santa Anna lost (an estimated) 2000 dead and wounded in the battle, the American casualties being 746. Northeast Mexico was conquered and Zachary Taylor returned shortly to the United States to oversee personally his campaign for the presidency.

Scott's campaign from Vera Cruz to the City of Mexico was out of the periphery of the American Southwest, but the Texas Rangers, under Hays and McCulloch, who were sent by Taylor to Scott, played a brilliant part in the series of maneuvers and battles and in the occupation of the capital. They became acquainted also with another young officer who later won considerable renown. He was Captain Robert E. Lee, who by a brilliant and audacious reconnaissance enabled Scott to win the Battle of Cerro Gordo. Later, General Robert E. Lee of the Confederate Army would greatly value the Texas troops during the Civil War.

CHAPTER SIX

Los Goddammies

OTHER parts of the Southwest had meantime been witnessing equally interesting activities from other American forces.

Polk, now that the war with Mexico had begun, "wanted the whole

hog, not just the trotters." Particularly he wanted California. He had
tried to buy it and failed. He hoped to get it by revolution, for the
Californios cared little for Mexican rule. When war came, he intended
to get it by conquest.

Captain John C. Frémont, the self-styled "Pathfinder," was in Oregon
with what appear to have been secret instructions to create an "incident" in California if war occurred. He did so and the so-called Bear
Flag Revolt followed, a rather ludicrous affair, in which some horses
were stolen and a hamlet and an abandoned fort were "captured."

Meanwhile, back in Missouri, something more important was getting under way. Colonel Stephen Kearny, ordered to organize an
"Army of the West," gathered what assuredly was one of the most
heterogeneous forces in history for a descent on New Mexico.

Kearny had 300 regulars of his own regiment, the First Dragoons.
Governor Edwards of Missouri issued a call for volunteers and enlisted
a regiment known as the First Missouri Mounted Volunteers. It numbered 856 men, divided (roughly) into eight companies, and its
elected commander was Alexander Doniphan, a thirty-eight-year-old
lawyer, whose entire military experience had been during the so-called
"Mormon War," in which members of that sect were expelled from
Jackson County, Missouri. Doniphan's chief contribution to that dis-
order was his refusal to obey the command of Governor Lillburn W.
Boggs to execute Joseph Smith, the Mormon "prophet." This insubordination saved Smith's life—thus giving him time to receive the celebrated "revelation" whereby polygamy became a popular feature of
Mormon life, until it was abandoned in 1890. Doniphan did not know
he was pushing back time for this purpose, but his act won him the
regard of all Mormons. And though his military training was hardly
impressive, he turned out to be a good soldier in a backwoods sort of
way; as well as an orator and something of a humorist.

Besides these units, Kearny had two companies of light artillery and
two battalions of volunteers, making a total of 1658 men and sixteen
cannon, which he mobilized at Fort Leavenworth.

The start for New Mexico was in June 1846. Kearny was to be followed by another Missouri regiment, commanded by Colonel Sterling
Price, and a unit even more remarkable—the Mormon Battalion, enlisted among the whiskery followers of that sect living in Iowa and in
a good many cases accompanied by their families, a total of 540 persons
of both sexes and all ages, shepherded rather than commanded, after
it reached Santa Fe, by a much-harried but excellent officer, Colonel
Philip St. George Cooke. The Mormon Battalion did no fighting, but
made its way by the extreme southern route along the Mexican border
to San Diego, California.

Preceding it, Kearny and Doniphan and the "Army of the West," marched some six hundred and fifty miles, accompanied by four hundred wagons of the annual Santa Fe trading expedition from the Missouri river towns, and camped, early in August, at Bent's Fort, where the Mormon Battalion caught up with them.

From Bent's Fort Kearny sent Cooke with twelve picked men, nominally as an "ambassador" to treat with Governor Armijo of New Mexico, but actually to escort James Magoffin, a Kentucky Irishman, much liked in Santa Fe as a trader for his bluff and jovial ways. Magoffin had been in conference some weeks before with President Polk in Washington, and had a secret mission—in which money was a large factor. With this advance party Kearny sent a proclamation, announcing the annexation to the United States of all New Mexico east of the Rio Grande—those shadowy claims of Texas again, which now had been espoused by the Union.

Exactly what happened in Santa Fe is not known to this day, but later on Congress appropriated $25,000 to Mr. Magoffin for "expenses and money expended by him" in this enterprise.

Perhaps Armijo's actions furnish some clue to those expenditures. The general, who was portly, and a scourge to the poor and helpless of his own province, was no fighter and held his title by courtesy. But he announced that he was going to "exterminate the invader" and marched with four thousand men and a couple of cannon. The men—mostly Indian or peon levies—were poorly armed. Half had muskets of ancient vintage and the other half carried pikes or spears, even bows and arrows. They proceeded to Apache Canyon to defend that strong point.

Kearny, by now at Las Vegas, New Mexico, issued a new proclamation "absolving" the people of New Mexico from allegiance to Mexico, and announcing himself as governor. But he still had to reach Santa Fe and the way led through Apache Canyon, where Armijo, even with ill-armed troops, might have made a strong resistance. But here Armijo's actions became passing strange.

Whether or not Magoffin's money was involved, the governor suddenly declared that all was lost and ordered a retreat. When some of his officers demurred, he threatened them with his cannon. The New Mexican army immediately retired, led by its showy commander, who paused in Santa Fe only long enough to gather up his valuables and continued the "retirement" all the way to Mexico. Among his valuables he did not include his wife, whom he left behind in his hurry.

Lieutenant George Frederick Ruxton, a British army officer with a taste for adventure and sport, who was traveling north to the buffalo plains and Indian country, encountered Armijo in Chihuahua and described him as "a mountain of fat." When Armijo asked what people were saying about his doings in Santa Fe, the bluff Britisher replied that there was but one opinion, expressed everywhere—that Armijo and the New Mexicans "were a pack of arrant cowards."

To this Armijo replied, "*Adiós!* They don't know that I had but seventy-five men to fight three thousand. What could I do?" And with that he continued his retirement, followed by a long line of wagons carrying his goods, which he disposed of at considerable profit in Durango. Later Ruxton saw the general's wife in Santa Fe, where her spouse had abandoned her. "I had a good view of the lady, who was once celebrated as the belle of New Orleans," he wrote. "She is now a fat, comely dame of forty, with the remains of considerable beauty, but quite *passé*."

After Armijo's retreat, Kearny marched through the dangerous canyon; entered Santa Fe without bloodshed; raised the flag of the United States over the governor's palace; appointed Charles Bent, a partner in the fur-trading firm of Bent & St. Vrain, governor of the new territory; began the construction of Fort Marcy; gave Doniphan orders to draw up a set of laws and then march south to join General Wool at Chihuahua City; and, having done all these things, hurried on westward with all his army except the First Mounted Missouri Volunteers.

His objective was California and his haste was occasioned by the fact that he encountered Kit Carson, riding east with dispatches telling of the "conquest" of California by Frémont and Commodore Stockton of the United States Navy. He persuaded Carson to turn around and guide him on the journey west; made the trip successfully, his cannon being the first wheeled vehicles to cross this part of America; and not only put down the real resistance which was engendered by Frémont's "Bear Flag" *émeute,* but court-martialed that vainglorious officer for insubordination, in spite of all the powers of nepotism as exemplified by Senator Thomas Hart Benton, Frémont's father-in-law.

In Santa Fe, Alexander Doniphan solved the necessities of law-making by declaring the statutes of the state of Missouri legal and binding, with a few exceptions covering *acequias,* land grants and other such matters, peculiar to New Mexico.

His men, meanwhile, quickly perceived that there were many ways of enjoying themselves. They also, from their constant use of certain favorite words, which they uttered on all occasions, whether happy or angry, laboring or at play, fighting or frolicking, gained for themselves a name by which they continued to be known.

They were called "Los Goddammies."

The New Mexicans had been led by Armijo to expect the worst at the hands of the Americans, and were pleasantly surprised when they found themselves treated as well as could be expected under martial law. The pretty women of Santa Fe began smiling upon the sons of the North and some interesting amours followed. The men, on the other hand, were almost obsequiously polite. Some of the wealthier families, which had fled from the city in terror of the "lewd and licentious soldiery," gradually returned—the more quickly since they discovered that, rather than seizing supplies, the American army was paying for them at a good round price.

A little overindulgence naturally took place. The Missouri volunteers were mostly backwoods boys seeing the world for the first time—both Doniphan's regiment and more particularly Sterling Price's Second Missouri Regiment, which presently arrived to take over the garrisoning while Doniphan went south. "Among the volunteers of both regiments," wrote Hubert Howe Bancroft, "there was much sickness, caused to a considerable extent by indulgence in the various dissipations of the New Mexican metropolis. Some 300 of the Missourians are said to have been buried at Santa Fe." Which was a rather high price, however you look at it, for New Mexican love and liquor.

It was time for Doniphan's boys to end their vacation. The lawyer-colonel, having provided New Mexico with a set of statutes, now had a more difficult problem. Since Kearny had undertaken, for the American army, to protect New Mexican citizens, it devolved upon the Missouri volunteers to make good on the promise.

Los Goddammies were equal to the job. The First Missouri Mounted Volunteers set out on far-flung expeditions into the desert and mountains, led by Fischer, Gilpin, Jackson, Parsons, Reid and other officers on the company commander level. They rode into the heart of the Indian country, rounded up chiefs, and talked turkey with them. So impressed were the Navajos by the cold-blooded audacity of the Missourians that they made and kept a rendezvous with Doniphan at Bear Springs, and promised not to raid the New Mexicans again—a promise they actually kept for a few months.

Now Doniphan felt free to leave Santa Fe to Sterling Price and march southward, invade Mexico proper, and make a juncture with the army of General Wool, which was supposed (erroneously) to be marching from the east to meet him.

Down the Rio Grande Valley straggled Los Goddammies. That is the only way it can be described, since to call it a march indicates some sort of military precision. Lieutenant Ruxton, encountering them on his northward trek, left the shocked impressions of a professional soldier of a European army concerning this amateur aggregation of frontiersmen:

"From appearances no one would have imagined this to be a military

encampment. The tents were in line but there all uniformity ceased.
. . . The camp was strewed with the bones of the cattle slaughtered
for its supply, and not the slightest attention was paid to keeping it
clear from other accumulations of filth. The men, unwashed and un-
shaven, were ragged and dirty, without uniforms, and dressed as, and
how, they pleased. . . . The most total lack of discipline was apparent
in everything. These very men, however, were as full of fight as game-
cocks, and shortly after defeated four times their number of Mexicans,
at Sacramento, near Chihuahua. . . . Of drill and maneuvering the
volunteers have little or no idea. 'Every man on his own hook' is their
system in action; and trusting to, and confident in, their undeniable
bravery, they 'go ahead' and overcome all obstacles."

Lieutenant Ruxton was a little hard on the Missourians, because
they did show some discipline, or at least regard for the commands of
their officers, a little later when, approaching El Paso, they encountered a Mexican army led by General Ponce de León. It was the afternoon of Christmas Day, and the boys were just making camp at
Brazito, on the east bank of the Rio Grande at the foot of the Organ
Mountains.

It is recorded that when scouts brought word of the approaching
enemy Colonel Doniphan and several of his officers and buck privates
—no distinction being accorded to rank on such occasions—were playing "three trick loo" to decide who would own a fine horse captured
that morning by the advance guard. When Doniphan saw he was
in the face of the Mexican army, he "sprang to his feet, threw down
his cards, grasped his saber, and observed, 'Boys, I held an invincible hand, but I'll be damned if I don't have to play it out in steel
now.'"

The Missourians were widely scattered, fetching wood and water
and caring for their animals, but they rallied around the nearest flag
in sight, regardless of units, each loading and looking to his gun. In an
incredibly short time, by this primitive and unmilitary method, Los
Goddammies were in line of battle.

León's battle line far outflanked the Americans, pinning them against
the river. He had 514 regular dragoons, 800 infantry, and four pieces
of artillery, with their companies, in all more than 1400 men. As usual
they were gorgeously uniformed. Whatever failings Santa Anna had,
he always costumed his soldiers picturesquely, and the dragoons in
particular were eye-filling in tall caps plated in front with brass and
plumed with horsehair, green coats trimmed with scarlet, and white
pantaloons. Against this combination of numbers and sartorial splendor
Doniphan could at the moment oppose only about 500 ragged and be-
whiskered men, the rest of his command not yet having come up, be-

cause of the habit of straggling for which the First Missouri was notorious.

Yet nobody on the American side doubted they would win; while the Mexicans, seeing the ill-disciplined and shabby force before them, were equally confident of victory.

A mounted officer, bearing a black flag on which were painted two skulls and crossbones, and the motto *Libertad o Muerte*—which, in the Mexican code, was a notification that no quarter would be given— galloped forward. Colonel D. H. Mitchell rode out to meet him. The Mexican ultimatum was surrender "at discretion." The Missouri answer was, "Go to hell, and bring on your forces!"

The Mexican officer rode back to his lines waving his black flag, a bugle sounded, and the Vera Cruz Dragoons charged the American left. They encountered a fire so withering that they fell back quickly, harried by Captain Reid and a squad of sixteen mounted men—the rest of the army fighting dismounted, horses to the rear. One company of dragoons, outflanking the Missourians, got in as far as the baggage train. But the muleskinners and packers carried shootin' irons too, and the rash dragoons, with losses, extricated themselves from that hot position with celerity.

Now the Chihuahua infantry moved forward. Advancing to within gunshot, they took cover in the chaparral, from which they fired three volleys at the Americans. Since they could see nothing to shoot at, the Missourians did not return the fire, but threw themselves flat on their faces, according to the frontier instinct to present as small a target as possible. High overhead the Mexican bullets sang without harm.

In the misguided belief that they had all but wiped out their enemies, since only a few Americans remained standing, the Mexicans rushed forward. They were treated to a most unhappy surprise. As soon as the Mexicans broke from the brush, Los Goddammies rose as one man, and the long, rippling fusillade of the rifles echoed from the mountains. Down went Chihuahuans by scores. There were yells of terror and the gaily uniformed lines reeled, then retreated in confusion.

Only one of León's four cannon had been brought into action—a six-pound howitzer. James Peacock, who was in the center, facing the gun, related afterward that when it was fired two or three times, its balls sailing harmlessly overhead, one of the Missourians, who had never seen a fieldpiece fired, asked, "What the hell do you reckon that is?"

"A cannon, I believe," said another.

"Let's go get it!" several cried.

A handful of Howard's company ran right into the Mexican lines, putting to flight the artillerymen. Los Goddammies had captured the cannon. Lieutenant Kribben was sent up to take charge of it, but before he could get it into action the whole Mexican array was gone—he had no target for his captured gun.

That ended the only battle of the Mexican War on New Mexican soil. Doniphan, who commanded with the greatest coolness, humorously belittled his own part in it. At a welcoming banquet given himself and his men when they returned to Missouri after the war, he described the Battle of Brazito in the following words:

"I remained behind, on the hill overlooking the battle, as any prudent commander would. I soon found the Mexicans were overshooting the boys who were below me. Their shot were falling thick all around me. I put spurs to my horse, charged to the front, hallowed, 'Come on boys.' . . . The boys thought I was brave as hell, but they did not know what drove me there."

The Mexican loss was 43 killed. About 150 were wounded, including General León. The Missourians had 7 wounded, all of whom recovered. They captured the Mexican baggage, ammunition and supplies, including "gourds of delicious wines of El Paso." That night they had a Christmas banquet on the captured delicacies and a frolic thereafter.

General León retreated all the way to Chihuahua, where he was arrested for cowardice. When he was shown the fortifications there, he is reported to have said, "Yes, those are all right; but those *Americanos* will roll over them like hogs; they do not fight as we do."

An uncomplimentary simile, but a correct prediction.

Doniphan occupied El Paso and remained there forty-two days, awaiting the arrival of artillery under Major Clark. The battery of six pieces arrived February 1, 1847, and the whole population of the city, together with all the Missourians, gathered to watch its entrance.

All at once a soldier suggested that a salute should be fired from the brass cannon captured at Brazito. Men hurried to carry out this inspirational notion. Into the gun they poured powder, but wadding of some kind was needed to make it a blank shot, and nothing could be found. Rising to the emergency, one of the men pulled off his socks and rammed them down on the powder.

So great was the hurry—and perhaps the men had taken a pull or two at El Paso *aguardiente*—that they paid little attention to the direction the gun pointed. When it was fired, the socks hit one of the incoming artillerymen in the face. He raised a loud outcry, even after it was found he was not in the least injured.

Asked why he kept bemoaning the matter, he replied that "he would rather have been shot with a solid ball than with a pair of socks worn from Fort Leavenworth to El Paso, without a change for eight months."

On such a note of incongruity ended the campaign of Los Goddammies through New Mexico, and perhaps it was fitting, considering the general humorous informality of the whole affair.

To sum up briefly the later career of Doniphan's Missourians: they marched down to Chihuahua; defeated with sheer exuberance and reckless courage an army of 4200 men commanded by General José A. Heredia; and occupied Chihuahua and found that General Wool, who was supposed to meet them there, was still lingering at Saltillo. Thereupon Doniphan marched his men from Chihuahua to Saltillo, all Mexican resistance being broken in his area. Wool, the regular, was scandalized when he reviewed Los Goddammies, "some dressed like Mexicans and some like Comanches."

Nevertheless they made a great marching and fighting record. Their one-year enlistments having expired, they rode jubilantly to the mouth of the Rio Grande, embarked to New Orleans, and thence went up the river to be received with barbecues and barn dances at home. They had covered thirty-six hundred miles by land and two thousand by water, won two battles against superior enemy forces, captured two provinces, and enjoyed an exuberant good time. Perhaps they were not soldiers, in the conventional sense, when they started, or even when they arrived home after their memorable campaign. But man for man they were as formidable fighters as then walked the earth.

The Mexican War came to an end with the Treaty of Guadalupe Hidalgo, February 2, 1848, whereby the United States gained undisputed possession of not only Texas but the territory covered by the present states of New Mexico, Arizona, Nevada, Utah and California, on the payment of $15,000,000.

CHAPTER SEVEN

The Last War of the Pueblos

ALREADY the new order of things was in effect to all appearances in New Mexico. Trade went on, young people made love, households took up the old familiar routine, and everything seemed peaceful.

Yet there were some who resented the American occupation. When Armijo fled from New Mexico, his second in command, Colonel Diego Archuleta, remained. Ashamed of his chief's cowardice, or venality, or both, Archuleta presently, with Tomás Ortiz, began to conspire against the conquerors. And since the New Mexicans had little apparent interest in warlike activity, Archuleta and Ortiz conceived the notion of stirring up an insurrection among the Pueblo Indians.

To Sterling Price, commanding the military forces at Santa Fe, it never occurred that he should watch the pueblos. Not in generations had those Indians caused trouble. The pueblo at Taos was particularly well known to Americans, many of whom—including Charles Bent, the new governor, and such men as Kit Carson, Judge Beaubien, Ceran St. Vrain and others—dwelt in the town nearby and were on familiar terms with the Indians.

Yet this very pueblo was chosen by Archuleta and Ortiz as the center of a witches' brew of evil they were concocting. In their plot they were aided by some padres who preferred the government of Catholic Mexico to that of the Americans. Since the Taos Indians trusted the padres, the latter were able to aid the conspirators greatly by acting as intermediaries with the natives.

The Mexican promoters of the rebellion displayed their usual incompetence. Plans miscarried; delay followed delay. Eventually the plot was exposed by a mulatto woman, wife of one of Armijo's disbanded soldiers. Colonel Price, learning of it, arrested some of the ringleaders. Both Archuleta and Ortiz, however, escaped and followed Armijo to Mexico.

But the mischief was done; the powder train was laid. Even with the archconspirators gone, the Taos Indians were so stirred up that an explosion only awaited some spark.

The inflaming act was supplied January 19, 1847, when three Taos Indians were arrested for theft. In a sullen crowd their fellow tribesmen gathered around the *calabozo* in the town of Taos and demanded their release. An angry dispute with the authorities followed.

All at once the Indians began to kill. Cornelio Vigil, the prefect, and Stephen Lee, the sheriff, were murdered first. Then the Indians spread through the town, looking for Americans who previously had been marked for slaughter by the conspirators.

Governor Charles Bent, a known friend of the Indians, was surrounded in his house by the blood-maddened mob. He refused to defend himself, saying when his wife brought him a pistol, "I will not kill any of them, for your sake. At present, my death is all these people want."

They broke into his room and riddled him with arrows and bullets. Tomasito, the Taos chief, scalped him. But because he made no resistance Mrs. Bent and the rest of his family were spared.

James W. Leal, the prosecuting attorney for the district, was tortured to death. Judge Beaubien was to have been a victim, but he had gone the day before on business to Santa Fe. Nevertheless, the Indians murdered his son, Narcisse, a promising youth who had just finished his education in the States. Only two Americans escaped death in the town. General Elliott Lee was saved by the intercession of a friendly priest, and Charles Towne rode out of Taos on a fast mule and carried the news of the uprising to Santa Fe. All other male Americans were killed.

Now fully launched, the insurrection spread over the country. On the road to Mora, Taos Indians and New Mexicans murdered eight Americans, and others here and there, the list of victims mounting hourly. At Turley's Mill, on the Arroyo Hondo—a place rather widely celebrated for the distilling of a brand of whiskey known as "Taos Lightning," were the owner, Simeon Turley, and eight mountain men who were his guests. The Indians surrounded the place and called on Turley to surrender.

But they were encountering here some gentlemen who were averse to having their scalps lifted without a contest. Nine men defended themselves in the mill against perhaps two hundred Indians. Before the building was at last set afire, the mountain men already had sent more than their own number of assailants "shouting home to glory," as the expression was. The fire forced the defenders to make a rush for safety after dark. Two broke through the cordon alive, one being Turley. He was betrayed by a Mexican who found him hiding, and killed. John Albert, a trapper, hid in the darkness and later made his way north. He encountered the peripatetic Britisher, Ruxton, camping near the present site of Pueblo, Colorado, and in his book, *Wild Life in the Rocky Mountains,* Ruxton preserved a spirited account of the fight at Turley's Mill, as told by Albert. Those who died there were Turley, Albert Tarbush, Bill Hatfield, Louis Tolque, Pete Roberts, Joe Marshall, Bill Austin and one other, not named. The Indians lost twenty warriors.

There were other murders and much looting. Then came retribution.

Charles Towne, who escaped from Taos, brought the report of the tragedy to Price next day, January 20. The colonel immediately began concentrating his forces and within three days was marching for Taos. A second detachment, under Captain Isaac R. Hendley, started from Las Vegas at about the same time. It was driven back from Mora in a sharp fight in which Hendley was killed. Captain Morin revenged him February 1 when he captured Mora and destroyed everything in it.

With 354 infantry, four howitzers and a company of "cavalry"—65 mountain men on horseback, led by the redoubtable Ceran St. Vrain, close friend of the murdered Charles Bent—Price marched up the Rio Grande Valley, brushed aside disorganized forces at La Cañada and Embudo, and reached Taos the afternoon of February 3.

The Taos Indians, deserted now by their Mexican allies, had retired to their pueblo. Then, as now, Taos consisted of two large structures, several stories high, flanked by a church and some lesser buildings. Between the two main edifices gurgled Taos Creek. It was in the larger, northern pueblo, and in the church, that the Indians made their stand.

At sight of Price's forces, the Taos warriors swarmed on the *azoteas,* yelling defiance. Price looked the place over, had his howitzers fire a few exploratory shots at the church, then fell back on the town to camp for the night. This movement was believed by the Indians to be a retreat, and loud were the taunts and jeers they sent after the Americans. With morning, however, they saw the soldiers returning.

This time Price—later a Confederate general—made his dispositions in a businesslike manner. St. Vrain and his mountain men were ranged on the eastern side, to cut off escape toward the mountains. Two of the howitzers, with Burgwin's dragoons, were stationed on the west, facing the church and corrals; and the infantry, with the two remaining guns, formed on the north, directly confronting the pueblo.

For two hours the heavy booming of the artillery echoed from the mountains. The church was the chief target but its thick spongy walls of adobe simply swallowed the cannon balls and refused to breach.

At eleven o'clock Price ordered a charge. Under a heavy fire the infantry swept forward from the north, while Burgwin and his dragoons made a rush from the west. Several men were killed in this attack, including Captain Burgwin.

But presently the soldiers broke into the church and its defenders fled in some cases to the pueblo and in others toward the mountains. The last was a fatal election, because on that side were the mountain men. Jesús Tafoya, one of the chief conspirators, was killed by St. Vrain himself. He was wearing the coat of the murdered Charles Bent and this circumstance did not make St. Vrain any more merciful to him. Of fifty-four fugitives who attempted to escape to the mountains, fifty-one were ridden down and slain. The mountain men took no prisoners.

The day ended, and with darkness the firing ceased, but this time Price kept his men about the pueblo. At dawn next day the Taos Indians, bearing white flags and crucifixes, came out and begged for mercy. Inasmuch as, of 650 persons in the pueblo, 150 were dead and many wounded, Price considered that they had perhaps been chastised sufficiently. He granted the plea for mercy, specifying that they should surrender their war captain, Tomasito, and others who were leaders in the massacre.

These were tried, and before Judge Beaubien, whose son had been murdered. Tomasito was shot while trying to escape and the others were hanged as murderers in Taos, February 9. It was the last flicker of resistance by the pueblo people.

But a more lingering and deadlier Indian war was shortly to begin. When Kearny's army marched across the deserts toward California, every foot of the way was paralleled by Apache scouts. The Americans stopped briefly at the Santa Rita copper mines and there Kearny was visited by the giant chief of the Mimbreños, Mangus Colorado.

Mangus highly approved of the war on Mexico and offered to furnish guides. One of his subchiefs addressed Kearny through an interpreter along the following lines:

"You have taken Santa Fe; go on and capture Chihuahua and Sonora; we will go with you! You fight for honor; we fight for plunder. So we agree perfectly. Let us punish the Mexicans as they deserve!"

The Apaches could not understand why Kearny would not join them in a war of extermination, yet it is a historic fact that, though Apaches were encountered along the way thereafter, this warlike people made no attacks on Kearny. In a perfect truce, almost the only one in the whole experience of the Southwest, he and also the Mormon Battalion marched to California and the first American invasion of Apacheria ended bloodlessly.

The truce did not last long. About to move west was the great tide of empire. On January 24, 1848, James W. Marshall, overseer of Sutter's lumber mill on the American River in California, found a glittering stone in the millrace. It was a gold nugget. Though he and John A. Sutter, the Swiss owner of the mill, tried to hush the matter, to keep such news from spreading was impossible. By May, all America knew that gold in fabulous quantities had been found in California.

Followed that strange, hysterical stampede known as the California Gold Rush. Cold, heat, hunger and every imaginable peril failed to stop it. Trampling their way westward, the gold seekers thrust out of their way, or slaughtered, the Indians who lived in the country. Almost overnight life changed for the aborigines, caught in the road of a crazed typhoon of humanity which charged deliriously west, deaf to every consideration except the desire to reach the coast—and dig gold.

War with the Indians was an inevitability. On the northern plains the Sioux were the white man's chief foes. In the deserts of the south the Apaches bloodily merited their name—Enemies.

BOOK 6

War
Between
the
States

Raiders and Traders

I T W A S some time after the Treaty of Guadalupe Hidalgo before New Mexico, which still included Arizona, was anything but a passive and none too happy appanage of the United States. The bulk of the people were Mexicans or Pueblo Indians, and after the brief Taos revolt they relapsed into subserviency made the more imperative by martial law under which the territory was ruled for the next four years.

Accustomed to tyranny, the peons did not complain overmuch at brusque military methods, and as a matter of fact their condition was somewhat improved. American soldiers might be a little hard-fisted, but systematic looting of the populace ceased, and a man's life and a woman's honor were safer than they had ever been before. Nevertheless, it was not until the complexion of the population was greatly changed by the infusion of newcomers from the States that New Mexico became thoroughly Americanized.

Texas, on the other hand, was American from the first—aggressive, self-confident and somewhat robustious. It believed in claiming everything in sight, and the more farfetched were these claims, the more loudly Texas upheld them. Right after the Mexican War, Texas reasserted its contention that it owned all of New Mexico to the Rio Grande. In March 1848 the Texas legislature created the "County of Santa Fe"—all of eastern New Mexico—and conferred on this "county" the privilege of sending one representative to the Texas legislature, passing ordinances relating to militia, establishing a judicial circuit, and paying taxes—to Texas.

New Mexico denied every Texas claim, and citizens (chiefly Americans) held indignation meetings to denounce the Texas assumptions. Texas was a slave state, in full sympathy with the South. New Mexico's still scanty American population was largely from free state areas.

What followed was a minor crisis, not without its ridiculous aspects.

Early in 1850, Texas sent Robert S. Neighbors into New Mexico as "commissioner," to divide the territory east of the Rio Grande into several counties and hold elections in them for county officers. Judge Beard also was sent to hold district court.

But New Mexico was under martial law; and the military rulers simply refused to pay any attention to Texas pretensions. Although Neighbors issued a proclamation fixing time and places for an election, nobody went to the polls. The military courts continued to try cases and Judge Beard appeared to be without jurisdiction. To cap all this, Colonel Munroe, commandant of New Mexico, ordered an election of a *territorial delegate* to the United States Congress.

This was a flat denial of Texas claims and erected New Mexico into an independent territory. Considerable heat developed in Texas and Governor George T. Wood made a ringing demand that his legislature put the whole military establishment of the state under his control so that he might *enforce* the sacred claims of Texas to New Mexico.

But from Washington, presently, came a terse warning that if Texans attempted to take forcible possession of the neighboring territory they would be "treated as intruders." Texas contemplated the exact meaning of those words, and armed intervention did not take place. Wood was defeated for re-election; and under his successor, P. Hansborough Bell, the vexing boundary questions were settled, the government paying Texas $10,000,000 to relinquish all claims outside of its present limits. The terms were not popular with many Texans. One of the factors in the settlement was the circumstance that Texas still possessed a "national debt" of some millions of dollars. The creditors, seeing a chance to recover their money, formed lobbies, both in Congress and in the Texas legislature, which had much to do with gaining the compromise—and the cash.

In Texas the population swelled. Where there were but 20,000 Anglo-American settlers at the time of the Texas revolution, a census in 1847 showed 100,508 persons of white blood, including European immigrants from England, Ireland and Germany. It was a motley combination of many racial, political and religious complexions, yet as Bancroft wrote:

"In their intercourse with each other and with strangers, they exhibited a freedom, and a want of the tinsel of politeness—so often the cloak of insincerity—which might not always have pleased the transient traveler; but if he possessed ordinary common sense, he soon discovered the virtues of frankness, truthfulness, and hospitality in the Texas settler."

The Texans were perhaps "frank, truthful, and hospitable" to one another, and to strangers (if white), but they showed less amenity toward the 4000 Mexican people living among them; and thorough enmity and ferocity—repaid, it must be admitted, in kind—toward the Indian tribes on their plains.

One of the important effects of the Treaty of Guadalupe Hidalgo was that it brought within the limits of the United States an estimated 120,000 additional Indians, some of them very savage and warlike. Of those on the Texas borders, the Comanches and their inveterate allies the Kiowas were the most actively hostile. To their hatred of the white man was added a profit motive—impelling even among savages —for continuous warfare and raiding on the Texas frontier.

That motive was supplied by a strange, shifty, yet colorful people known as *Comancheros* (those dealing with the Comanches). They were chiefly Mexican, though unscrupulous white men and even some semicivilized Indians took part in their transactions. New Mexican by origin, their activities may have been inspired somewhat by detestation of the Texans, which they felt before and after the American occupation.

At first they had gone out on the plains from the New Mexican settlements as *ciboleros* (buffalo hunters), selling the dried meat of the bison as *carne seca,* an important article of commerce in the early days. Camping along the streams under the cap rock of the Staked Plains, they met the nomadic tribes and a small trade sprang up. Gradually this trade grew more important, until the original object, buffalo hunting, was forgotten, and the former *ciboleros,* now called *Comancheros,* went forth each year with caravans of pack burros and loaded *carretas* for the sole purpose of trading with the Indians.

Rendezvous were established and there were even camps or villages of a more or less permanent nature in strategic places, where the Indians came to barter. At first, in the 1820s, such trading was mostly for furs and meat; but by 1832 it had taken on a more sinister character, the most valuable commodities the Indians offered being loot from the Texas settlements, chiefly horses and cattle.

That year, 1832, Albert Pike crossed the Staked Plains with a party of traders, noted the trails over which the Mexicans journeyed, and himself had commerce with the Comanches. Josiah Gregg, in 1839, wrote of the "rude indigent" residents of some New Mexico villages, who traded with the Plains Indians. Kendall told of encountering some of these traders on the ill-fated Texas-Santa Fe expedition of 1841, and Captain R. B. Marcy, in his Red River expedition of 1849, saw camp sites along the Canadian River and cart trails leading west.

Between 1850 and 1870, Comanche raids for loot and livestock to trade to the *Comancheros* grew in magnitude and terror. In those twenty years an estimated hundred thousand cattle and horses were driven across the Staked Plains from Texas to New Mexico. Texans angrily charged that white persons, including officials and even army officers in New Mexico, were financing the traders in this nefarious practice. It was profitable, for the Indians sold cheap—for liquor, gunpowder, red calico, knives, guns, lead, beads and gaudy decorations.

Nobody ever tried to total up the human lives taken, but in addition to the sale of livestock there grew up a traffic in prisoners. Captive white women and children sometimes were "ransomed" by the *Comancheros*—who expected a wide profit on their "investment" before they returned them to their relatives. Mexican women and children also were taken, and the *Comancheros* often bought these captives of their own race and kept them as slaves, the women and girls sometimes for immoral purposes, and with no more compunction than if they had been dumb brutes.

Some interesting place names were left in the western Texas plains through *Comanchero* activities. For example, Canyon Rescate means "Canyon of Ransom"; Las Tecovas Springs got its name from the *tecovas,* or buffalo-hide sacks in which dried meat was stored; Valle de las Lágrimas—"Valley of Tears"—was where the Comanches, returning from their raids, separated weeping captive mothers from their children; Rio de las Lenguas, or Tongue River, was an important rendezvous where the Comanches, Kiowas and other Indians, together with Mexicans and renegade whites, gathered to barter, with a resultant babel of languages.

While the Comanches made a hell of the Texas frontier, the Apaches and Navajos were busy in northern Mexico, also finding a market for stolen livestock and captives among the unscrupulous traders of New Mexico. Over the long years the Apaches had come to regard their raids for murder and plunder into Sonora and Chihuahua as a legitimate occupation; and the Navajos had grown rich, by Indian standards, with livestock carried off from southern *ranchos.*

After the Mexican War, in 1851, J. R. Bartlett, at the head of the American Surveying Commission, with a military escort, began the survey of the Gadsden Purchase, territory bought at a price of $10,000,000 paid to Mexico, to straighten out the southern border of New Mexico and Arizona and obtain a feasible railroad route.

When he arrived at the ruins of the village of Santa Rita del Cobre and camped near there, he was visited by a considerable personage, Mangus Colorado. Bartlett assured the giant chief that the Americans were there only temporarily and Mangus departed with promises of friendship.

Shortly thereafter three Mexican traders came to the camp, bringing with them a Mexican girl about fifteen years old, named Inez Gonzáles.

She had been kidnaped by Pinal Apaches, who sold her to the traders, who in turn, with the callousness of their breed, were conveying her to Santa Fe, to sell her or make a prostitute of her. Bartlett intervened and released her, under the provisions of the treaty whereby the United States agreed to free such captives and suppress traffic in them. Parenthetically, the subsequent career of the fair Inez, as recorded by J. P. Dunn, is of some interest.

"Inez was returned to her parents by the commissioner when he arrived in Santa Cruz [Mexico]. She subsequently became the mistress of Captain Gomez, who commanded the troops in northern Sonora. He married her on the death of his wife, and after his death, Inez married the *alcalde* of Santa Cruz, her social standing not having been at all affected by her romantic adventures."

The case of Inez was not unique. Since their system of peonage amounted to life servitude in most cases, Mexicans could never see any great evil in slavery—of their own variety—and there was no particular sentiment against devoting women to debauchery.

In his report of 1850, John C. Calhoun, the first Indian agent in New Mexico, had this to say: "The trading in captives has so long been tolerated in this Territory that it has ceased to be regarded as a wrong; and purchasers are not prepared willingly to release captives without an adequate ransom. . . . Unless the Mexicans are paid for such captives as they have purchased and now have in possession, very few of them will be released."

In the New Mexico market, female slaves were more sought after than male. "A likely girl, in her teens, often brings three or four hundred dollars. The men are valued less." The reason is self-evident.

Without emotion the Apaches observed the release of the girl. But a few days later this policy came home to them. Two Mexican boys, Savero Aredia, thirteen years old, and José Trinfan, eleven, darted into Captain John C. Cremony's tent, begging protection. He took them to Bartlett.

Shortly a delegation of Apache chiefs appeared, headed by Mangus Colorado, to demand the return of their property, the boys having been captives in their camp. Mangus, as the spokesman, said in part:

"You came into our country. You were well received. Your lives, your property, your animals were safe. . . . We were friends—we were brothers! Believing this, we came among you and brought our captives, relying on it that we were brothers and that you would feel as we feel. . . . We believed your assurances of friendship, and we trusted them. *Why did you take our captives from us?*"

Bartlett's position was awkward, for at the very moment there were millions of Negro slaves in the American South. But the treaty was binding. After a long argument, he prevailed on the Indians to take about $200 worth of trade goods for the boys. The Apaches departed sullenly.

Still they kept their peace. Then, July 6, Jesús Lopez, a Mexican laborer employed by the commission, shot an Apache during a petty argument. At once the chiefs came, demanding the murderer's life. But Bartlett could not summarily execute Lopez, guilty as he was. He could only promise a fair trial and execution in Santa Fe, if the man was found guilty.

This by no means coincided with Apache ideas. "Apaches will not be satisfied to *hear* that the murderer has been punished in Santa Fe," said Ponce, one of the chiefs. "They want to *see* him punished here, at the copper mines . . . where all Apaches may see him put to death."

Bartlett suggested that he would keep the prisoner in chains, make him work, and give the money he earned to the family of the slain man.

"Money will not satisfy an Apache for the blood of a brave," said the chiefs with scorn.

Bound by American law, Bartlett was forced to refuse their demands. The Apaches left his camp scowling. Shortly thereafter, horses and mules began to disappear from the expedition's herd, until within a month nearly two hundred were gone—taken by the Mimbreños. Bartlett attempted no retaliation. Greatly handicapped by the loss of so many riding and pack animals, the commission moved on about its business. The Apaches believed they had driven the white men away.

Unfortunately for everyone concerned, some white men remained in the country. While the boundary commission was at Santa Rita, gold was discovered at Pinos Altos, not far away. When Bartlett moved on there were 140 miners at the diggings and they stayed. Their presence was a source of deep anxiety to the Apaches. After a time, Mangus Colorado went to their camp and gave the miners to understand that he could show them much more *oro* (gold) elsewhere than could be scratched out at this place. Quite probably the chief was making an honest offer. There was considerable gold in the country and it would not be strange if he knew where some of it was. He explained that he only wanted them to leave his hunting grounds and go to the land of the Mexicans, where he would show them the better gold.

But the miners could only think of treachery. To "teach the big buck a lesson" they overpowered him, tied him to a tree, and cut his back to ribbons with a blacksnake whip. Then they released him and jeered him as he staggered out of camp.

They could not have made a greater mistake. Mangus Colorado never forgot that whipping, the greatest humiliation an Indian could suffer. How many white lives paid for each stroke of the lash on his bare back can never be known, but the number was not scant.

CHAPTER TWO

Secession and Sam Houston

A TALL gangling lawyer named Abraham Lincoln was stumping Illinois in 1858, and holding a series of debates with Stephen A. Douglas, whose admirers called him the "Little Giant." The tall man lost the election, but he put his opponent in such a dilemma on certain aspects of the slavery issue that, though Douglas went to the Senate, he was finished as a presidential prospect, while Lincoln emerged as the sign and symbol of a new party, opposed to secession and slavery.

There were rumblings in the South and dark clouds of war brooded over the nation. In this time of crisis Texas called back to public service Sam Houston, electing him governor once more, in 1859.

Now sixty-six years old and looking even older because of the strenuous life he had lived, Houston took over the government at the most difficult of times. Texas was secessionist, bound by ties of blood and ideas to the South. But a strong minority in Texas opposed the withdrawal from the Union which was being openly advocated. Chief of these was the veteran governor, who remained true to his principles learned under Andrew Jackson, that passionate believer in a united and powerful America. His victory at the polls was believed by some to be a victory for Unionism, but in reality it probably was a tribute to his personal popularity.

Shortly after Houston assumed office, John Brown raided Harper's Ferry and was captured and hanged. The always inflammable South Carolina passed startling resolutions in both branches of its legislature, affirming the right to secede, charging that the rights of Southern states were being threatened, and calling on all slave states to meet and adopt united action.

Sam Houston, on receipt of these resolutions, sent a well-reasoned message to the Texas legislature in January 1860, opposing secession. One paragraph of the message contains much of the gist of his belief:

"The union was intended as a perpetuity. In accepting the conditions imposed prior to becoming a part of the confederacy, the states became part of the nation. What they conceded comprises the power of the federal government; but over that which they did not concede, their sovereignty is as perfect as that of the union in its appropriate sphere."

The legislature debated and resolutions were adopted, but in the main the majority were in harmony with Houston's views for the time being.

To complicate Houston's problems, Texas was undergoing at this time various excitements not connected with the national issues. The Comanches had increased their attacks so that on March 20, 1860, Houston reported that in four months fifty-four persons had been murdered and as many more wounded or carried away as prisoners, the raiders hardly ever being punished, so rapid was their escape.

And clear across Texas, in the lower Rio Grande Valley opposite the Comanche plains, life was at the same time being enlivened by the so-called "Cortinas War."

Juan Nepomuceño Cortinas, commonly called Ceño, was a Mexican criminal who had murdered an American named Somerville in 1847, stolen his mules, sold them to the government on the American side, and escaped into Mexico before his crime was discovered. For some years he lived as a bandit in Tamaulipas, stealing cattle and horses, robbing travelers, frequently crossing over into Texas—where his mother owned the Rancho del Carmen, about nine miles above Brownsville—to raid with his following of outlaws.

Then, July 13, 1859, occurred an incident which suddenly changed Cortinas' status from that of a shabby desperado into a cactus country Robin Hood—in the opinion, at least, of many Mexicans. Cortinas and some of his men were in Brownsville when one of his followers was arrested for disturbing the peace by Adolph Glaevecke, the city marshal. Cortinas interfered, shot Glaevecke through the shoulder, and carried his follower triumphantly out of Brownsville, mounted behind him on his horse, followed by his whooping, sky-shooting *compadres*.

Such a feat of derring-do made Cortinas a hero among Mexicans on both sides of the river. He received ovations, gifts and "enlistments" for his outlaw band. Encouraged by all this, he rode boldly into Brownsville with his mounted banditti, the morning of September 28, killed three Americans and two Mexicans, and terrorized the town before he withdrew upriver to the Rancho del Carmen, which he turned into a "military camp."

There he issued his first "proclamation," announcing that he was the defender of his "persecuted people," the chastiser of their enemies and the righter of their "wrongs." The proclamation was worded in just the kind of lofty and glittering phrases that appealed to the peons and *vaqueros* and aroused among the semioutlaw Mexican population a prideful enthusiasm.

American authorities did not share this enthusiasm. Neither did Mexican authorities south of the Rio Grande, for that matter. The commandant at Matamoros, in fact, sent a detachment of soldiers across the river to protect Brownsville from further "chastisement" and kept them there for some days.

About October 12 a sheriff's posse rode for the Rancho del Carmen. Cortinas and most of his men hurriedly departed and recrossed the Rio Grande. A man named Thomas Cabrera, said to be Cortinas' lieutenant, was not quite fast enough and the posse scooped him up. At once Cortinas sent a message to Brownsville, saying he would "lay it in ashes" unless the prisoner was released. But Captain Tobin's company of Texas Rangers arrived in the city and the citizens, encouraged by this circumstance, took Cabrera out of jail and quietly lynched him.

With a roar Cortinas rode back into Texas, where his forces were augmented by scores of Mexicans from the American side. He defeated two posses sent against him and issued a second "proclamation" in which he announced that a secret society had been organized for "the extermination of the tyrants." Captain Tobin with his Rangers and a crowd of volunteers from Brownsville attempted to oust Cortinas from the Rancho del Carmen, November 24, but the "Protector" was well intrenched, had cannon which he had captured, and Tobin was forced to fall back.

This series of "victories" boosted Cortinas' stock to the sky. He now had between four and five hundred followers, from both sides of the border, including a number of dangerous criminals who escaped from the Mexican prison at Victoria.

But his triumph was near an end. On December 5, Major S. P. Heintzelman—later a Union general—arrived in Brownsville with 165 officers and men of the regular army. With these and Tobin's Rangers, he attacked Cortinas and the rancho was captured with expedition. The "Protector" retreated up the Rio Grande Valley, devastating the country as he went. But, on December 27, Heintzelman caught up with him, soundly whipped him in a fight outside Rio Grande City, and chased him across the river.

In his report Heintzelman said: "The whole country from Brownsville to Rio Grande City, 120 miles, and back to the arroyo Colorado, has been laid waste. There is not an American, or any property that could be destroyed, in this large tract of country. Business as far as Laredo, 240 miles, has been interrupted or suspended for five months. ... There have been fifteen Americans and eighteen friendly Mexicans killed. Cortinas has lost 151 men killed; of the wounded I have no account."

To follow Cortinas' career as little further: So strange are the turnings of events that this bandit, hunted alike by Mexican and American authorities, joined the revolution of Juárez, became a general in the Mexican army and at last governor of Tamaulipas.

Elsewhere in Texas affairs grew progressively hotter. Lincoln was nominated for the presidency by the Republican party at Chicago and the campaign created unexampled bitterness.

Some of the more extreme secessionists determined to push matters to a crisis. To do so they revived a curious secret organization, the Knights of the Golden Circle. Formed years before, its original purpose was almost ridiculously visionary: the formation of an "empire," including all the lands within a great circle, the center of which would be Havana, Cuba, and which would include everything between the Isthmus of Panama on the south and the Pennsylvania line on the north—taking in the West Indies and islands of the Caribbean Sea, a large part of Mexico and Central America, the northern tip of South America, all Texas and the South, and even generous portions of some Northern states. The foundation of this eccentric realm, enclosed arbitrarily in a circle without regard to geographic, ethnic, political or other considerations, was to rest on the institution of slavery. Its impracticality is evident, yet all the filibustering movements from 1850 to 1857, including the expeditions of the gasconading William Walker, were associated with it.

With its main purpose defeated, the order was in danger of being entirely forgotten, until the secession movement gave it new motive for action. It began to grow wonderfully, rapidly forming "castles" (lodges), in every important town and city of Texas. It provided "vigilance committees," flogged and terrorized unionists, burned property of free state advocates, and committed some lynchings. Very definitely its activities created a shift in sentiment in Texas, the secessionists becoming emboldened, the antisecessionists afraid to speak their opinions.

In the midst of this turmoil Abraham Lincoln was elected President, November 6, 1860, and his victory inflamed the South. Heavy pressures were exerted on Houston to call a special session of the legislature and he at last unwillingly did so, setting the opening of the session for January 21, 1861. The Knights of the Golden Circle, to which many if not most of the legislators belonged, had the upper hand, called a highly informal state convention, voted it lawfully constituted over the protests of Houston, who declared it illegal, and when he vetoed it, overruled his veto.

This convention, only about half of its members duly elected, on January 28 passed the ordinance of secession by a vote of 167 to 7, subject to the ratification of the people at an election to be held February 23.

Before that, however, the Knights of the Golden Circle, numbering three hundred or more men, led by Ben McCulloch—who was destined to die a Confederate general at the Battle of Pea Ridge—took possession of the Alamo and the main square of San Antonio. The maneuver was to provide General David E. Twiggs—a Southern sympathizer who was in command of the national troops in Texas—the excuse of "a show of force," upon which he surrendered the troops, forts and military supplies in the state to the Confederates. Thus twenty-two hundred soldiers wearing the uniform of the United States became on February 18, 1861, the first prisoners of the Confederacy, which was not yet actually organized. Twiggs was dismissed from the United States Army but was given high rank in the Confederate Army in the war that followed.

One soldier who did not surrender at Twiggs's command was the gray-bearded colonel of the Second Cavalry, the former commander of the Department of Texas, who quietly took a stage to Indianola, where he boarded a ship for New Orleans, and thence traveled to Washington for an interview with his commander-in-chief, General Winfield Scott. The Texas uprising did not comport with his notions of honor and, though he was threatened with arrest, he rejected Texas demands that he declare for the Confederacy. In Washington, however, face to face with his superior and in the seat of government, he felt free to tender his resignation and go to his own state, where shortly he began to play a rather important role. He was Robert E. Lee, of Virginia.

A few days before the popular vote on the ordinance of secession was taken, February 23, old Sam Houston made a grave and ominous speech from the balcony of the Tremont House in Galveston, warning his people of the consequences of secession. His friends tried to prevent him from doing so, fearing that in the excited state of public opinion violence might be done to him. But Sam Houston never stood back because of a threat of danger to himself.

In prophetic language he pictured the dark future, the loss of life, the destruction of property, the sacrifice of treasure and the small chance of winning Southern independence even after all this.

"I tell you," he said, gloomily as a latter-day Jeremiah, "that while I believe with you in the doctrine of states' rights, the North is determined to preserve this union. They are not a fiery and impulsive people as you are, for they live in cooler climates. But when they begin to move in a given direction, where great interests are involved, such as the present issues before the country, they move with the steady momentum and perseverance of a mighty avalanche, and what I fear is that they will overwhelm the South in ignoble defeat."

His address had little effect. At the polls Texas voted 53,256 to 13,841 for secession. Houston refused to take the oath of allegiance to the Confederate government and was deposed from office March 18, retiring to private life. Followed Lincoln's decision to send an expedition to relieve Fort Sumter, the firing upon the flag of the Union April 12, 1861, and the cataclysm of civil strife, the bloodiest and most destructive of wars.

Before the Civil War ended, every warning Houston gave his people was proved true and all the tragic consequences he foresaw were being suffered by the South. But Sam Houston did not live to see the end. Even his own family was divided. His son, Sam, Jr., was a Confederate soldier, wounded and in a Northern prison, which embittered his last days. On July 26, 1863, the steadfast old patriot, architect of Texas independence and guide of its crucial years, died at his home in Huntsville, Texas.

CHAPTER THREE

Texas Invades New Mexico

THE great War Between the States overshadowed all lesser events. Vast eruptions of blood and fire, such as the battles of Bull Run, the Seven Days, Fredericksburg, Chancellorsville, Antietam, Gettysburg and the Wilderness Campaign in the East; conflicts of equal ferocity, such as Shiloh, Vicksburg, Chickamauga, Chattanooga and Atlanta in the West; Sherman's "scorched earth" march to the sea; and Lee's final defeat and surrender to Grant at Appomattox, made anything that happened west of the Mississippi seem unimportant by comparison.

Yet the Southwest was not entirely devoid of excitement. Texas did not suffer in the same sense that the rest of the Confederacy suffered. There were a few battles along her coast, of secondary importance, and chiefly of a naval-landing-party nature; her ports were blockaded; and Galveston was captured by a federal fleet and later recaptured for the Confederacy by General Magruder. Otherwise Texas soldiers fought chiefly on other ground than their own.

Under General John B. Hood, the Texas Division made an everlasting reputation for hard and heroic fighting in Lee's Army of Northern Virginia—and, incidentally, introduced to the world the shrill Texas war cry which became celebrated as the Rebel Yell. Texans were a redoubtable part, also, of the Confederate Army of the Tennessee, and took an important part in the western operations of the war.

And as a state Texas came to the long-delayed grapple with its neighbor, New Mexico. Ever since the first days of Texas independence it had been building up. The cruelties toward the Texas-Santa Fe expedition, the evil activities of the *Comancheros*, the claims to territory made by Houston and his successors and rejected by New Mexico, all caused Texans to regard with considerable animosity the territory just on the other side of the Staked Plains.

This was given point by plans of wider strategy made by the Confederate high command. At the outbreak of the war the capture of all the Southwest was envisaged, chiefly for the purpose of reaching and taking possession of California, with its gold fields, which would greatly aid the financing of the Confederate cause. There was supposed to be strong Southern sentiment in California, but it did not importantly materialize. Union supporters dominated the state, in point of fact, and sent military aid eastward as the sequel will show.

In this scheme of things Arizona had no especial value, except that through it lay the route to California; and New Mexico hardly more, save that besides lying across the California road it might also serve for a flanking movement against Union forces along the Missouri River.

New Mexico itself, except for its comparatively small American population, had a *"Quién sabe?"* attitude toward the issues which had riven the nation. Although a census showed fewer than one hundred Negro slaves held in the territory, the institution of peonage existed and Indian captives were held as slaves, so that New Mexicans found themselves unable to work up much excitement over the controversy that inflamed both North and South. Since many Americans in the territory had Southern backgrounds and traditions, it was supposed that when Confederate troops came the people might support them. But nothing like that occurred.

These were *Texans* who were invading! The old fear and hatred, arising out of the Mexican War and the territorial claims of the Lone Star State, reasserted themselves. New Mexicans did not even remain neutral—they enlisted in droves, furnishing between five and six thousand Union volunteers. To be sure, some of them were a trifle volatile, and had a tendency to go elsewhere when needed, so that Colonel E. R. S. Canby cautioned his subordinate officers, "Place no reliance on the New Mexican troops except for partisan operations, and then only when the main operations will not be affected by the result." But at least they showed their loyalty and provided a friendly country for the operation of Union forces, and furnished supplies (at wartime prices). They didn't like Texans.

Handicapped by the Confederate misjudgment of the temper of New Mexico, Lieutenant Colonel John R. Baylor crossed the state line from El Paso, July 25, 1861, and occupied Mesilla. Major Isaac Lynde, commanding the Union forces in that part of New Mexico, advanced on Mesilla with seven hundred men.

There is a fairly well substantiated story that Lynde's warlike followers on the way to Mesilla, by a brilliant maneuver, "captured" a saloon and "confiscated" its whiskey supply, so that many of them were more convivial than bellicose when they encountered Baylor's Texans. A brief skirmish took place, with few casualties, although "dead soldiers" (empty bottles) lay thick upon the field. Major Lynde surrendered his men. They were at once paroled and sent marching back to Albuquerque by the Texans, who seemed to fear that they might assail the visible whiskey supply of Mesilla if they remained there. Lynde was later dismissed from the United States Army for lack of zeal in fighting the enemies of his country.

Having achieved this notable victory, the Confederates prepared to further their plan of occupation of New Mexico, Arizona and California. General H. H. Sibley, an officer who had fought in the Seminole and other Indian wars, was sent to take command of the forces of occupation.

Sibley was opposed by an old comrade-in-arms of the Seminole campaigns, Colonel E. R. S. Canby, who later became a general in the Union Army and was murdered by Modoc Indians in 1873. Finding matters badly disorganized in New Mexico, Canby worked feverishly to prepare the territory for defense. His persuasions, with those of Governor Henry Connelly, swelled his forces to about four thousand men, some of whom, however, were not worth much as fighters.

Against him Sibley marched up the Rio Grande with 1750 men, including some hard-bitten Texas Rangers, accustomed to Indian warfare and hard campaigning. At the same time Sibley dispatched a small force westward, under Captain Hunter. This detachment occupied Tucson, where it remained until the California Brigade began its march eastward from Yuma, two months later, at which time Captain Hunter retired to New Mexico and thence to Texas.

Canby concentrated his forces at Fort Craig, on the west bank of the Rio Grande, just north of the Jornada del Muerto, a severe desert stretch which Sibley must cross. The post was situated opposite a basaltic mesa which created steep banks forty to eighty feet high, down which there were only one or two bridle paths, and nowhere a place suitable for fording the river or even watering an army's horses and mules. This stretch of inaccessible bank reached from the Pandero crossing, seven miles below the fort, to the Valverde crossing two or three miles above it. Fort Craig was supposed to cover both these fords; and since Sibley was east of the river, Canby believed his foe would attempt to cross at this point.

He was right. With considerable sweating and swearing, Sibley's command at last dragged its way across the Jornada del Muerto by mid-February. After a feint at the Pandero ford, where a picket skirmish was fought the morning of February 16, the Confederate commander moved north toward the Valverde crossing, which was better suited for getting his army, and particularly his supply train and artillery, across the river.

Canby guessed the maneuver and Major Benjamin S. Roberts, with a strong force, was guarding the ford. On the afternoon of February 20 the advance guard of Texans appeared and camped across the river after a brief engagement in which Roberts withdrew to his own side of the stream.

Warfare in the Southwest was bound to be informal. In Canby's little army was Captain James Graydon, better known as Paddy Graydon, who commanded an independent company of scouts. Graydon, among various quaint traits, had an ingenious method of keeping his ranks filled. Whenever he lost a man, by death, capture or desertion, he would ride up to the next simple peon he saw, accost him by the missing trooper's name, and promptly put him in the ranks, in spite of the despairing and often tearful protests of the man thus "enlisted." As a result, when his company was mustered out it had a full complement; and judging by its roster, the same identical men who originally enlisted in it.

The night of the twentieth Paddy Graydon was the hero of one of the more bizarre episodes of a campaign filled with the bizarre. Looking across the Rio Grande at the Confederate campfires, he suggested to Major Roberts a night attack which was, to say the least, ingenious and original in plan. Permission was granted.

Taking two old mules, unfit for service, Graydon had them loaded with explosives, to which were attached fuses, and led them as near as he could, with safety, to the Confederate camp. When he thought he was close enough he lit the fuses and drove the animated land torpedoes toward the hostile lines. Thereupon, he and the men with him began to withdraw to a safe distance to await the expected explosion.

But horrors! The two old mules were accustomed to Paddy Graydon and his men. They would have nothing to do with those Confederates, who were total strangers to them. No sooner did they see

Graydon and his men fall back than they also turned and sought to rejoin their masters.

Graydon's men quickened their withdrawal. The devoted mules broke into a trot, then a gallop, to overtake them. The fuses were burning short and now Graydon and his command were in a panic.

Whip and spur were frantically applied, but the too faithful mules, with a burst of speed of which nobody could have suspected them, appeared about to overtake the stampeding scouts.

Just as they reached the Rio Grande and plunged their horses headlong into its waters—not an instant too soon—two giant explosions lit up the night and deafened everyone near. The mules were obliterated. Fortunately Paddy Graydon and his men had been able to keep a sufficient interval between themselves and the animals so that nobody was actually hurt. Of course the Confederate camp was fully aroused and no surprise was possible for the rest of the night. "Graydon's charge" (for the river, with two mules pursuing) became a topic for many a delighted quip among Canby's soldiers.

Next morning Roberts crossed the river, attacked the Confederate advance party, and drove it back. Toward noon Sibley's main force came up, and about the same time Canby appeared with reinforcements and took charge of the Union operations. Sibley was sick, so that he could not sit his saddle, and the direction of the Texas forces was relinquished by him to Colonel Thomas Green.

At once the engagement became general, the Texans having the greater incentive—they were mighty thirsty and wanted to reach that water. On Canby's left, Hall's battery hammered the gray lines, and on his right McRae's battery was equally busy with grape and shell. The two battle lines took such protection as they could behind sand hills and lava beds, and in groves of trees that dotted the field.

A feinting charge by the Texans on the Union left drew off troops from the right. Then, suddenly, from behind sand hills and a thick bosque, the Texas cavalry burst out and thundered down upon McRea's guns.

"The charge was most desperate," wrote A. A. Hayes, a member of Canby's force, "the men [Confederates] relying principally on revolvers and bowie knives, and being maddened by thirst."

The guns were taken, the captain being killed with many of his men. Some of the New Mexico militia stampeded. Colonel Kit Carson, the old frontiersman, who commanded a regiment he had himself raised, held firm in the center; but Canby was forced to withdraw across the river and retreat to Fort Craig.

The Texans had won the ford, and a victory. They drank muddy Rio Grande water until all the wrinkles were smoothed out of their bellies. Canby reported his casualties as 68 dead, 160 wounded, and 35 missing, a total of 263. Green gave the Confederate loss as 36 killed, 150 wounded, and 1 missing, a total of 187.

Not bothering to reduce Fort Craig or further deal with Canby, Sibley marched on up the Rio Grande Valley. Without much opposition Albuquerque and Santa Fe were occupied. But Sibley's real objective was farther along.

At Fort Union, about thirty miles north of Las Vegas, was an important concentration of military stores. Since the post was not heavily garrisoned, no real trouble was expected in taking it, and Sibley dispatched a force of about a thousand men, under Colonel W. R. Scurry, to seize all that luscious matériel. To reach the fort, Scurry must pass through Apache Canyon, the gateway through the Sangre de Cristo Mountains. The Texans reached the mouth of the canyon March 10.

At Fort Union there was something like despair. Major Gabriel R. Paul, sure that he could not defend the post, mined it, prepared to blow it up and destroy the military supplies, and retreat north. But at the last moment help arrived.

Down from Colorado was marching a force of volunteers, composed chiefly of hard-rock miners from the Pikes Peak region, the toughest kind of fighting men, not taking too kindly to restraints or discipline, but eager when the bullets began to fly. At times whole companies of these miner-soldiers were under arrest for mutiny, but when word was passed that they soon would be going into battle they behaved well, as if this was what they had been waiting for.

Colonel J. P. Slough was their commander, but the man who was forever connected with their name, for good or ill, was a robustious, fanatical, fearless, Bible-pounding, presiding elder of the Methodist Church, Lieutenant Colonel J. M. Chivington. It was this same Chivington who two years later directed the massacre of peaceful Cheyennes at Sand Creek, for which history has never forgiven him; and who coined the bloodthirsty slogan, "Kill and scalp all [Indians], big and little; nits make lice."

He had been one of Jim Lane's bushwhacking Jayhawkers in the border troubles of Kansas and Missouri during the John Brown days, alternately preaching brimstone-and-damnation and cutting throats. When the Colorado volunteers were mustered he was in Denver, and he spoke to them with such fire-eating eloquence that he was offered the chaplaincy of the regiment. He refused. "If I go with the soldiers, I am going to fight," he said. Governor Gilpin of Colorado gave him a major's commission, and eventually he became colonel of the regiment. War—whether against Hell, the Missourians of the Kansas border, Indians, or the Texas invaders of New Mexico—gave his extraordinarily belligerent nature the strife it enjoyed.

The Colorado troops descended to the foot of Raton Pass in northeastern New Mexico, March 7. A message reached them March 12 from Fort Union calling for help. In the next twenty-four hours they made a march of sixty-four miles, arriving at the fort March 13, when the Confederates were preparing to ascend Apache Canyon to Glorieta Pass.

Colonel Slough had a total force of 1342 men, including his hardrock Pikes Peakers, 300 regular infantry and two batteries of artillery. With these he plunged into the eastern end of Apache Canyon to stop the invaders.

The first brush occurred March 26, near the summit of Glorieta Pass, at the ranch of a Frenchman named Alex Valle, a colorful character who bore the nickname of Pigeon because of his enthusiasm in "cutting the pigeon's wing"—one of the more violent maneuvers in frontier dances, in which the dancer leaped in the air and cracked his heels together. His ranch was called Pigeon's ranch and the engagement fought on it often is given that name.

The headlong Chivington was in command of the advance guard which encountered the Confederate van. At the appearance of the Union troops two Confederate fieldpieces began to boom, sending grapeshot and shells screaming down the defile but not causing much damage. Chivington acted at once.

Deploying his infantry across the canyon and posting about a hundred cavalry behind a spur of the cliffs, he attacked. It was the first battle for the Colorado soldiers, but their deportment was far from that of ordinary green troops. With muskets rattling and the big guns creating thunderous echoes in the defile, they began a forward movement so businesslike, and a fire so deadly, that presently the Confederate commander limbered up his guns and prepared to fall back.

At that Chivington sent an order to his concealed cavalry. Out from their canyon pocket swept the horsemen, and down on the enemy's flank with yells and a flashing of sabers, "running over and trampling them under their horses' feet."

The Confederates retreated in full flight down the canyon, having lost 32 killed, 43 wounded, and 71 taken prisoner. Chivington, with a loss of only 5 killed and 14 wounded, did not pursue.

"It now being sundown, and we not knowing how near the enemy's reinforcements might be, and having no cannon to oppose theirs, hastened to gather up our dead and wounded and several of the enemy's, and then fell back to Pigeon's ranch and encamped for the night," he reported in a rather involved sentence, which nevertheless made sense.

All the honors of the brisk little skirmish rested with Chivington and his Colorado hard-rock men. A Texan, writing to his wife, described them: "Instead of Mexicans and regulars, they were regular demons, that iron and lead had no effect on them, in the shape of Pikes Peakers from the Denver gold mines."

Said Alex Valle, the ebullient, heel-cracking Frenchman, "Zat Chivington, he poot 'is 'ead down, and fought loike mahd bull!"

Next day Slough, with the main Union force, came up and joined Chivington at Pigeon's ranch. Scouts reported the approach along the canyon of considerable numbers of Confederates. It was the main Texas force under Colonel Scurry and the hour had come for a conclusive engagement.

The night of March 27, Slough detached Chivington with 440 men to make a steep and dangerous detour through the mountains and if possible fall on the Confederate rear. The following morning Slough moved forward and encountered the enemy in force just beyond Pigeon's ranch. It appears to have been something of a surprise to the Federals, and Slough later reported, "Having met the enemy where he was not expected, the action was defensive from its beginnings to its end." As a matter of fact, the action became a rather hasty retreat, with the Texans driving the Union troops a considerable distance along the canyon in this contest for Glorieta Pass.

It was, as Colonel Scurry asserted in his report, a Confederate victory. Yet just when he should have made another, and perhaps decisive, attack, a flag of truce instead was sent forward, asking an armistice for the burial of the dead. This was agreed to by the Federal commander. The following day, at the expiration of the armistice period, the gray-clad forces were in full retreat from the canyon.

Why this surprising withdrawal, after the Federals had been whipped and driven? The activities of the bellicose parson, Chivington, provided the answer to that question. Guided by Lieutenant Colonel Manuel Chavez, who was a native of the country and knew the remote trails, he led his 320 Colorado volunteers and 120 regulars over treacherous paths across the rugged mountains.

About noon he reached a point where, from the heights of precipitous cliffs, he could look down on Johnson's ranch, at which were assembled the supply trains, ammunition wagons, one piece of reserve artillery and the transport livestock of the enemy, under a guard of about two hundred men.

Chavez indicated the steep and dangerous path down. Chivington nodded. In single file, horses sometimes sliding, sometimes almost toppling over as they fought to keep their footing, the whole command began the descent. All reached the bottom safely.

The appearance of Federals almost literally from the clouds took by complete surprise the Confederate rear guard, which did not imagine a blue uniform within miles. Chivington led the charge. The Confederates were briskly swept back, finally routed.

Chivington proceeded systematically to destroy everything of military value. All ammunition, supplies, rations, even surgical stores were demolished. He later reported that his men bayoneted eleven hundred mules and burned sixty-four wagons with their contents, besides spiking the gun they captured.

It was a messenger from his defeated rear guard, flying to Scurry with this news, who caused the Confederate colonel to ask for the armistice and retreat. Chivington, meantime, climbed up the mountains, retraced his path of the night before, and joined the Union Army where it was camped on the pass.

The fight at Glorieta Pass was the high-water mark of Confederate advance in the Southwest. What began as an invasion turned into a retreat. His ammunition gone, Scurry and his Texans fell back on Santa Fe. Colonel Slough wished to pursue him, but received orders to remain and protect Fort Union at all hazards. In disgust he resigned and Chivington became colonel of the regiment. It was a rank he certainly had earned, for that little side operation of his was the decisive blow of the entire New Mexico campaign.

His army defeated, its supplies gone, Sibley retreated from Santa Fe, harried every step of the way by the Colorado soldiers and by Canby, until early in May they were out of New Mexico. So ended the Texas invasion of New Mexico, threatened since the days of Santa Anna. Of the force sent out to capture the territory, more than half were left behind in killed, wounded or captured.

In his general report, written May 4, Sibley made clear his feelings:

"I cannot speak encouragingly of the future, my troops having manifested a dogged, irreconcilable detestation of the country and its people."

The "dogged, irreconcilable detestation," he might have added, was contributed to, in no small degree, by the Colorado hard-rock men.

CHAPTER FOUR

Reaping the Whirlwind

ALTHOUGH Mangus Colorado had long been on the warpath against the white men, Cochise, chief of the Chiricahua Apaches, while always ready to raid against the Mexicans, held back from fighting the Americans.

The Chiricahua Mountains of Arizona, which were the camping and hunting grounds of Cochise's people, are pierced by the steep-sided and narrow Apache Pass—not to be confused with the Apache Canyon of New Mexico—the only natural highway through the great barrier and therefore the route of the Butterfield mail stagecoaches. About halfway through the pass stood a stone stage station, the keeper of which, a man named Wallace, gained the friendship of the Chiricahuas and contracted with them to furnish wood for his station. So loyal was Cochise to this agreement that the sage line operated without molestation through the very heart of his country.

Some time previously a comely Mexican woman had been captured by the Apaches and kept by them for a year or two before she was ransomed or rescued. During this period she gave birth to a child, of which one of the Apache warriors was the father. The lady retained her comeliness; and after her return to her people, Johnny Ward, a bachelor, took her to his ranch shack on the Sonoita River, where she lived with him and her small son in evident content.

But in October 1860 a band of Apaches raided the ranch, burned Ward's house, ran off his cattle, and carried away the child. This child, incidentally, grew up among the Apaches and is believed to have been Mickey Free, who gained some renown in later years, during the Geronimo days, as a scout and interpreter for the United States Army.

When report of the raid reached Fort Buchanan, Lieutenant George N. Bascom set out with sixty men to recover the boy and the livestock. Bascom was just out of West Point and knew a lot about spit and polish but less than nothing about handling Indians.

Told that there was an Indian camp in Apache Pass near the stage station—where Cochise and his band lived for convenience in supplying the station with wood—Bascom led his men directly there, without bothering to ascertain whether or not those particular Indians were guilty of making the raid. At his summons, Cochise and several of his

leading warriors came to the stage station. Bascom began by demanding that they return the missing cattle and the child to him, and ended
by peremptorily ordering the arrest of Cochise.

At first the Apache chief could not believe the officer was serious,
since he himself had been noted for his peaceful policy toward the
white man. But when he saw Bascom's men advancing to arrest him,
he led a dash for freedom in which, though wounded, he escaped,
with all his warriors except five, who were captured and held.

From that moment began the hostility of one of the deadliest Apache
leaders. Firing broke out along the canyon sides, to which the soldiers
in the bottom replied as well as they could, inasmuch as they could see
nothing of their enemy, concealed in the trees above. Bascom lost
several men. In the midst of this the five captured warriors tried to
escape. Two were killed and the other three overpowered.

That night a stagecoach reached the station. It was the last to
traverse Apache Pass in many long months. It had been attacked, but
the driver cut loose a horse shot down in its traces and managed to get
to the shelter of the stone station.

On the third day Captain B. J. D. Irwin—later a general—arrived
with fifteen men to reinforce the soldiers in the canyon and take command. Irwin had captured three Apaches on his way up, so now there
were six prisoners. The troops at the stone station were suffering from
thirst and there were wounded to be attended.

Next night a wagon train, unaware of the suddenly created hostility
of the Chiricahuas, was cut off and eight persons killed, while three
were carried away as captives. Matters were becoming desperate. At
last Wallace, who knew the Indians, said he would try to talk with
Cochise and see if he could get a peaceful settlement. With two of the
stage employees he went up in the woods. They did not return. So
hostile had the Indians become that they seized their former friends,
the stage people, and held them.

Next day Cochise brought his six captives into view of the soldiers
and offered to exchange them for his six warriors. Irwin and Bascom
feared treachery and would not make the exchange.

That night Cochise tortured his six prisoners to death.

The providential arrival of two companies of cavalry from Fort
Buchanan saved the survivors in Apache Pass. As they retreated down
the gorge they found the bodies of the six white men who had been
put to death. In reprisal they hung the six Apache warriors and left
them for Cochise to cut down.

A blundering West Point shavetail had started something greater and
more terrible than he could have imagined—a general Apache war.
From this time forth Cochise gave full co-operation to Mangus Colo-

rado, and for the next twenty-five years the Apaches as a people never really ceased fighting.

In western Texas the Mescalero Apaches, under their chiefs Cadete and Nicolás, kept Fort Davis, occupied by the Confederates in the Big Bend country, in a state of siege. They wiped out the settlements along the Rio Bonita, ambushed and destroyed a column of Confederate cavalry under Lieutenant May, and depopulated the entire area.

In New Mexico, Mangus Colorado attacked his old enemies of the Pinos Altos mines and cut off a wagon train, but was forced to draw away by the timely arrival of a party of the highly informal Arizona Rangers. The chief was not, however, through with the mining settlement. Balked of direct attack, he began the same sort of siege he had formerly thrown about Santa Rita del Cobre—a silent, unseen watch, warriors prowling in concealment, keeping all supplies from reaching it, and cutting off any who ventured out from it, except in strong parties. Slowly Pinos Altos starved.

Elsewhere in their country the Apaches were supreme, so that Colonel Baylor, appointed Confederate military governor of New Mexico and Arizona during the brief months of Sibley's campaign up the Rio Grande, recommended that every Apache man, wherever found, be killed on sight, and the women and children sold into slavery. President Jefferson Davis promptly rejected the policy and demanded an explanation. To justify himself, Baylor wrote to General Magruder, commanding in Texas, including a ghastly exhibit, the scalp of a Miss Jackson, which had been taken by the Indians, with a request that it be forwarded to Davis. His letter said:

Arizona has been kept in poverty by Indian depredations . . . and the general belief among the people is that extermination of the grown Indians and making slaves of the children is the only remedy. This system has been practiced in New Mexico. There is not a family of wealth in that country but has Indian slaves derived from that source. In fact so popular is this system of civilizing the Indian that there have been several efforts to pass a law in the New Mexico legislature, making all Indians slaves for life.

Davis, far from agreeing with Baylor's "civilizing" method, removed him as governor. But shortly after, the Confederates ceased to be a factor as Chivington and Canby drove them out of the territory.

Early in April, California, having settled within its own borders the question of loyalty to the Union, sent eastward a little army of about fourteen hundred men under the command of General J. H. Carleton.

Mangus Colorado and Cochise had due notice of their coming. In fact Carleton himself supplied the warning. He sent three express

riders with dispatches for Canby from Tucson, June 15. The men were
Sergeant Wheeling, Private John Jones and a Mexican guide named
Chavez. In a running fight the Apaches killed Wheeling and Chavez,
and though Jones, "almost by a miracle"—to use the words of Carleton's
report—succeeded in escaping to the Rio Grande, he was captured by
the Confederates.

Realizing from the incident of the three dispatch bearers that something was happening toward the west, the Apaches scouted in that
direction, discovered Carleton's force advancing from Tucson, and prepared to resist it in Apache Pass.

On June 12, Carleton forwarded another set of dispatches to Canby,
this time by Lieutenant Colonel E. E. Eyre and an escort of 140 men.
The size of the escort is sufficient evidence of the gravity of the Apache
peril. While camping near the abandoned stage station in Apache Pass,
Eyre had a parley with the chief of a band of about seventy-five warriors—undoubtedly Cochise. The Apache leader asked for tobacco and
food, and departed after viewing Eyre's detachment, which was too
strong for his immediate force of warriors. As he went, however, he
cut off three men and killed them. Eyre ordered a pursuit but the
Indians easily outdistanced it. Later the same day they did some
sniping from the top of the canyon wall, wounding Surgeon Kittredge
and killing a horse. The Apaches were not yet ready for a full-dress
battle, and Cochise did not molest Eyre further as the latter went on
and joined Canby. Probably at this time Cochise was awaiting the
arrival of Mangus Colorado and his Mimbreños.

By the time Carleton's main army neared Apache Pass the Indians
were ready. As the advance guard of three hundred men, under Captain Thomas Roberts, started up the gorge toward the stage station and
its springs, the Apache yell was suddenly raised, and bullets and
arrows came whizzing down from the canyon walls where, according
to Roberts, "several hundred Indians" were concealed.

Although he lost only two killed and two wounded in the first fire,
Roberts fell back from his position, which was untenable. But he had
to reach the water and he had the answer to an Indian ambush. Bringing up two howitzers, he began shelling the heights. To the Apaches
the experience was novel and terrifying, since they never before had
encountered the "wagon guns that shoot twice"—a reference to the
shells, which exploded after being fired. In astonishment and some
panic they retreated far enough up the canyon so that Roberts could
reach the springs on which the army depended for water.

A messenger, escorted by a small detachment of cavalry, was sent
back to Carleton, requesting reinforcements, and Roberts prepared for
the next day's fighting, which he supposed would be a real and perhaps

costly battle. But when morning came the Apaches had disappeared. The whole army marched on through the pass without seeing another Indian.

Two miles beyond the pass they found what was left of nine men from the Pinos Altos mines. Carleton's report said, "One of them had been burned at the stake; we saw the charred bones and the burnt ends of the rope by which he had been tied." It was another of Mangus Colorado's little attentions to Pinos Altos. His back still smarted from that flogging.

But what happened to create such a different situation in Apache Pass? Why did what appeared to be a formidable fight turn out to be no more than a preliminary skirmish? The resolute behavior of one man, and a stroke of luck, brought about the surprising change.

When Roberts sent his message back to Carleton, Indians on horseback tried to cut off the small escort. In the running chase they killed the horse of Private John Teal. His comrades could only ride for their lives with the message, which was imperatively important, leaving him to his fate.

Teal prepared to die gamely, crouching with his carbine behind his dead horse. At a fairly long range about him galloped the Apaches, preparing for the scurrying charge by which they would close with him. The trooper noticed that their leader was an exceptionally large man, but did not dream that this was the famous Mangus Colorado himself. He aimed at the giant with great care and pulled the trigger. The huge warrior tumbled out of his saddle.

To Teal's amazement, the Apaches at once seemed to lose all interest in him. They gathered about their fallen leader and bore him away, their voices "growing fainter in the distance." After a time, it having grown dark, Teal rose and walked unmolested to camp, carrying his saddle with him.

It was the wounding of Mangus Colorado that ended the Apache Pass fight. From their positions in the heights the Indians withdrew, leaving the way open. Southward to Janos, a Mexican town, they carried their chief, and occupied the streets while the inhabitants cowered in their homes. A Mexican doctor was confronted by some of the warriors, bearing the wounded Mangus Colorado.

"Make Indian well," said the spokesman curtly. "He die, everybody in Janos die. He no die, everybody live."

No physician ever exerted more prayerful care, perhaps, than this one as he treated his savage patient. Fortunately the rawhide constitution of the sufferer was in his favor. The bullet was extracted, the wound bound up, and Mangus lived. The people of Janos watched thankfully as the unwelcome visitors departed without any new scalps.

But the chief, who was growing old, never fully recovered from his wound.

Meantime, Carleton and the California column, safely through the Chiricahua Mountains, reached New Mexico, where Carleton took over the command from Canby.

One of his acts was to send a strong detachment under Lieutenant E. D. Shirland to convey food to the people at Pinos Altos, who were starving under Mangus Colorado's siege. The rescue force reached the mining settlement August 6, with five beeves, six hundred pounds of pemmican, three thousand pounds of flour and fifteen hundred pounds of *panocha* (Mexican sugar), and found the people in terrible destitution. Shirland reported there were "about thirty Americans, French, Germans, &c; two of the Germans with families; all the rest were Mexicans . . . received . . . little assistance before our arrival, before which time they had been living on purslane and roots, and several had become insane from hunger."

Mangus Colorado's dealings with those he hated were not light.

With New Mexico secure from the Confederates, Carleton, who was no lover of Indians, turned his full attention to the Apaches. The Mescaleros in west Texas and southeast New Mexico were the objectives of three columns sent against them, all with identical orders: "The men are to be slain whenever and wherever they can be found. The women may be taken prisoners, but, of course they are not to be killed."

Captain McCleave with two companies of Californians encountered the Mescaleros in Canyon del Perro, shot it out with them, and routed them. The Indians knew when they had enough. They also knew better than to surrender to the Californians. Instead they fled to Kit Carson, who was in their country with five companies, and surrendered to him.

Cadete, whose Indian name was Gian-na-tah (Always Ready), made a short speech to Carson, which is preserved and is reminiscent of the famous "From where the sun now stands" utterance of Chief Joseph of the Nez Percés on a similar occasion: "You are stronger than we. We have fought you as long as we had rifles and powder; but your weapons are better than ours. Give us like weapons and turn us loose, we will fight you again; but we are worn out; we have no more heart; we have no provisions, and no means to live; your troops are everywhere; you have driven us from our last and best stronghold and we have no more heart. Do with us as may seem good to you, but do not forget that we are men and braves."

Carson, the old frontiersman, understood the Indians. He took the liberty of disobeying Carleton's extermination orders. Instead he sent the Mescaleros to the Bosque Redondo reservation.

Carleton with equal assiduity devoted himself also to the western Apaches—the Mimbreños, Chiricahuas and other bands. Results against those desert sidewinders were at first disappointing. But suddenly, in January 1863, came a windfall for the white man.

Prospectors were encouraged by Carleton to go in strong parties into the Indian country, looking for gold or silver, because this gave him an excuse to ask for more troops to hunt down the Indians for the "protection" of the gold seekers. One such party, under Captain Joseph Walker, camping near Fort McLean, learned that old Mangus Colorado was in the vicinity with some of his Mimbreños. That day E. D. Shirland, the rescuer of Pinos Altos, now a captain, visited the prospectors with a detachment of soldiers. Walker conferred with him and suggested to him a plan to "eliminate" the Apache chief which would have made a Judas blush. Shirland, however, was no Judas. He agreed promptly, and without blushing.

Under a promise that peace would be made between the white men and his people, Mangus Colorado, sick and aging, was induced to come alone into the camp. Once they had him among them, the soldiers and prospectors disarmed him and made him understand that he was a prisoner.

When word of this reached Colonel J. R. West, commanding at Fort McLean, he rode over to the prospectors' camp with an escort. Arriving after dark, he surveyed the great-limbed Indian captive by the light of a campfire, where he was being guarded by Shirland's soldiers, and gave instructions to two of the guards, Privates James Collyer and George Mead.

"Men," he said, "that old murderer has got away from every soldier command, and has left a trail of blood for five hundred miles on the old stage line. I want him dead or alive tomorrow morning. Do you understand? *I want him dead.*"

That night, according to a witness, D. E. Conner, one of the prospectors, the soldiers heated their bayonets in the fire and burned the feet and legs of the sleeping prisoner. When Mangus Colorado rose on his left elbow in pain and angry protest, they shot him to death. Colonel West reported that the prisoner was "killed while attempting to escape."

So treachery ended the life of the Apache who could not be conquered by honest force of arms. Mangus Colorado had made a vast contribution to the history of his race. Captain John C. Cremony, who knew him and his people well, wrote of him, "He was the greatest and most talented Apache of the Nineteenth Century. . . . His sagacious counsels partook more of the character of wide and enlightened statesmanship than those of any other Indian of modern times. . . . He found means to collect and keep together, for weeks at a time, large bodies of savages, such as none of his predecessors could assemble and feed . . . and taught them to comprehend the value of unity and collective strength. . . . Take him all in all, he exercised influence never equalled by any savage of our time."

Later Apaches, such as Cochise and Geronimo—who waged war on the whites when the writing of sensational Western literature became popular—received more publicity than Mangus Colorado. But Geronimo never was more than a minor outlaw raider; and Cochise never did a tithe of the warlike damage to white interlopers that Mangus Colorado did. Cochise was present and unhurt when Mangus was wounded at Apache Pass; yet so much greater did Mangus Colorado loom in the minds of the Apaches that they desisted from the battle and bore him away. He was the rimrock Apache, the greatest figure of his race.

A disgusting detail of the murder of the old chief was that the head was severed from the body by a surgeon and the brain taken out and weighed. The head measured larger than that of Daniel Webster and the brain was of corresponding weight. For a time the skull ornamented the phrenological museum of Professor O. S. Fowler. It is said now to be in the Smithsonian Institution, in Washington, D.C.

The final comment on him by J. P. Dunn was: "It was time for him to die. He was about seventy years old, and had secured all the revenge to which one man is entitled."

After the death of Mangus Colorado, the Apaches took to their hiding places and there was a cessation of raids on the border. But the extermination policy continued. One of its ugliest episodes was the so-called "Pinal Treaty," January 24, 1864. Colonel King S. Woolsey, with thirty Americans and fourteen Pima and Maricopa Indians, encountered a band of Pinal Apaches, led by a chief named Par-a-muck-a. When he invited them to come in and make peace, thirty-five of them did so. Woolsey seated them, and announced with a vicious sort of irony—which escaped them—that he would "give them certificates of good conduct such that no white man would ever molest them." The Indians remained seated while Woolsey's followers gathered about them, making ready for the "treaty." When his men were posted, "Woolsey drew his revolver and gave Par-a-muck-a the Arizona certificate of a 'good Indian' at the first shot. His men signed on the bodies of others. Only one Indian—a lame man who could not run away—affixed his signature. He did it with his lance, on the person of Mr. Cyrus Lennon."

The Apaches were for the moment relatively inactive, but the Navajos frisked wild and fancy-free in northern New Mexico and Arizona. They made numerous "peace treaties," beginning with Doniphan, but found it inexpedient to keep any of them. The Navajos warred on the Mexicans, and the Mexicans on the Navajos, "the common opinion being that the Navajos captured the greater number of sheep, and the Mexicans the greater number of slaves."

Navajo slaves were in demand, "on account of their tractable nature, intelligence, light skins, and the voluptuousness of the females." One writer, Dr. Louis Kennon, said between five and six thousand Navajos were held as slaves at this period. "I know of no family which can raise $150 but what purchases a Navajo slave," he recorded, "and many families own four or five—the trade in them being as regular as the trade in pigs or sheep."

Kit Carson was the man most conversant with Indian ways, and at last Carleton called on him to solve the Navajo problem. During the winter of 1863–64 the Navajos retreated as usual to their stronghold, the Canyon de Chelly. The canyon is one of America's natural wonders, rivaling in some respects even the Grand Canyon in spectacular features. Its sheer walls of red sandstone reach a height of nearly fifteen hundred feet in places, and it is so narrow at certain points that a stone can almost be thrown from one precipice lip to the other. In only a few places can it be entered by men, and in even fewer by animals. The bottom of this great chasm is flat and sandy, with the waters of Chelly Creek flowing through it.

Before the Navajos occupied the canyon the Cliff Dwellers lived there, and their deserted habitations may still be seen in niches high on the canyon walls. On the floor of the gorge the Navajos had their little orchards of peach trees and herded their sheep, while there and above, on the level desert, were their *hogans,* the distinctive moundlike dwellings of logs and earth which they build. In Canyon de Chelly the Navajos believed themselves safe for the winter, as they always had been.

But Kit Carson had another notion. He knew where the canyon was, and though neither he nor any other officer had much knowledge of its topography or the difficulties which confronted an expedition to it, he decided that winter was the time to strike the Navajos there.

With 390 officers and men he left Fort Canby, January 6, 1864. It was a season of bad weather and snows which exhausted animals and men, and would have appalled anyone except the old Indian fighter. Even he had to abandon part of his supply train, but he pushed on, reaching Canyon de Chelly January 12.

That day his scouts, under Sergeant Andrés Herrera, jumped a party of Indians, killed eleven, and captured two women and two children. Carson next day divided his command in three divisions, one on each rim of the canyon, the other on its bottom. They moved the entire length of the great fissure in the earth, fought two or three skirmishes and, as Carson reported, killed 23 Navajos, captured 234, seized two hundred sheep, and destroyed about three thousand peach trees in the canyon.

In despair over this destruction, the Navajos asked how they could have peace. Carson told them to go to the Bosque Redondo, a reservation on the Pecos River. It was named from a round grove of trees and was said to have been visited by both Coronado and Espejo in early explorations. Later it was a trading post. In 1862, Fort Sumner was erected there and the Mescaleros established on a reservation near it, Captain Cremony becoming agent for them.

Kit Carson's "long walk"—as the Navajos still call it—had a most salutary effect. The Indians began coming into the Bosque Redondo in such numbers that Carleton's resources were heavily taxed to support them. By the following July more than seven thousand of them had surrendered and were living off the government. They stayed at the Bosque Redondo until 1878, when they were removed to their present reservation. Exit the Navajos from history as enemies of the white man.

But the Apaches were of different stuff. They refused to surrender even though the Indian hunt went on throughout the dreadful sixties. The number of encounters which took place with them is illustrated by the fact that six pages of fine type were required to enumerate them in the General Orders of 1865. By that time official reports showed 363 Indians killed and 140 wounded; 7 soldiers killed and 25 wounded; 18 civilians killed and 13 wounded.

In spite of this progress along the road toward extermination, however, the Apaches still bushwhacked and ambushed, made it almost impossible to maintain the stage routes, scalped and raided and escaped. While the Apaches were on the loose, settlement in southern Arizona was virtually impossible.

BOOK 7

Epic
of
Horn-spiked
Herds

In Spite of Hell and High Water

O N A P R I L 9, 1865, General Robert E. Lee, after an incomparable defense for four years against great odds, surrendered what was left of the Confederate Army of Northern Virginia to General Ulysses S. Grant, whose hammer blows at last had crushed him. It was the end of the Civil War, although other Confederate armies made their surrenders later.

The last shot fired in hostility between the North and South was an engagement in Texas, at Palmito, near the scene of Zachary Taylor's Mexican War victory of Palo Alto, May 12, 1865. It might, incidentally, be called a Confederate victory, since the Union force under Colonel Theodore H. Barrett was forced to retreat. If there was any consolation to the Southern cause that it won the final battle, that was about the only grain of satisfaction remaining. The South was completely beaten and prostrate.

In Texas, with the coming of peace, came also those years of bitterness, misrule, strife and readjustment known as the Reconstruction. For five years Texas drained the bitter cup of Carpetbagger rule to the dregs. Then, in 1870, having complied with the statutory requirements, the state was readmitted to the Union. The Amnesty Act, signed by President Grant in 1872, re-enfranchised all in the South except for a few who had been especially prominent as leaders in the Confederacy; and even these gradually were readmitted to citizenship by special acts, and at last by the general Amnesty Law of 1898.

Aside from Texas, the Southwest was little affected by the Reconstruction and other postwar problems. One aftermath of some importance in New Mexico was the abolishment of peonage, or debt service, by Congress March 2, 1867—a tardy reform, brought about by the emancipation of Negro slaves, of an abuse which had continued in one form or another since the first Spanish occupation of the territory.

Meanwhile something else was taking place; something having nothing to do with laws or lawmakers, elections or race problems, but which intimately affected the whole Southwest, starting with Texas and extending to New Mexico and Arizona—which had become separate territories in 1863—spreading eventually over the entire West. In its way it had greater influence on history than the gold rushes and its effect was infinitely more permanent. It brought about indirectly the subjugation at last of the warlike Indian tribes, the arrival of civilization in the farthest confines of the nation, and put the stamp of the Southwest on a full half of the continental United States.

It was the sudden, strange extension, amounting almost to an explosion, of the cattle range in America.

From the very first arrival of the white man, cattle were part of the authentic Southwest scene. That visionary explorer, Coronado, when he made his long and disappointing march through the pueblo country and on up into the high plains, had large herds of slaughter animals, including sheep, hogs and cattle, driven at the rear of his army. Such of his cattle as survived the journey up through New Spain, and the necessity of the mess kettles, were the first to cross the present borders of the United States.

It has been theorized that some of Coronado's horses and cattle escaped and lived to perpetuate their breeds, thus being the ancestors of the wild herds of mustangs and longhorns which later were so typical and colorful a part of the wilderness. This speculation, unfortunately for romance, is hardly acceptable. Coronado's soldiers were Spaniards, and the Spaniard had a preference for stallions as steeds. The padres rode mules, when they did not walk "in the apostolic manner." Arthur H. Aiton, who made a study of the Coronado muster rolls, discovered that there was an accurate count of horses, with a distinction between *caballos* (stallions) and *yeguas* (mares). Only two mares were listed, wherefore, as he pointed out, "the possibility, biologically considered, that stray horses from Coronado's expedition stocked the plains is slight." As to cattle, when the expedition, disillusioned and bitter at its failure to find the cities of gold, returned to New Spain in 1542, the record says "no slaughter animals were left."

But if Coronado did not bring cattle and horses permanently to the American West, others soon did. In New Spain cattle *ranchos* spread rapidly from the time of the final conquest of the Aztec Empire, the nature of the country and people being favorable to them.

Indian slaves were the first herdsmen and became the forerunners of the *vaquero*, and hence of the cowboy. And here arises an interesting speculation. When the Spaniards at last wearied of slaughter, in the bloody conquest of Tenochtitlán, they took thousands' of captives. These Cortés caused to be branded on the cheek with a G, for *Guerra*

(War), and sold as slaves. That was in 1519. The first tiny seed herd
of cattle was brought to New Spain by Gregorio de Villalobos two
years later. It can be surmised almost with certainty that Villalobos
had a herdsman to care for his cattle who wore an angry red G scarred
on his brown cheek. If so, by a curious twist, the first "cowboy" in this
hemisphere bore a brand before the first cow.

In the beginning the Spaniards made it unlawful for a native to ride
a horse, and the first herdsmen worked on foot. But after a time this
prejudice was erased, the advantage of the horse in handling cattle
being so obvious, and gradually certain characteristics were developed
by the *vaqueros*, through generation after generation, which became
part of the cattle tradition. Loyalty to the outfit, reckless disregard of
personal danger, wonderful skill and dexterity with the lariat, a prejudice against walking when one could ride even a short distance, pride
in the ability to mount and stay on anything with four legs and hair—
these grew up in the cattle country of New Spain. Some principles also
were established. Water rights, for one thing, whereby possession of
water was tantamount to possession of the range surrounding it. Also
the sacredness of the brand.

The *vaquero* provided also a distinctive argot for the range. Spanish-
Mexican influence is seen in words like corral, tapaderas, remuda,
segundo, bronco, jinete (bronco buster), orejano (unbranded steer),
frijoles, hombre, loco, arroyo, and morral, which are almost pure
Spanish. Other words were more or less twisted in transition to the
American tongue. There is little difference between *lazo* and lasso,
la reata and lariat, *rodear* and rodeo, *adobe* and doby, *pinta* and pinto,
or *rancho* and ranch. But there were further distortions. The cowboy-
ism "cavvy yard," for instance, is from the chaste Spanish *caballado*.
Vaquero was turned into buckeroo. *Mesteño* became mustang. The
Mexican word *cocinero* (cook) wound up as coosie. The Spanish
jáquima was corrupted into hackamore. *Chaparreras* was shortened
to chaps. There are many others, among which one of the strangest is
the mutation of the name for the act of wrapping the lariat two or three
times around the saddle horn when roping an animal, in order to throw
it. The Spanish phrase for this was *de la vuelta* (a turn). On the tongue
of the American cowboy this degenerated into an approximation in
sound if not in written appearance—dolly welter, or simply dolly.

Oñate brought the first permanent cattle herd of record across the
line in 1598. Thereafter cattle spread quite rapidly. A vital part was
played by the missions, which encouraged livestock culture. Every
mission outpost had its herd and its native *vaqueros*.

By the time Austin's first Anglo-American colonists settled along the
Brazos in 1821, lower Texas swarmed with cattle. Most of the first

settlers became cattle owners for a good reason. Mexican land grants had this peculiarity: if a married colonist declared his intention to farm only, he received one *labor* (177 acres) of land. If, on the other hand, the same man declared his intention to raise livestock as well as farm, he was granted one *sitio* or square league (4438 acres) of grazing land, besides the *labor* of tillage land—adding up to 4615 acres. These grants were modified as time passed, but the distinction, which was based on a consideration of what land a farmer could till to crops, as contrasted with what a rancher could utilize, gave impetus and character to the whole economic life of Texas.

Taxes were paid in Texas on the following numbers of cattle, not including "wild cattle," in the years indicated:

1848	382,873
1855	1,363,688
1860	3,786,443

During the Civil War, ranches, unable to sell their increase, saw their herds grow to such an extent that when the ranchmen returned from the Confederate Army they found the cattle roaming wild in vast numbers, and so valueless that rounding up and branding them was almost a waste of time and labor.

It was a period of intense gloom and discontent in Texas. "Cattle poor" was the phrase of the day. Thousands of head were slaughtered for their hides and tallow, the carcasses being left to rot or be consumed by the buzzards, coyotes and other carrion eaters. Small packeries which rendered tallow, salt-cured hides, and pickled a little beef, were known as "hide and tallow factories." But they offered a market so small that the surface of the supply was hardly touched.

Yet through these clouds of darkness for the ranchers was coming a ray of light and hope. In the North, during the war, an industrial revolution had taken place. Military orders, greatly stimulating manufacturing, brought tens of thousands of people, who otherwise would have been raising food on the farms, to industrial cities. At the same time the nation became transportation-conscious. In the military campaigns railroads had played a part so vital that their importance was dramatically emphasized. It became apparent that the Pacific coast and the East must be linked, and in 1862 Congress passed the Union Pacific Act, offering government assistance to the proposed railroad which was to be built across the continent.

The war prevented construction of more than a few miles of this line, but after the war Congress passed other laws, whereby ten sections of public lands and a loan of $16,000 per mile of construction in United States bonds were offered as a stimulus to railroad building.

By 1866 a construction race was under way, two great rival rail interests fighting for the government bounty by seeking to outdistance each other in ground covered, as they hammered their way toward a common meeting place. Gangs of Irish immigrants pushed the steel westward from the Missouri and gangs of Chinese coolies pushed it eastward from the Pacific. The railheads met in Utah, at Promontory Point, and with the driving of a golden spike the continent was joined from coast to coast by rail.

That golden spike symbolized an event of far-reaching consequence to the West. In the postwar era of inflated prosperity the country was seized by a railroad-building mania, so that within a decade the nation's map was crisscrossed by the greatest web of rails anywhere on the globe; and as vast distances shrank because of regular and faster transportation, the United States became closely knit instead of widely scattered and provincial. One of the westward-pushing railroads was the Kansas Pacific, and Texas was the first of the Western states to profit greatly from the transportation it offered.

Long before the war some Texas cowmen had tried the experiment of trail-driving cattle to distant markets. As early as 1842 a rancher took a herd all the way to New Orleans. Shreveport became something of a market. And there is one strange story, shrouded in complete absence of details, and contained in a newspaper item quoted by the United States Department of Agriculture in 1855, which mentions that a drove of several hundred cattle from Texas was passing through Indiana County, Pennsylvania, on the way to New York City. Who were the adventurers who made that epic journey? What difficulties and perils did they meet? And what, in the end, became of their cattle? History is silent.

After 1849 a few daring Texas cattlemen, attracted by the market created by the gold stampede to California, trailed herds westward across the desert country, fighting Indians and hunting water as they went. Most went by the "northern route"—following the Rio Grande north to the mountains, crossing the continental divide in southern Colorado, angling again north to the California Overland Trail in northern Utah, and following that southwest across the Nevada flats and over the high Sierra passes, to San Francisco. It took two years for a trail herd to make that march, which was a lot of time, but on the northern route you avoided the Apaches.

There was a "southern route," too, by way of Albuquerque, across Arizona, and to the Mother Lode country of California by way of Walker's Pass over the Sierras. It was shorter by months than the northern route, but such unpleasant personages as Mangus Colorado, Cuchillo Negro, Delgadito and their various Apache bands might be encountered while traveling it, and the scalp of a man with the temerity to go that way sat uncomfortably loose on his skull.

Yet some Texans had the nerve to try it. One was Jack Cureton, a Ranger captain who took an outfit and a herd across the Indian-infested desert to California's lush pastures. He paid $10 a head for cattle in Texas, and sold them for $30 a head in California, which left him a neat profit even after deducting strays and deaths. But most men with a lingering prejudice in favor of living to a reasonable old age eschewed the Apache country. All in all, those first blind drives had little effect on the mounting numbers of cattle in Texas.

With the Civil War came one of those industrial miracles wars some-times bring. P. D. Armour, a square-set, side-whiskered man, who bet on Grant and the Union Army by selling pork short during the last stages of the conflict, cleaned up $1,500,000, and with his partner, John Plankinton, decided to establish a beef-packing business at Chicago, where the Union Stockyards, greatest of all livestock delivering and holding points, were completed Christmas Day, 1865.

The war had cleaned most of the cattle out of the East, while at the same time increasing the per capita demand for meat. Soldiers had dis-covered that beef was both satisfying and strengthening as food. Armour concluded that the West was the source to which the nation must look for its beef supply and acted accordingly. Others decided similarly, notably G. F. Swift. Competition grew up among them, so keen that they went to incredible lengths to utilize every bit of a car-cass, and at the same time cut prices to a point where their actual profit came from the by-products, the meat of the carcass little more than paying expenses. Refrigeration was introduced. Freight costs were studied and the westward march began. In 1869, to be still nearer the supply, Armour established the first packing plant in Kansas City. The American factory hand and clerk found that they could afford to eat meat, and with the middle years of the 1860s the packing com-panies had not only evolved cheaper meat for their customers but created a vastly increased demand for the steers of the cattleman—and a great industry, to go hand in hand with the spreading ranges of the West, was born.

Word of this trickled down into Texas, where war-worn Confederate veterans were wondering what to do with their enormous and appar-ently worthless herds.

Texas cattle were mostly true longhorns, products of climate, soil and surroundings, as well as of mixed bloods, and evolved by Nature to fit their environment and the conditions confronting them. They were not ideal for butchering, being bony, long-legged and tough. In color they ranged from brown, dun, red, black, occasional yellow, even

white, to curious combinations of all colors. It was their horns, out-
rageous and unbelievable, that gave them their names. These grew to
lengths and shapes that tax the credulity. Sometimes they corkscrewed.
At others they made prodigious sweeps. At still others they extended
almost straight out from the sides of the head. The longhorn steer
reached his full growth when he was about ten years old, but not so his
horns. They continued to lengthen and spread as long as the animal
lived. Old steers often carried horns seven feet from tip to tip. There is
a reliable record of seven feet, nine inches, by "pole measurement"—
straight across the tips of one pair of horns—and about nine feet following the curves of that particular pair. J. Frank Dobie, the greatest
authority on the longhorns, believes the most magnificent pair of horns
was worn by a steer named Champion. No measurement was attested
by affidavit, but the steer was exhibited in the East and Midwest, and
Chicago papers published an account of him, stating that his horn
spread was nine feet, seven inches. "A steer hitched to a pair of horns"
was a saying for the longhorn. Yet these cattle, turned loose to shift
for themselves, developed the endurance and the ability to survive
which alone fitted them for the great trail drives that were about to
begin.

In the spring of 1866 many stockmen simultaneously decided to
drive cattle north to the markets then centering in Chicago. There also
were some venturesome speculators from the North who went down
into Texas and by purchase made up herds for the drive.

The shocking state of cattle prices that year was shown by Joseph G.
McCoy in his *Historic Sketches of the Cattle Trade*. A buyer looked
over a herd of 3500 Texas steers and struck the following bargain: he
would purchase 600 head of his choice at $6.00 a head, and a second
600 at $3.00 a head. He thus took the 1200 choicest cattle from a herd
of 3500, at an average of $4.50 a head, or about 40 cents a hundred-
weight, gross.

Between 225,000 and 260,000 Texas cattle crossed the Red River and
strung out on their way north to a hoped-for market in the early months
of 1866. They were guided and guarded by bronzed riders, many of
whom had just exchanged the cavalry saddle for the stock saddle, and
wore their holstered six-shooters—and sometimes used them—with
practiced ease.

But that drive of 1866, with a few exceptions, proved to be a vast
failure and disappointment. The herds were preyed upon and stampeded by Indians in the Indian Territory. At the border of Kansas and
Missouri they were stopped by "committees" of grangers, who feared
the "Spanish fever"—later identified as being caused by blood ticks—
which the Texas cattle would transmit to domestic stock.

To the legitimate opposition of the farmers was added guerrilla work by bands of outlaws, the product of the war, known as Jayhawkers. These sometimes extorted bribes before they would permit cattle to pass; sometimes stampeded herds so that they could make off with part of the scattered animals; and abused, flogged, and even murdered trail drivers who would not accede to their demands.

South of the Kansas border the herds piled up, ate off all the grass, and countless cattle died of starvation. Others were disposed of by their despairing owners for little or nothing, and even these owners were sometimes defrauded by glib-tongued strangers who gave them bogus checks or drafts. Of more than a quarter of a million Texas longhorns which were driven north with infinite labor and peril that year, very few were sold at anything approaching a profit.

One trail driver of 1866 kept a diary—the only one, so far as is known. He was George C. Duffield, a young Iowan, and his journal was published in the *Annals of Iowa* in 1924. Since it gives a firsthand picture of trail-driving conditions, it is worth glancing at.

It was on April 29, 1866, that he and his partner Harvey Ray, with a herd of cheap cattle bought in Texas and an outfit of Texas cowboys, began what was to be a hard and exasperating northward journey. Stampedes occurred May 1, May 6, and very frequently thereafter. By May 9 young Duffield was wishing fervently that he was through with his task, as his entry on that date shows: "Still dark & Gloomy River up everything looks *Blue* to me." Four days later, in a thunderstorm, another maddening stampede added to his gloom, although he recovered all but fifty of his steers: "all tired Everything discouraging."

When he reached the Brazos real trouble began. It took three days to cross his approximately one thousand cattle, and his camp outfit and remuda. The animals swam and the provisions and camp equipment were rafted over. Unhappily, most of the "Kitchen furniture such as camp Kittles Coffee Pots Plates &c &c" were lost in the stream. After rounding up the cattle on the other side of the river, "all Hands gave the Brazos one good harty dam," and rode away, without joy.

Rain fell, the wind blew almost continuously, and some of the Texas herders grew sulky and quit. On May 20, Duffield wrote: "Rain pourd down for two hours Ground flooded Creeks up—Hands leaving Gloomey times as ever I saw."

Most of their few remaining cooking utensils were lost crossing the Trinity, and the following night, May 23, "Hard rain that night & cattle behaved very bad—ran all night—was on my Horse the whole night & it raining hard. Glad to see Morning come counted & found we had lost none for the first time—feel very bad."

At the Red River three more days were required to put the herd across. And here a cowboy named Carr, caught in a whirlpool while working with the swimming herd, was drowned. To make matters worse, the perverse longhorns stampeded the night after the crossing. Duffield wrote: "hard rain & wind Storm Beeves ran & had to be on Horse back all night. Awful night. wet all night clear bright morning. Men still lost quit the Beeves and go Hunting Men is the word—4 p.m. Found our men with Indian guide & 195 Beeves 14 miles from camp. allmost starved not having had a bite to eat for 60 hours got to camp about 12 m *Tired.*"

For a few days things went a little better, although the country was boggy with heavy downpours and the rivers and creeks gave constant trouble. But on June 12 came the following entry: "Hard Rain & Wind Big stampede & here we are among the Indians with 150 head of Cattle gone hunted all day & the Rain pouring down with but poor success Dark days are these to me Nothing but Bread & Coffee Hands all Growling & Swearing."

It was enough to make them swear, but their troubles were only beginning. On June 17 they reached the Arkansas where Duffield spent four days swimming the herd across that flooded river. "Worked all day hard in the River trying to make the Beeves swim & did not get one over," wrote the doleful chronicler at the end of the first day's effort. "Had to go back to the Prairie Sick & discouraged. Have *not* got the *Blues* but am in *Hel of a fix.*"

Eventually the cattle were crossed and they reached the vicinity of Baxter Springs, Kansas, July 10. There Duffield found the cap of his misfortunes. The Jayhawkers were swarming on the border. Duffield encountered several cattle herds being held on the grass and heard from their drivers disquieting reports of the Jayhawker activities. One cowboy already had been killed and many cattle stolen. Anger and discouragement prevailed.

For several days Duffield tried to negotiate a way through the barrier. He faced an impossibility. But he had plenty of courage, for all his woeful feelings. On July 25 his entry was: "We left the Beefe Road & started due west across the wide Prairie in the Indian Nation to try to go around Kansas & strike Iowa. I have 490 Beeves."

His herd was reduced by more than half, but with pleasure one reads on that he made the western circuit around the settlements of eastern Kansas, reached the Missouri River early in September near Nebraska City, and ferried his herd across to the promised land in Iowa. Even with his losses he must have made a worth-while profit on the dolorous expedition.

CHAPTER TWO

Cattle Take Over the West

SOME Texans sought other outlets. One pair, as salty a team of cattlemen as ever forked saddles, was that of Charles Goodnight and Oliver Loving. Goodnight had been a freighter, bullwhacking out of Fort Worth, and during the Civil War served four years with the Texas Rangers, fighting Indians, Mexican bandits, renegade cattle thieves and road agents. His partner, Loving, was one of the most experienced trail drivers in Texas. He was first to take a herd north through the Indian Territory to Quincy, Illinois, establishing the Sedalia route. Two years later, in 1860, he took a herd to Colorado, where a gold rush was on, and during the Civil War drove cattle for the Confederate armies—going broke when the Confederate currency in which he was paid became worthless.

Together these two, knowing there must be a government market which had suddenly been created by Kit Carson's gathering of several thousand Navajo and Apache Indians at the Bosque Redondo, decided to take a herd thither in 1866.

It was an ordeal sufficiently severe to have daunted most men. They had, first of all, to pass through the Comanche country. Then there was a deadly drive of ninety-six miles, from the middle Concho to the Horsehead crossing of the Pecos, without a drop of water on the entire route. The first chuckwagon in all history was designed by Goodnight for this journey, built of tough Osage orangewood and equipped with water barrels, covered with a canvas tilt, with a chuck box at the rear, containing dishes and cooking utensils, the lid provided with a folding leg so that when it was lowered it formed a table on which the cook could work. So excellent was the idea that it became universal in the range country.

Since the probabilities were strong that they might have to fight Indians, Confederate veterans were chosen exclusively for trail drivers —men who could handle shooting irons and weren't afraid of being shot at. The drive began in June. Fortunately, at that season the Comanches were elsewhere, and they escaped Indian trouble. But they had enough woes of other kinds to make up for it.

When they reached the head of the middle Concho River the cattle were rested for three days and encouraged to fill their hides with water for the dreaded ninety-six-mile dry leg of the drive which was about to begin. At last the herd was strung out and the brutal test began. All day the cattle and the drivers toiled across the plains. And again the next day, the men riding with neck handkerchiefs masking their faces to the eyes so that they could breathe in the stifling dust. By the second night the beasts were suffering, restless and bellowing with thirst. Next morning the partners decided they would not dare to camp again.

On the third evening the outfit presented a pitiable spectacle. The men were haggard, with lips cracked and bloodshot eyes; the cattle so gaunt that their ribs stood out like basketwork, tongues lolling from their mouths, and a continual bawling and moaning sound coming from them in their misery of thirst. But they had to be kept moving, because if they ever lay down they would never rise again. So above the noise of the herd rose the yells and whistles of the cowboys as they urged on their charges.

On the fourth morning they entered Castle Gap, an opening through the Castle Mountains, and debouched down into the Pecos Valley, where they saw the river twelve miles away. Only the exhaustion of the cattle prevented a stampede at the smell of water. As it was, Goodnight later said, when they reached the river, "They had no sense at all. They stampeded right into the stream, swam right across it, and then doubled back before they stopped to drink."

Three hundred of the weaker cattle lay dead along that dreadful back trail, but the rest of the herd, which originally numbered two thousand, after being allowed to rest and graze for a time to put back some of the lost tallow, was driven on to Fort Sumner, where the seven thousand Indians of the Bosque Redondo, who were almost starving, greeted it with whole-souled yowls of rejoicing. Beef was so scarce in New Mexico that it was selling for sixteen cents a pound, dressed. The partners got eight cents a pound on the hoof—say $13,000 for their herd—a price unheard of for Texas cattle in that day.

They had made history, and having proved the Horsehead crossing possible, pioneered a flood of cattle which would make both New Mexico and Arizona cattle domain, and would vastly change the aspect and history not only of those territories but of Colorado and all the northern plains.

One other epic exploit of trail driving.

Up in Montana the discovery of gold had caused a lurid, mushroom growth of population in the mountains which hitherto had been exclusively Indian hunting grounds. The fabulous strikes in Grasshopper Gulch and elsewhere created in rapid succession Bannack City, Virginia City, Helena and other booming mining camps. By the end of

1865 the successive gold excitements had brought into those areas a population so large that the problem of feeding it became acute.

Nelson Story, a man of some prominence in Montana—having been a leader of the Vigilantes who broke up the Plummer gang of desperadoes by hanging twenty-two of its members on assorted trees and barn girders—conceived the idea of bringing beef from Texas all the way to Montana. After cleaning up $30,000 in a placer mine he rode south in the spring of 1866 and put part of his money in a cattle herd.

Hiring hard-bitten Texas trail drivers, he started the herd north, swimming turbulent rivers, dodging Indians who wanted to collect toll in the Indian Territory, evading thieves, heading off stampedes, and at last arrived at the Kansas border without losing a man—which was a wonder—and with very few of his cattle missing.

There he discovered, as had many others, that the Jayhawkers were swarming on the border. But Story merely swung his herd west. Ten thousand miners were in the Montana towns—and beef was mighty scarce there. His Texas cowboys were nothing loath. They hankered to see Montana anyhow. So out of the jam below Baxter Springs Story headed his steers around the settlements—making a side trip to purchase a wagon train loaded with groceries and supplies at Leavenworth—and then with his cattle and this train took the Oregon Trail along the Platte.

When the caravan reached Fort Laramie, Wyoming, army officers shook their heads and warned Story not to go any farther north. The Bozeman Trail, the only feasible route, was swarming with Sioux on the warpath, led by Red Cloud. They were besieging Fort Reno and Fort Phil Kearny—and so ferociously that the following December was to occur the disaster in which Captain William J. Fetterman's entire command was annihilated.

But Nelson Story didn't scare, and neither did his men. There were twenty-seven of them, and he armed them all with Remington breechloaders, besides the Colt revolvers they already carried.

Northward they swung. Near Fort Reno Indians attacked them, wounded two cowpunchers with arrows, and drove away part of the herd. Story's ex-Confederates followed them, recovered the cattle, and "dealt" with the Indians. One of the riders, John B. Catlin, described the operation years later.

"How many cattle did you lose?" he was asked.

"Not a single head. We just followed those Indians into the Bad Lands and got the cattle back."

"Did they yield the steers willingly?"

"Well, you might say so. We surprised them in their camp and they weren't in shape to protest much against our taking the cattle."

Story left his wounded men at Fort Reno and drove the herd on. When he reached Fort Phil Kearny, General H. B. Carrington ordered him to stop and proceed no further without permission, because of the danger of the Indians. Story obeyed just long enough to find that he risked destruction if he stayed where he was, because the fort could not protect him since he must graze his herd at some distance away. On the night of October 22 he slipped around the fort and was gone up into the Sioux country.

From then on every hour was filled with tension. Story trailed his herd only at night and herd-guarded them by day, gradually making his way through the rough country. Near Clark's Fork of the Yellowstone River the Indians killed a cowboy who was hunting about a mile away from the herd. But after scalping him the band of warriors rode away.

Story was lucky. Red Cloud and most of the Sioux, numbering thousands, were at this time considerably to the south, preparing for conclusions with Fort Phil Kearny, and except for an occasional flying band of young scalp-hunting braves—who developed discretion about tangling with the Remington-armed herd guards—they were unmolested.

On December 9 the entire herd and the trainload of groceries rolled into Virginia City, where Story was greeted by his young wife, whom he had left there, and also by a whooping celebration by the whole bonanza town. It was a record-breaking drive. Not for four years would another trail herd make that trip. The Sioux made it look too much like suicide.

Individual trail-driving exploits like those of Duffield, Goodnight and Story were successes, but in the main the great effort of Texas cattlemen in 1866 was a failure. Nevertheless, the fact that even a few drovers made a profit lifted the spirits of Texas cowmen and in the spring of 1867 they were busy again, gathering herds for the great gamble, on the slim hope that somehow a market would open up for them to the north. For this and the next several years, gathering cattle and driving them up the trail was a major activity in the state.

And in that year, 1867, the man and the need met; and the range industry not only was saved but was given a tremendous impetus. In Springfield, Illinois, a young cattle dealer named Joseph G. McCoy dreamed of establishing a railroad market which would take Texas cattle and transport them readily to the great packing plants. His scheme met rebuffs and discouragements without number, but it was of the stuff of which empires are created.

He finally built a shipping yard and offices in Abilene, Kansas, then a wretched little hamlet of a dozen ramshackle log huts, with a single street "so lacking in traffic that a busy and populous prairie dog town existed in the middle thereof." There also he erected a three-story frame hotel, the Drover's Cottage, installed a set of Fairbanks scales; and from there he sent emissaries south to meet the northward-wending herds and tell their owners of opportunity awaiting them where, to use his own words, "Southern drover and Northern buyer would meet upon an equal footing, and both be undisturbed by mobs or swindling thieves."

He received some cattle, but by no means all he wanted, that first year of 1867. But the experiment worked; word went back to Texas, and in 1868 his shipping yards did a capacity business, so that the Kansas Pacific Railroad, which ran through Abilene, realized at last the immense value to it of this form of livestock freight. Abilene became the first of the booming cow towns.

It was succeeded, as the railroads discovered belatedly an eagerness to win the cattle freight business, by other towns as the railheads progressed west. Ellsworth, Newton, Wichita, Fort Hays, Dodge City and their kindred communities sprouted, mushroomed, and withered as cattle capitals. Each of them encountered the effervescence of the wild riders who came up from Texas with the herds; and each had its lurid chapter of lawless, six-shooter domination; and also its town marshal, grown legendary now, who upheld the peace with smoking revolvers.

Abilene had Bear River Tom Smith and Wild Bill Hickok; Ellsworth had Chauncey Whitney; Newton had Mike McCluskie and Jim Riley— who fought out Newton's "General Massacre" in which nine men were killed or wounded in a saloon, the bloodiest fight in all the cattle country's history—and Jack Johnston, who enforced law with a lightning draw; Dodge City had Bat Masterson, Wyatt Earp—who would be heard from elsewhere and later—Mysterious Dave Mathers and others. And so on. The exploits of the gunfighters were spectacular and have been recounted with sufficient detail in countless books, yet they provided little of importance to history, save for local narrative; and though there will always be dispute between Texas and Kansas as to which had the deadlier gunman, the former upholding John Wesley Hardin and the latter Wild Bill Hickok, there is so much legend surrounding them now that the truth probably never will be discovered.

Without exception each railroad town, as it became the goal of the Texas cowboys, had its district of vice. It was Texas Street in Abilene, Nauchville in Ellsworth, Hide Park (from the bare skins of the ladies of the evening) in Newton, and Delano in Wichita. Dodge City provided a generic name, used the world over now, the Red Light district —arising from the old Red Light, a sporting house with a blood-red glass in the front door through which the light shone in lurid welcome

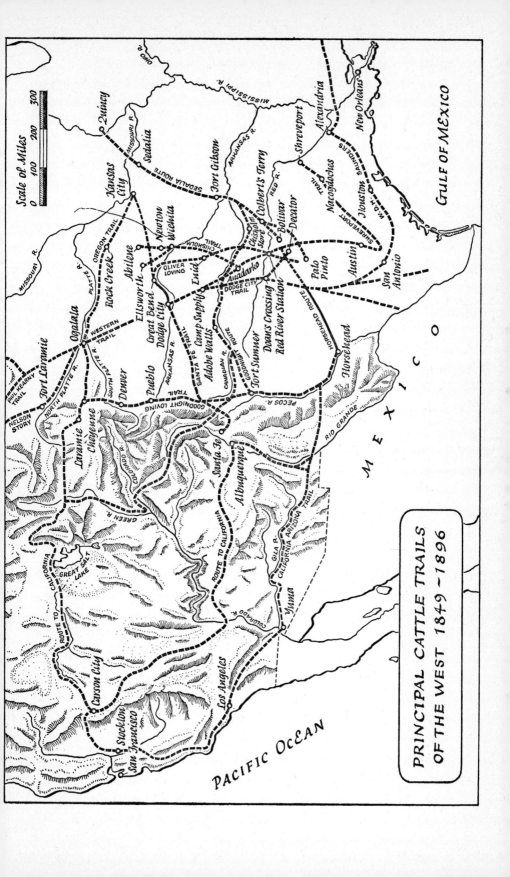

PRINCIPAL CATTLE TRAILS
OF THE WEST 1849~1896

to the cowboys, and which gave its distinctive title to all the saloons and bawdy houses gathered about it, south of the tracks. Dodge City, incidentally, provided another widely used name—Boot Hill. It buried its dead who passed suddenly to their reward with their boots on— hence by "lead poisoning"—on a low hill, which soon became rather populous with the dear departed. So appropriate was the designation that Boot Hills afterward were designated all over the West.

But all of this was incidental to the great surge of cattle driving, whereby Texas projected its vast reservoir of livestock into the remotest corners of the Western country from the Canadian to the Mexican line. From driving to immediate market, Texas cowmen began seeking pasturage north and west. When the United States Army finally put the Sioux, Cheyennes and Arapahoes of the Dakotas, Wyoming and Montana on their reservations in 1876–78, this movement was accelerated. What had been buffalo country became cattle country, as the hide hunters wiped out the great bison herds. Ranchers, pushing ever farther and farther, ferreted out each watercourse, valley, mountain pass and stretch of grass; and threw their cattle across the continent, thus bringing civilization (of a sort) all the way up to Calgary, in Canada.

Repeatedly the cattle trail was swung farther and farther westward, until at last it culminated in Miles City, Montana. How many cattle went up that shifting trail nobody will ever know. But a single firm, headed by Captain John F. Lytle, sent 450,000 over it in a period of several years, and in a single season Colonel Ike T. Pryor drove 30,000 cattle north. When one considers other names equally notable—like Shanghai Pierce, Captain Richard King, Mifflin Kenedy, Colonel D. H. Snyder, to name only a few of the giants of trail-driving days—besides scores of less famous drovers, the numbers become fabulous. George W. Saunders, himself one of the great drovers and later president of the Texas Trail Drivers' Association, made the following estimates, which probably are as close as anyone will ever get to the totals:

Saunders said that approximately 12,000,000 cattle and horses were driven north during the trail-driving period. Of these about 6,000,000 crossed the Red River at Doan's Crossing for the Western trail; 5,000,000 at Red River station, farther east, for the Chisholm Trail and the Kansas rail markets; and 1,000,000 at other points for various goals. The sale of these vast herds brought approximately $250,000,000—a very tidy sum in the dollar of that day, bringing prosperity where there had been ruin in Texas.

Trail driving lasted less than thirty years—until settlement spread westward so far that it was no longer possible to drive great herds of cattle because of towns and fenced farms. The last great Texas trail herd was an XIT bunch which was driven north in 1896, with John McCanles as trail boss. The drive was one long continued, exasperating battle with farmers and city constables, but McCanles finally delivered his herd.

Before this, however, trail driving had practically ceased. The railroads had equalized the cost and Northern ranches were pretty well stocked. Trail driving became history as rapidly as it developed, but the impetus from Texas made Texas talk, dress, actions, modes and habits of thought the familiar fare of all the great plains northward.

Meantime an equally vital trend had been established directly west of Texas. Goodnight and Loving, pioneering the Horsehead route, provided the spur to other cattlemen. While cattle had always been raised in New Mexico, the ranching industry assumed no considerable proportions until after that famous drive of the adventurous partners. Thereafter, however, many drovers competed with Goodnight and Loving; and when more cattle were in New Mexico than its ranges needed, the herds were driven north to Colorado, or still farther west into Arizona, even to Nevada and California.

A certain stimulus was given to this westward movement by those freebooters, the *Comancheros,* who encouraged the Comanche Indians to steal Texas cattle and horses, bought the livestock from the raiders, and trailed the stolen herds across the Staked Plains to New Mexico. In 1872 two Texas ranchers, John Hittson and H. M. Childress, with sixty hard-visaged riders, and armed with powers of attorney from many ranchers in the Lone Star State, suddenly descended on New Mexico, swept through the Pecos Valley, and repossessed cattle wherever good ownership credentials could not be shown. They overawed small ranches which had cattle with Texas brands, so that not a shot was fired; and rode back with 11,000 head they had recovered—all of it, presumably, from the *Comanchero* trade.

CHAPTER THREE

The Buffalo and the Indian

FOR much of the plains country, cattle ranching was at first impractical because of the enormous herds of buffalo which occupied the vast open stretches. Not only did the migrating bison destroy fields and fences, encompass and move off livestock herds, and make settlement almost impossible, but they were the key to the Indian problem.

It is difficult in this day to comprehend the numbers of buffalo existing in the great herds at their height. Alvarado, Coronado's captain, rather helplessly reported, "There are such multitudes of them that I do not know what to compare them with unless it be the fish of the sea." E. T. Seton, the naturalist, estimated that 75,000,000 ranged from north New Mexico to central Canada, and from the Alleghenies to the Cascades, in the period just before the Indian acquired the horse. In the 1860s General Sheridan computed 100,000,000 on the southern plains alone.

The wild Indians depended on the buffalo, which furnished them everything they needed for subsistence—meat, robes, tepee covers, bone utensils, sinew for cordage, and countless other articles of savage life. With this ready commissary at hand the Indians could, and did, devote a great deal of their time to warfare against the white man. And it appeared to most persons that the very numbers of the buffalo made it unthinkable that they ever would be eliminated from their feeding grounds.

Yet this seemingly insuperable problem was solved in a single decade, and in a manner so cold-bloodedly methodical that it left the world aghast at the slaughter of those vast herds. The millions of buffalo were wiped out: not by the Indians who lived on them; not by the soldiers who wanted them out of the way to make easier the defeat of the hostile tribes; not by cattlemen who desired room for cattle range, or farmers who wished to preserve their fields from being trampled; but by a new and potent army, which appeared and disappeared with equal suddenness—the hide hunters.

Fearless, armed with rifles shooting a very heavy bullet, they were from all walks of life. One of them, killed by Indians near Adobe Walls in 1874, was an heir of a noble British house whose death created serious diplomatic complications. Among them were men of high character, like Billy Dixon, Pat Garrett, J. Wright Mooar and others. But many also were fugitives from justice—murderers, thieves and outlaws.

Sudden discovery in 1870 that buffalo hides were commercially usable sounded the death knell of the bison. In that year J. Wright Mooar sent a shipment of hides experimentally to a New York tanning firm, which found them of value, particularly for machine belting.

Followed as terrible and indiscriminate a destruction as the world ever witnessed. By the thousands hide hunters went out on the plains. A good hunter could kill 150 to 200 animals a day; the number limited only by the ability of his skinners to keep up with him—and the skinners, using horses to strip off the hides, worked fast. So many hunters were at work all the time that old-timers recalled that on a clear morning the firing sounded like a fair-sized battle in progress. The stupidity of the animals made the slaughter possible. If they did not see the hunter, or smell him, as he crouched behind some obstruction or perhaps in a buffalo wallow, they would mill around while, one after another, they sank to the ground before the merciless buffalo gun, only a few fleeing at last.

Their rotting carcasses created an overpowering stench over great stretches of the fairest plains; buzzards, ravens, coyotes and other creatures gorged fat on their carrion; and when their bones whitened they became a source of revenue to men called "bone pickers" who went about with wagons, gathered the skeletal parts strewn everywhere, and shipped them to Eastern fertilizing companies. By 1889, fifteen years after hide hunting ceased for lack of sufficient animals to hunt, Dr. William T. Hornaday, in a continental survey, found only 1091 American buffalo still in existence. He awakened the public consciousness, fortunately, in time. Today the bison is secure from extermination, although his fate for all time is to occupy game preserves and parks.

Slowly the Indians began to realize that their natural commissary was disappearing. The army was fighting a desultory and not very successful war with the Sioux and Cheyennes of the northern plains when, in October 1867, representatives of the southern tribes gathered on Medicine Lodge Creek in southern Kansas, to make a peace treaty.

General W. T. Sherman, commanding general of the army, and General Phil Sheridan, commander of the Division of the Missouri, scoffed at the peace effort as a waste of time. Nevertheless a commission, headed by Generals Harney and Sanborn, met with the Indian tribes which had been doing most of the damage in the Southwest. The record shows that of the Comanches there were 150 lodges; of Kiowas 150; of Arapahoes 175; of mixed Kiowas and Lipan Apaches 85; and of Cheyennes 250—a total of 810 lodges, or more than 4000 Indians, figuring the usual average of five persons to a lodge. The Comanches had only about 750 persons present—a significantly small representation from that populous tribe.

From the chiefs at council the commissioners received promises of peace, agreement to relinquish their hunting grounds in the Texas Panhandle, and assurances of willingness to abide on reservations in the Indian Territory assigned to them. In return for this the commissioners divided among the Indians a wagon train of provisions and clothing, and—most delightful of all to the red men—large quantities of ammunition and arms.

It was assumed that the "Medicine Lodge Peace Treaty" would end

Indian troubles in the Southwest. What happened, of course, was the reverse, just as Sherman and Sheridan had predicted. Arms and ammunition furnished by the government figured prominently in the Indian wars that followed. The Cheyennes scourged Kansas and Colorado. The Comanches and Kiowas, far from relinquishing the Texas Panhandle, continued to frequent it. Raids on cattle ranches and settlements went on as before.

"So boldly has this system of murder and robbery been carried on that, since June 1862, not less than 800 persons had been murdered, the Indians escaping from the troops by traveling at night, when their trail could not be followed, thus gaining enough time and distance to render pursuit, in most cases, fruitless," wrote Sheridan in 1868. "This wholesale marauding would be maintained during the seasons when the Indian ponies could subsist upon the grass, and then in the winter, the savages would hide away, with their villages, in remote and isolated places, live upon their plunder, glory in the scalps taken, and in the horrible debasement of the unfortunate women they held as prisoners. The experience of many years of this character of depredations with perfect immunity to themselves and families, had made the Indians very bold. To disabuse their minds of the idea that they were secure from punishment, and to strike them at a period when they would be helpless to move their stock and villages, a winter campaign was projected against the large bands hiding away in the Indian Territory."

Followed the Washita campaign of General George A. Custer, who later was to be the chief figure in the total destruction of his United States cavalry force by the Sioux, on the Little Bighorn River of Montana. In the dead of winter Custer, with his Seventh Cavalry, marched south from Camp Supply, Indian Territory. There was a foot of snow on the ground and the weather was bitter cold when he struck an Indian trail left by a band of warriors who had killed mail carriers between Dodge City and Larned, an old hunter near Dodge City, and two of Sheridan's dispatch carriers.

On the night of November 26, Little Beaver, an Osage scout, smelled smoke. He told Custer an Indian camp was near. With the scout, Custer crept to the top of a low snowy hill, from which his straining eyes made out a dark blotch on the snow—an immense pony herd. Significant noises reached his ears—dogs barking, a bell tinkling in the herd, the faraway wail of an Indian baby. He was right on top of a big Indian village.

Returning to his command, he split it into four detachments—three troops under Major Joel Elliott, two each under Captains Thompson and Myers, and four troops under himself. He was dividing his forces in the face of an enemy, a violation of an old military rule, and the same tactics cost him his life and the lives of his immediate command later at the Little Bighorn when the Sioux defeated his detachments in detail; but on this occasion the plan worked.

Just as the first light of morning broke a bugle sounded and Custer and the Seventh Cavalry rode down on the village from every side. With startled yelps the Indians bolted from their tepees, some running stark naked into the icy waters of the Washita. A few fought and were slain where they stood, but for the most part the troopers simply killed fugitives, including women and children, and mostly unarmed.

The village was Cheyenne, under a chief named Black Kettle. It was pretty thoroughly obliterated. Custer's men killed 101 Indians and captured 53 squaws and children. They destroyed more than a thousand buffalo robes, five hundred pounds of lead, an equal amount of powder, four thousand arrows, all the lodges, and slaughtered seven hundred captured ponies.

But in the middle of the morning, when the fight should have been over, more warriors were seen riding up the valley. Custer did not know it then, but the village he had attacked was only one of several strung up and down the Washita, including Kiowas, Arapahoes, Comanches, Lipans and Cheyennes. There were perhaps two thousand warriors within riding distance.

The Indians cut off and killed Major Elliott and fourteen troopers, but Custer extricated the rest of his force and retreated. Including the Elliott group, he lost 21 officers and men dead, and 14 officers and men wounded.

Two other columns under Colonel A. W. Evans and General Eugene A. Carr, at about the same time, scouted up and down the Canadian River in Texas, where they made the country so unhealthy for Indians that a large number of hostiles came in and went on the reservations assigned to them.

But the next year, 1869, the hostile tribes again ranged all over the plains from north of the Platte to the Mexican border, and 1870 saw more of the same. In New Mexico the stage routes were closed. Thirty separate raids and engagements with Indian war parties were recorded in Texas and New Mexico in those two years, an unrecorded number of American and Mexican settlers were murdered, and hundreds of head of livestock driven away, to say nothing of ranches looted and burned.

But the tide was about to turn. In 1871 General Sherman made a personal tour of inspection of the frontier posts. He was critical of the carelessness of the border ranchers. "They expose women and children singly on the road and in cabins far off from others, as though they were safe in Illinois," he wrote. "If the Comanches don't steal horses, it is because they cannot be tempted."

He saw no Indians who could be described as hostile until he reached Fort Sill, Indian Territory, but while on his tour, at Fort Richardson, Texas, a man named Thomas Brazeal staggered in with a gunshot wound in one foot. He told of an attack by Indians on a wagon train a few miles from where Sherman had slept that night. Four men escaped the Indians, three of them, including Brazeal, being wounded. Seven were killed. The bodies of the slain men, all mutilated, and one charred and suspended face down over a fire by a chain on a wagon pole, indicating that he was tortured to death, destroyed any skepticism Sherman might have had concerning the ferocity of savage warfare.

When he reached Fort Sill, he at once asked Lawrie Tatum, the Indian agent, if any Indians recently had been off the reservation. Tatum thought a few Kiowas had gone. When these Indians arrived a couple of days later to draw their rations, Sherman had the agent bring some of them to the headquarters of the fort.

The general began by asking which of them were involved in the destruction of the wagon train near Fort Richardson. To his amazement, Satanta, one of the chiefs, said he was the leader of the attack. "He openly admitted the affair," Sherman wrote, "and described the attack exactly as the man did to me at Fort Richardson, only denying that anybody was tied to the wagon wheel and burned; but as Gen'l MacKenzie found the body, it does not admit of dispute."

With that, Sherman ordered that Satanta and two other chiefs, Satank and Big Tree, be arrested and sent to Texas to be tried for murder.

William Tecumseh Sherman was internationally famous as a soldier, the commanding general of the United States Army, and being mentioned at the time as presidential timber. But in those next five minutes he stood as tensely close to death as ever in his career.

At mention of arrest, Satanta threw back his blanket and grasped the handle of a revolver at his belt. He could have killed Sherman and nobody could have stopped him.

But for some reason the Indian hesitated. As cool as if he had all day, Sherman gave an order, and the windows of the headquarters building opened, revealing a squad of soldiers with leveled carbines.

Satanta said, "No shoot!" and took his hand off his gun.

But Kicking Bird, another chief, began to harangue, saying that he had been a good friend to the white man—which was true—and asking that his three chiefs be released.

Sherman stood grimly firm. "I am going to take them with me to the place where they killed those boys," he said. "There they will be hung, and the crime will be paid for."

Kicking Bird grew excited. "You have asked for those men to kill them!" he exclaimed. "I will not let you have them. You and I are going to die right here!"

At this juncture, Big Tree attempted to escape. He knocked down a trader and dove through a glass window headfirst. Soldiers pursued him, firing, and a bullet creased his scalp. He stopped running and surrendered.

Meantime Lone Wolf, one of the most dangerous fighters in the Kiowa tribe, came to the porch carrying two Spencer repeating carbines, a bow and quiver, and a revolver. He distributed these weapons among the Indians crowding about the porch, saying as he handed the revolver to one of them, "If anything happens, make it smoke."

Stumbling Bear, who received the bow, promptly strung it and put an arrow to the string. "I want to kill the big soldier chief," he said, and drew the arrow to the head, pointing it at Sherman. But as he released the shaft someone knocked the bow up and the arrow sailed harmlessly overhead.

Lone Wolf aimed his carbine at Sherman, but Colonel B. H. Grierson, commandant at Fort Sill, seized him and fell with him, kicking on the floor.

A flurry of shots sounded. Near the guardhouse some Kiowas had fired on a group of soldiers, wounding one. The soldiers shot back, killing one of the Indians.

Through all this furious excitement, amidst the yelling of the Indians, the shots and the scuffle, the one person who remained completely calm was General Sherman. He had looked death in the eyes three times in five minutes, and he did not turn a hair.

His monolithic coolness subdued the Indians. Leaving their chiefs, Satanta, Satank and Big Tree, manacled, they departed for their camp.

While being taken to Texas, Satank "committed suicide" in a novel manner. He sang his death song, told another Indian that by the time they reached a certain tree he would be dead, then somehow managed to free himself from one of his manacles, wrenched a carbine from a soldier, and stabbed a corporal in the leg with a knife he had secreted. A moment later he was dead as he predicted, with seven bullets in his body.

Satanta and Big Tree were not executed, but were confined in the Texas penitentiary at Huntsville.

Even the presence of Sherman and his awesome display of intrepidity in the face of deadly peril, followed by the arrest of the Kiowa chiefs, did not, however, bring any betterment of conditions on the plains. Many of the Comanches had never gone on the reservations, and this contingent, the Quahadas, was led by Quanah Parker—son of Cynthia Ann Parker by Peta Nokoni—who had developed into the chief daredevil of the Comanche people. Late in September 1872, Colonel Ranald S. Mackenzie surprised a Quahada Comanche village on Mc-Clellan Creek and routed the Indians, killing 23 and capturing more than 100, with a loss of only 3 killed and 7 wounded. He rounded up the herd of Indian ponies and let his Tonkawa scouts take the pick of them for racing and hunting steeds.

That night, however, Quanah Parker led his braves in a wild dash through Mackenzie's camp, ringing horse bells, blowing whistles, yelling, and dragging bouncing buffalo robes at the ends of lariats. The whole horse herd "spooked" and stampeded, and the Comanches got not only their own animals but all the horses of the Tonkawa scouts as well. Next morning Mackenzie faced his chagrined Indian allies, who had only a solitary and forlorn burro left, of all their animals.

Mackenzie's punishment, while severe, did not drive the Comanches on their reservation. They still hid their villages on the breaks of streams coming from the great canyons in the escarpment of the Staked Plains, and caused continual trouble. Then, after two years of prison, Satanta and Big Tree, the Kiowa chiefs, were released in October 1873, over the protests of Agent Tatum, who resigned because of it. The Kiowas had behaved themselves, believing their chiefs were being held as hostages. But with the return of the two, they shortly drifted away from the agency and out on the plains. And in the spring of 1874 all hell broke loose.

Destruction of the buffalo herds caused the final desperate flurry of fighting. By 1874 the hide hunters had done their job of extermination so well that only a few stragglers of the once teeming millions remained on the southern plains. It upset the whole way of life for the Indians, and together they rose—Comanches, Kiowas, Cheyennes, Arapahoes and Lipans—with a fury and unanimity as shocking as it was surprising.

Through New Mexico, northern Texas, Colorado, Kansas and the Indian Territory their war parties swept; and a partial list of their victims among the settlers, including no casualties of soldiers or scouts, shows 190 killed.

Chief resentment of the Indians was against the hide hunters. And the hide hunters had a stronghold—a primitive outpost of a few sod and long structures whose outer walls formed a palisade—situated near the juncture of Bent's Creek and the Canadian River, near which stood an old trading post built and long ago abandoned by the fur company of Bent & St. Vrain. The ruins were called the Adobe Walls, and from them the fort took its name.

About the middle of June, when the hunters were scattered at their killing, the war parties began their work. Here and there they surprised and killed hunters. The survivors found the bodies of their friends and partners butchered and scalped, and took the hint. From every direction they hurried to the fort.

The night of June 26 was sultry, with heat lightning playing on the horizon. At Adobe Walls that night slept twenty-eight men and one woman—Mrs. William Olds, wife of a man who ran a sort of restaurant for the hunters. In the darkness Comanches, led by Quanah Parker and Isa-tai, a medicine man who promised them invulnerability against the white man's bullets, Cheyennes under Iron Shirt, and Kiowas and Lipans under Satanta and Lone Wolf, stole up around the post.

A remarkably timely accident saved the white people. One of the structures at the post was a sod house, in which James Hanrahan ran a saloon. The roof was of slabs of sod, so heavy that the cottonwood ridgepole was too weak to uphold it. That ridge pole selected as its time to break, with a loud crack, two o'clock on the morning of June 27.

The people in the post were aroused, and since the whole roof threatened to collapse—on all that precious whiskey!—everyone took a hand in repairing it. So all were awake when the first pink light of pre-dawn tinged the eastern sky, and Billy Dixon, a great hunter and scout, stepped out of the fort to get his pony from the corral. It was he who discovered the Indians and, firing his rifle, gave warning.

As soon as they knew they were seen, the Indians, believing in their "medicine" of invulnerability promised by Isa-tai, charged with remarkable boldness directly at the fort. Two hunters, the Shadler brothers, who had slept outside because of the heat, were shot down or lanced before they could reach safety. Then the Adobe Walls blazed with the roar of the hunters' heavy guns.

In the little fort were some of the finest shots in the world. Indians fell fast. They rode into the stockade and hammered on doors and windows of buildings with their rifle butts, but the hunters inside never ceased spreading death.

Very quickly the warriors retired from that hot enclosure, amazed and angered at seeing so many of their best fighters dropping, and more than dismayed by the failure of Isa-tai's promise. For a time they tried a long-range duel with the hide hunters, but there the hunters held all the top cards. Their rifles outranged those of the Indians and about four o'clock in the afternoon, carrying off all their dead and wounded whom they could reach, the hostiles withdrew.

The hunters had four dead, including William Olds, husband of the only woman in the post. Nobody learned the extent of the Indian losses, but thirteen dead warriors were found close about the fort in spite of daring efforts made by the Indians to carry them away. The heads of these thirteen decorated posts of the palisade when, a few days later, a relief expedition reached Adobe Walls from Dodge City.

After the bloody repulse, the allied tribes went out for revenge. Not a road in western Kansas, eastern Colorado, the Texas Panhandle or the Indian Territory was safe. Agencies, ranches, even military posts were attacked and wagon trains ambushed and their drivers butchered. The frontier yelled for the army, and the army took the field.

General Nelson A. Miles campaigned in the Sweetwater Valley, and a detachment of his men under Lieutenant Frank D. Baldwin smashed the village of Gray Beard, sending these Indians back to their reservation and securing also the release of four white girls, sisters by the name of German (or Germaine). They were Catherine, seventeen years old; Sophia, fifteen; Julia, ten; and Adelaide, five. All had been captured in a Cheyenne raid near the Smoky Hill River, in Kansas.

The experiences of the girls, particularly the older ones, were terrible, of course; and when the Cheyennes surrendered, the men were lined up and the girls pointed out a number of them, who had been chiefly guilty in the murders of their parents, and in offenses later while the girls were prisoners in the Indian camp. These men were sent to Fort Marion, Florida, to be imprisoned. Great pity was aroused over the girls, but General Miles became their guardian, sufficient funds were taken from the Cheyenne annuities to support them, and all of them lived normal and happy lives, married, reared families, and survived to a ripe old age.

But the heaviest blow was struck by Colonel Mackenzie. Hunting Indians in the Staked Plains, he encountered José Tafoya, a *Comanchero* who had grown rich buying blood-spattered Indian loot and was heading out with his caravan to make some more profitable transactions. Mackenzie questioned him. When the old *Comanchero* refused to talk, Mackenzie had a wagon tongue propped up and from it suspended Tafoya by the neck. As his breath grew short the *Comanchero* recovered the use of his tongue. Through him Mackenzie learned that the hostiles were in Palo Duro Canyon.

Led by his scouts to the rim of the great chasm in the night of September 26, he sent his men clambering down a precarious trail to hit the big Indian village which was in the canyon. Before they reached the bottom they were discovered and shooting began; but the main body of Indians was farther along the gorge, and though bullets smacked the rocks about them or ricocheted off through the darkness, howling like lost souls, the soldiers reached firm ground on the bottom before they were seriously attacked.

Now powder smoke made a gray cloud in the gloom-filled gorge and the multiple clatter of rifles was doubled and trebled by the sounding echoes. Mackenzie drove the Indians, but encountered fierce resistance. The camp was Lone Wolf's Kiowa village and the chief managed to get the squaws, children and most of their lodges and equipment out, although it cost him some warriors. The troops captured and burned about a hundred tepees and killed some fourteen hundred captured ponies.

After the Palo Duro fight the Kiowas and Cheyennes surrendered by hundreds and when winter came in 1874 the war was practically over. A few Comanches still remained out, but in February 1877 one of the last of these bands encountered and was severely defeated by forty-five hide hunters led by Hank Campbell. They lost thirty-five dead in the little fight on the Staked Plains, and when Captain P. L. Lee, with a troop of the Tenth Cavalry, rounded them up weeks later near Lake Quemado, they were ready to surrender.

The Comanches never went on the warpath again. They and their allies were convinced there was no place for them to hide any longer, and peace was their only course. The buffalo were gone, the Indian menace abated, and the cattle moved in.

CHAPTER FOUR

"The Incorrigibly Hostile"

I N   T H E farther Southwest the problem of hostile Indians was even more difficult. There were, to be sure, fewer of the Apaches than of the Comanches and their allies of the plains, but what they lacked in numbers they made up for in sheer endless murderousness and in the skill with which they used the desert reaches for their warlike purposes.

As nearly perfect at self-subsistence as any fighting man in the world's history was the Apache warrior, even though his chosen campaigning ground was ferociously sterile desert. No clumsy commissary accompanied him, nor any pots, frying pans or other utensils, save for the knife sheathed at his belt. In addition to the white man's sheep and cattle, which he took without hesitation or qualm of conscience, his range was the habitat of many kinds of game—deer, *javalinas* (desert peccaries), rabbits, wild turkey and desert mountain sheep. Nor was he dainty in his tastes. When other meat lacked he did not disdain mice or pack rats, dug from their small lairs, or lizards killed with a switch, or even the gray flesh of the coiling rattlesnake. When all else failed, his pony always was a last resource. Killed when perhaps too exhausted to move farther, it furnished a stock of jerked meat and a unique water carrier—the long intestine, which, cleaned (after somewhat rudimentary Apache notions of cleaning), could be filled with water and wound several times about the body of another horse, to furnish life-giving if somewhat offensively smelling and tasting water for days. It is no wonder that the frontier troops, handicapped by pack trains and equipment, had difficulty in coping with their wily and resourceful foe.

But the Apache was more than a mere Spartan in his living. He took and utilized every modern implement of war on which he could lay his hands. The best rifles and revolvers were his—by capture, or by purchase from sneaking traders who got the highest price for their illegal merchandise—and the Apache knew how to use them to deadliest effect. He cached spare ammunition and arms at strategic hidden places, so that he usually could get new supplies when needed. He even had field glasses—the finest—to supplement his already marvelous eyesight. And he was a master at camouflage and concealment.

His natural ferocity was brought to peak by treacheries such as the murder of Mangus Colorado, the "Pinal Treaty," the scalp hunters' slaughters, and the Camp Grant massacre, in which, on April 30, 1870, a camp of Aravaipa Apaches, who had surrendered, was attacked by a mob from Tucson, and eighty-five of them slaughtered, all but eight being women and children.

Most active and murderous of the Apaches for a time were Cochise and his Chiricahuas. A spare, gray-eyed, slightly stooped, sandy-haired man, with a five-foot-seven-inch frame of whalebone endurance, was their ablest and most untiring foe. He was Lieutenant Howard B. Cushing, member of a famous military family.

For a time the honors were with Cushing in his duel with Cochise. But Cochise had the last say. On May 5, 1871, the Chiricahua chief lured his archenemy and twenty-two men into an ambuscade near Bear Springs in the Whetstone Mountains. So perfect was the trap that Cushing and his men did not even suspect it until they were well within it. At the tearing volley from the Indians, Cushing dropped dead. Down the sides of the canyon bounded the yelling Apaches, fighting the soldiers hand to hand. Half the soldiers were dead and most of their horses lost when the survivors escaped, leaving their fallen leader behind.

The following July, General George Crook took command of the Department of Arizona. Before he could move, however, President Grant appointed Vincent Collyer to go to the Southwest with plenary powers to bring about peace with the Apaches. Collyer knew the President's kindly attitude toward the Indians and worked hard, though without complete success.

One paragraph of his report indicates that the Apaches had good reason to hate the white race: "The Apaches were friends of the Americans when they first knew them . . . the peaceable relations continued until the Americans adopted the Mexican theory of 'extermination,' and by acts of inhuman treachery and cruelty made them [the Apaches] our implacable foes; . . . this policy has resulted in a war which, in the last ten years, has cost us a thousand lives and over forty millions of dollars, and the country is no quieter nor the Indians any nearer extermination than they were at the time of the Gadsden purchase."

Collyer did induce Cochise to quit the warpath. Early in September, after some negotiations, the Chiricahua chief met General Gordon Granger and a peace commission in the Cañada Alamosa. One of those present, Dr. A. N. Ellis, described this remarkable Indian as he sat in council: "Evidently he was about fifty-eight years of age, although he looked very much younger; his height, five feet, ten inches; in person lithe and wiry, every muscle rounded and firm. A silver thread was now and then visible in his otherwise black hair, which he wore cut straight around his head about level with his chin. His countenance displayed great force."

Cochise's speech revealed the essential sadness of the red man and his perplexity at facing the insoluble problem of white encroachment. Toward the close he said: "When I was young I walked all over this country, east and west, and saw no other people than Apaches. After many summers I walked again and found another race of people who had come to take it. How is it? Why is it that the Apaches want to die —that they carry their lives on their finger nails? They roam over the hills and plains and want the heavens to fall on them. . . . Tell me, if the Virgin Mary has walked through all the land, why has she never entered the lodge of an Apache? Why have we never seen or heard her?"

He finished by promising to remain peaceful, stipulating that his reservation should be the territory about the Cañada Alamosa. This was promised—and the promise promptly broken. Told he must go on the Tularosa reservation, Cochise simply took to the mountains with his people and war flared all over the Southwest again. In the next year fifty-four Indian attacks were made in Arizona alone, forty-four soldiers and civilians killed, sixteen wounded, several children taken captive, and hundreds of head of livestock stolen, besides other damage.

Cochise, however, was getting old and found less zest in the labors and self-denials of the warpath. A few months later General O. O. Howard arrived in Arizona, with orders to find Cochise, rectify the errors made concerning him, and bring him back once more to peace.

The only white man who could claim friendship with Cochise was Tom Jeffords, a lean, tall frontiersman, with red hair which he generally wore about as long as any Apache, and a dangling red beard which no Apache could match. He was given to sartorial eccentricity —no matter if he was on the roughest kind of border scouting duty, he wore a black derby hat and a long-tailed black frock coat, both somewhat rusty as to hue and frayed by use, which give him a most incongruous appearance among the scouts, Indians and soldiers. He had won the regard of Cochise, even—according to one account—becoming blood brother with him "through the mystic ceremony of commingling and quaffing each other's blood."

Enlisting the help of this whimsical and droll personage, Howard sought out the camp of Cochise in the Dragoon Mountains and talked peace with him. The chief was conciliatory. He had two demands— that his people have their reservation in the mountains and valleys of their present hunting grounds, and that Jeffords be their agent. When this was agreed, Cochise said, "Hereafter, the white man and the Indian are to drink of the same water, eat the same bread, and be at peace."

He was true to his word. As long as he lived—his death came June 8, 1874—his Chiricahuas stayed on the reservation, as a people; although some of the young braves perhaps "wandered off" occasionally to join some of the "bronco" Indians.

With the most formidable Apache chief pacified, Crook reorganized his forces, enrolling numbers of Apaches as scouts, and announced a policy of dealing justly with peaceful Indians while proceeding to "punish the incorrigibly hostile."

The "incorrigibly hostile" were many and agile as fleas, but Crook was one of the greatest of all Indian fighters. He was a lean, quiet, muscular man, with chin whiskers and mustache, and averse to outward insignia. When not absolutely obligatory he never wore a uniform, and in his campaigns usually was attired in a duck suit and white canvas helmet.

Crook's first move was against the Apaches of the Tonto Basin. There were several depredating bands there, led by daring chiefs such as Del-she, Chuntz, Nata-totel and Naqui-naquis. November 15, 1871, was chosen as the start of the campaign because it was the beginning of winter and snows in the higher mountains made it difficult for the hostiles to climb into them, while campfires were necessary, with resultant smoke which could be spotted by Crook's keen-eyed scouts. To sweep the Tonto Basin clear the general sent out several columns, each self-sufficient but operating on a central plan.

Results were immediate and decisive. On December 27, Major William H. Brown, with a battalion of the Fifth Cavalry and 140

Indian scouts, surprised Chuntz's band of Tonto Apaches in the Salt River canyon. The Indians took refuge in a large rock cave, but the soldiers killed 74 of them and captured 18. Chuntz, the chief, escaped and next day joined Del-she's band.

Chuntz and Del-she raided south toward Wickenburg, where they overwhelmed a party of young Englishmen who had just come into the country. Most of the party were killed at once, but two were tortured to death. Wrote Captain John G. Bourke: "The assailants . . . tied two of them to cactus, and proceeded deliberately to fill them with arrows. One of the poor wretches rolled and writhed in agony, breaking off the feathered ends of the arrows, but each time he turned his body, exposing a space not yet wounded, the Apaches shot in another barb."

It fell to Major George M. Randall to pursue these raiders, who took refuge on top of Turret Butte, a mountain named from the fact that it resembled a turret on an old-style battleship, with very steep walls and a comparatively flat top. Up the sides of this primitive Gibraltar Randall sent his men clambering the night of April 22, 1872. Their arrival at the top in the darkness took the Apaches by surprise. In a few blasting volleys the fight was over. Some warriors, in despair, leaped over the precipice and were dashed to death hundreds of feet below, but most of the band, including Chuntz and Del-she, surrendered.

The Turret Butte fight cleaned out the Tonto Basin. Crook dealt fairly but firmly with his captives, setting them to work on irrigation projects for their own benefit, and paying them for their labor. Abuses by white men continued, but so long as Crook remained in Arizona comparative peace existed. The Indians themselves dealt with outlaws among them. On one occasion, a group of scouts came to the general and dumped out from a sack they carried seven bloody, grinning, human heads. They had been told to bring in the renegade Apaches, dead or alive and, lacking other proof that they had disposed of them, brought in their heads.

But Crook was transferred, in March 1875, to the Department of the Platte, far to the north, where already ominous signs foretold the outbreak of the Sioux, which would climax in 1876 at the Little Bighorn.

After his departure things grew worse in Arizona. On June 7, 1876, a band of Chiricahuas—deprived now of Cochise's steadying influence —killed a corrupt stage station agent named Rogers and another man named Spence, who had been selling them bad whiskey, and, fearing punishment, left their reservation. There were seventy-five or eighty warriors, with their women and children, led by two new chiefs named Geronimo and Juh. The first of these was to win especial lurid fame in history. Not for many months were the Chiricahuas brought back on the reservation. Geronimo, an ugly and morose Indian, was for a time lodged in jail, which did nothing to improve his temper.

At this time, however, he was overshadowed by a Mimbreño chief named Victorio, who jumped his reservation at Ojo Caliente, when told he must move to the hated San Carlos. Victorio had been trained under the great Mangus Colorado and knew every trick and stratagem of Apache fighting tactics.

From the time he first crossed over into Mexico, in April 1879, until his finish, he provided the most baffling series of maneuvers the army ever had to combat in Indian campaigns. Toward the Mexican sheep-herders and small ranchers he pursued a settled policy: so long as they furnished him with arms, food and ammunition Victorio allowed them to live. When they ceased doing so they died. All of them knew this, and when the savages, with their steel-trap mouths, rode up, the Mexicans gave them anything they demanded, being only too glad to get off with their lives. Replenishing his supplies thus, and knowing every foot of the country, Victorio for many months out-witted and outfought the best the United States and Mexico could send against him.

In September he crossed from Mexico into the Big Bend country of Texas, made a sweep westward into New Mexico, fought three detach-ments of white men and defeated them each time, killed twenty-six persons and wounded many more, captured scores of horses and other booty, and picked up reinforcements of warriors who joined him from the reservations—all without losing, so far as is known, a single brave.

Returning safely to Mexico, he trapped a body of men from Car-rizal who were out looking for him, killed all fifteen of them; then, with cunning such as would hardly have suggested itself to any other Indian, used the dead bodies of the first party to catch a second party from Carrizal. These went out to discover what had happened to the first group. They found the dead bodies and began burying them, not dreaming that Apaches lay all around them. At Victorio's signal the deadly fire broke out and every man of the second party died.

Now began the biggest man hunt in the Southwest's history. Back and forth, crisscrossing the international boundary, went Victorio, always throwing off his pursuers, sometimes fighting them, seeming to grow more savage as the pursuit continued. Upwards of a hundred Mexicans and Americans were officially listed as killed in this cam-paign by the Apaches, and the fate of many others was never known.

At last, however, Victorio was forced back into Mexico and to his fate. By accident, rather than design, a large force of Mexicans caught him in a canyon in the Tres Castillo Mountains and killed him with many of his warriors.

Ralph Emerson Twitchell, in *Leading Facts of New Mexican History*, made this comment: "He [Victorio] outwitted two generals of the American army and one in command of the Mexican forces. . . . He and his warriors killed over two hundred New Mexicans, more than one hundred soldiers, and two hundred citizens of the Mexican republic. . . . This war was the result of the greed of the settler and the corrupt policy of the government in the management of Indian affairs in the Southwest."

Yet though their ablest chief was dead, the Apaches still remained "incorrigibly hostile." In July 1881 occurred a raid into the United States led by Nana, a superannuated old chief about seventy years old, short, fat, wrinkled and much troubled by rheumatism, so that he usually moved slowly, often feebly. On occasion, however, he was capable of tremendous energy, as he now proved. With forty warriors he swept through New Mexico, killing sheepherders and ranchers. After a skirmish July 17, with a detachment of cavalry, and pursued by converging columns of soldiers, the Apaches reached the San Andreas Mountains, evaded the troops sent to catch them there, surprised a civilian posse in the San Mateo Mountains, killing eight of them, and left the soldiers plodding in frustration in their rear. After two skirmishes with Ninth Cavalry detachments, Nana and his warriors disappeared into Mexico, leaving only a mocking trail fading in the dust. In two months they had raided over a thousand miles of territory, fought eight battles and won them all, killed anywhere from thirty to fifty enemies, captured not less than two hundred horses and mules, and eluded pursuit by more than a thousand soldiers and perhaps four hundred civilians—with a force never exceeding forty warriors and sometimes as few as fifteen. Their only loss was four men wounded, and they all got back to Mexico.

In the spring of 1882, after Nana's wild ride of 1881, Loco, another Mimbreño chief, fled the San Carlos reservation and made for Mexico. He beat off an attack by General George A. Forsyth in the Steins Peak range, and, crossing into Mexico, thought himself safe. There, however, he was cut off by Colonel Lorenzo García with 250 Mexican soldiers. In a furious battle in which García lost 19 killed and 16 wounded, the Mexicans killed 78 Apaches, chiefly women and children. Most of the warriors escaped, including Loco, but it was the most severe defeat the Apaches had suffered in years.

It was followed by another setback, when White Mountain Apaches, under Nan-tia-tish, broke off their reservation July 6, 1882, ambushed J. L. (Cibicu Charley) Colvig, agency police chief, and killed him and seven of his Indian scouts, then rode wildly north. They destroyed property worth many thousands of dollars and murdered eight ranchers before ten troops of cavalry brought them to bay in Chevelon's Fork of the Canyon Diablo, a gigantic slash through the Mogollons, which in places is fully a thousand feet deep and has sides so steep that they frequently overhang.

Nan-tia-tish, who had only fifty-four warriors, tried to set an ambush for the troops, but under Captain Adna R. Chaffee's directions the soldiers, outnumbering the Indians ten to one, outflanked them, and in the spitting, snarling rifle duel that followed, twenty-six Apaches were killed, including Nan-tia-tish. The rest, many of them wounded, hastened back to their reservation and the White Mountain uprising was over. The troops, with overwhelming superiority in fire power, lost only two dead and seven wounded.

In the midst of these difficulties General Crook returned from the Sioux campaigns to resume command in Arizona, September 4, 1882. At once he set out to rectify wrongs. White squatters and unauthorized miners were expelled from Indian lands, trusted officers were placed in charge, the growing of crops and livestock was encouraged again. The Indian Ring—of government contractors and traders—took the usual dim view of this, since if the Apaches became self-supporting the profits to the Ring would cease. Began again the long-drawn political fight which ended only when Crook left the territory.

Yet Crook almost succeeded in pacifying the Apaches: he would have done so had it not been for Geronimo. That Indian, whose real name was Go-ya-thle (He Who Yawns), hated all peoples who were not Apaches and he had a long record of blood, particularly in Mexico. Crook called him "the human tiger." General Miles referred to him as "the worst Indian who ever lived." He was cunning, bloodthirsty, incredibly cruel, and combined many savage talents. Though he gave an impression of cowardice with his skulking tactics, on occasion he was courageous. Of his appearance, Charles F. Lummis wrote:

"He was a compactly built, dark-faced man of one hundred and seventy pounds, and about five feet, eight inches in height. The man who once saw his face will never forget it. Crueller features were never cut. The nose was broad and heavy, the forehead low and wrinkled, the chin full and strong, the eyes like two bits of obsidian with a light behind them. The mouth was a most noticeable feature—a sharp, straight, thin-lipped gash of generous length and without one softening curve."

Geronimo was in the fastnesses of the Sierra Madre of Mexico when

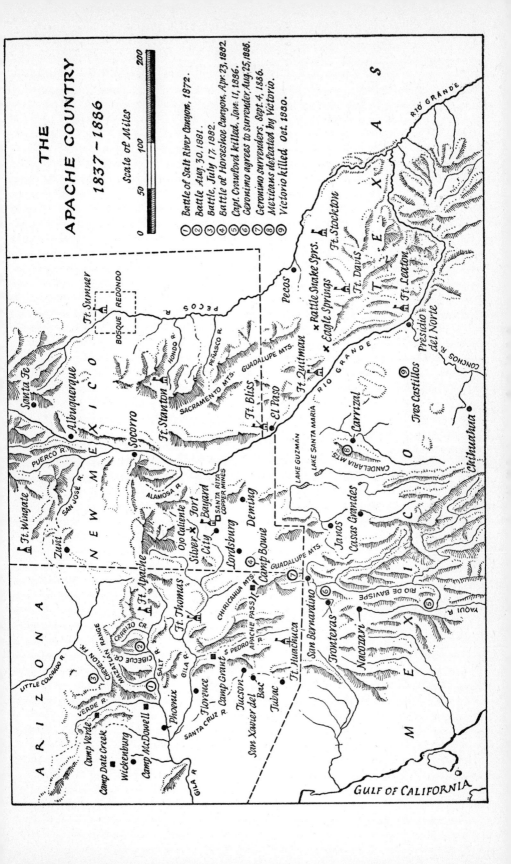

THE
APACHE COUNTRY
1837 – 1886

Scale of Miles

0   50   100   200

① Battle of Salt River Canyon. 1872.
② Battle Aug. 30. 1881.
③ Battle, July 17. 1882.
④ Battle of Horseshoe Canyon. Apr. 23. 1882.
⑤ Capt. Crawford killed. Jan. 11. 1886.
⑥ Geronimo agrees to surrender, Aug. 25. 1886.
⑦ Geronimo surrenders, Sept. 4. 1886.
⑧ Mexicans defeated by Victorio.
⑨ Victorio killed out. 1880.

Crook returned to Arizona. In March 1883 one of his chiefs, Chato (Flat Nose), raided north of the border. In this raid the Indians killed seven persons. Most notable of their victims were Judge H. C. McComas and his wife. Judge McComas was a federal judge and Mrs. McComas, cultured and accomplished, was a sister of Eugene Ware, the then popular poet "Ironquill." Their little son Charley was carried away. The McComases were driving by buckboard for a session of court at Leitendorf, near Silver City, New Mexico, when the Apaches attacked them.

Owing to the prominence of these victims, a national sensation was created and Crook was ordered to pursue the raiders, punish them, and try to recover the little boy. Taking advantage of a treaty recently signed with Mexico, whereby troops were permitted to cross the border in pursuit of hostile Indians, Crook was in the Sierra Madre by May 8. Captain Emmett Crawford, with a company of Indian scouts, surprised a camp high in the mountains May 15 and defeated the hostiles. Shortly after, most of the Apaches, including Geronimo, Nana, Chato and Loco, surrendered and returned to their reservation.

Charley McComas was not recovered. Crook was told by the Indians that the child was dead, but there is a strange story, at least partly substantiated, that the boy lived and grew up among the Apaches in Mexico, eventually became a chief in the wild bands of the Sierra Madre, and died only comparatively recently.

With the exception of a few bronco (outlaw) bands, all the hostiles now were back on the reservation. Many even of those came in later, for Juh, the last chief of consequence who remained out, got drunk and unromantically drowned when he fell from his horse while fording a river near Casas Grandes, Mexico.

The breathing spell did not last long. On May 17, because their agent told them to stop drinking *tiswin*—a native beer that made them ugly and quarrelsome—thirty-two warriors, eight well-grown boys and ninety-two women and children left the Fort Apache reservation and headed for Mexico. At their head was Geronimo. With him went Nana, Nachite (son of Cochise), Mangus (son of Mangus Colorado), Chihuahua and Ulzana, all notable leaders, besides the pick of the warlike Apaches.

Army pursuit was prompt and vigorous but pretty futile. In the next six months of campaigning the troops and their Indian allies killed six warriors, two women and a child of the Apache outlaws. In the same period, according to the official records, seventy-three soldiers and settlers and twelve reservation Indians were slain by the hostiles in American territory besides an unknown number of *vaqueros,* sheepherders and peons below the Mexican border.

Most spectacular episode of this period, and worth special examination because it so well illustrated the peculiar aptness for murder and stratagems of the Apaches, was Ulzana's raid.

A dour fighter and cunning as a wolf, Ulzana with ten warriors slipped across the international line into Arizona early in November 1884. In the full knowledge that they were braving the efforts of two thousand soldiers and many Indian scouts, as well as all the settlers and ranchers in the country who were unanimously anxious to cut them off and exterminate them, the eleven Apaches traveled over the roughest mountains to the Gila River. There, the hue and cry having been raised, they scattered and disappeared. The pursuit was called off, simply because there was nobody to look for.

Nothing was heard from the Apaches for nearly three weeks, while Ulzana hid in the mountains of New Mexico, planning his foray. Then he gathered his braves, and on the night of November 26 he struck.

The renegades were bitter against their kinsmen who refused to join them and that night Ulzana descended on a village of White Mountain Apaches near Fort Apache, Arizona. Guns thudded, white-hot flashes lit the gloom, there were wild yells and scurrying figures in the darkness. Before the cavalry could come from the fort Ulzana was gone, leaving the bodies of twelve Indians friendly to the whites, and one of his own warriors, who had been killed by a reservation Apache with an ax.

From then on Ulzana's band, now numbering exactly ten warriors, led a career both bloody and thrilling. Flashed by telegraph, news that the terrible Apaches were on the prowl again went to every fort and town in the Southwest. Troops swarmed to the pursuit from Fort Apache, San Carlos, Fort Thomas, Camp Grant and Fort Bowie.

At first Ulzana made for Mexico via the old route between the Dragoon and Whetstone mountains which had been used ever since Coronado first came that way centuries before. On December 2 he was in the vicinity of Solomonville, on the Gila River, signalizing his arrival when his warriors killed two brothers named Wright near that town and Dick Mays next day on the Coronado ranch.

Knowing Apache ways, Crook concealed five companies of soldiers in the valley between the Whetstones and Dragoons; but Ulzana perceived and was contemptuous of this obvious device. Instead of continuing south he turned east up the Gila and crossed into New Mexico with cavalry and scouts pressing on his trail.

Pursuit he really did not fear, since he changed the horses of his band every time a new ranch herd came into view, while the troops were forced to husband the strength of the animals they rode, no remounts being handy for them. So on December 9 and 10 the Apaches stopped on the upper Gila long enough to kill four ranchers. Then, abandoning their horses and much of the plunder they had picked up, they scattered like so many coyotes. Once more Ulzana's band had disappeared as if into thin air, and nobody could tell where or when it would next assemble.

Wildest panic, by this time, prevailed in Arizona and New Mexico. Every effort was made by the government and by private citizens to notify all ranchers, farmers, prospectors and travelers of the presence of Apache death in the country, but to reach all was impossible.

Ulzana manifested himself again December 19, when he and his braves fought a brief little battle with a detachment of the Eighth Cavalry in Dry Creek Canyon. Dr. Maddox, an army surgeon, and four enlisted men were killed. The Apaches suffered no losses. Evidently the hostiles once more were heading south, and Crook, who had not for one moment relaxed his grim alertness, posted five companies of cavalry between the Chiricahua and Peloncillo ranges, while he kept a company of Navajo scouts, under Lieutenant Scott, pushing behind the raiders to keep them from turning back.

Two men, named Snow and Windham, were killed by the hostiles near Carlisle, New Mexico, November 26, and the same day they crossed over into Arizona and butchered two more men near Galeyville. One was Caspar Albert. The other has not been identified to this day.

At this point it appeared that Ulzana and his warriors were caught between Scott's scouts and Crook's cavalry. But at the last minute, just before the nutcracker closed, a heavy snowstorm began. It lasted for three days. To trail the Indians now was manifestly impossible. Sometime in that period Ulzana, using an unknown game trail over the mountains, passed through the military screen and was once more out of the reach of the troops in the Sierra Madre of Mexico.

In four weeks Ulzana had led his men not less than twelve hundred miles through enemy country, maintaining himself and his warriors as he went. His band killed thirty-eight persons, captured and wore out two hundred and fifty horses and mules, changed mounts at least twenty times, twice left all their animals and scattered on foot to evade pursuit; and yet, in spite of the efforts of two thousand soldiers, many Indian scouts and hundreds of civilians, eventually got back to Mexico with the loss of only one brave—killed by a White Mountain Indian near Fort Apache.

Crook was convinced by the Ulzana raid that he could not catch the will-o'-the-wisp Apaches when they made their lightning forays into the United States. He reorganized his plan and prepared to send detachments down into Mexico after them.

Best of his Indian fighters was Captain Emmett Crawford, who with a contingent of lean, fierce Apache scouts was the chief spearhead of the pursuit. Crawford almost caught Geronimo. He did capture the renegade's camp, with all his supplies, and a squaw came as a messenger from Geronimo, suggesting a peace talk. Delighted, Crawford agreed. But he never held the conference. Next day, January 11, 1886, a Mexican contingent was encountered in the mountains. The Mexicans thought Crawford's scouts were hostile Apaches. In the confusion shots were fired and Crawford was mortally wounded. Furious at the fall of their leader, the scouts returned the fire, and killed two officers and two enlisted men of the Mexican force.

Carrying their captain, who died a few hours later, the scouts fell back toward the American line. That night Geronimo met Lieutenant Marion P. Maus, who succeeded Crawford in command, and promised to confer with General Crook, "in two moons." At the same time old Nana, weary of war, surrendered with eight other Indians and returned with Maus.

True to his promise, Geronimo and his warriors met Crook and an escort of officers, men and scouts at the Canyon des Embudos, south of the Mexican border. Followed a long, three-day council, at the end of which Geronimo shook hands with Crook. "Two or three words are enough," he said. "I surrender myself to you. Once I moved about like the wind. Now I surrender to you and that is all." Again he shook hands with the general.

But a conscienceless, money-grabbing white man spoiled everything. An American bootlegger named Tribolet sneaked into the Apache camp that night and began selling liquor to them. Before morning Geronimo, in the light of his new alcoholic courage, repented of his peace agreement and skipped out with Nachite and twenty warriors, thirteen women and six children. All the others of his band, including the ferocious Ulzana, kept their promise and returned to their reservation.

The escape of Geronimo, the dreaded, aroused a typhoon of angry criticism of the commanding general in Arizona. Crook, who had been hectored by the Indian Ring throughout his tour of duty, had enough. He wired General Sheridan a long message, outlining his policy of fairness both to red men and white, and ended by requesting to be relieved of command.

Next day, April 2, General Nelson A. Miles was assigned to command the Department of Arizona. A famous and successful Indian fighter, who had campaigned against the Comanches, Sioux, Nez Percés and other tribes in wars extending over more than a decade, Miles set out to capture Geronimo.

It was a big problem, yet actually the Apache was doomed. In twenty-five detachments, Miles set his troops to combing the country. Every water hole, no matter how small, and every ranch had its garrison. Flying columns penetrated into Mexico. Mountain peaks were equipped with heliograph stations, from which the campaigning units were kept informed of every report concerning their enemy.

Yet once more Geronimo swept into southern Arizona. On April 27 he butchered several cowboys on the Peck ranch in the Santa Cruz Valley and compelled the rancher, Peck, to witness the torture of his wife until he went temporarily insane. The superstitious Indians released the crazed rancher but carried away his thirteen-year-old daughter.

Pursuing with a company of scouts, Captain H. W. Lawton recovered the girl, but the Apaches were back in Mexico, leaving a trail of blood. They killed seven Mexican irregular soldiers south of the border, five or six Mexican placer miners a little farther on, seven woodchoppers next, and thus continued into Sonora with murders marking their passing.

In the Pinito Mountains Geronimo repulsed a cavalry attack, and again did so between the San Pedro and Santa Cruz rivers. But Lawton had begun what was to be an endless pursuit. For three months it continued, a never ceasing, bloodhound following of the hostile's trail, with the heliograph signals always directing him. Pressed as he was, Geronimo vented his hate in slaughter. During his pursuit Lawton picked up as many as ten butchered Mexicans a day, and Governor Luis E. Torres of Sonora reported between five and six hundred of his people killed during the campaign.

On June 6, Lawton captured Geronimo's camp with most of the Apaches' ammunition. Late in July two squaws stole into Fronteras, Mexico, with word that the hostiles wanted to give up. Lieutenant Charles B. Gatewood, best liked by the Indians of the army officers since Crawford's death, with two Indian scouts, went on an assignment of immense peril—to find Geronimo and verify the message of the squaws.

Gatewood met the chief at last, and boldly laid down Miles's terms. "Surrender and you will be sent with your families to Florida, there to await the decision of the President as to your final disposal. Accept these terms or fight it out."

Geronimo passed his hand over his eyes, and as he did so, Gatewood saw it tremble. The iron chief was shaken at last.

On September 3, 1886, Geronimo and his band met Miles and his escort at a place named as if by inspiration for such a scene—Skeleton

Canyon. There the final fragment of a warlike race and the sole remaining fighting chief of the Apaches surrendered.

The captives were sent to Fort Marion, Florida, from which after many years the survivors were removed to Fort Sill, Oklahoma. A lasting infamy is the fact that many Chiricahua and Mimbreño Indians, who had remained peacefully on the reservation, including some of the very scouts who bravely helped capture Geronimo's band, were lumped in with the renegade prisoners and all shipped away together, to exile and misery.

Old Nana died at Fort Sill, at a great age, saying, "I feel that I have no country." Geronimo died there also, in 1909. Peace, as far as the Indians are concerned, has reigned in the Southwest for three quarters of a century. But because of that final episode it can hardly be called peace with honor.

CHAPTER FIVE

Six-shooter Vendettas

THE invention by Samuel Colt of the repeating pistol with a revolving cylinder revolutionized the firearms industry and had a mighty effect on the history of the West. Colt revolvers first became popular in Texas as early as 1839, because they were ideal horseback weapons, could be put in action quickly, and hence were, as one Texas Ranger said, "the best answer to a Comanche." The handiness of the new firearm soon caused it to supplant the bowie knife as the universal weapon of the frontier. So much a part of the equipment of every range rider did it become that until comparatively recently a cowboy felt hardly decently garbed without his cartridge belt and six-shooter.

After the destruction of the buffalo herds and the subduing of the hostile Indian tribes, a tidal wave of cattle swept out from Texas. Within a little more than two decades the thrust of ranching expansion occupied the whole of the unsettled portions of the United States, bringing the half-outlaw precursor of civilization to a territory comparable in size to that which required three centuries to win east of the Mississippi.

To cattle and sheep ranching was added gold prospecting, and mines of many minerals were developed in the Southwest, among which silver and copper were the most important. In such a period of vast enterprise and exploitation, when rights to properties of great value were in frequent dispute, and where almost every man carried a lethal weapon on his hip, violence was inevitable. Outlawry was common, robbery and murder frequent, and the six-shooter was very often the arbiter of disputes in the mountains and on the plains. Feuds broke out—between ranch and ranch, between big operators and little ones, between claim owners and claim jumpers, between cattlemen and sheepmen, between stockmen and rustlers, between man and man.

Though the army finally cornered the last of the hostile Indians, it by no means followed that there was peace in the Southwest. Revolvers barked out their staccato messages of death in saloons and dives, along the trails and in the open. Road agents and rustlers fought posses, town marshals sought to enforce peace with bullets, men sometimes shot it out in simple rivalry over which had the greatest lethal virtuosity with the nimble weapon he swung at his belt. In this era it was notable that bullies were scarce in the West; and that a high degree of almost stately politeness existed between men. This was for the reason that all were measured by the standard of the six-shooter, and a big man could be cut down as quickly as a little man by a leaden slug.

Billy the Kid was an undersized youth, physically no match for any able-bodied man of normal size and strength, yet he was a terror in half of New Mexico and part of Texas. Doc Holliday was a skeletonic consumptive, but his name brought respect from men far bigger, healthier, and fully as brave as he. The holstered death at their sides made these two—and others—greater than themselves. In the West they spoke of the six-shooter as "Colonel Colt's Equalizer."

A long struggle took place before law and order were brought to the land and men were induced to lay down their weapons. In Texas the Rangers proved themselves a holy terror to evildoers, and although they could not quite boast that they always got their man, chiefly because of state and international boundary lines across which they could not operate, they imprisoned or killed men like John Wesley Hardin, Sam Bass, Juan Flores—and in later years Bonnie Parker and Clyde Barrow—to name only a few. They broke up county feuds and suppressed banditry by both American and Mexican outlaws, until Texas became relatively law-abiding.

Elsewhere no such efficient peace-enforcement weapon as the Rangers existed, and feuds and factional "wars" were correspondingly explosive. In the Pleasant Valley War of Arizona, from 1887 to 1892, for example, between twenty-eight and fifty men were killed before the last man of the Tewksbury faction slew the last man of the Graham faction and thus brought to an end, by sheer attrition, the feud.

Among the hundreds of episodes in which the six-shooter played its deadly role, the two most celebrated serve to give a general example of all: the Lincoln County War of New Mexico, 1876–78, and the Earp-Clanton feud of Tombstone, Arizona, 1880–81.

The Lincoln County War begins with John Chisum and Major L. G. Murphy. Chisum, a considerable cattleman from Texas, established his ranch on the Pecos River and gained possession of riparian rights—by squatter claim—on both sides of that stream, from Fort Sumner to the Texas line, two hundred miles southward. His cattle holdings were said at one time to be the largest in the world. Murphy operated a store, saloon, hotel and flour mill at the little town of Lincoln, about sixty miles west of Chisum's headquarters. In addition to these enterprises the major had some cattle in the hills, and since his herd multiplied far faster than natural increase might account for, Chisum, a forthright personage, accused him of rustling from the Chisum herd.

Bitterness between the two men was increased when Alexander A. McSween, a young lawyer from Kansas who once had hoped to enter the ministry and still had pronounced views on ethics and violence, refused to defend some of Murphy's men who were charged with cattle theft, and shortly after began to represent Chisum instead. When McSween set up a store in rivalry to Murphy's emporium in Lincoln, the major felt even more aggrieved, for he charged that Chisum was behind the enterprise. This McSween denied, saying that his only backer was a young Englishman, J. H. Tunstall, who was enamored of the American West and had bought a ranch on the Rio Feliz, thirty miles from Lincoln. Some of Murphy's ire turned on Tunstall.

The major was a political as well as a financial power. He controlled the town of Lincoln, which was the county seat of Lincoln County, then including the present New Mexico counties of Lincoln, Chavez, Eddy, Otero and part of Doña Ana—one fifth of the state, an isolated mountain country, cut off from outside civilization by barriers of desert. Its people traded naturally at Lincoln and prior to McSween's mercantile venture Murphy controlled that trade, as he controlled the votes of the area. The sheriff, James A. Brady, was his man.

One of Tunstall's cowboys was a youth named William Bonney, much better known as Billy the Kid, a name given him with indulgent humor by his fellow cowboys before he became terrible. About Billy the Kid there was nothing to impress one who saw him. A damaged photograph of him exists and it coincides with a description of him given by a man who knew him well, Frank Collinson, of El Paso, Texas:

"A slight, boyish-looking chap, badly weather-beaten . . . not much to look at. About five feet seven or eight inches, not over one hundred and forty pounds at the outside. Rather sloping shoulders, no chin, good nose, very good blue-gray eyes . . . everything he wore, from his old black hat to his boots wouldn't have cost ten dollars all together when new."

Yet this unlikely-looking individual was, in many respects, the most notable six-shooter killer of history.

The Kid was born in New York's Bowery and was taken, as a baby, by his parents to Coffeyville, Kansas, a tough border town where later the Dalton bandit gang was wiped out in a street battle. His father died and his mother took him to Colorado, where she married a man named Antrim. Later they moved to New Mexico and the Kid is said to have killed his first man at the age of twelve—a Silver City blacksmith who spoke slightingly of his mother.

Thereafter the boy took to the hills. He never saw his mother again. In the next years he roamed the Southwest, becoming an unparalleled expert with the six-shooter, almost equally dexterous with cards, doing some cattle rustling, and killing a man now and then in saloon fights— a deadly youth, whose moods and technique men learned to dread and respect. Yet he had some good points, too. Women often idolized him, and some men remained faithful to him to the death. He had a certain oblique code of honor and made good his word, whether it was a threat or a promise. Above all he possessed superlatively the virtues that counted most in the wild cattle land—nerve and courage.

Tunstall had befriended Billy the Kid; and the Kid, in turn, idolized the bluff Englishman. What took place February 13, 1878, therefore, drove the youth berserk.

On that day Murphy sent a posse to the Rio Feliz ranch to take over Tunstall's property, in lieu of a debt the major alleged was owed him by McSween, the Englishman's partner in the Lincoln store. Tunstall indignantly objected. The possemen were drunk and irresponsible. They shot the Englishman and left him lying dead. Over Tunstall's grave, later, Billy the Kid said with chill solemnity, "I will kill every one of the men that had a hand in this murder, or die trying. You were the only man who ever treated me like I was freeborn and white."

Those two sentences, uttered by a lonely youth to a man in his grave, constituted the declaration of war in Lincoln County.

Through his lawyer, McSween, Chisum managed to get Dick Brewer, Tunstall's foreman, appointed constable. That made two rival law-enforcement heads in Lincoln County—Murphy's Sheriff Brady and Chisum's Constable Brewer. Wild to avenge Tunstall, Brewer appointed as his deputies some of the choicest desperadoes in the West. Among them were Billy the Kid, Charlie Bowdre, Tom O'Folliard, Doc Skurlock, Hendry Brown, Frank McNab, Jim French, John Middleton and George and Frank Coe.

A few days after Tunstall's murder, Brewer's men captured two members of the posse that had killed him—Billy Morton and Frank Baker. The prisoners were fearful that they would be lynched. As they rode toward Lincoln a member of the posse named McClosky tried to reassure them by saying that before they were harmed he would have to be killed first. He uttered his own death sentence. Another posseman, Frank McNab, shot McClosky dead off his horse. Knowing that their own death was certain, the two prisoners spurred to get away, but Billy the Kid, sitting in his saddle, fired twice. Morton and Baker spun lifeless out of their saddles. Leaving the three bodies to the buzzards, the Brewer deputies rode back to Lincoln.

March passed. On April 1, as Sheriff Brady, with Deputy George Hindman, Billy Matthews, the court clerk, and George Peppin—all Murphy men—walked past the McSween place in Lincoln on their way to open court, a clatter of shots echoed from the canyon wherein stood the town. Down went Brady, dead in the dust. Hindman, mortally wounded, with a bullet between his shoulders, crawled in a trail of blood to the steps of San Juan church, where he died. The other two, dodging and bounding, reached safety around a corner.

Over the patio wall vaulted the Kid and Fred Wayte. The Kid wanted Brady's guns. As he stooped over the fallen man, Matthews, from the door of a Mexican house, fired and wounded Wayte in the thigh, the same bullet cutting a slight flesh wound in the Kid's hip. The two jumped back to the protection of the wall, but the Kid stopped long enough to gather up the guns and fire a *coup de grâce* shot into Brady's head. Charlie Bowdre, Tom O'Folliard, Jim French and Frank McNab took part in the ambush, with the Kid and Wayte. But the Kid personally accounted for Brady, the man who had sent out the posse that murdered Tunstall.

Thereafter things happened rapidly. With a posse of thirteen men, Brewer tried to arrest Andrew J. Roberts April 14. The "wanted" man was known as Buckshot Roberts because of the amount of lead he carried in his frame owing to a career as a soldier and Texas Ranger, and he was marked as a Murphy partisan. They found him at Blazer's mill on the Mescalero reservation, but he refused to surrender. Though mortally wounded by a bullet fired by Bowdre, and hemorrhaging to death, Roberts propped himself up at a window and fought like a dying wolf. One of his bullets passed through Jack Middleton's body. A second took off George Coe's trigger finger, knocking the revolver out of his hand. A third, fired from a huge-bored buffalo gun, neatly removed the top of Brewer's head and with it his life.

The posse withdrew with its wounded. Roberts quietly bled to death in the mill. Next day he and Brewer were buried side by side—some say in the same grave—near the scene of their battle.

Brewer, leader of the McSween faction, and Brady, head of the Murphy people, were both dead. But instead of ending, the war spread. Out on the range shootings occurred. McNab, who had killed McClosky, was himself killed and two or three other men wounded in a clash between rival posses in Bonito Canyon. The Kid, with five or six followers, fought a long-distance gun battle with a posse that tried to arrest him on the Chisum ranch; and then escaped with his men to the refuge of the McSween house in Lincoln.

There, the night of July 17, George Peppin, who had been appointed sheriff after Brady's death, surrounded them with sixty men. Shortly afterward McSween rode into town with reinforcements—perhaps twenty men. Though still far outnumbered, the Kid laughed scornfully at Peppin's call to surrender.

McSween, with both legal and moral scruples against violence, begged for a peaceful adjustment, but he was caught in a storm of conflicting forces over which he had no control. Even as he pleaded, the first shots crackled out, and the "Three Days' Battle," as famous as any in Western history, was on. Billy the Kid was only eighteen years old. Yet he was the dominating figure, the leader, the maker of decisions, to whom men greatly his senior in age and experience turned for orders, in the fighting that followed.

Although the shooting was rather continuous nobody at first was hit on either side, because these men were too adept at finding and using cover. The Kid did no firing for a time. He was a little bored and said with a yawn, "I'm waiting till I get a good square crack at someone." To poor McSween, imploring him to trust the Lord and keep the peace, he said, "Go ahead and trust the Lord. The rest of us will trust our six-shooters."

A small peak lifts its head just above the town and when night fell, silencing the guns, two of Sheriff Peppin's best shots, Lucio Montoya and Charlie Crawford, posted themselves there. From it they could look down into the patio of the McSween house.

As dawn came a man crossed the yard. Both Montoya and Crawford fired at him, but missed. He dodged back into safety.

Down in the patio, Fernando Herrera, an old Mexican buffalo hunter who had espoused the cause of "the Keed," crouched with his heavy Sharp's rifle. When Crawford raised his head to look down from the pinnacle, which loomed about a quarter of a mile distant, Herrera's gun boomed, and Crawford, a bullet through his skull, toppled over lifeless and rolled all the way down the cliff. Montoya, in his excitement, leaned over to see where his companion had fallen and a second slug from the buffalo gun smashed his leg.

From then on both sides took added care to keep in concealment, and though windows were smashed and doors punctured, nobody was wounded in the long hours of the day. The second night came and again the guns ceased speaking, although everyone was tensely watchful. On the third day, July 19, the shooting began again, an indeterminate stalemate now, until a new force appeared in the afternoon.

Notified of the battle in Lincoln, Colonel N. A. M. Dudley rode into the town with two troops of Negro cavalrymen and a couple of Gatling guns. After he conferred with the leaders on both sides, he withdrew and camped outside the hamlet. He had concluded, as he later reported, that the legal sheriff of the county, with a legitimate posse, was in combat with men who were at least technically outside the law. It was a civil affair and Dudley could interfere only if asked to do so by the proper authorities. Peppin, who seemed to be the "proper authority," wanted no help, and certainly no interference, from the military.

The parley occurred toward evening. While all attention was focused on it, some of the Peppin men crept to the rear of McSween's house and set it on fire. After the soldiers departed and the shooting again began, the flames were suddenly discovered. Efforts to control them were vain, because water was lacking. The beleaguered forces of the Kid had to burn to death, surrender, or fight their way through the cordon surrounding them.

Mrs. McSween and two other women came out of the blazing building. Not a shot was fired as they hurried to safety.

But with the men it was different. Harvey Morris and Francisco Semova made the first dash for life. Outlined in the glare of the flames, they fell dead, riddled by bullets. Vicente Romero was next to try—and die. Then McSween stepped forth. He carried his Bible in his hand and called, "Gentlemen, I am McSween." It was no use. A dozen rifles from the darkness crumpled him lifeless on the ground.

Suddenly the men in the burning and untenable house came hurtling out in every direction, running for life. So unexpected was the rush, and the fugitives burst forth in such numbers, that it seemed to confuse the Peppin men. A ragged volley roared out, but only two of the fugitives were hit, both wounded. The others, leaping and dodging, threw themselves over the adobe wall at the rear and plunged into the safety of the brush along the Rio Bonito which cut through the town.

Last to emerge was Billy the Kid. With a revolver blazing in each hand, he sprinted across the McSween patio, bullets singing and thudding about him. Bob Beckwith pitched forward, dead from one of the Kid's leaden slugs. Two other Peppin men were wounded. Then the Kid was gone—diving headlong down into the ravine and lost in the brush. Guts and murderous skill with his six-shooters had saved him.

The three-day fight produced six corpses and several wounded. It firmly established Sheriff Peppin in power, but it did not end the feud. Hatreds grew worse, if anything. Out in lonely canyons and on wild sagebrush flats cowboys were "dry-gulched." Rustlers continued to steal cattle and herders died defending them. Billy the Kid, small, slope-shouldered and deadly, led and directed the outlawry.

General Lew Wallace, governor of the territory—and then working on his famous novel, *Ben Hur*—sent for the Kid, under a promise of safe-conduct, and, when the latter showed up, offered him amnesty if he would leave New Mexico. The Kid shook his head. "This is my country," he said, "and I'm staying in it."

He still had some accounts to square for the killing of Tunstall. Revenge was the great driving motive of his life. He left the governor and rode back to his wilds.

But a new adversary entered the arena when a six-foot-four-inch former buffalo hunter, Pat Garrett, became sheriff in place of Peppin. Garrett knew Billy the Kid and had once been his friend, but when he accepted his office he solemnly accepted with it the duty of bringing in the outlaw. Months passed in a widespread man hunt and the Kid killed and killed, until his total of dead was nineteen. At last Garrett's relentless pursuit cornered him. Surrounded in an abandoned stone house by a posse, the Kid at first fought back, but when his two companions, Bowdre and O'Folliard, were killed, he surrendered.

Tried at Mesilla and sentenced to hang, he was returned to Lincoln for execution. But the Kid wasn't ready to die yet. While Garrett was out of town—making arrangements for the gallows—the young outlaw took advantage of the carelessness of one of the two deputies set to guard him, and managed to get the man's own revolver and kill him. Then he shot the other guard from the window as he came running from where he had been eating lunch. With a Winchester in his hands, taken from the jailer's gun rack, the Kid cowed the crowd of people that gathered at the shots, made someone free him of his manacles and leg irons, and, commandeering a horse, rode away.

Garrett's work was all to do over again. Doggedly he began it and for months he maintained his hunt, knowing now that it was Billy the Kid or himself—one or the other must die before it was over.

Billy the Kid's one weakness—for a woman—finally undid him. A girl who lived at Fort Sumner fascinated him. He went to see her. Learning of it, Garrett followed and on the night of July 14, 1881, stole into the house of Pete Maxwell where the Kid was staying.

In the darkness his presence was felt rather than seen by the outlaw. "*Quién es?*" called the Kid.

Two instantaneous flashes lit the interior for the wink of an eye as Garrett pulled his trigger twice.

Billy the Kid plunged lifeless to the floor. He was just twenty-one years old.

How many men died in the Lincoln County War nobody will ever know. The Kid's own total of killings was twenty-one—a man for every year of his life—but of these only eight died by his hand in the Lincoln County feud. The authenticated list, starting with Tunstall, is in the neighborhood of twenty. But this does not take into account killings which took place out in the hills and canyons, of which no record was kept, and which perhaps were never known except to the slayer, until someone stumbled across a whitened and unidentifiable skeleton in later years.

Meantime, while the later stages of this stark vendetta of the hills were being enacted, a feud equally as spectacular began in another frontier town, hundreds of miles to the west.

A prospector named Ed Schieffelin had discovered a fabulous silver lode in southern Arizona in 1877. In that year the Apaches still were very active in the area. When Schieffelin told his friend, Al Sieber, chief of the army scouts, that he was going to prospect for "stones" (quartz specimens), the latter said, "The only stone you'll ever find out there is your tombstone." Because of that remark Schieffelin sardonically named his diggings Tombstone.

In the rush that followed his discovery the town of Tombstone grew up nearby, with other mining towns, such as Bisbee, near. The mushrooming growth of population created a market for beef, and certain gentry made shift to provide that beef—by stealing cattle in Mexico and driving them north over the border. The stolen cattle were held in southern Cochise County, then a wild stretch of mountains, gulches and desert on the international boundary, where men who did not particularly wish to have their past known found a convenient hiding place.

Headquarters for these stock thieves were at two ranches: the Clanton ranch in the San Pedro Valley, where N. H. (Old Man) Clanton and his three hard-eyed, hard-shooting sons, Ike, Phin and Billy, held sway; and the McLowery ranch, run by the brothers Frank and Tom, both quick and deadly on the draw. About these gathered as malign a group of desperadoes as ever lived, including men like Curly Bill

Brocius, John Ringo, Joe Hill, Jim Hughes, Pony Deal, Frank Stilwell, Billy Claiborne, Zwing Hunt, Billy Leonard and others, all killers, all outlaws, living in that rustlers' paradise.

After Old Man Clanton and four of his men were waylaid and killed by Mexicans while running stolen cattle across the border, Curly Bill Brocius assumed the leadership of the rustlers and Clanton's sons carried on with him, the McLowerys and the others. Not only cattle theft but other crimes, including stage robbery, murder and a reign of terror in all southeastern Arizona, emanated from the outlaw domain of Cochise County.

A deputy United States marshal named Wyatt Earp arrived in Tombstone December 1, 1879. Remarkable even on the border, which had many remarkable men, was Earp. When he arrived in Tombstone he was thirty years old, but already he was famous as a gun fighter, having served as a peace officer in Ellsworth, Wichita, Dodge City and other Kansas cow towns in the era of trail driving and six-shooter law. A tall, loose-limbed, powerful man with lightning reactions, his face was unforgettable, with its grim jaw, sweeping blond mustaches and blue-gray eyes, piercing, cold, continually watchful.

He was shortly joined by three others—his brothers Morgan and Virgil, and a close friend of all of them, John H. Holliday, always known as Doc, lean, consumptive, sardonic and deadly. The brothers, Morgan and Virgil—and Warren, who came into the picture later— were similar in mold to Wyatt: tall, mustached men, but a little less striking than he. All four Earps were fond of and intensely loyal to each other, a loyalty joined in by and extended to Doc Holliday.

Concerning the feud that followed there is to this day an extremely wide divergence of opinions. Billy Breakenridge, who later became sheriff of Cochise County, wrote a book called *Helldorado*, in which he referred to the Brocius-Clanton-McLowery crowd merely as "cowboys" and stigmatized the Earps as aggressors, mistreating the inoffensive sons of the saddle until they were goaded into action. On the other hand, such writers as William MacLeod Raine, Walter Noble Burns and Stuart Lake take the position that the Earps were peace officers legitimately fighting crime and the Cochise County crowd were rustlers, desperadoes and outlaws—in which the record rather seems to back them up. In the Southwest these differences in belief still hold true, but the fact remains that the Earps broke the power of outlawry and when they moved on the clean-up that followed was possible.

In the summer of 1880 the Bisbee stage was held up and Sheriff Johnny Behan arrested Frank Stilwell and Pete Spence, of the Brocius-Clanton crowd, for it. After they were arraigned and about to be released on bond, Wyatt Earp, as deputy U.S. marshal, rearrested **them** for robbing the United States mails, for which they were again arraigned and bonds much heavier placed upon them. The friends of the two considered the second arrest gratuitous and Earp began to receive threats.

Into Tombstone, the evening of October 27, rode a crowd of men. Curly Bill Brocius was at their head. He was accompanied by Ike and Billy Clanton, Frank and Tom McLowery, Frank Patterson, Pony Deal, and a few others. By the time they had made a round of the saloons they were drunk and ugly. Fred White, the city marshal, set out to arrest them, and asked Wyatt Earp to help him.

Tragedy followed. In a struggle for Brocius' gun, White was shot through the bowels and carried away dying. Earp "pistol-whipped" Brocius, dragged him unconscious to the jail, and locked him up. Then he set out grimly to arrest the other ringleaders. One after another he hunted down Frank Patterson, both McLowerys, Pony Deal and Billy Clanton. Each he handled in the same way—a tremendous blow on the skull with the barrel of his pistol, then a cell for the senseless man.

Before he died, however, Fred White exonerated Brocius, saying the shot that killed him was accidental. The prisoners were freed and rode back to their ranches, furious at Earp and with aching heads.

Feeling now was tense but almost a year elapsed before the climax came. On October 25, 1881, the Clantons and McLowerys once more rode into Tombstone and began to "licker up." Ike Clanton and Doc Holliday met in a saloon and exchanged fiery words, but were parted.

Early next morning the Earp brothers were notified that the Clanton gang was gathering. There had been some loud talk and threats with guns on the street. Finally direct word came, to the following effect:

"Tell the Earps that we're waiting at the O.K. Corral, and if they don't come down and fight it out, we'll pick them off the street when they try to go home. If Wyatt Earp will leave town, we won't harm his brothers, but if he stays the whole outfit will have to come down and make its fight."

It was a formal cartel of the West. In the O.K. Corral waited Ike and Billy Clanton, the two McLowerys and Billy Claiborne, five very dangerous gunfighters. To meet them went the three Earp brothers and Doc Holliday, refusing an offer by some of the citizens, who had formed a vigilance committee, to go down and disarm the troublemakers.

There, in the O.K. Corral, the five Clanton gunmen were confronted by the four Earp fighters. A sudden shattering clatter of many guns fired at once—and save for a haze of smoke drifting slowly across the corral, it was over in sixty seconds.

Morgan Earp had a bullet in his shoulder and Virgil Earp one in his leg. But Frank and Tom McLowery were dead, Billy Clanton was dying of hemorrhage, and Ike Clanton and Claiborne were running for their lives.

By no means, however, was the feud over. Weeks later Virgil Earp was wounded again, by an unknown sniper. Morgan Earp, five months after the corral battle, was killed by a shot through a window as he was playing billiards.

The surviving Earps grimly began to collect blood-payment. Within forty-eight hours, in Tucson, Wyatt Earp killed Frank Stilwell, who, he believed, had murdered Morgan Earp. Sheriff Behan made a half-hearted effort to arrest Wyatt, but public opinion favored Earp and other officials refused to co-operate. Warren Earp, the fourth brother, arrived in Tombstone to take Morgan's place and the hunt went on, as the Earps, with a posse of fighting men, rode relentlessly through the wilds of Cochise County.

Indian Charlie, a half-breed member of the rustler crowd, was killed at the camp of Pete Spence. Before he died he said that it was Spence who had killed Morgan Earp—for which Spence later served a penitentiary sentence.

Curly Bill Brocius elected to fight it out with Wyatt Earp at Iron Springs. He got in the first shot but was cut down by a blast of buckshot from Earp's shotgun. Other leading rustlers, including Ike and Phin Clanton, John Ringo, Hank Swilling and Pony Deal, scampered into Mexico.

Their work was done and the Earps left Tombstone. They encountered legal difficulties over their killings, but the governor of Colorado refused to honor a request for their extradition and later all charges against them were dropped. A few years afterward Wyatt Earp was offered the position of U.S. marshal for Arizona by President McKinley, but refused it on the ground that he did not want to stir up old hard feelings. Wyatt Earp lived to be more than eighty years old. He became fairly wealthy in oil and died peacefully at his home in Los Angeles, California, January 13, 1929—one of the few frontier gunfighters to attain a considerable age.

The record of what happened to the once powerful rustler crowd shows the thoroughness of the Earps' campaign. Old Man Clanton and Billy Clanton were dead. So were both McLowerys. Ike and Phin Clanton were in Mexico; but Ike was killed soon after, along with Pony Deal, by Sheriff Commodore Owens, and Phin went to the penitentiary for stealing cattle. Curly Bill Brocius was dead and also Frank Stilwell. John Ringo, Harry Head and Billy Leonard were killed later. Joe Hill surrendered and confessed to some of the activities of the gang —incidentally exonerating Doc Holliday of all connection with an attempted holdup which enemies of the Earps had attempted to pin on him. Others simply disappeared and made themselves "mighty scarce" in Arizona thereafter. Law and order had come to Cochise County . . . after a fashion.

CHAPTER SIX

"The Night Sky Blazed Noon-day Bright"

SIXTY and more years have passed since the end of the last great outlaw vendetta—the Pleasant Valley War—and settlement, civilization and law have come to the Southwest. Rangers, sheriffs, marshals and vigilance committees, backed by public opinion, played their part here and there; and courageous and often highly informal courts—people's tribunals, convening in the back room of a saloon or store, with the presiding officer's revolver butt as a gavel and the nearest cottonwood tree or windmill as a gallows—dealt sternly with outlaws and criminals.

Picturesquely whimsical characters sometimes dispensed justice (of a sort), like the one in Langtry, Texas, whose sign read, *Judge Roy Bean, Notary Public—Justice of the Peace—Law West of the Pecos— Ice Beer.* There were ferocious ones, too, like Judge Isaac Parker, "the hanging judge," of Fort Smith, Arkansas, the scourge of the outlaws of the Southwest who made the almost unorganized Indian Territory their haven; in twenty-one years on the federal bench Parker sent eighty-one men to the gibbet; and he twice had six, and three times five, culprits executed at the same time and on the same gallows— which were built, at his order, to accommodate as many as twelve at once, if necessary. And there were grave judges whose sense of duty impelled them to defy threats and even murder in dispensing justice, and whose monument is a land of peace and safety.

The nation fought wars in those sixty years. In the war of 1898 against Spain, the Southwest's old suzerain, the most widely publicized single regiment in American history—the Rough Riders—was recruited chiefly from the cattle ranches, mining camps and law-enforcement bodies of the Southwest. Headed by fiery and colorful Colonel Theodore Roosevelt, its personnel offered brilliant copy to the uncensored and uninhibited war correspondents of the era. In the Cuban campaign, from Las Guásimas to San Juan Hill, the Rough Riders lived up to their advance publicity, and though the fighting methods of the Southwest troopers were sometimes unconventional, they were usually highly successful. And they provided a springboard from which Roosevelt went on to the presidency.

Later, in 1912, trouble flared south of the border when the twenty-six-year despotic rule of Porfirio Díaz was broken in Mexico and warring factions struggled for power. Most theatrical of the bandit-generals who campaigned gleefully for loot and ascendancy was Pancho Villa, whose operations close to the American border made continuous trouble. Villa's bullets frequently flew across the international line, as at El Paso when he captured Juárez just across the Rio Grande; Villa's *charros* made incursions into Arizona and New Mexico, looted ranches, and killed American citizens; and at last Villa, infuriated at the recognition by the United States Government of General Venustiano Carranza, his enemy, as *de facto* president of Mexico, attacked Columbus, New Mexico, in the dark hours of early morning, March 9, 1916.

The attack was a surprise, accompanied by no declaration of war, and Villa, stealing up with between four and six hundred men on the unsuspecting town, burned the hotel and several other buildings, and killed seven soldiers of the garrison and eight civilians, besides wounding five soldiers and two civilians (one a woman). But the Thirteenth Cavalry, which was in barracks at Columbus, fought back savagely and Villa discovered he had stirred up a wildcat. He retreated precipitately back across the border, pursued by the raging Thirteenth, and leaving forty-three dead to be picked up after the battle, besides suffering other losses never ascertained in dead and wounded who were carried away.

The American people yelled for revenge after the Columbus raid. The patience of President Woodrow Wilson was exhausted. A punitive expedition under General John J. Pershing, later commander of the American Expeditionary Force in World War I, chased Villa five hundred miles down into Mexico, fought six skirmishes, lost about twenty men killed and fifty wounded, and killed and wounded an indeterminate number of Mexican *bandidos*. But nobody in the expedition even caught sight of Villa himself.

The expedition cost about $150,000,000. It was almost a complete failure, and Pershing found his job more difficult than when he later commanded the A.E.F. The Mexican people were understandably exercised over the invasion by the American troops. Even if Villa was a bandit he was *their* bandit and they wanted to deal with him themselves. Pershing and his men were ordered back to the United States as a result of diplomatic representations by the Carranza government, and returned with a profound feeling of frustration.

Nevertheless, two important results were gained: Villa's prestige received a blow from which it never recovered; his career went down-grade from then until he was killed in 1923. And as a result of the raid the National Guard was mobilized and set to guard the entire border of the Southwest. The latter event was of profound importance in our national history. It was the beginning of the new era in national defense, led to congressional action whereby National Guard units became federal instead of state troops, and vastly increased the combat value of those units for the coming test on the battlefields of France in 1918.

In the two World Wars and the Korean War, young men from the Southwest did magnificent service in the armed forces—at places sometimes so far from their homes that they had never heard of them before they battled for them. But these wars, insofar as the Southwest itself was concerned, were remote and part of the national rather than the regional history.

Meantime population grew, cities sprang up and developed in some cases to immensity, universities, schools, hospitals, scientific centers, art colonies and industries—the evidences of settled civilization—flourished. And New Mexico and Arizona—separate territories since 1863—became states in 1912, New Mexico on January 6 and Arizona on February 14.

Some of this spectacular development was due to a new factor which entered the life of the Southwest. "Rock oil"—later called petroleum, which means the same thing, or simply oil—had been a subject of interest financially and otherwise since the first commercial well was drilled in Pennsylvania in 1859. Oil had been known in America through seepages since prehistoric times. Indians in California used crude oil and asphalt to waterproof baskets and to caulk boats. Among Eastern Indians, particularly the Senecas, oil was esteemed as a medicine; and this admiration was shared by some white men—medicine show operators and other dealers in nostrums—who gathered it from the surface of springs from which it seeped, and sold it in bottles gorgeously labeled "Seneca Oil," advertising it as a cure for almost any malady known to man.

But the Industrial Revolution was in full swing. Whale oil was insufficient to grease the wheels of manufacture, and various vegetable oils, such as that from the castor bean, proved equally inadequate to meet the growing demand. If some plentiful and cheap lubricant were not discovered, machinery could never run in the mighty harmony of industry that was building up.

The invention of the kerosene lamp, and the discovery that petroleum could be broken into numerous by-products of commercial value, at once gave a vast impetus to the oil industry and provided a solution, at least potentially, for industry. Lubrication could be brought from the bowels of the earth. If only enough of it could be discovered, it was the answer. Over the country spread the search for oil.

Petroleum had been known in small quantities in the vicinity of Nacogdoches, Texas, since 1887. In Corsicana, the city fathers in 1894 decided to drill an artesian well for a municipal water supply. At 2480 feet the well suddenly filled with oil. Citizens of Corsicana were quite bitter about the "failure" of the well and the "waste" of money on it, and the city fathers who failed to get the water had a rocky political road to ride. But a few men saw value in the greasy substance, organized a company, and drilled another well, finding oil again. At first there was little market for it, but presently Eastern capital became interested, a small refinery was built, and Corsicana became the first Texas commercial oil field.

So far the oil industry was puny. But Texas has a way of doing things in a fabulous manner. A retired Austrian naval officer, Captain Anthony F. Lucas (an Americanization of his original family name of Luchich), had ideas about finding oil arrived at through his experiences in drilling for salt. He believed that under the earth there were salt plugs about which petroleum might gather.

South of Beaumont, near the marshes of Galveston Bay, stood a low hill called Spindletop. Lucas obtained a lease and began to drill the hill, late in 1899. He found a little oil but ran into trouble and lost his hole, being forced to give up drilling in March 1900.

Already he had put all his own money into the venture, and he and his wife, who was a member of an aristocratic Georgia family, lived in a shack, the furniture of which consisted of cracker boxes for chairs and a plain carpentered table of yellow lumberyard pine. Nevertheless, Lucas would not give up. Somehow he managed to get more financial backing and tried again, this time with the newly devised rotary drilling method.

What followed is history—perhaps the most important event not only in Texas oil but anywhere in the nation's petroleum industry. On the morning of January 10, 1901, the men working in the derrick on Spindletop saw mud coming up from the well. They fell back. Suddenly, with a roar like an express train, a column of liquid driven by terrific pressure shot four tons of pipe out of the hole and clear up through the crown block of the derrick, spraying the ground about for scores of yards. It was oil, heavy and green, a stream six inches thick, spurting more than a hundred feet over the top of the derrick, and spouting an estimated 75,000 to 100,000 barrels a day.

The famous Spindletop strike, the first immense oil gusher in America, was the genesis of many things. It solved the lubrication problem for industry. More importantly, the theory and methods it proved assured a veritable ocean of petroleum, which meant the beginning of the liquid fuel age and therefore the introduction of the era of the automobile and airplane (there were 5000 motorcars in America in 1901, where there are 50,000,000 or more today). It revolutionized warfare on land, on the sea and in the air, and made it infinitely more terrible and devastating to civilian populations as well as combat forces. It ushered in a new era for the oil industry itself, and created overnight fortunes the like of which the world had hardly ever witnessed before. It changed the whole way of life of America and much of the rest of the world.

From the day the Lucas well blew in on Spindletop, oil became the biggest thing in Texas. Other great fields quickly were discovered—Sour Lake and Saratoga in 1902, Batson in 1903, Humble in 1904, and so on—each boosting the state's production of oil until in 1905 it produced 28,136,000 barrels.

And still Texas found more oil. Across the vast state geologists, lease hounds and wildcatters went. The oil fields straddled the state. Out in the Panhandle—where Coronado once rode drearily in the belief there was no treasure to be found there—great oil and gas fields were discovered. Westward, almost all the way to El Paso, another vast producing area was developed. As if all this were not enough, the East Texas field was found near the Louisiana border—the biggest yet. In less than nine years that single field produced 1,281,226,000 barrels—more than the whole of Europe (excluding Russia), together with Africa, Japan and assorted other countries, had produced in all of history. And back and forth between these outposts, hundreds of separate fields spread out—an incredible outpouring of wealth and useful resources.

Scrofulous little shack towns sprang up in the new fields, and crime and vice flourished as always in such communities, whether in cow towns, mining camps or oil dumps. And wars were fought for titanic stakes—for oil leases and drilling rights, for distribution areas, for refinery sites, and for competitive markets—interests that ran into the billions of dollars and dwarfed any other quick wealth in the world's history. Yet physical violence played no part in these property wars. A new kind of fighting had come in. There was skulduggery of countless varieties: cheating by slick lease men to get control of fields; money barons selling each other out to ruin; cutthroat price wars on the high national marketing levels; a whole new and complicated network of legal tactics, precedents and statutes, the astute oil lawyer slashing his opponent with suit and countersuit as remorselessly as ever a Spaniard slashed an Indian with his sword for gold, real or imaginary. It is said

—and probably quite accurately—that far more men have been ruined in oil than have profited from it. But the public has gained unquestioned mighty benefits.

The oil craze lapped over into New Mexico. In 1922 the Hogback field was found in the northwestern corner of the state, and on the Navajo reservation west of the famous natural landmark, Shiprock. But the real play developed in the southeast corner—the old stamping grounds of Billy the Kid. First the Artesia field came in near the Pecos River, on what was once part of the old Chisum cattle baronry. Then, almost on the Texas border, the Eunice, Jal and Hobbs fields were discovered. New Mexico became a major oil state, producing more oil than her parent, Old Mexico, and ranking sixth in the nation in spite of self-limiting her production.

But Texas was, and is, first. She produces nearly a quarter of all the oil in the world, over twice as much as all Russia produces, and about a third of the nation's entire production—something around half a billion barrels a year. Today oil derricks sprout like strange forests all the way from Texarkana almost to El Paso and from Dalhart to the gulf coast. The Texas oil millionaire has become a recognized form of fauna as typical of the state as the Texas cowboy. Nor is the Texas oil epic nearing an end. It may be only beginning. Each year new fields are discovered, new reserves mapped out. And the celebrated tendency of the sons of the Lone Star to speak with some exaggeration of their native state and all it does hardly can keep pace with the reality of this modern miracle.

Out of what the oil wells represent came a factor which did more than all the six-shooters and sheriffs' badges to tame the Southwest— the motorcar and the paved highways which lace across the open spaces, bringing every ranch and hamlet to comparatively near companionship with the rest of the nation. The breezy son of the Southwest considers a man who lives a hundred miles away a near neighbor and thinks no more of clambering into his car and scooting fifty miles over smooth concrete or blacktop to eat breakfast with a friend than if that friend's house was next door. Airplanes skim the skies, and radio and television echo the banalities of crooners and soap operas in shanties and oil kings' palaces alike, bringing their contribution to the homogeneity which makes forever impossible the return of the old, wild days.

No longer is it a test of courage and physical ability to venture out into the country of mesas and deserts, Indians and cattle, vivid colorings and strong sun. The Southwest has become one of the nation's favorite playgrounds. Instead of lifting scalps, Indians—particularly Navajos and Pueblos—are prime tourist attractions in the great railroad stations and the observation cars. At countless places in Texas, New Mexico and Arizona, luxurious hotels and dude ranches do a thriving business in tourist trade, besides providing, on occasion, gaming devices for the quick abstraction of money from their guests.

All this is recent, and it is part of another kind of history than this. But there is a final chapter that belongs here.

On the night of July 15, 1945, thunder and lightning rumbled and flashed, and rain fell in the dark hours, as if all nature were ominously concerned over what was taking place. The United States was at war. Germany had yielded, but Japan still fought on in the Pacific. In an old ranch house at the Alamogordo proving grounds in southern New Mexico, a tense group of men, dressed in dungarees or jeans, watched the cool, methodical work of one of their number, bending over an odd contraption.

In spite of their rough garb, these were scientists—American, British, Canadian, and refugees from warring European nations—the most brilliant experts in chemistry, physics, explosives and weapons who could be mustered. With them were important military officers, as gravely concentrated as any of them, perhaps more so.

Not one of those men was sure what was in store for him in the next couple of hours. But every one of them was certain that what was about to occur might be of near cataclysmic import. They were watching the final assembly of the first atom bomb in history by Dr. Robert Bacher, of Cornell University, after the parts had been devised and manufactured under the direction of Dr. Robert Oppenheimer, nuclear expert of the University of California. It was to witness the explosion of that engine of dreadful portent that they were gathered.

Once something jammed—a vital part of the mechanism. There was a catch of breath by the watchers. Unruffled, Dr. Bacher reassured his colleagues and went on with his work. Presently he freed the mechanism and there was a long sigh as he stepped back and announced that the preliminary assembly was done. The bomb, whose potentialities no man could surely foretell, was ready for its detonation.

Like a smoothly oiled machine, the team of top experts now took over their predetermined roles. One oversaw the setting of the timing mechanisms. Another gave his attention to the delicate task of mounting the bomb on a steel tower which had been erected for it. Others checked instruments, already in place, to record the effects of the explosion.

Zero hour was near. Scientists and military personnel went to their assigned observation posts, which were placed at distances ranging from five to ten miles from the tower. Following carefully rehearsed instructions, they donned dark glasses and lay flat on the wet ground with their feet toward the tower, to protect themselves from the blinding flash and other manifestations expected from the bomb.

Rain beat down on their faces and thunder echoed over the desert, with lightning now and then luridly lighting the mountains and momentarily revealing nearer countenances, queerly drawn and intent as the final instant approached. What would happen? Would the result of this experiment with cosmic forces by puny man be outside of and beyond all calculation?

There was a line of speculation to the effect that the discharge of the atom bomb might set off a chain reaction of inconceivably widespread and disastrous effects. The scientists here present discounted that, but it represented one extreme of thinking. At the other extreme lay the possibility that, after all, the bomb might perhaps not work— and all the great effort and treasure poured into it would be wasted. Somewhere between these poles of thought was the very real sense of personal danger experienced by each man. Nobody knew the extent of the coming explosion or how it would behave. They could only wait and see.

With hearts perhaps beating a little faster than usual, they listened as the voice of Dr. Samuel K. Allison, of the University of Chicago, heard over radio speakers placed near every observation post, counted off the time lapse.

"Minus fifteen minutes . . . minus fourteen minutes . . . minus thirteen minutes . . ."

At minus forty-five seconds a robot mechanism took over.

Minus thirty seconds . . . minus ten seconds . . . minus three seconds . . . minus two seconds . . . minus one second—

Every watcher held his breath.

Suddenly there was a brilliant flash of an intensity beyond any description. At Albuquerque, more than a hundred miles away, one account said "the night sky blazed noon-day bright."

The flash was instantaneously followed by the bursting out of a luminous, expanding sphere, several hundred feet in radius from its center—the fireball.

Then came chaos—a numbing, mighty detonation—a sustained roar of sound, shaking the earth, the greatest voice ever loosed on this sphere, up to that moment.

And with that the blast wave, leveling everything in its immediate periphery—followed by a tornadic wind, greater than the fiercest hurricane, screaming out in every direction.

Gasping, awed, almost stunned by what they themselves had set into action, the observers gazed up and saw—*the cloud.*

Gigantic. Incredibly malignant and towering. Colored with the brilliant polychromatic hues of every form of heat—white-hot fury, dull red, oranges, yellows, ultraviolets—swirling with awesome turbulence and charged with radioactive death in amounts beyond comprehension, it tore its way up, through the overcast, into the stratosphere where the now familiar mushroom top spread itself forty thousand feet above the surface of the ground.

Where the steel tower had stood was a prodigious crater and the tower itself was utterly vaporized by the heat of the explosion, fierce as at the center of the sun.

Slowly the scientists crawled to their feet and stared at the dreadful pillar, held motionless for the moment by awed fascination as they tried to measure in their minds this titan of catastrophe. Perhaps after that came the feeling of triumph—followed almost instantly by speculation, even fear, of the future.

The first atom bomb had been successfully exploded. The war with Japan already was as good as ended, for two of these bombs, dropped on the cities of Hiroshima and Nagasaki, would swiftly bring that empire to its knees. And the most important problem facing the human race was posed—how to control this new giant of atomic energy, both as a destructive and as a constructive force.

It was thus that the Southwest, which had witnessed so much of violence and change in its four hundred years of strife, became once again a frontier of vast consequence: the theater for the launching of what has been called "the second epoch in history."

Today many things are changed in the Southwest, but even with the coming of the atomic age many things also remain individually and harmoniously unchanged, and in this is a feeling of comfort to the human heart.

In the deserts and canyons the Navajo still watches his herds of sheep and his wife croons as she weaves the brilliant and beautiful rugs for which their people are celebrated. Pueblo farmers labor in their irrigated fields or make pottery and silver jewelry of rare charm and elegance.

Vaqueros still ride the range and the voice of the coyote is heard at moonrise of nights. Guitars and soft singing voices sound from little adobe *casas* in Mexican villages in the darkness, and when the dawn comes the mountains and deserts are illumined by a wonder of sunrise such as is seen almost nowhere else on this globe.

You will be greeted, often as not, with a flashing smile and a Spanish *"Buenos días,"* when you meet one of the people of the Southwest upon the road.

And when you part, you will hear the old beautiful Spanish farewell: *"Vaya con Dios*—Go with God."

Some Books to Read

THE list of sources used in preparing this volume is long, and he who wishes to embark upon the Spanish and French archives, to say nothing of those written in English, could well devote many years to them. For him who has less time, but wishes to read further, I suggest here a lesser list of books which I can endorse both for interest and for a general background of information.

The starting place for one who wishes to steep himself in the history of the Southwest is Coronado, and of the books on Coronado's grand exploration the best for general purposes is *Coronado on the Turquoise Trail*, by Herbert E. Bolton, a great scholar on the early phases of the Southwest's exploration. Similarly, Bolton's translation and editing of *Kino's Historical Memoir of Pimería Alta* is the best available English version of that remarkable missionary's adventures.

For the period of early Spanish colonization I commend *After Coronado*, by Alfred Barnaby Thomas, a translation and excellent editorial summary of important material from the archives of Spain, Mexico and New Mexico. A handy volume covering the suppression of the Pueblo Revolt is *Diego de Vargas and the Reconquest of New Mexico*, by Jessie Bromilow Bailey.

Concerning La Salle's tragic effort on the Texas coast, nothing better has been written than *La Salle and the Discovery of the Great West*, the classic account by Francis Parkman. On the whole French episode —and the Spanish also—the monumental works of Hubert Howe Bancroft are almost fundamental, particularly his *New Mexico and Arizona*, and the two-volume *North Mexican States and Texas*.

The rise of Texas and its struggle for independence are well told in a number of historical works. Among these, Henderson Yoakum's *History of Texas* and William Kennedy's *Texas*, although differing from each other in some particulars, are close to the times. Francis White Johnson's *Texas and Texans* is interesting also, as containing much of the early Texas correspondence and papers. In this connection I strongly recommend the reading of *The Raven*, Marquis James's magnificent biography of Sam Houston.

The period of the Mexican War has been thoroughly covered in many histories of the nation, but Bernard De Voto's discerning dissection of the period, *The Year of Decision*, is fascinating reading. An earlier and highly interesting account of American operations is *Doniphan's Expedition*, by William Elsey Connelley.

The War of the Rebellion, an Official Compilation of the Records of the Union and Confederate Armies, available in most important libraries, is diffuse and hard going, but gives the gist of the operations in New Mexico and Texas during the Civil War. As for the long Indian difficulties, the reader cannot go wrong on *Massacres of the Mountains*, by J. P. Dunn, *Carbine and Lance*, by Captain W. S. Nye, which deals with the Comanche-Kiowa-Cheyenne wars, *The Apache Indians*, by Frank Lockwood, and my own *Death in the Desert*, republished recently with a companion volume, *Death on the Prairie*, under the new title, *The Indian Wars of the West*.

For general reading concerning the Southwest, J. Frank Dobie's writings are a mine of entrancing information. *Coronado's Children*, telling of the lost gold and silver mines, *The Longhorns*, and *The Mustangs*, all by Dobie, will introduce the reader to his peculiar kingdom of fact and folklore.

The chronological story of the cattle industry is told in my own book, *The Trampling Herd*, and there is an infinitude of works dealing with separate facets of that fascinating phase of history, including *Historic Sketches of the Cattle Trade*, by Joseph G. McCoy, and *Cattle*, by William MacLeod Raine and Will C. Barnes.

As to the period of the range wars, there are innumerable books, but to name only a few of the best, I suggest: for the Lincoln County War, *The Saga of Billy the Kid*, by Walter Noble Burns; for the struggle to bring law to Cochise County, *Wyatt Earp, Frontier Marshal*, by Stuart Lake; and for the Pleasant Valley War, *Arizona's Dark and Bloody Ground*, by Earle R. Forrest.

This is only to touch the surface of the literature available. It is my hope that it will stimulate the reader to delve more deeply into the fascinating story of the Southwest.

Index

The FRENCH and SPANISH Frontier